FIRST CORINTHIANS

A Shorter Exegetical and
Pastoral Commentary

FIRST CORINTHIANS

A Shorter Exegetical and
Pastoral Commentary

Anthony C. Thiselton

WILLIAM B. EERDMANS PUBLISHING COMPANY
GRAND RAPIDS, MICHIGAN

Wm. B. Eerdmans Publishing Co.
4035 Park East Court SE, Grand Rapids, Michigan 49546
www.eerdmans.com

Published 2006
Paperback edition 2011
Printed in the United States of America

26 25 24   18 19

Library of Congress Cataloging-in-Publication Data

Thiselton, Anthony C.
    First Corinthians: a shorter exegetical and pastoral commentary /
    Anthony C. Thiselton.
        p.   cm.
    Includes bibliographical references and index.
    ISBN 978-0-8028-4036-3 (pbk. : alk. paper)
    1. Bible. N.T. Corinthians, 1st — Commentaries. I. Title.

BS2675.53.T44 2006
227'.2077 — dc22

                                        2006028679

Contents

Contents

Preface

This commentary is in no sense a mere summary or abbreviation of my earlier, longer commentary on the Greek text, which was published in December 2000. I have reflected on this epistle for five more years, and I have accorded priority here (1) to stating my own views rather than examining a variety of possible interpretations, and (2) to giving an even higher profile to how this epistle engages with pastoral and practical issues in the church and the world today.

The impetus for writing a second, shorter commentary on 1 Corinthians emerged at two levels, one serious and the other not-so-serious. The latter arose from some banter with the Bishop of Truro, Bill Ind, a former colleague on the Church of England Doctrine Commission some twenty years ago. The Bishop collared me one day, two or three years ago, with the comment, "I saw you had written a commentary on 1 Corinthians. I thought, 'I'll buy that'. Then I noticed that the reviewer said, 'On page 1,371. . . .' Can't you write a commentary that's a sensible size?"

More seriously, while numerous scholars, theological teachers, and senior clergy have expressed very generous and warm appreciation of the longer commentary, many clergy, pastors, and leaders of church Bible study groups have spoken of the need for a shorter commentary that would (like the larger one) show pastoral as well as scholarly concern but make more allowance for the pressures of time that they face. Further, the Bible Society in the United Kingdom, who had generously assisted with funding for research for the larger commentary, also expressed their desire and hope for a work designed more directly to serve church life. The William B. Eerdmans Publishing Company also very generously warmed to the idea, on the condition that the shorter commentary would not merely replicate the larger one on a small scale. I have carefully honored this agreement.

I seldom had either my earlier commentary or any other open on my desk as I wrote this one. A lifetime of research on 1 Corinthians allowed me to simply "think" as I wrote. Needless to say, this work presupposes and builds upon these many years of research and reflection, but I have simply asked myself (1) what the text means; and (2) how it applies to pastoral and practical issues today. Some will recall that many other questions were brought to the larger commentary.

The exegetical or expository sections, printed in standard type, were relatively easy to write, although I have revised them and simplified their vocabulary three times. The difficult part was to write the fifty-two sections that follow each block of text and exegesis with "Suggestions for Possible Reflection" on the passage or section in question. These fifty-two sections appear in smaller print after the exegesis of each section.

"Possible" signals my hesitancy at so daunting a task, especially since "practical" comments are often either banal or wander too readily from the point of the passage. My first attempt was too "pious" and sermonic, verging too much on the hortatory. After all, the gospel is a celebration of transformative good news, not a catalogue of "how to do better." My second draft majored on formulating questions. But everyone knows the pitfalls here. Either they are so transparent that they are downright patronizing ("the answer is in v. 7"), or they are so opaque in their open-endedness that readers are uncertain how to address them.

After much anguish and many full wastebaskets, I undertook a third rewriting. I have tried to offer a mixture of reflections and questions designed to avoid the pitfalls mentioned above. "Possible" signals: "Who am I to say all this?" But I fervently pray that the "Reflection" sections will facilitate a practical and formative impact for thought and life today that genuinely arises from careful exegesis of the text. I hope that for some they even facilitate sermon preparation in a busy, pressured ministry. The early chapters have been road-tested in my parish church in outer Nottingham in Bible studies led by others.

The Introduction is selective. Its aim is to shed practical light on how the epistle as a whole is to be understood. With Schleiermacher I lament that too often "Introductions" are dull and academic when they should fire a vision for reading the text. I hope that those who seek practical help will not ignore the Introduction. It is designed to transport readers into the "worlds" of Corinth and of Paul, and to explain why this church and this apostle think, feel, act, and write as they do. Hence in the Introduction I have included a map of the geographical situation of Corinth and seven photographs of remains of the ancient city.

I need to comment on the English translation from the Greek text that I use here. Among the many reviewers of my larger commentary, a number expressed particular appreciation for my English translation, which was entirely new or original. In this shorter commentary I have reproduced this translation except for some occasional minor rephrasing where my earlier attempt to be rigorous and accurate left an English phrase somewhat too cumbersome or clumsy. Bearing in mind a broader readership, I have smoothed the translation here and there. At only one point has it substantially affected the meaning. After I had completed my earlier commentary, Bruce Winter published his persuasive understanding of 12:3, which I have broadly adopted in my translation here. Occasionally I have called attention to small differences of wording.

Some of you may find the extensive Bibliography of Works Cited unduly intimidating. But I have cited only those authors whose work is so much a part of my thinking on a passage that it would suggest a lack of professional integrity not to acknowledge their influence. In the commentary itself I have used only very short, abbreviated titles with page references. The full publication data can be found in the Bibliography of Works Cited. I have included no book or article that I have not explicitly drawn on in the text. Thus if any major study has been omitted, this is not because I fail to value it but because I wanted to keep scholarly allusions to a minimum. If the book or article was published not later than 2000, it was almost certainly included in my larger commentary.

This commentary runs to barely one-sixth of the larger work in length, but since I have added many "Suggestions for Possible Reflection" the exposition or exegesis is considerably shorter, and, once again, different. The questions and agenda with which I have approached the text are not those that I had in mind when I wrote the longer commentary.

Finally, I acknowledge with grateful thanks the help of my wife Rosemary, who had long hoped that I would write a much shorter, practical commentary, even if it was based on work for the longer commentary. She arduously deciphered my handwriting to type it. This is my ninth book, and time away from the family is one unavoidable price I pay. I thank my family (which includes three children and five grandchildren to date) for their understanding. Mrs. Sheila Rees has also kindly and freely given her time in checking references and proofreading. I am deeply grateful to all who have encouraged me in this work, and I pray that it may help many who wrestle with this wonderful epistle to find new light for their way.

ANTHONY C. THISELTON
Department of Theology,
University of Nottingham, and
Department of Theology,
University of Chester

Introduction

I. The City and the Culture of Corinth: Distinctive Features That Assist an Understanding of the Epistle

A. Corinth as a Prosperous, Bustling, International Center of Trade and Industry

Corinth is situated on a narrow neck of land in Greece with a harbor on each side of it. On the east side the harbor of Cenchreae faces across the sea to the Roman province of Asia and Ephesus. On the west side the port of Lechaeum faces Italy and ultimately Rome. Yet at the narrowest point of the isthmus the distance between the two seacoasts is barely nine kilometers, or less than six miles. Corinth was thus a major center for international east-west trade.

This favored location for east-west trade was matched by an almost equally favored position between northern and southern Greece. To the north lay the Province of Achaea, and yet further north, Macedonia, which included Philippi and Thessalonica. To the south lay the Peloponnese, down to the shores of Cape Malea. Corinth stood at the crossroads or intersection between north and south and between east and west for business and trade (see the map below). In Paul's time it had become a busy, bustling, cosmopolitan business center. By comparison Athens might have seemed a slumbering university city, dreaming of its greater past.

Those who traded between Asia and the west preferred to use the two port facilities of Corinth rather than to travel by ship around Cape

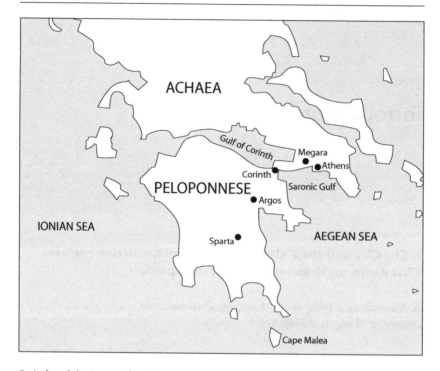

Corinth and the Surrounding Area

This map shows the strategic location of Corinth at the crossroads or intersection of east-west trade, and also between north and south. Not for nothing was it called "wealthy Corinth" in the classical and Hellenistic eras. It stood on an isthmus only about four miles or so across. On the west (strictly the northwest), about a mile and a half distant, stood the harbor of *Lechaeum*. This overlooked the Corinthian Gulf, facilitating trade with Rome and Italy. On the east, over-looking the Saronic Gulf, stood *Cenchreae,* facilitating trade with Ephesus and Asia. Corinth also stood between the routes to the north (Athens, Achaia, and Macedonia), and to the south (the Peloponnese).

Malea, where winds and tides were often hazardous off the southern shores of Greece, especially in winter. If they used light cargo ships, sailors or traders could transport even the ship on rollers over the paved road, the *diolkos,* that linked the two harbors. Alternatively they could unload cargo at one port and reload it at the other (see fig. 1). In either case toll fees or carriage charges swelled the income of Corinth and its officials.

Figure 1. The Modern Canal and the Ancient *Diolkos*

The *diolkos* was a paved roadway dating from the sixth century B.C. It served for light ships to be moved on rollers between the two ports to the east and to the west. Sailors and merchants preferred to pay a toll to Corinth to use the *diolkos* rather than to sail around the treacherous Cape Malea in the south of the Peloponnese. This would not only take an additional six days but would also involve facing gales up to above Beaufort Force 6. Sailors had a saying, "See Malea twice and die." *The modern canal* follows roughly the route of the *diolkos*. The Romans attempted digging a canal in the ancient world, but without success. Nero "opened" one such attempt using a golden trowel. The *diolkos* can still be seen for most of the route, but the canal dates from the nineteenth century.

3

B. Corinth Inherited a Large Income from Tourism, Business, and Manufacturing

Tourists flocked to Corinth not least for the famous Isthmian Games, which were held every two years. Second only to the Olympic Games, the Isthmian Games were among the three great games-festivals of the whole of Greece. They attracted participants, spectators, and other visitors from all corners of the empire between Rome and the east. Archaeologists have recovered coins that witness to the range of international visitors who came to the Games.

When he arrived in Corinth, Paul would probably have seen whatever booths and stands remained from the Games of A.D. 49, while they would have been in full swing during his ministry there in A.D. 51. By the middle of the first century the Games had expanded to include a multiplicity of competitive and sometimes spectacular events. In addition to chariot races, athletic events, competitions in trumpet, flute, and lyre, poetry readings, and other events, Corinth or Isthmia had unusually introduced athletic contests for women, and the *apobatikon* in which a rider would leap from one team of horses to another. During this period Corinth managed the Games, and reaped a vast income from them.

In addition to competitors and spectators, businesspeople, traders, and especially individuals with entrepreneurial skills or hopes visited what constituted a hub of opportunity for new commercial contacts and ventures, new possibilities of employment, quick person-to-person agreements or transactions, and a large cosmopolitan pool of potential consumers. These visitors brought money to rent rooms, to buy necessary or exotic products, and to hire dockers, porters, secretaries, accountants, guides, bodyguards, blacksmiths, carpenters, cooks, housekeepers, and both literate and menial slaves. They sought to employ or to hire managers, craftsmen, and people who could repair wagons, tents, ships, or chariots.

Paul would have spent many long, hot hours in a workshop probably close to the Lechaeum road (see fig. 2) or on the north, sun-drenched side of the *Agora* or Forum. Archaeologists have excavated shops or workshops of some thirteen feet by eight feet, some with sleeping accommodations above, which Aquila and Priscilla may well have used as their quarters (cf. Acts 18:3).

Figure 2. The Road from Lechaeum, with the Background of Acrocorinth

This is probably the most familiar view of Corinth, showing the road to and from Lechaeum, with Acrocorinth dominating the scene. (Ben Witherington)

C. Corinth as a Roman Colony and the New Settlers

Corinth's geographical position as an international center for trade, together with its attraction for business and economic prosperity, already sets the stage for regarding it as a deeply competitive, self-sufficient, and entrepreneurial culture marked by ambitions to succeed and what we nowadays term a cast of mind shaped by consumerism. But two further factors add decisively to this growing picture.

First, Corinth had been resettled in 44 B.C. as a *Roman* colony. The history of Corinth goes far into earlier centuries as a Greek city-state, but in the second century B.C. it became embroiled in political struggles that related to Sparta and also to Rome. In 146 B.C. a Roman army sacked the city, and they left it virtually in ruins for some two hundred years. Yet such a prime location for defense, trade, and economic power could not remain neglected forever. In 44 B.C., the year of his assassination, Julius Caesar refounded Corinth as a Roman *colonia* for veterans from his legions.

The new Corinth was initially resettled chiefly by Roman soldiers, Roman freedpersons, and Roman slaves, and was very soon swelled by tradespersons and business entrepreneurs from various parts of the Roman Republic. The government and laws of the new city were established on a fully Roman pattern. Loyalty to Rome was fundamental, for the settlement of the veterans and loyal Roman citizens made Corinth a secure strategic base for possible future campaigns against Parthia, Dacia, or further east. The new name of the city honored Julius Caesar, *Colonia Laus Julia Corinthiensis* in full or *Corinth* for short. The massive Acrocorinth, adjacent to the city and of some 570 meters, had served as a citadel for defense during the early Greek period, and it still provided a structure for defense if ever this was needed (see fig. 3).

The well-ordered colony attracted an increasing number of immigrants, who came in the hope of making their fortune. Every condition was right: a cosmopolitan international center under secure Roman government order, with shipping routes to Rome and Ephesus and to the east; a plentiful supply of natural resources for manufacturing; and a vibrant business culture where quick success (or sometimes failure) was part of the cultural ethos. *Competition, patronage, consumerism, and multiform layers and levels of success* were part of the air breathed by citizens of Corinth.

D. Corinth as a Hub of Manufacturing, Patronage, and Business

As if all this were not enough, Corinth enjoyed spectacular natural resources for the production of goods. First and foremost the almost limitless supply of water from the Peirene Fountains not only provided the domestic needs of a large, vibrant, expanding city but was also a necessary component for the manufacture of bricks, pottery, roof tiles, terracotta ornaments, and utensils (see fig. 4 below). Other needed components were available: a very large deposit of marl and clay; light sandstone to be quarried for building on a large scale; and a harder limestone for the durable paving of streets and roads.

Even in the earlier Greek period Corinth had been called "wealthy Corinth." Now in its first-century Roman period the city hummed with economic wealth, business, and expansion. Businesswomen like Chloe, we may surmise, sent their middle managers to Corinth to deal

Figure 3. Acrocorinth

Acrocorinth, here in the background, formed the original citadel of ancient Corinth in the Greek era. It dominates the territory of Corinth and stands at a height of 474 meters, or approximately 2000 feet. In the Greek period before the second century the notorious temple of Aphrodite stood at the summit, but it lost much of its influence in the Roman period.

on their behalf (1:10). Aquila and Priscilla saw Corinth as a prime location for leather goods or tentmaking when Claudius expelled Jews from Rome in A.D. 49. They probably arrived, already as Christians, shortly before Paul, and set up their workroom-cum-shop either on the north side of the Forum or among the shops and markets of the Lechaeum road.

It is not surprising that the culture of the day in Corinth expressed a degree of *self-satisfaction,* if not *complacency,* alongside a drive *to compete* and *to succeed.* The culture was one of *self-promotion* alone. When Paul carried the gospel to Corinth, it is not surprising that he "came . . . with

Figure 4. The Peirene Fountains

This source of water was vital to the prosperity of Corinth. The rate of flow has been calculated at eighteen cubic meters per hour, which is said to be enough to supply the needs of a large city. The springs also resourced the manufacture of clay pottery, roof tiles, and terra-cotta objects. The use of water for washing, drinking, and other purposes made these springs a social center as well as a resource for the city. Paul and the earliest Christians would have frequented it. (Ben Witherington)

much fear and trembling" (2:3). For the gospel of a humiliated, crucified Christ was *an affront* to people who cherished *success* and who loved *winners*. Paul himself refused to carry himself like a professional lecturer or rhetorician, but insisted on working as an artisan in a leather worker's workshop and leather-goods shop. Paul "did not come with high-sounding rhetoric or a display of cleverness"; but this consumer-oriented culture wanted precisely what Paul refused to give. His only selling point was the one thing that nobody would want: to speak "only of a crucified Christ" (2:2). No wonder that "the proclamation of the cross is, for their part, folly to those who are on their way to ruin," even if it is "the power of God to us who are on the way to salvation" (1:18).

II. The Ethos That Permeated the Church, Largely Derived from the Social, Political, and Economic Culture of Corinth

The content of our epistle makes it clear that Christians in Corinth still carried over into their Christian existence many of the cultural traits that characterized their pre-Christian culture. This is almost always the case in a diversity of cultures. No doubt when he thanks God quite genuinely for their gifts of "speech," which could sometimes but not always be *wise speech* and includes "all kinds of knowledge" (1:5), Paul has in mind among other things their potential for traveling to other cities of the empire with the gospel, and communicating it with initiative and articulate persuasion. But there were also serious reverse sides. Of these we may mention especially the problems and destructive tendencies set in motion by (a) a drive toward *competitiveness, self-achievement, and self-promotion;* (b) an attitude of *self-sufficiency, self-congratulation, and autonomy* and entitlement to *indulge freedoms;* and (c) the tendency to *overvalue gifts of "knowledge," "wisdom," and "freedom"* over and above more basic gifts in everyday life such as *love and respect for others.*

A. Competitiveness, Self-Achievement, and Self-Promotion

(1) The people of Corinth were in general terms a thrusting, ambitious, and *competitive* people. The *competition for success* was everywhere apparent: in the Isthmian Games, in business and trade, in social status, and in economic power. *Entrepreneurs* do not always follow conventions and "order"; they feel "free" to cut corners and to find shortcuts if or when this brings instant success. They use social networks of influence, not least in Corinth through the Roman system of patronage, where choosing the right patron could ensure rapid promotion through the influence of the patron rather than strictly on personal merit. "Getting ahead" was the order of the day.

While Paul feels able to thank God for their gifts of speech and "knowledge" (1:4-7), other cultural inheritances are less admirable in the context of Christian faith: "Where jealousy and strife prevail among you, are you not centered on yourselves and behaving like any merely human person?" (3:3). Paul needs to appeal "that there be no splits among you" (1:10). He declares, "Let no one be self-deceived. If

9

any among you thinks he or she is wise in terms of this world order, let that person become a fool in order to become wise. . . . 'God catches the clever in their craftiness'" (3:18, 20). "Let no one glory in human persons" (3:21). "'All of us possess "knowledge."' This 'knowledge' inflates; love, on the other hand, builds" (8:1).

Comparisons of a competitive nature also too readily lead to "putting down" others and to boasting or bragging about one's own achievements. "The eye cannot say to the hand, 'I do not need you,' or the head cannot say to the feet, 'I have no need of you.' On the contrary . . . those limbs and organs . . . which seem to be less endowed with power or status than others are essential'" (12:21, 22). "Love does not brag — is not inflated with its own importance" (13:4).

(2) If Corinth enjoyed "success"-oriented or triumphalist versions of religion, the proclamation of a humiliated and a crucified Christ was viewed as inexpressibly "shameful," disgraceful, and "foolish"; indeed, it was both "folly" and an "affront" (1:18, 24). The proclamation of the cross could have only the inevitable affect of *subverting* and *reversing* the value system that dominated Corinthian culture. "The foolish things of the world God chose to shame the clever; and the weak things of the world God chose to shame positions of strength; . . . and . . . to bring to nothing the 'somebodies'" (1:27-29). "We are fools on Christ's account, but you are wise. . . . We are weak, while you are strong. . . . We have become, as it were, the world's scum, the scrapings from everyone's shoes" (4:10, 13). This approach and value system is entirely at odds with the cultural expectation that competition and the high evaluation of initiative and cleverness sent the "weakest" to the wall.

(3) The culture of Corinth, and certainly of its aspiring "climbers," was one of *self-promotion*. Ben Witherington sums this up very well: "In Paul's time many in Corinth were already suffering from a self-made-person-escapes-humble-origins syndrome. . . . [Paul's] self-humiliation, his assumption of a 'servant role,' contradicted expected values 'in a city where social climbing was a major preoccupation'" (*Conflict and Community*, pp. 20-21). (All works cited in the text have full details in the Bibliography of Works Cited near the end of this book.)

This assertion receives full support from two factors that we consider further below: rhetoric in Corinth and archaeology. Rhetoricians provided precisely the kind of profile and "spin" that we associate today with the mass media. They declared the achievements of benefactors or rising stars, often with more concern for effect than for truth. Further archaeological remains also testify to this passion for recognition and public honor. Probably the most celebrated example is that of the two inscriptions relating to Gnaeus Babbius Philinus found in the *Agora* or Forum. The one that was once at the head of the columns of a structure now ruined reads: "Gnaeus Babbius Philinus, aedile and pontifex, had this monument erected at his own expense, and he approved it in his official capacity of *duovir.*" So eager was Babbius to insure recognition in the present and future that he sought appointment to the office that would monitor and approve benefactions to the city, and paid also for two declarations of his beneficence for posterity.

B. Self-Sufficiency; Local Autonomy and Freedom

Corinth, as we have noted, had everything that it needed: the Peirene Fountains provided an almost inexhaustible water supply; Acrocorinth could provide a citadel for defense if necessary; trade between east and west and north and south was abundant and assured; manufacturing and exports prospered; the Isthmian Games brought in more consumers than could readily be supplied; the natural resources of clay, marl, and limestone were abundant; employment of multiform variety was available; trade and production flourished; it was a provincial center for rhetoric; it drew people from all parts of the Eastern Empire to admire its facilities and spectacles.

It is no surprise that when they became Christians, many people of Corinth carried over attitudes of self-sufficiency and Corinthian pride. Many wanted and expected a *"Corinthian" spirituality* that we might describe in today's fashionable language as *contextually redefined for Corinth.* Paul has spoken of "wisdom," "knowledge," "Spirit," "spiritual," "free," and "saved." All of these terms, it seems, became redefined to match a Corinthian understanding and context. Hence in several parts of the epistle *Paul redefines them* again in accordance with the *received apostolic gospel.*

Thus Paul writes: "We do communicate wisdom, . . . but it is a wisdom which is not of this present world order" (2:6). "We speak God's wisdom," which is "too profound for merely human discovery" (2:7).

"'All of us possess "knowledge"'" (8:1) — but "if anyone thinks he or she has achieved this 'knowledge', they have not yet come 'to know'" (8:2). The Holy Spirit is not an instrument for self-promotion as "spiritual" people, but is "the Spirit who issues from God" and brings "Christ's mind" (2:12, 16). "For my part, my Christian friends, I could not address you as people of the Spirit.... You are still unspiritual" (3:1, 3). "'Liberty to do all things' — but not everything is helpful" (6:12; cf. 10:23). Christian believers are "on the way to salvation" (present tense, 1:18).

The Corinthian concern for "autonomy" led them to devalue the translocal character of Christian identity. In his very opening address Paul reminds them that they are "called to be a holy people, together with all who call on the name of the Lord ... in every place, both their Lord and ours" (1:2). It can be no accident that he makes the point three times within a single verse: "all who call on the name in every place; their Lord and ours." It is an overture for a theme that will come more fully in the body of the epistle.

The clearest question mark against claims to both general and local self-sufficiency comes in 4:7-8: "Who sees anything different in you? What do you have that you did not receive? If, however, you received it [i.e., as a gift from another], why do you boast as if you did not receive it?" Paul quotes their own triumphalist slogan with heavy irony: "'We have been made rich! ... We reign as kings'" and comments, "If only you did 'reign as kings,' ... we, too, could reign as kings with you!" (4:8). The apostles, however, still struggle with weariness and wounds in the gladiators' arena while the Christians in Corinth look on and applaud (vv. 9-12). The apostles are "the world's scum" (v. 13). Paul's irony escalates: "We are fools; you are wise.... We are weak; you are strong. You are honored; we are disgraced" (v. 10). Yet he does not want *to shame* them for the sake of it; only *to warn* them (v. 14). It is the "proclamation of the cross" and God's sovereign grace that provides and constitutes the ground of their being and their identity as Christians (1:18-25).

C. Wisdom, Knowledge, and Freedom: Further Comments

We have already noted Paul's redefinition of a Corinthian reuse of "wisdom" and "knowledge." Paul refers positively to the wisdom of *God*, not to that of the world. Clearly *knowledge* and *wisdom* in the sense of knowing the right people, knowing the markets, and operating the right strategies of success are necessary qualities for success in the rough-and-tumble of the world of trade, business, manufacturing, promotion in employment, and even a slave's desire to improve his or her situation (cf. 7:21). Paul does not belittle wisdom as such, but wisdom is more than mere cleverness, especially if cleverness is used for self-interest.

The relation between knowledge, freedom, and moral conduct emerges in chapter 6, while a contrast between knowledge and freedom on one side and love and respect for "the other," on the other side, emerges in 8:1–11:1. Christians in Corinth who perhaps designated themselves as "the strong" (i.e., in knowledge and/or in social and economic influence) claimed that *knowledge* encouraged a more enlightened attitude toward taking part in festivals and meals in the precincts of pagan temples. This was the case, they urged, whether or not the meat served there had originally been part of sacrifices offered to idols. Knowledge informs us that "'An idol has no real existence,'" for "'There is no God but One'" (8:4). So Christians may on this basis maintain their business and social contacts. But, Paul replies, there is a problem: "It is not everyone who possesses this 'knowledge!' Some are still gripped by the idol through force of habit even now, and they eat meat as an actual idol sacrifice" (8:7).

Paul tries to steer a middle but firm course that is uncompromising about nonparticipation in actual idol sacrifices but allows a degree of freedom on the basis of this knowledge in certain specific situations. Christians need to mix with Gentiles when this can be done without compromise. But *love* must rule their conduct in relation to other Christians. "You who 'possess knowledge'" (8:10) must not bring *destruction* upon "the brother or sister for whom Christ died" (8:11). To do so would be "to sin against Christ" (8:12). This emphatically qualifies and constrains a supposed "'right to choose'" (8:9). Indeed, the slogan beloved in Corinth, "'Liberty to do all things'" (6:12a), receives firm qualification and firm boundaries because "not everything is helpful" (6:12).

Love remains a broader and more positive theme in chapters 11 to 14. *"Knowledge"* not only risks inflating the ego of the one who lays claim to it (8:1); it also risks dividing the community of the church into the "informed," "mature," "strong," or "secure" in their faith and those who are supposedly ill informed, less mature, "weak," or insecure (in the sense of uncertain) in their belief system and Christian identity. Against this, Paul insists that the core quality of love entails *building* "the other" (8:1) in such a way as to *respect* the other even where the other may be different. Hence in 11:2-16 Paul emphasizes complementarity, reciprocity, and mutuality in gender attitudes, in contrast to assimilation of differences or uniformity; 11:17-34 protects the socially vulnerable in the context of the Lord's Supper: 12:1-14 stresses the twin axes of unity and diversity in the church, but with important "house rules" to restrain and "order" the parading of "gifts" by self-styled "spiritual people" over against those whom they make to feel inferior.

The chapter on love (13:1-13) stands at the very heart of the theology of this epistle. Virtually all the qualities ascribed to love resonate with features (or the absence of these features) in Corinth. "Love shows kindness. Love does not burn with envy; does not brag — is not inflated with its own importance. It does not behave with ill-mannered impropriety; is not pre-occupied with the interests of the self" (13:4b-5a). This governs the "courtesies" or good manners enjoined in chapter 14 about not speaking too long when another feels God's call to speak; or when someone imposes inarticulate noises upon the congregation when the speaker cannot express what moves him or her to communicate this clearly to others for them to share in the praise (14:1-33a).

III. Other "Corinthian" Traits Relevant Today: The Rhetoric of Audience Approval and Resonances with Consumerism and Postmodernity

A. Classical Rhetoric and Audience-Pleasing Rhetoric: Corinth versus Rome

The almost obsessive concern in Corinth about status, recognition, and self-promotion went hand-in-hand with a high regard for a certain kind of *rhetoric*. It is essential, however, to observe a distinction between two different types of rhetoric. The *"classical"* tradition of rhetoric goes back to Aristotle and was taught by the Roman orator Cicero (106-43

B.C.) and later by Quintilian (A.D. 40-95). This had as its aim not only the art of persuasion but also the *effective communication of truth.* By contrast some provincial centers, especially Corinth, were influenced by a kind of rhetoric that was more concerned *with "winning" than with truth.*

Bruce Winter and others have demonstrated the influence on the Corinth of Paul's day of the Sophists, or "the Second Sophistic" (Winter, *Philo and Paul,* esp. pp. 1-15 and 126-202). "To win admiration" was the aim of the Sophists; to present truth persuasively and clearly was the different aim of the classical rhetoricians of Rome. Sophist rhetoricians aimed to win competitions; the School of Cicero, Quintilian, and Seneca the Elder (ca. 55 B.C.-A.D. 40) aimed to serve education, society, and truth.

Quintilian expresses serious disquiet about those less-educated rhetoricians who separate truth context from rhetorical form or effect. Some "shout on all and every occasion and bellow their utterance 'with uplifted hand' (to use their phrase), dashing this way and that, panting and gesticulating wildly . . . with all the frenzy of people out of their minds" (Quintilian, *Institutio Oratoria* 2.11.9-11). Nothing could be further from Paul's disclaimer, "We do not proclaim ourselves" (2 Cor. 4:5), for these rhetoricians performed showpieces for the admiration of their listeners. When Paul rejected the way of "high-sounding rhetoric or a display of cleverness" (1 Cor. 2:2), he was rejecting the status accorded to a Sophist rhetorician to which the Christians in Corinth wanted him to aspire. They were embarrassed by a leather worker or artisan, and wanted a "real professional" with all the status that this would bring with it.

Quintilian laments the prostitution of rhetoric into the status of "mere performance" by media stars and public cult figures. They behave like athletes or singers; their oratorical flourishes and "spin" are "greeted with a storm of . . . applause . . . shouts of unseemly enthusiasm. . . . The result is vanity and empty self-sufficiency. . . . [They become] intoxicated by the wild enthusiasm of their fellow pupils," and truth is sacrificed to what the audience wants to hear (Quintilian, *Oratoria* 2.2.9-12). Quintilian is not alone in such a complaint. Seneca complains that too often the goal is "to win approval for yourself, rather than for the case" (Seneca, *Declamationes Controversiae* 9.1).

B. Rhetoric, Social Construction, and a "Postmodern" Ethos: Corinth versus Paul

In incisive and convincing studies two writers among others find resonances between this pragmatic, audience-pleasing, sophistic rhetoric
and the mood of many postmodern attitudes and values today. The
older classical rhetoric still shares a concern for truth that also characterizes the "best" of modernity, whatever its failings in giving undue
status and privilege to "scientific" method. Sophistic rhetoric is
largely concerned with the verdicts and applause of communities of
power and influence, adopting a radical "antifoundational" (not simply non-foundational) stance, "constructing" texts and truth "only
within social-linguistic worlds" (Pogoloff, *Logos and Sophia*, p. 27). This
approach to knowledge becomes "radical by nature, since the axioms
of rational thought are not rationally demonstrable, but are held only
by persuasion" (p. 29). The assimilation of truth into techniques of
persuasion evaluated by audience or consumers betrays a different
"worldview" that stands "in contrast to modernist epistemologies"
(pp. 27 and 30).

The very word "recognition," so highly prized in Corinth, confirms this point. It is the audience or "consumer" who grants or with-
holds *recognition*, irrespective of whether it is deserved or corresponds
with the truth. The fame of media stars and sports heroes is *contrived
and constructed* by audience votes and consumer purchases in the marketplace. *Value* is determined by a consumer market. But the consumer
market is not "free" or value neutral. It is manipulated and shaped by
sophistic rhetoricians in ancient Corinth, and by the "spin" of mass
media in the postmodern world. Do teenagers genuinely *choose* whether
an item of designer clothing that is *de rigeur* among their peer group is
really "what they need" or "what is best"? Sophistic rhetoricians were
like the mass media of today: they did not describe, they promoted.
Their concern was not truth content; they devised seductive, persuasive
strategies of presentation. (See further, Thiselton, *Thiselton on Hermeneutics,* essays 30-36.)

In addition to Pogoloff's incisive and convincing study John D.
Moores offers a parallel analysis (*Wrestling with Rationality in Paul*, pp. 5-
32 and 132-60). Paul, Moores writes, appeals to Scripture and to reason,
as well as to common apostolic traditions within the church, as the ba-

sis on which to promote truth. If he uses classical rhetoric, he deploys its devices strictly within this frame. He never invites the audience "to weigh the gospel evidence on probability scales"; as if to suggest that it is the audience that constructs what counts as "gospel" (pp. 21-23). Indeed, Paul remains on the watch for "code switching" by the audience (i.e., changes of linguistic code that give new meanings to a familiar vocabulary).

Paul argues from premises shared by Scripture, reason, and the apostolic community, that is, *enthymemes* or shared convictions stated as presuppositions. Moores declares, "[Paul] does not think . . . that the identity of the message . . . is in any sense determined by what it means for those at the receiving end. For him it is rather *their* identity than that of the message which is determined by their response. To subject him to the criteria of present-day reader-response theory would be to turn his ideas on the subject upside down" (pp. 133-34). In 1 Corinthians 1-2 it is beyond question that Paul regards the gospel of the cross as "the ground and criterion" of apostolic and Christian identity (Schrage, *Der erste Brief,* vol. 1, p. 165). Christians do not set themselves up as criteria of what counts as gospel proclamation. But this is at odds with sophistic rhetoric in Corinth.

Moores shows how credibly Paul can claim that a version of the proclamation of the cross engineered by audience and readers would "empty" it of content and power (2:4, 5). For if words are redefined by "code switching" (using the same vocabulary with a different meaning), the communication will cease to be communicative and become a mere "performance" or operation in which words simply chase words in a circle of self-reference. Like Wittgenstein, and like Paul, he insists that extralinguistic reference must be anchored in human behavior and lifestyle. This is precisely what Paul does when he expounds "the mind of Christ" (2:16) in terms of apostolic labor (3:5–4:21). Moores finally relates this, again rightly, to the need for articulate speech urged by Paul in 1 Cor. 14:6-32. "If the trumpet produces a sound which is ambivalent as a signal, who will prepare for battle?" (14:8).

Many readers today will recognize these paragraphs as sketching out the less desirable features of a postmodern, consumerist-oriented pluralism. We cannot simply redefine truth in terms of what appeals to "our" community. Two of the most influential American postmodernist writers today are Stanley Fish and Richard Rorty. From the side of postmodern neopragmatism Fish approves the stance of "rhetorical man" as against "serious man." "Rhetorical man is trained not to discover reality but to manipulate it. Reality is what is accepted as reality, what is useful" (Fish, "Rhetoric," in *Doing What Comes Naturally*, p. 483; also citing Richard Lanham). Some may regard this as the only viable alternative to a *theistic* worldview, but it has more in common with Corinth than with Paul.

The same might be said of Rorty's claim that there is no task of "getting reality right" because "there is no Way the World Is" (*Truth and Progress*, p. 25). Truth is no more than what can be "justified" as useful to this or that "local" community (p. 21). Not surprisingly, Rorty shares with the spirit of first-century Corinth the view that a "local" community, in effect, can define its own criteria of truth since no criteria apply to all contexts. Paul, by contrast, perceives the cross as the "ground and criterion" for the Christian identity of "male and female, slave and free, Jew and Gentile" (Gal. 3:28; see further Thiselton, *Interpreting God and the Postmodern Self*).

C. Does Paul Use Rhetoric? What Kind of Rhetoric?

Paul's rejection of *sophistic*, audience-pleasing rhetoric is clear, and is strikingly apparent in 1 Cor. 2:1-5. Nevertheless, Paul does draw upon those standard forms and devices of *classical* rhetoric that clarify argument and articulate truth persuasively. One outstanding example comes in the chapter on resurrection. As we suggest in our commentary below (on 15:1-58), the declaration of the common apostolic tradition begins a statement of what is the case (the *narratio*, 15:1-11). Paul's exposition of the consequences of denying the resurrection constitutes a first rhetorical *refutatio* (vv. 12-19), involving the genre of deliberative rhetoric. This device outlines the advantages or disadvantages of accepting certain beliefs or of practicing certain conduct (cf. Mitchell, *Paul and Rhetoric*, and Eriksson, *Traditions as Rhetorical Proofs*). The next section affirms positive declarations and arguments about Christ's resurrection as the ground for the future resurrection of believers, and this constitutes a rhetorical *confirmatio* (vv. 20-34). The chapter continues in this vein.

Paul is also comfortable with using parody and self-parody to press a pin into the inflated pomposity of some of his readers. Wuellner and McCant show convincingly that much of 1 Cor. 4:1-21 and 9:1-23, embodies not only irony (e.g., "Without us you came to 'reign as kings' — if only you did 'reign!'" 4:8) but also parody and self-parody. Self-parody is "fun-making" that makes delicate and subtle alterations to what would otherwise be a solemn self-defense. "A parodist manipulates various related genres including satire, burlesque, irony, and sarcasm" not least to puncture the pomposity of "pretentious people" (McCant, "Paul's Parodic Apologia," in *Rhetoric,* p. 179). Paul pretends to take high ground, but he is not really interested in whether the Christians in Corinth accord him high status, so offering a parody of a pretentious rhetorical defense that provides fun for those with eyes to see it.

One clear example of this technique comes in 2 Corinthians. In 2 Cor. 11:1 Paul signals that he will use a different genre by asking his readers to "bear with me a little in my weakness" (NRSV). "If I may boast a little. . . . I am saying [it] as a fool" (11:17). "For you gladly put up with fools, being wise yourselves" (v. 19). "Speaking as a fool, I also dare to boast" (v. 21). "Three times I was beaten with rods; once I received a stoning" (v. 25). "In Damascus . . . I was let down in a basket through a window in the wall and escaped" (v. 32). As Edwin Judge observed, in the ancient world to be "first over the wall" in attacking a besieged city, risking burning oil and the first strikes of the defenders on the wall, was indeed a hero's venture worthy of boast. Paul declares that he was "first over the wall" — but in the reverse direction of escape! Here indeed is self-parody within the "game" of "boasting" and self-promotion (cf. Phil. 3:7-11, esp. v. 8). How easily Paul *could* have played the Corinthian game of rhetorical self-glory!

IV. Some Remaining Issues of Introduction That Shed Further Light upon the Text

A. Archaeological Corroboration of the Roman Character of Corinth

The site of Corinth and its surroundings is particularly informative for our understanding of the city, its life and culture, and Paul's epistles.

The first fact to strike the modern visitor is the *dominating preponderance of Latin inscriptions over scarcely a single Greek inscription* in the Pauline period. If, like Paul, one arrives in Corinth from Athens, where inscriptions are in Greek, the contrast is all the more striking. This confirms the *Roman* character of first-century Corinth, and the need to reject some of the popular illusions or myths about Corinth that might apply only to the earlier Greek period.

Three examples of seeking to understand the text of this epistle emerge with force. (1) First, this Roman background sheds light on 1 Cor. 6:1-8. While Roman criminal law was administered with a reasonable degree of impartiality, *civil law* was usually a different matter. Those with financial resources, business or social influence, or wealthy or influential patrons, were in a position to offer incentives to judges or juries to find in their favor. Hence Paul's indignation that a Christian should take a fellow Christian to law is not a prohibition to resort to the law as such, but a repudiation of a Christian's taking advantage of his or her superior social or economic position *to manipulate* another believer through a use of power; and thereby to force them to part with goods or property unfairly. Some claim that the evidence is not sufficient to warrant this interpretation (Hall, *Unity,* pp. 76-77), but it reasonably fits the situation.

(2) The second example comes in 11:17-34. It concerns dining arrangements in a villa used for the administration of the Lord's Supper as if it were a banquet in the house of a householder. The excavation of a villa in an outer suburb at Anaploga reveals a dining room *(triclinium)* where invited guests would recline on couches of about 5.5 × 7.5 meters, while the hallway *(atrium),* including its space for the collection of rain, was about 5 × 6 meters (see fig. 5). Given Roman dining customs, it is plausible that "first class," favored guests reclined in the triclinium with an excess of good-quality food and wine, while "hangers on," or "the others," stood in the atrium and fed on inferior fare or even went hungry. Again, Hall expresses scepticism about this scenario (*Unity,* pp. 64-74), but his aim is to attack Theissen's reconstruction, and many have broadly accepted this account. The Roman framework of dining customs explains this background well.

(3) A third example comes from 11:1-16. Aline Rousselle and Dale Martin have shown that in Roman society for a married woman to appear in public without head covering would send out signals of her be-

Figure 5. Villa Mosaic

Archaeologists have excavated two Roman-style villas from the mid- or late-first century at Anaploga in the outer suburbs, west of the Forum. The mosaic formed the floor of the main room, the *triclinium*. The dimensions are approximately 7.5 × 5.5 meters, or roughly 24 × 18 feet. Allowing for the space taken by couches, this might accommodate some fifteen or more guests, while the *atrium* (a kind of lounge-hallway of about 6 × 5 meters, or 20 × 16 feet) might hold thirty to forty guests even allowing for the central pool of water collected from the roof (the *impluvium*). Some scholars argue that this arrangement sheds light on the problem seen in 1 Cor. 11:17-31, where some diners feel "second class" in relation to more favored guests: they might have eaten in the atrium.

ing an "available" woman, that is, available "for friendship or more." A respectable married woman, loyal to her husband, would not wish to dispense with her hood or veil in public. Paul's concern is for "respect and respectability" in public worship. We will comment further when we reach these passages.

B. *Pluralism, Benefaction, and Self-Promotion: Archaeological Corroboration*

(1) Archaeology also witnesses to the pluralism of religions in Corinth. Ruins of a *temple of Apollo* still stand, and the temple would have been ancient even in Paul's day (see fig. 6). Excavations of the temple of Asklepios revealed numerous terra-cotta models of body parts, presented in thanksgiving to the god of medicine for healing of those organs. There were also covered colonnades and courtyards where diners might invite friends or business colleagues to join them for a celebratory or companionable meal. It is not surprising that some of the more influential or self-aware Christians would have been reluctant to miss such social occasions as business opportunities or to maintain friendships. But it is equally unsurprising that many "weak" Christians felt squeamish about entering the precincts of a pagan temple where an "idol" presided. Paul had to apply pastoral judgment with both firmness and flexibility (8:1–11:1).

(2) *The Babbius monument* is one of the most intriguing archaeological remains. We noted it above. It probably belongs to the period of Tiberius, perhaps twenty years or so before Paul's visit. It witnesses both to benefaction and to self-promotion. Babbius probably rose from the ranks of the *nouveau riche* and was determined to leave his mark on the city and his name for posterity. No fewer than two inscriptions survive that tell us that he erected the monument "at his own expense," and one tells us that he approved the benefaction also. Some argue that he may well have begun as a freedman, since it has been shown that freedmen could rise to the office of *duovir* (Wiseman, "Corinth and Rome," p. 498). Thus some individuals in Corinth achieved a rapid rise to power and influence, amid a climate of highly competitive self-promotion.

(3) Another key monument lies outside the formal boundaries of the Corinth Museum and the official site. A slab of limestone, originally from Acrocorinth and once with the letters filled with bronze, reads: "*Erastus* in return for his aedileship laid [this] at his own expense." The date is generally placed around the middle of the first century. It is highly likely that this refers to the Erastus of Rom. 16:23, "Erastus, the city treasurer, . . . greets you."

(4) Paul knew nothing else but "pluralism" in every city of the em-

Figure 6. Temple of Apollo
Paul would have been amazed that some people today consider "pluralism" an obstacle to the credibility of the gospel. Every "deity" had a temple! Some of these temples were already ancient when Paul came to Corinth. (Ben Witherington)

pire, and not least in Corinth. Only perhaps among communities of very strict Judaism was it otherwise. However, today with the breakup of monolithic "modernity" into the fragmentation of the postmodern condition, some Christians lament that cultural diversity and "pluralism" constitute almost insuperable obstacles to the proclamation of the gospel. It defies imagination what Paul might have thought about these twenty-first-century defeatist laments over "pluralism" when the more monolithic traditions of the medieval and modern worlds represent only a passing era in the history of the West, unknown to Paul.

C. Paul's Arrival in Corinth, His Ministry, and Its Date

As Engels observes, Corinth was a logical choice to establish a strong Christian church since its numerous trade connections assured a rapid propagation of the gospel, and it also included a synagogue and Jewish community (*Roman Corinth*, p. 20). Those who became Christians there appear to have covered a wide social spectrum, from such named officeholders or householders as Erastus and Stephanas to many who had little social status, and included slaves as well as those who were poor, and freedpersons.

Paul traveled to Corinth from Athens. The comparison would have been startling. "Corinth offered advantages which Athens lacked. . . . Athens was no longer either productive or creative . . . a mediocre university town," while Corinth was "a wide-open boom town" (Murphy-O'Connor, *Paul*, p. 108). Paul's journey was one of some fifty miles. By the end of the first day on foot, he would probably have reached Megara, but the second day's travel would have been more hazardous until he reached the outer bounds of the Corinthian *territorium*.

Soon Paul would encounter jostling crowds, the paved *diolkos*, and traces of the Games of A.D. 49. Finally, he would take the Lechaeum road past markets and shops to the Forum. He would have passed the temple of Asklepios, the Peirene Fountains, and the triumphal arch. In the Forum he would have seen imposing administrative offices on the south side, and offices, shops and booths on the north. Traders, tourists, craftspeople, street hawkers, officials, messengers, slaves, and householders would have thronged the streets and Forum at busy times.

If Paul's first preaching was "in weakness, with much fear and trembling" (2:2-3), it is possible that (as Schweitzer and Dibelius suggest) Paul had arrived in poor health. At all events he soon began spreading the gospel focussed on "Christ crucified" (2:2), choosing to renounce the audience-pleasing "cleverness" and rhetoric that so many in Corinth would have preferred (2:1, 5). He settled in with fellow Christians Aquila and Priscilla, who shared the same trade (Acts 18:3, 11; cf. 1 Cor. 16:9), communicating the gospel as he plied his trade in their combined shop and workshop, although presumably also at the market, at the fountains, and elsewhere. It is possible that Stephanas and his household were the first converts following Paul's arrival (16:15; cf. 1:16). Gaius and Crispus were also among the early converts (1:16). Paul left Corinth after some eighteen months by ship from Cenchreae for Ephesus (cf. Acts 18:11-19). Paul's ministry in Corinth would have been from around March A.D. 50 to around September 51.

The archaeological evidence for dating includes a letter from the

Figure 7. The Bema

This site is usually regarded as the "judgment seat" at which Paul appeared before the Roman Proconsul Gallio (cf. Acts 18:12-17). Prior to 1905 there was some scepticism about this Gallio allusion in Acts, but in 1905 four fragments of a letter of the Emperor Claudius relating to Lucius Junius Gallio were discovered. They were published in 1913. Two further fragments were published in 1967. The letter reflects a date of April or May A.D. 52 (or August 52 at the latest). The letter is a report, and dates Gallio's proconsulship in Corinth from *either* July 51 to June 52 *or* July 50 to June 51. Either way it situates Paul at Corinth in A.D. 51. In turn, 1 Corinthians might be dated between A.D. 53 and 55, probably 53-54. Paul returned to Ephesus probably in August or September 52, where he stayed for the most part for eighteen months. During this period he wrote 1 Corinthians. (Phoenix Data Systems, Neal and Joel Bierling)

Emperor Claudius to Governor Gallio, before whom Paul appeared in Corinth (Acts 18:12-13; see fig. 7). Some fragments of the letter were first discovered in 1905; then three more in 1910, and the last two fragments in 1967. I discuss this evidence in my longer commentary (*First Epistle,* pp. 29-32).

D. *The Writing of the Epistle: Its Occasion, Date, and Unity*

After he left Corinth in A.D. 51, Paul made Ephesus his pastoral and missionary base through the period 52-53, or perhaps up to the summer of 54. (Some scholars believe that Paul wrote the Epistle to the Galatians there in A.D. 53, but others place it earlier.) From Ephesus Paul revisited the Christian communities in Galatia, Antioch, and elsewhere. Meanwhile Apollos visited Corinth and then returned to Paul in Ephesus with disturbing news. This may well have provoked the writing of the "previous" letter before 1 Corinthians, to which Paul clearly refers in 1 Cor. 5:9, "I wrote to you in my letter not to mix indiscriminately with immoral people." Almost certainly this previous letter became lost, although some identify it with 2 Cor. 6:14–7:1.

By around A.D. 54 (or possibly 53) Paul received news of Corinth from two further sources. An oral report reached him through "Chloe's people" (1 Cor. 1:11). These may have been agents working for Chloe, and were presumably members of the church in Ephesus. Paul also received a letter of inquiry from Christians in Corinth. This raised questions about marriage and celibacy (7:1), about food offered to idols (8:1), about the gifts of the Holy Spirit (12:1), and other issues. Our "1 Corinthians" combines responses from Paul to both sources. His response to the oral report is more clear-cut and at times stern (1:10–6:20). His replies to questions from Corinth recognize the complexity of sensitive areas where often something has to be said on both sides, especially in chapters 7–10.

Paul sets everything in the light of the cross and of a crucified Christ, and toward the end he expounds the resurrection. Throughout the epistle Paul needs to redefine terms that Christians in Corinth had begun to distort or to use in "Corinthian" ways, in effect to deconstruct and reconstruct "spirituality" on their own terms. Although some writers have suggested the contrary, the unity and integrity of the epistle is inescapable. It fits together as a single, coherent exposition of God's *grace* and the centrality of the *cross* and the resurrection. Throughout the epistle *love* is a unifying theme. Love *builds* (8:1).

Every quality attributed to love in chapter 13 applies to the church in Corinth. Love "does not burn with envy; does not brag — is not inflated with its own importance. It does not behave with ill-mannered impropriety; is not preoccupied with the interests of the self. . . . It never tires of support, never loses faith, never exhausts hope, never gives up. Love never falls apart. . . . Tongues . . . will stop. . . . 'Knowledge' . . . will be rendered obsolete. . . . The greatest . . . is love" (13:4, 5, 7, 8, 13). Even the supposed constraints governing the conduct of public worship are to promote respect for "the other," to build the whole church, and to spread the gospel to others.

All the same Paul does not want the Christians in Corinth to live with inhibitions and moralistic rules. His concern is that their grounds for joy, glory, and "boasting" should not lie in illusory claims about achievements and "success" judged in terms of competitive human comparisons. If they glory, they are to glory in God (1:29-31; 3:21). The invitation to glory solely in God and in what God has given as sheer gift is another way of expressing the truth of justification by grace. In this epistle this is expounded not as an abstract doctrine, but as an axiom of Christian identity that applies to every aspect of Christian life as this is lived out in the rough-and-tumble of the everyday church and world.

Text and Commentary

I. Address, Greeting, and Thanksgiving (1:1-9)

A. Address and Greeting (1:1-3)

1 Paul, called to be an apostle of Christ Jesus through the will of God, and our dear Christian brother Sosthenes, 2 to the church of God which is in Corinth, to those who are sanctified in Christ Jesus, called to be holy people, together with all who call on the name of our Lord Jesus Christ in every place, both their Lord and ours. 3 Grace and peace be to you from God our Father and from the Lord Jesus Christ.

Apostle (v. 1) will prove to be an important word in this epistle. Paul attaches importance to it in 9:1-3 ("Am I not an apostle? Have I not seen Jesus our Lord?"), in 12:28 ("God placed in the church, first, some who are apostles"), 15:8-9 ("least of all the apostles"), and elsewhere. Traditionally many commentators, including Calvin, argue that this allusion to **apostle** is "to gain authority." This is true in part, for Paul does not write to Corinth merely to offer personal opinions, or on his own initiative. He writes as God's spokesman, commissioned to undertake a task given rather than sought. Nevertheless, recent research on apostleship confirms that **apostle** points away from the self to Christ, to whom apostles bear witness. Crafton helpfully observes, "Apostles are . . . windows on God's design. . . . [Their] agency is inherently transparent (*The Agency of the Apostle*, p. 63).

Apostleship does not promote an obtrusive self-importance. It provides an uninterrupted view of Christ. The only stumbling block should be that of the cross (1:18), not the distracting, self-important, or sometimes unattractive personality of a witness. In this sense all Christian witness should be "apostolic." Since it rests entirely on God's *grace* (1 Cor. 15:10) apostleship also precludes personal merit as its basis. Chrysostom observes, "Now here of Him that calls . . . everything; of him that is called, nothing . . . but only to obey" (*Homilies on 1 and 2 Corinthians,* Homily 1).

Apostolic witness testifies both to belief *that* Christ died and was raised (9:1-3; 15:8, 9) and to belief *in,* that is, to a personal, firsthand sharing in Christ's mission and work. Hence witness to Christ and to the cruciform gospel entails proclamation by both word and lifestyle. In chapter 9 and elsewhere (e.g., 4:8-13) apostolic lifestyle forms part of the apostolic witness. Those aspects of apostleship that relate to the apostles' unique role as the first witnesses to the resurrection remain foundational, unrepeatable, and universal. On the other hand, aspects of apostleship that "back" the apostolic message by an apostolic lifestyle also characterize apostolic faith and life from generation to generation.

Paul stresses that his **call to be an apostle** was not something that he had sought for himself. He was pressed into the service of Christ by **the will of God** (v. 1). It was not his choice. This is even clearer from 1 Cor. 9:15-18; Acts 26:14; and Gal. 1:15. These passages reflect the call of Jeremiah (Jer. 1:4-10; 20:7-9). Jeremiah, like Paul, insists that his is no self-chosen task. He has been *called* to it. Paul implies that he would never presume to write to the Corinthians in the way that he does unless God had laid upon him this task.

Paul's desire not to be unnecessarily obtrusive coheres with his use of *the conventional form of greeting and introduction* shared by most Greek letters of the day. To be sure, he fills out this conventional form with added Christian content. All the same, Paul does not regard the gospel as necessarily countercultural. Exceptions occur only when some external cultural norm genuinely conflicts with the values or ethics of the gospel. Thus on one side in 6:1-8 he rejects any Christian use of unfair influence or patronage to gain personal advantage over a fellow Christian (see below) because here is a cultural clash with the gospel. But on the other side in 8:1-13 Paul warns against an over-scrupulousness that would remove Christians of social or business influence from friends and contacts that might involve dining in the precincts of pagan temples where some social events might conventionally be held (see below on ch. 8).

Called to be holy people, together with all who call on the name of our Lord Jesus Christ (v. 2b) brings into focus the vocation of all Christian people, in parallel with Paul's vocation, **called to be an apostle** (v. 1). However, these two callings or "vocations" overlap, and are not mutually exclusive. The notion that Christians are called to be what God has already made them (**to those who are sanctified in Christ Jesus**, v. 2a) reflects the kind of logic that characterizes the command to ancient Israel to go in *"to possess"* the land, for God *"has given* you" the land (Josh. 1:1-3, 11-12). Here the emphasis of the word *holy* lies primarily in the notion of *belonging to God* as his own special, distinctive people. In the sense of being "set apart," it has rightly been said, "Holiness is received, not achieved" (Conzelmann, *1 Corinthians*, p. 21). Paul does not imply that Christians are already morally perfect. Another writer well expresses the point that "the church is a school for sinners, not a museum for saints." Nevertheless, Christian discipleship involves striving to become that which in terms of status God has already given. Practical holiness entails being transformed in Christ-likeness and goodness day by day. This is living out in practice what *belonging to God* means.

Yet steady growth in love, goodness, and Christ-likeness occurs mainly within a community. Only more exceptionally does it relate to a Christian as a lone individual. These opening words form an overture to Paul's consistent attacks upon undue individualism. Even apostleship involves "co-workers" (3:9). Paul emphatically rejects the notion that the local church in Corinth may view itself as self-sufficient, in isolation from other Christian communities. They belong to the wider Christian church. The readers are called to be holy **together with all who call on the name of our Lord Jesus Christ in every place, both their Lord and ours** (v. 2b).

Paul rejects all claims by the Corinthian church to be autonomous. Too often they seem to imagine that they are the only pebble on the beach; that they can think and live, or sink or swim, without regard to the traditions and practices of other Christians in other places. Throughout this epistle Paul utterly rejects such "local" thinking. "We are also a part of a universal church. . . . We must feel a sense of oneness with every other confessing and worshiping believer in Christ" (Johnson, *1 Corinthians*, p. 38).

The phrase **their Lord and ours** has invited more than one explanation. Some ascribe it to an indignant scribe, or possibly to Sosthenes, who is outraged by the exclusivism with which many in Corinth seek to monopolize Christ as *"their* Lord," in isolation from the experience and allegiance of other Christians. The point remains the same, however, whether it is Paul or another who makes the comment. No Christian, or group of Christians, possesses a monopoly of the presence, wisdom, or power of Christ. This is why in 1:13 Paul indignantly exclaims, "Has Christ been apportioned out?" That is to say: Has Christ become the exclusive property of some specific group of Christians rather than of all?

The temptation to assume a monopoly of Christ's presence and authority may take various forms. One such self-preoccupied church officer visited Charles Spurgeon, the great nineteenth-century preacher. On being told that Spurgeon could not see him yet, the church officer replied, "But tell Mr. Spurgeon that the Lord's messenger awaits him." A maid returned to the door with the message, "I am sorry, sir, but Mr. Spurgeon says that he's engaged with the Lord!" In the same vein the Christian who misses a flight on a plane doomed to crash may be tempted simply to thank God afterward for a personal deliverance, with not a thought for the passenger who took his or her seat. The **call to be holy** entails looking beyond individual or corporate self-centeredness.

Sosthenes is Paul's **dear Christian brother** (v. 1). We have added "dear" to **brother** in v. 1 because in many contexts found in Greek texts the word conveys bonds of warmth, intimacy, and collegiality that the English "brother" alone may seem to miss. Paul cites this family bond in 8:11 ("the brother [or sister] for whom Christ died").

To **call on the name of the Lord** (v. 2b) reflects the promise of Joel 3:5, which Paul will repeat in Rom. 10:13. "To preach Jesus as Lord" (2 Cor. 4:5) is a summary of the proclamation of the gospel, while "Jesus is Lord" is arguably the earliest Christian creed. **Name** denotes reputation or character. **Lord** denotes the one to whom absolute, unconditional trust and obedience are due (see on 12:3). Both terms together invite unreserved trust and confident commitment from those who, as "slaves of Christ" (6:20), "belong" fully and totally to him.

Grace and peace (v. 3) complete the conventional *form* of the greeting "writer to recipient, greeting," which is then customarily followed, as here, by a thanksgiving. However, it is the form rather than the *content* that is merely conventional. **Grace and peace** here are more than a greeting. A number of writers use the phrase "wish prayer" to denote the multiple functions of these words. All three acts, greeting, wishing, and praying, may be thought of as *actions*. The technical term for this is "speech acts" because speech here does more than merely convey information. It is the language of transaction that *does* something: it *conveys* grace and peace.

Grace (v. 3) denotes God's free, unmerited, sovereign gift, but here especially the gift of God himself: grace is inseparable from God's own presence. As Karl Barth rightly observes, the Corinthians all too readily exulted in "gifts" and "experiences" rather than in God. God's gifts *are* God himself. Hence, Barth insists, the phrase *"of God"* is the central nerve of this epistle (*The Resurrection of the Dead,* p. 18). **Peace** (v. 3) is more than a subjective feeling of inner tranquility. The Greek translation of the Hebrew *shālōm* denotes an objective state of well-being. In a distinctively Christian context this includes most especially a state of harmony with God, who is the source of peace or well-being.

Paul names **God our Father and the Lord Jesus Christ** (v. 3b) as respectively the ultimate source and mediating channel of this **grace and peace**. They come *from* **God**, *through* **Christ**. This very close association between God and Christ as co-givers has sometimes been said to point, for Paul, to "the Christlikeness of God." The nature of God's gifts is to be seen in the light of the person and work of Jesus Christ.

1. SUGGESTIONS FOR POSSIBLE REFLECTION ON 1:1-3

1. *On Christian calling (vv. 1-2):* Calling, like "apostolic" work, applies both to being called as Christians to witness to Christ and to being called to serve God in a particular way. To hear God's call may require careful attentiveness and willing openness, although Paul was otherwise pressed into God's service. Is there a difference between putting oneself forward in the hope of self-fulfillment and responding to God's call for what God wills? Should Christians today reflect more on "vocation"?

2. *On apostleship (v. 1):* Apostles are to point transparently to the focus of apostolic witness, namely, to *Christ.* Does overly ready language about "claiming authority" sometimes distract the eye from Christ to the agent?

3. *On churches "in every place" (v. 2):* Some Christians seem to want to learn only from their own patch: from their own era, their own culture, their own local church. What do they lose by shutting their eyes to the experiences and lifestyle of Christians and churches in other times and places? Could this narrow even intercessory prayer as being only for "people like us"? Might some extreme forms of contextual theology give too much privilege to the local over against "all the churches"?

4. *On using conventions and courtesies (v. 3):* Paul used the letter conventions of his day. Overly eager notions of the church as a "counterculture" can sometimes lead to brushing aside conventions, courtesies, or forms of address that are expected in the everyday world. Might this damage, rather than enhance, Christian witness, at least for some?

B. Thanksgiving (1:4-9)

4 I give thanks to my God always for you on the ground of God's grace given to you in Christ Jesus, 5 because in every respect you were enriched in him, in every kind of speaking and with all kinds of knowledge, 6 as the witness to Christ was confirmed among you, 7 so that you fall short in no gift, while you wait for the public revealing of our Lord Jesus Christ. 8 He will keep you firm to the end, free from any charge, on the day of our Lord Jesus Christ. 9 Faithful is God, through whom you were called into communal participation in the sonship of Jesus Christ our Lord.

Thanksgiving constitutes the first theme of this section. It includes at least three distinctive features that invite pastoral reflection. First, while **I give thanks** (v. 4) corresponds with the conventional form of ancient Greek letters, in such letters the writer customarily give thanks for health, safe travel, or some other personal benefit. Here, however, Paul's thanksgiving is not for personal benefits for him, but for what *God has given to others.* The welfare of others, rather than simply his personal well-being, is his major cause for **giving thanks**. Paul also gave thanks **always** (v. 4), that is, on every occasion.

Second, this thanksgiving has a distinctively Christian basis, namely, the *undeserved grace of God.* Paul introduces an economic metaphor of **enrichment** or riches (cf. 4:8), which he also expounds elsewhere. The readers have "nothing that [they] have not received" (4:7). In due course he will replace their favored term "spiritual [gifts]" (Greek *pneumatika*) with the more theological, less experience-oriented term "freely given [gifts]" (Greek *charismata*). Gifts, given without strings, invite the **giving of thanks**. *Grace* plays no smaller part in this epistle than it does in Romans.

Third, perhaps the greatest surprise is that Paul genuinely and generously thanks God for the very gifts that caused him the greatest problems in Corinth: divisions, disappointments, competitive comparisons, and the illusion of being self-sufficient or "special" in a self-affirming sense. Later he will warn them that **knowledge** (v. 5) too often "inflates" the ego or "puffs up" the self (8:1; cf. also 14:4). Yet Paul holds on to the positive potential of such gifts, and he **gives thanks** for them. If they are used in accordance with Christ-centered criteria and love (expounded in chs. 12-14), these **gifts** (v. 7) may constitute a positive blessing to the church as a whole.

The second theme turns on the repeated use of the name **Christ**. The first ten verses of this chapter contain no fewer than ten occurrences of the name. Every gift and blessing is given in **Christ** (vv. 4-7); the apostolic gospel witnesses **to Christ** as its content (v. 6); Paul appeals to his readers "in the name of Christ" (vv. 7, 10); the Christian life is lived in **communal participation in the sonship of Christ** (v. 9). Christians wait for the **public revealing of Christ** (v. 7). Christian faith finds its focus not in ideas or systems, but in the *person* of Christ in whom God meets us.

If God as Father is the source and ground of all that is good, Christ is the mediator or channel of these gifts. Christ's work is of cosmic significance and embraces more than personal forgiveness. Since all Christian life is Christomorphic and cruciform, Paul makes his appeal "in the name of Christ" (v. 10). In consumer markets, brand products rely on their *name:* Christ's *name* conveys his limitless love and outstretched arms. How can Christians at Corinth place self-esteem and competitive power play above all that this name should call to mind? Furthermore, Christians have a deeper involvement in this *name* than simply "fellowship" (NRSV). The Greek word *koinonia* (v. 9) entails the notion of being a shareholder, or a stakeholder, or (perhaps best) having **communal participation in the sonship of Christ** (v. 9), that is, living out the status of a derived sonship that draws its character from what it is for **Christ** to be God's **Son**. Our "sonship" is *defined* in terms of Christ's sonship.

Christians **wait for the public revealing** [Greek *apokalypsis*] **of our Lord Jesus Christ** (v. 7b), not least because they eagerly await the full, public vindication of Christ's work and the full, public disclosure of Christ's glory. This introduction prepares the way for 13:9-10, "We know in fragmentary ways; we prophesy part by part. But when the completed whole comes, what is piece by piece shall be done away." Present discipleship may be marked by certain ambiguities, but there is always sufficient light to take the next step in faith. Thus Christians long for the curtains to be flung open wide, for the sun to stream in upon the whole of reality, and for Christ to be seen by all as he truly is. Meanwhile, faith a step at a time calls for a certain humility in which a brittle, cocksure, arrogant certainty about everything would be out of place. Again, Paul prepares for what he says in 8:1: "'Knowledge' inflates; love builds."

The third theme of this section relates to *God's faithfulness and God's gifts.* The use of "all," translated here as **in every kind of speaking and with all kinds of knowledge**, is *qualitative,* not quantitative or numerical. We might say of a social event "everyone was there," without implying a *numerical* totality. Paul gives thanks for the *range* of gifts of speaking and apprehending in their many modes. In the modern West we tend to limit "speaking" to speaking *to* an audience *about* God. As Barth and Bultmann insisted, God-given speech is primarily speech *from* God rather than merely speech *about* God; and, we may add, it also includes Spirit-prompted speech *to* God, of which many of the Psalms offer a model.

Inspired or (better) *"given"* speech may include teaching, preaching, and personal witness, but no less adoration, intercession, thanksgiving, petition, confession, absolution, declaration, celebration, expressions of lament, yearning, or longing, and many more modes of vocalization or communication. Although Paul is not the author of the Epistle to the Hebrews, Heb. 1:1-13 provides a marvelous example of the opening of a sermon that includes praise, confession, exposition, declaration, theology, hymns, and other multidimensional modes, which put to shame in their richness our overly worn distinctions between "sermons that proclaim" and "sermons that teach."

Yet because rhetoric played an undue part in cultural concerns for competitive achievement and power play in the city of Corinth, even these gifts of God were capable of abuse. The very "richness" (**you were enriched**, v. 5) of this multidimensional phenomenon (see chs. 12-14) could bring side effects of competitive status-seeking and a chaotic lack of orderedness in worship. If God gives without strings, it does not detract from the value of the gifts if human persons use them irresponsibly or even for self-aggrandizement.

Precisely the same principle applies to **knowledge**. Sometimes Paul uses the term as if it carried quotation marks. "Knowledge" inflates (8:1). The noun (Greek *gnōsis*) often carries an illusory or pejorative sense, in contrast to the verb, as most especially in "coming to know God" (Greek *epignōsomai*) in 13:12. "Knowledge" is sometimes used as it is here, in a wide, general sense that embraces wisdom, understanding and reason. In many contexts it remains essential to conserve the distinction between *being wise* and using reason, information, or cognitive knowledge. Here, however, **knowledge** is used in a nontechnical sense to denote a general gift of understanding that, on one side, provides a condition for wisdom but on the other side can lead to arrogance, self-importance, and individualism. Paul thanks God for this gift, given to others, leaving aside for the present whether or not others proceed to abuse it.

Paul places the emphasis on the theme of *gift* and *giving* through a combination of nouns (Greek *charis* or *grace*, v. 4; *charisma* or *freely given gift*, v. 7) and verbs, *to give* and *to make rich* (v. 5). This excludes *self-achievement*: "What do you have that you did not receive?" (4:7). In chapters 12-14, as we have noted above, Paul replaces the Corinthians' preferred term *"spiritual [gifts]"* (Greek *pneumatika*) with his own preferred term *"freely given gifts" (charismata)* to make this point.

God's giving is part of his **faithful** provision on the ground of which believers will be **kept firm to the end, free from any charge, on the day of our Lord** . . ." (v. 8). When **charges** may be put forward at the last judgment, Christians cannot be accused because in Christ they are unimpeachable or legally blameless. Everything has been "put right." If they need "gifts" to insure that their final salvation is secure, God sees to it that they **fall short in no gift** (v. 7). This epistle constantly anticipates the Epistle to the Romans on grace, and on justification by grace through faith alone. It is no less robust on this subject.

2. Suggestions for Possible Reflection on 1:4-9

1. *On thanksgiving (vv. 4-7):* The greatest cause for thanksgiving as Paul sees it is God's *grace,* or his love without strings. But he is as warm in his thanks that God gives this to other Christians as in his gratitude for what God gives to him. Do Christians thank God warmly enough for blessings given to *others?* Do we also give thanks for "mixed" blessings (e.g., when the gift of speech in Corinth was both a blessing and a snare)? Can thanks ever be self-centered (e.g., when one person receives something at the expense of another's losing it)?

2. *On the repeated use of the name of Christ:* "Christ" is used five times in these six verses. Do concerns about doctrines, ideas, and practices ever serve to divert the central focus from *Christ?*

3. *On God's faithfulness:* Christians are invited to rest securely on God's promise that he will keep us "to the end" (v. 8). Such freely promised security may meet with three different responses: from some, doubt; from others, presumption; from still others, trustful faith. Martin Luther writes, "Faith is a living, daring confidence in God's grace, so sure and certain that a man would stake his life on it a thousand times. . . . It makes men glad and bold and happy in dealing with God and with all his creatures" (*Preface to the Epistle to the Romans,* 1522).

II. Causes and Cures of Splits in the Church (1:10–2:5)

A. Report of the Situation: The Scandal of Personality Cults and Power Play (1:10-17)

10 I ask you, brothers and sisters, through the name of our Lord Jesus Christ, that you all take the same side, and that there are no splits among you, but that you be knitted together again with the same mind-set and with common consent. 11 For it was made clear to me about you from Chloe's people, my dear Christian family, that there are discords among you. 12 I mean this: each of you says, "I, for one, am one of Paul's people"; "I, for my part, am for Apollos"; "I am a Peter person"; "As for me, I belong to Christ." 13 Has Christ been apportioned out? Surely Paul was not crucified for you, was he? Or were you baptized in the name of Paul? 14, 15 I give thanks that I baptized none of you except

Crispus and Gaius, so that none of you can say that you were baptized in my name. 16 Well, I did also baptize the household of Stephanas; for the rest, I do not recall whether I baptized anyone else. 17 For Christ did not send me to perform baptisms, but to proclaim the gospel — not with clever rhetoric lest the cross of Christ should be nullified.

A key word in this passage is **splits** (v. 10; Greek *schismata*). We risk losing the point if we translate the Greek by a more formal word such as *divisions,* for these are not divisions of doctrine. Welborn observes that the problem is "a power struggle, not a theological controversy" (*Politics and Rhetoric,* p. 7). The word **split** (in the Greek) denotes a *tear* in a fishing net that needs to be mended (Mark 1:19), or a *rending apart* that has to be "put back to order" (2 Cor. 13:11). The word may be used metaphorically of a political divide. In the Fourth Gospel the preaching of Jesus provokes a *split* among the crowd of hearers (John 7:43; 9:16). It is very serious when **splits** or *tears* appear in the church. Since Paul calls the church Christ's body, it is almost as if this power play tears apart the limbs of Christ (1 Cor. 12:27; cf. 11:18).

Paul never defends those who say, "I am for *Paul*" (1:12). If the splits were doctrinal, we would expect him to do so. All of these subgroups or splinter groups are condemned wholesale, without discrimination.* In the face of this, Paul appeals or **asks** that the Christians in Corinth **all take the same side** (v. 10). This phrase takes up their "political" language. As Christian believers on the same side they share the same *grace as their basis of life* (1:4-9), and thus should exhibit **the same mind-set** (v. 10b). Paul will later explicate this as "the mind of Christ" (2:16). Here he appeals, or makes his request, in the **name of Christ** (v. 10a). The **name** constitutes a reminder of Christ's character and rep-

---

*Technical Note: This point remains important since in 1831 F. C. Baur proposed a speculative but influential theory based on the assumption that the "Christ party" at Corinth inclined toward a quasi-Judaizing opposition to claims for gospel freedom and emancipation from the law put forward by a supposed "Paul party." In the second half of the twentieth century, by contrast, a series of writers, including J. Munck and N. A. Dahl, urged that these groupings were not "parties" or "factions," but cliques gathered around certain personalities or reflecting a certain ethos. During the 1990s several writers, including L. L. Welborn and Margaret M. Mitchell, perceived a "political" dimension that reflected a power struggle for influence within the church, supported by a use of rhetorical confrontation. This complements rather than excludes Munck's approach.

utation as self-giving, sacrificial love for "the other," even at a cost to the self. Christians pray in this **name** with confidence.

To translate the Greek as "speak the same thing" (AV/KJV), "be in agreement" (NRSV), or "agree" (NIV) accurately reflects the word-for-word meaning but underplays the importance of the political or social context. Paul does not require uniformity or replication in every detail of doctrine, but a noncompetitive attitude that sets aside all hint of power play. J. B. Lightfoot suggested "free from factions" or "making up differences" (*Notes,* p. 151). Polyphonic harmony does not require dull unison but contributes to the beauty and coherence of the whole. The thrusting, competitive culture of the city of Corinth since its re-founding as a Roman *colonia* in 44 B.C. makes it all the more certain that competitive power play on the part of one group against another was the root problem in the church.

The names **Paul, Apollos, Peter,** and perhaps even **Christ** (v. 12) are a focus for political slogans rather than actual affiliations to those named. David Hall may well be right to urge in a recent study that here **Paul, Apollos, Peter,** and **Christ** are disguised references to *other un-named leaders* or teachers (*The Unity of the Corinthian Correspondence,* pp. 4-25). He argues persuasively largely on the basis of 4:6, where Paul speaks of making a "disguised" allusion to Apollos. In any case, Paul empha-sizes that he and Apollos are entirely "one in the work" (3:9), playing complementary and mutually supportive roles. So any pitting of one against the other in Corinth is either manipulative or misconceived.

If the four names were actually on the lips of Christians in Cor-inth (and we cannot be certain about this, although Hall's suggestion may be right), perhaps some thought to gain prestige by claiming some link with Peter the "senior" apostle, on whose confession Jesus had "founded" the church, while others may have imagined that a direct ap-peal to **Christ** might suggest a hyperspiritual bypassing of all merely human ministers. We know that in Corinth many sought to improve their status by finding respected and influential patrons. Plutarch speaks of those who, like ivy, sought to gain height or eminence by winding themselves around some figure of stature to climb upward (Plutarch, *Moralia,* lines 805 E, F). Perhaps in the same vein, some Chris-tians sought to gain reflected glory by involving leaders whom they may never have met or heard firsthand.

Paul finds such attitudes wholly incompatible with a Christian faith based on the proclamation of the cross. If Christ is "**split** up," so that each **split** claims to have a monopoly of Christ, how can anyone receive Christ in his wholeness and fullness (cf. 12:12)? Paul addresses an ironic question to what is supposedly "his" (Pauline) group: **Surely Paul was not crucified for you, was he?** (Greek *mē Paulos . . .*). Are you putting a human leader or patron in the place of Christ, and looking to him for your salvation through the cross? The allusion to **baptism** reinforces the point by considering the question: *to whom* was your *allegiance* made when you became Christians? Here is the ironic denunciation of all "personality-centred politics . . . characteristic of the surrounding Graeco-Roman society" (Clarke, *Secular and Christian Leadership,* p. 92).

Paul is so deeply distressed by misplaced statements of "allegiance" to human leaders, rather than to Christ, that he expresses relief that he did not risk more "Pauline allegiances" by conducting numerous baptisms (vv. 14-17). There was always the danger that the president or minister of a sacrament might be perceived as having a special bond with the person to whom they ministered. Paul's one settled, determined goal when he was in Corinth was to proclaim a crucified Christ, and this alone (2:2, 3). For his part, his sole "boast" is in the cross of Christ (Gal. 6:14). In Galatia he publicly "placarded" only Christ as crucified (Gal. 3:1).

3. Suggestions for Possible Reflection on 1:10-17

1. *On power plays in the church:* Power plays within the church can result in obscuring the centrality of Christ and perhaps unwittingly causing "splits." Are there traits in our own secular culture that draw Christians into such power plays? What happens to the vulnerable when church-people play this role? What might prevent people's "using" respected ministers, or their names, as convenient rallying points for divisive crusades or personal agenda?

2. *On agreement and a common mind:* Do we have to agree with everything that other Christians say to be "of one mind"? Are Christians ever guilty of unwittingly claiming a monopoly, in effect, of "the mind of Christ"? Do those who minister in the church sometimes encourage or discourage the kind of personal allegiance that would be at the expense of a more bal-

anced or rounded discipleship and the unity of the church? Too often good-hearted attempts to reform committees or church infrastructure may also lead, less happily, to divisive church power plays. These verses might help to prevent this.

B. The Criterion of the Cross: Power and Wisdom, Weakness and Folly (1:18-25)

18 For the proclamation of the cross is, for their part, folly to those who are on their way to ruin, but, for our part, the power of God to us who are on the way to salvation. 19 For it is written, "I will destroy the wisdom of the wise, and the shrewdness of the shrewd will I nullify." 20 Where is the sage? Where is the expert? Where is the debater of this world order? Has not God made a fool of the world's wisdom? 21 For since in God's wisdom it was not through wisdom that the world came to know God, it pleased God to save those who believe through the foolishness of what is proclaimed. 22 Since Jews asked for signs and Greeks seek wisdom, 23 but we proclaim a crucified Christ: to the Jews an affront; to Gentiles, folly; 24 but to those who are called, a Christ who is God's power and God's wisdom. 25 For God's foolishness is wiser than human wisdom, and God's weakness is stronger than human strength.

Perhaps surprisingly for modern readers Paul begins this section with a fundamental contrast not between **power** and **weakness**, but between **power** and **folly** (v. 18). The Christians in Corinth undoubtedly carried over from the culture of their city notions of power as influence or force, on the analogy of social or economic power, just as today many understand **power** from the analogy of the force of machinery, the power of electrical or electronic operations, the political power of votes, or the power of armed conquest or armed forces. This may lead to an overly hasty identification of **power** as the miraculous or the overwhelming. Paul speaks of **the power of God** in different terms.

The power of the cross is not that of sheer force, or of the big battalions. Jesus rejected such notions of **power** in his resistance to the messianic temptations, each of which enticed him to adopt a crude shortcut to raw power, especially through the use of the spectacular to manipulate belief by quasi-mechanical or "rhetorical" persuasion. Most characteristically in Paul **power** denotes that which is *effective*.

The proclamation of a humiliated, crucified Christ, whose manner of death was too shameful for mention in polite conversation (see below), had nothing to do with the spectacular or manipulative. But it *effectively empowered,* most especially as *power for,* rather than as a Christianized version of secular power *over.* The point is implicit in Luther's contrast between an inauthentic theology of glory and an authentic theology of the cross.

Hence what stands in contrast to God's **power** is not merely weakness. Indeed, Paul will later talk of power-in-weakness. The contrast is with **folly**, because folly leads to striving that is *ineffective, fruitless,* and *empty.* That this characterizes **those who are on their way to ruin** (v. 18) logically fits with this. The ineffectiveness and emptiness of foolish journeying (**on their way to** renders Paul's important choice of a *present* participle, *in process of . . .*) lead to the nothingness of an abyss in which the self is *"lost."* Folly brings self-destruction. However, Christian believers for whom the proclamation of the cross becomes an *effective reality* (**the power of God**) are turned away from such a fate and find themselves by God's grace **on the way to salvation** (another carefully chosen present participle that denotes a continuing *process*).

To those who think of Christian believers as "the saved" Paul's choice of the continuous present to denote the *process* of *being* saved may seem less than robust and confident. But Paul expounds salvation in terms of three tenses. A well-known analogy depicts those rescued from a sinking ship by a lifeboat as: (1) those who have been *saved:* they have been rescued from peril; but (2) as the lifeboat moves to the shore, they are *in process of being* saved. Finally, (3) they look ahead with longing to the lifeboat's reaching the solid shore. Then they *will be* saved. The Christians in Corinth took their salvation too readily for granted. "Already," states Paul with heavy irony, "you have been filled; already you have been enriched; without us [our pastoral support and teaching] you have ascended your thrones and 'reign as kings'! *If only it were so!*" (4:8). The readers are still on the journey; one that requires self-discipline, reflection, further understanding, and humility.

Paul now cites Isa. 29:14 to link these thoughts with God's unavoidable judgment upon human pretentiousness (v. 19). People are wrapped up in illusions of **wisdom** while living in **folly**. **The cross** now becomes a sifting *criterion* that exposes the difference between **folly** lived in an *illusion* of **wisdom** and a humble, realistic appropriation of the *true* **wisdom** of God, which is effective in leading to salvation. Through what is proclaimed concerning **a crucified Christ** (v. 23, not at this point a triumphalist Christ) God exposes the folly of the foolish and the effectiveness of true **wisdom** (vv. 20-21).

It is of critical importance to emphasize that this proclamation of **a crucified Christ** (v. 23) constitutes the greatest **affront** (Greek *skandalon*) to all except those who appropriate what is proclaimed. Martin Hengel's work is most instructive here (*The Cross*, pp. 93-263). Death on a cross was regarded in Roman society (and Corinth was a "Roman" city) as brutal, disgusting, and abhorrent. It was reserved for convicted slaves and convicted terrorists, and could never be imposed upon a Roman citizen or more "respectable" criminals. It was so offensive to good taste that crucifixion was never mentioned in polite society, except through the use of euphemisms. For Gentiles who might imagine a "divine" savior figure, and for Jews who expected a Messiah anointed with power and majesty, the notion of a **crucified Christ**, a Messiah on the cross, was an **affront** and an *outrage*. Alluding to Goethe, Nietzsche, and Marx, Jürgen Moltmann rightly warns us (also citing H. J. Iwand) that by "surrounding the scandal of the cross with roses," we too often forget its ugliness and shame (*The Crucified God*, pp. 35-36). After this commentary had been sent to the press a work by L. L. Welborn appeared, which presses this point even further. He argues that the "affront" was not primarily that a crucified Christ seemed anti-rational; it conveyed social stigma and vulgarity. "In the cross of Christ God has affirmed nothings and nobodies" (Welborn, p. 250).*

It is entirely understandable that Jews and Gentiles who were not believers should find the proclamation of the cross grossly offensive. But Paul's argument in this epistle suggests that *even some Christians in Corinth had tried to move "beyond" the centrality of the cross,* perhaps to a more Spirit-centered, more triumphalist religion. Against this attitude Paul insists that the cross of Christ constitutes the criterion and foundation of their very identity as Christians. The gospel itself *is the* **proclamation of the cross** (v. 18): folly to many it may be; but effective reality and transforming power it is to those who are **on their way to salvation**.

---

*Technical Note: L. L. Welborn, *Paul, the Fool of Christ: A Study of 1 Corinthians 1-4 in the Comic-Philosophical Tradition* (London and New York: T&T Clark/Continuum, 2005). I thank the publishers for allowing this late insertion.

Such Christians, Paul insists, need to hear afresh the effective reality of the cross as a *reversal* of all "natural" human values. For what the world naturally perceives as sheer **folly** is in fact divine **power** and divine **wisdom**. For **God's** so-called **"foolishness" is wiser than human wisdom**, and **God's** supposed **weakness is stronger than human strength** (v. 25). This act of "reversal" exposes the limitations of human perceptions and the fallibility of human knowledge. Two "worlds" confront each other at the foot of the cross, with diametrically opposing expectations and claims to "knowledge." Illusory or misguided "knowledge" inflates self-importance and self-reliance (8:1). Appropriation of the affront of the cross brings self-reliance to nothing and turns attention wholly to Christ as the source and channel of effective reality as God reveals it.

Even the world's **sages** and the world's **experts** are caught by this reversal of values and "worlds" (v. 20). As Dietrich Bonhoeffer observes, Paul's "reversals" simply reflect those of Jesus in the Sermon on the Mount. Jesus ascribes good fortune or "blessedness" not to the successful, not to the "powerful," not to the self-confident, but to the bereaved, the persecuted, and the poor (Matt. 5:3, 4, 10) because they are driven to abandon self-reliance, to seek the grace of God on God's own terms. Bonhoeffer writes: "If it is I who say where God will be, I will always find there a God who . . . corresponds to me, is agreeable to me. . . . But if it is God who says where he will be, . . . the place is the cross of Christ" (*Meditating on the Word,* p. 45). The proclamation of the cross replaces an emphasis on *achieving* with an opposing emphasis on *receiving* (as noted above). As Alexandra Brown aptly observes, the criterion of the cross "turns things upside down." This includes "the Corinthians' ways of knowing." The cross does this by projecting a new world founded upon having *the mind of Christ* (2:16; Brown, *The Cross,* pp. 33, 81, and 139). The cross, with the resurrection, is "Paul's point of departure" (Crocker, *Reading 1 Corinthians,* p. 2).

4. Suggestions for Possible Reflection on 1:18-25

1. *On being on the way to salvation:* Are some so hesitant to perceive themselves as "on the way to salvation" that they verge on the sin of despair, without assurance? Are others, on the contrary, so glibly certain that they have "arrived" that they are in danger of committing the sin of presump-

tion, suggesting a triumphalism that conflicts with the cross? "The three tenses of salvation" nurture sober confidence without triumphalism.

2. *On God's power:* Does the promise of "power" sometimes awaken desires that belong more closely to "folly" than to "the power of God"? Even Christians can still seek "power *over*" people rather than "power *for*" salvation, holiness of life, and God's service. The cruciform "mind of Christ" brings about a *"reversal"* of how the world perceives power. Nevertheless, God-given, legitimate "power" may sometimes *also* entail taking responsibility for a given task or situation. Might some be tempted to use "power in weakness" as an excuse to opt out of courageously accepting such responsibility? To suffer the cross entailed moral and physical courage as well as "weakness."

3. *On the cross:* Why might it be that *even Christians* drift into finding the cross an embarrassment or even an affront? If this occurs, what happens to our identity as Christians? Are there perhaps Christians today who appeal to an emphasis on the Holy Spirit to promote a supposed "advance" upon the centrality of the cross, when in reality it is to retreat? Bonhoeffer wrote that to seek to meet with God on our own terms rather than on God's terms at the cross leads to illusion and to a kind of self-constructed idolatry (cited above). The cross can never be a vehicle of self-affirmation (as some in Corinth seemed to think). Compare Nietzsche's critique of Christians: "'the salvation of the soul?' — in plain language: 'The world revolves round me'" (*The Antichrist,* aphorism 43). The cross delivers Christians from such self-preoccupation. On the cross Christ did for me what I could never have done for myself.

C. The Criterion of the Cross Applied to the Readers' Social Status (1:26-31)

26 Think about the circumstances of your call, brothers and sisters, that not many of you were intellectuals as the world counts cleverness, not many held influence, not many were born to high status. 27 But the foolish things of the world God chose in order to shame the clever; and the weak things of the world God chose to shame positions of strength. 28 The insignificant of the world and the despised God chose, yes, the nothings, to bring to nothing the "somebodies"; 29 so that all kinds of persons should not pride themselves before God. 30 It is as a gift from him that you are in Christ Jesus, who became for us wisdom

given from God: our righteousness and sanctification and redemption, 31 in order that, as it is written, "Let the one who glories, glory in the Lord."

The principle of "reversal" expounded in 1:18-25 finds further expression in the readers' own situation and experience in Corinth. In terms of the criteria of value that the world and the general culture of Corinth applied, many (although not all) of the Christians at Corinth were social **nothings** (1:28). Why should they wish to use the world's criteria of value when **not many of you were intellectuals as the world counts cleverness, not many held** [social] **influence, not many were born to high status** (v. 26)?

In fact, their sole claim to be *anything* or a "**somebody**" (v. 28b) rests upon God's new world of reversed values, within which they derive from or through Christ new **wisdom: . . . righteousness and sanctification and redemption** (v. 30). Through sheer **gift** (v. 30a) they *receive* from God an acceptance, a position, and a status that reverses their previous status as "nothings." If they reject, or fail to appropriate, the reversals brought about by God's act in Christ, they have undermined their own very ambition to achieve or to gain status. But this must come about *only through God's chosen method of gift; not through their preferred method of self-promotion.*

Translators have attempted to place due emphasis on the phrase **from him** (God) (v. 30). Hence REB renders the succinct Greek **from him** *(ex autou)* by a verbal phrase "by God's act." Merklein comments that Paul presses the point that the "reversal" is "no product of human effort. . . . It is through the initiative of God" without whom the Christians in Corinth would have remained "nothings" (*Non-beings*, v. 28; *Der erste Brief,* vol. 1, p. 200).

The role of this section within the broader argument is also instructive. Several recent commentators argue that Paul carefully deploys standard tools of classical rhetoric to present a coherent appeal to truth. The statement on *the splits* (1:10) provides a major *premise* (or *propositio*). Paul next gives an *exposition* of the premise (1:11-17; i.e., a *narratio*). He finally presses home a clear logical argument by means of a *demonstration* (an *argumentatio*) of the point in three blocks or strands: on the nature of the cross as the criterion of Christian identity and the power of God (1:18-25); on the reversal of the low status of many Christians in Corinth by God's sheer grace (1:26-31); and on Paul's own ministry in Corinth as a demonstration of cruciform criteria and "power" (2:1-5).

If this is valid (and it fits well with "good" classical rhetoric) Paul conscientiously prepares his approach to present as clear and as coherent an argument as possible, even if in the rush of actual dictation he also adapts some phrases as he goes along, for example, about his memory of whom he baptized (1:15-16). It is likely that *Paul respects careful preparation and reflection prior to communication,* although he does not allow this to tie his hands.

The phrases **not many held influence . . . not many were born to high status** (v. 26) have generated much debate. In summary, New Testament scholarship has passed through three phases. Adolf Deissmann *(Light from the Ancient East)* insisted that the overwhelming majority of Christians in the Pauline churches were drawn from the most underprivileged social classes. He insisted equally that the Greek of the epistles is the nonliterary everyday language of the people. In the 1960s counter-indications received more attention. Paul observes only that **not many** (v. 26) came from wealthy, influential, or well-born family backgrounds. E. A. Judge urged that Christians significantly included a "pretentious" section of the population of big cities *(Social Patterns,* p. 60). Such Christians as Crispus and Erastus (Rom. 16:23) owned property and held high office.

From the 1970s to the present there emerged a general recognition of widespread variations of social status. Gerd Theissen led this consensus with his essay "Social Stratification in the Corinthian Community" *(The Social Setting of Pauline Christianity,* pp. 69-144). Ben Witherington endorses this approach. He writes, "The social level of the Corinthian Christians apparently varied from quite poor to rather well-off . . . a fair cross-section of urban society" *(Conflict and Community in Corinth,* pp. 23-24). In terms of Christian apologetics it is constructive to recall that converts to the Christian faith included all types, all classes, all temperaments, all backgrounds, male and female, young and old. There is no single social or psychological "type" for whom the gospel held particular appeal. It has universal relevance. Within the church, however, tensions that may characterize social differences present a perennial pastoral challenge, just as they did at Corinth, not least in 8:1–11:34. However, the debate about the social mix of the earliest Christians still goes on.

Whether Christians are well off or in poverty, the direction of emphasis in 1:26-31 is indicated by a threefold repetition of **God chose** (vv. 27-28). It is God who by sheer gift raises the **nothings** to people who are accepted and accorded a status as the **redeemed** (v. 30). Even the better off remain relatively the **nothings** in the great reversals of the cross: **so that all kinds of persons should not pride themselves before God** (v. 29). The doctrine of God's sovereign grace remains no less central in this epistle than it is in Romans: "What do you have that you did not receive?" (4:7). If the Corinthians are hungry for status, true (rather than illusory) status can be found only "in Christ," by sharing derivatively what Christ imparts. Here is the Christian's ground of "boasting," and here alone. In v. 29 *"all flesh"* (Greek *pasa sarx*) is best understood in its generic sense to denote **all kinds of persons**. The phrase is often used in this way, and this meaning fits the context and Paul's main point.

Righteousness (v. 30) is used not to denote a level of moral achievement but God's acceptance of one whose *standing* has been "put right with God." Similarly, **sanctification** does not denote here a state of advanced moral or spiritual growth, but the status of *belonging* to God, or *nearness* to God. **Redemption** does not denote deliverance into some *autonomous* freedom, as Deissmann urged. It denotes rescue from hostile structural forces, including sin as a power of bondage, to a new state in which the redeemed *belongs* to Christ as *the Lord who has purchased the redeemed.* We explain this point more fully in the comments on 6:20, "You were bought with a price." All of these terms point to a new status and new security as accepted members of Christ's household or family. The *basis* of it all remains clear: "**Let the one who glories, glory in the Lord**" (v. 31). Paul is probably citing a version of Jer. 9:22-23. In spite of some claims to the contrary, Stanley argues, "Paul does not appreciably change the meaning of the verse" (*Paul and the Language of Scripture*, p. 188). In Greek literature, characters "glory in" what gives them most delight. Odysseus glories in his cunning, and Achilles in his strength. Christians find their ground of delight **in the Lord** rather than in qualities or supposed achievements of their own.

5. SUGGESTIONS FOR POSSIBLE REFLECTION ON 1:26-31

1. *On grounds for glorying:* To glory in our home, children, achievements, or possessions may range from innocent pleasure to illusion and self-

indulgence. In Homer's *Iliad,* Odysseus gloried in his guile, and Achilles in his strength. But for Paul one test of where our heart lies is whether our pride and delight is the generous grace of God in Christ. Jesus said, "Where your treasure is, there will your heart be too" (Matt. 6:21). Is God's grace the prime ground for finding it good to have been created?

2. *On trying to compensate for an undistinguished past:* Might humble origins or blighted backgrounds tempt us to look for compensatory ways of acquiring esteem within the church? Do "church activities" provide opportunities for power and influence that otherwise would not come? This would not fit well with sharing the shame and humiliation of the cross and with our Christian identity as those "in Christ" crucified.

3. *On social differences within the church:* Do social and economic differences between fellow Christians influence attitudes toward them in the church more than they should? These differences can become either potential sources of cliques and divisions within our church, or opportunities for Christian love and care that embraces all regardless of background.

4. *On redemption:* Do we regard "redemption" as freedom to do whatever we like, or as purchase from bondage to "belong" to the Lord who now takes responsibility for us? If the Lord now has the care of us, and we belong to him, does this release us from anxieties over self-blame or self-reproach, or from undue self-praise?

D. The Criterion of the Cross Applied to Paul's Mode of Preaching (2:1-5)

1 As for me, when I came to you, brothers and sisters, I did not come with high-sounding rhetoric or a display of cleverness in proclaiming to you the mystery of God. 2 For I did not resolve to know anything to speak among you except Jesus Christ, and Christ crucified. 3 I came to you in weakness, with much fear and trembling. 4 My speech and my proclamation were not with enticing, clever words, but by transparent proof brought home powerfully by the Holy Spirit, 5 that your faith should not rest on human cleverness, but on God's power.

Paul turns from the past experience of his readers in Corinth to his own experience there, comparing both of these experiences in relation to the cross of Christ. Paul did not come to Corinth to display his own achievements as a rhetorician or professional lecturer (v. 1) but to focus *only* on **Jesus Christ, and Christ crucified** (v. 2). Indeed, superficially the kind of *power* that some expected to overwhelm the hearers, whether by triumphalism, manipulative rhetoric, or spectacular miracles, appeared to have been absent: **I come to you in weakness, with much fear and trembling** (v. 3). Paul renounced the seductions of "spin" or audience-pleasing devices (v. 4). For if the birth of Christian faith depended on such manipulative methods, the genuineness of such a response might be open to question. Nevertheless, his preaching did exercise formative power to change lives. The basis of his hearers' turning to Christ rested on *God's effective action* (see on *power*, above). This "gospel power" is defined in terms of the cross, and is mediated through the effective agency of the Holy Spirit (v. 5). The Spirit renders this truth transparent and capable of personal appropriation.

Such an understanding of Paul's **weakness** receives corroboration from other parallels. 1 Cor. 2:1-5 does not stand alone. Paul's preaching in Galatia was marked by the physical weakness of poor health (Gal. 4:14), and later in Corinth his bodily presence and oral speech were deemed "weak" in contrast to his more forceful or effective letters (2 Cor. 10:10). Numerous writers substantiate the case that Paul deliberately distances himself from the rhetoric of "display" associated with the Second Sophistic movement in provincial cities. We refer to works cited in the Bibliography, including Bullimore, Pogoloff (esp. pp. 97-172), Litfin, and Winter (*Philo and Paul among the Sophists,* pp. 113-61).

Paul does not oppose the use of honest, "good" rhetoric, for he uses its forms in this epistle, partly in 1:18–2:5 but especially in chapter 15. Nevertheless, he utterly rejects *manipulative* and *audience-dominated* rhetoric. This was frequently attention seeking and aimed simply to persuade people, regardless of the truth of the matter at hand. "Good" classical Roman rhetoricians, most notably Cicero and Quintilian, would have endorsed Paul's disdain for those in Corinth who regarded rhetoric as a competitive "performance" designed to elicit applause, approval, and status from audiences. Plutarch attacks those self-absorbed, competitive rhetoricians who seek the status of "stars," comparable in this respect to audiences' favorite actors or gladiators. The more such popular stars argued persuasively against all reason and truth, the more thunderous the applause, Plutarch observed, that greeted their performance.

Many Christians in Corinth wished that Paul would show such

qualities. It would boost the status of the church if their leaders could compete with other professionals on the platform. Part of the reason why Paul could accept funding from Philippi but not from Corinth (1 Corinthians 9) related to these expectations of a more "professional" standing as well as to obligations to the more wealthy Christians who promoted the funding. So Paul speaks plainly of the events of the gospel of Jesus Christ as a humble leather worker or tentmaker, to the embarrassment of some of the professional classes in Corinth.

"Rhetoric" in the medium of oral monologue may not be the primary medium of manipulative communication today. A closer parallel might make certain uses of music and lighting, electronic simulation, or whatever might divert attention from Christ and the cross to the antics and style of the speaker. Sometimes this might be bullying or wheedling. Against this, Paul declares that his only resolve was to proclaim **Christ, and Christ crucified** (v. 2).

Paul's rejection of self-promotion and attention seeking proves that his **fear and trembling** (v. 3) had nothing to do with overly great concern about what his audience would think of him. Rather, he felt the burden of proclaiming Christ effectively without the rhetorical tricks of the trade when so much was at stake. **Fear and trembling** is the very opposite of the bland self-confidence of the Sophist rhetorician. In view of an allusion to ill health in Gal. 4:13-14, we should not exclude the possibility that Paul did not feel physically fit (see also 2 Cor. 12:7-10, where God does not answer affirmatively Paul's prayer for the removal of "weakness").

6. Suggestions for Possible Reflection on 2:1-5

1. *On "manipulative" ways of proclaiming the gospel:* The cross provides a criterion not only for *what* Christians say of Christ but also *how* they say it. Does preaching, teaching, or witness sometimes draw more attention to the speaker than to Christ? Some Christian preachers use manipulative devices or methods that are unworthy of an honest proclamation of the cross. Might certain ways of using music, lighting, or bullying or wheedling rhetoric risk bringing discredit to the gospel, and encourage "conversions" that are only skin-deep (v. 5)?

2. *On the centrality of the cross and respect for truth:* These verses do not provide any argument against disciplined, rigorous, and reasonable communica-

tion of the gospel. "Only Christ, only the cross" offers no approval of sloppy presentations of Christian truth. Paul rejects "pleasing the audience" because then the audience would be constructing or reshaping the gospel. But how could he be said to retreat from reasonable argument and careful communication when he uses so much argument in his epistles?

3. *On fear and trembling:* Why should anyone present gospel truth with "fear and trembling"? Is this sometimes fear of what others might think? Or would experiencing no fear suggest that the preacher has forgotten how much is a stake? Might experiences of "weakness" become occasions for experience of God's resurrection power? (See 2 Cor. 1:9; 11:30; 12:8-10.)

4. *On the peril of preaching "another gospel" without the cross:* Christ and the cross take center stage as Paul's focus of proclamation. Has the church lost some of Paul's zeal and passion about the folly of preaching "another" self-constructed gospel "to please people" (Gal. 1:8-10)?

III. The Holy Spirit and "Spirituality": The Mind of Christ (2:6-16 and 3:1-4)

In these sixteen verses Paul draws on a vocabulary and catchphrases that were favorite terms among the Christians in Corinth. The Corinthians relished such themes and terms as *wisdom, knowledge, spiritual,* and *mature.* Paul takes all these on board, but decisively *redefines* what they mean for Christians. Most notably and centrally, to be *"spiritual"* is not to draw upon an innate "higher" capacity of the human soul; it is to be moved, activated, and transformed by the Holy Spirit of God. In technical terms, Paul unfolds the transcendent and Christomorphic character of the work of God's Holy Spirit. Paul urges that the Spirit comes, as it were, from "Beyond"; the Spirit **issues forth from God** (v. 12). Further, the Spirit's work may be recognized by his effect of promoting **the mind of Christ** (v. 16). Far from showing a supposed **maturity** that moves "ahead" of the cross, Christians at Corinth remain for the most part still **childish** and even **unspiritual** (3:1-4). In our day, too, "spirituality" has become too readily disengaged from its transcendent and Christ-like dimension, as if it were "produced" not by the Holy Spirit of Christ but by innate human capacities.

A. True and False Wisdom: The Cross and "Maturity" (2:6-9)

6 Yet we do communicate a "wisdom" among the mature, but it is a wisdom which is not of this present world order, nor of the rulers of this world order who are doomed to come to nothing. 7 Well, we speak God's wisdom in discourse too profound for merely human discovery, a wisdom that was hidden, which God marked out beforehand, before the ages, for our glory. 8 None of the rulers of this present world order had come to know this. For if they had known it, they would not have crucified the Lord of glory. 9 However, as is it written, what eye did not see, and ear did not hear, and what no human heart conceived — how very much — God prepared for those who love him!

Paul begins this section by reinforcing the contrast between two different kinds of thing that go under the name of "wisdom." He takes up 1:19-21: "I will destroy the wisdom of the wise. . . . Where is the sage? Where is the expert? . . . Has not God made a fool of the world's wisdom?" He cannot leave matters there. For while a *false* wisdom, or the so-called wisdom of the world, proves to be self-defeating, the **hidden wisdom of God** (v. 7) is *true* wisdom. There is one kind of so-called wisdom that is pretentious, self-affirming, and seeks to operate by means of human achievements; and there is a God-given, received, revealed wisdom that nurtures and directs the life of the people of God, and (in sometimes hidden ways) also the world as God's creation.

As for Christian **maturity** (Greek *teleios,* "mature," v. 6), this denotes not some supposed second or advanced stage that has left the cross behind, but growth in Christ-likeness (v. 16). Since the framework of thought remains that of a *crucified* Christ in these chapters, this turns Corinthian notions of maturity as "advanced" spirituality upside down. Once again the *reversals of the cross* operate with incisive and transforming logic.

The use of the plural "we" in place of the singular "I" may indicate that Paul initially shares the terminology that he is about to use with his Corinthian readers. But the meaning that Paul ascribes to **wisdom** is very different from assumptions about its meaning in Corinth. There may well be irony in Paul's taking up their word **mature** or *adult* in v. 6. For Paul insists that the self-centered "cleverness" beloved at Corinth is a product of the very opposite quality, namely, "childishness" (see 3:2). It is childish to use "cleverness" to score points or to engage in power play (1:10-12) or self-promotion. Children are often attention seeking. **God's** *true* **wisdom**, Paul counters, is *strictly for adults* who want to learn rather than to show off.

This adult wisdom is given, not achieved, by revelation. Hence even the structural powers of this world order cannot find access to it on their own terms (vv. 6b and 8). The phrase **the rulers of this** present **world order** (vv. 6b, 8) has been variously understood to mean either demonic powers or earthly, human rulers. Some argue that these "rulers" (Greek *archontes*) are both supernatural and political.* However, the main emphasis of this allusion to "rulers" may best be understood as referring to political, social, and spiritual structures that overwhelm the powers of mere individuals, leaving open whether this includes demonic agencies also. Paul has considerably less interest in "demons" than many attribute to him.

The central point for Paul is that while what is **too profound for human discovery** (v. 7) and **what no human heart conceived** (v. 9) can be apprehended only by *revelation,* if some at Corinth reserved such esoteric revelation for a second-stage elite ("the mature"), Paul places all Christians on the same footing, as long as they are "adult" enough to want to receive and to learn in due humility. We may compare 3:18, "he must become a fool if he is to become wise." Jesus and Socrates support this axiom. If the cross places all Christians on the same level as in equal need of divine grace, the gift of **wisdom** also operates on this basis. The source of the quotation from the Old Testament is disputed, but Paul probably combines at least two sources: Isa. 64:4 and 65:17.

---

*Technical Note: Origen and many other Church Fathers view these powers as demonic, and in modern times C. K. Barrett, H. Conzelmann, and W. Schrage support this interpretation. A. Wesley Carr argues a contrary view in *Angels and Principalities* (Cambridge: Cambridge University Press, 1981). However, O. Cullmann, *Christ and Time* (Eng. tr.; London: SCM, 1951), pp. 191-201, and George B. Caird, *Principalities and Powers* (Oxford: Clarendon, 1956) argue that both supernatural and political or structural evil forces may be intended. The view we propose comes nearest to that of Walter Wink, *Naming the Powers* (Philadelphia: Fortress, 1984) and *Unmasking the Powers* (Philadelphia: Fortress, 1986), and Neil Elliott, *Liberating Paul,* pp. 114-24.

7. Suggestions for Possible Reflection on 2:6-9

1. *On the difference between wisdom and information:* Wisdom is different from knowledge or information. People readily confuse the two, especially if they strive for even more information before they have applied wisdom to what they may already know. Gaining wisdom might well be more costly than the sheer labor of compiling information. Wisdom entails a willingness to *receive* and to *listen* in sensitivity to "the other," and the will to apply it. In what ways is this costly?

2. *On the wisdom of the world, or false wisdom:* "Wisdom" harnessed wholly to personal ambition can degenerate into a self-defeating, illusory cleverness. How often does this characterize the outlook of those who have power in the world?

3. *The wisdom of God as true wisdom:* If human discovery is largely a matter of work and achievement while divine revelation comes as a gift, how may we *acquire* divine wisdom (as Paul and the book of Proverbs enjoin us to do)? Is it, like justification by grace, to be received as a gift but appropriated day by day?

B. *The Criterion of the Spirit's Action and Presence (2:10-16)*

10 God revealed these things through the Spirit to us! For the Spirit searches out everything, even the depths of God's own self. 11 For who among human beings knows what pertains to the person in view except that person's innermost self? Even so, no one knows what pertains to God except the Spirit of God. 12 Now, as for us, it is not the spirit of the world that we received, but the Spirit who issues from God, in order that we may know the things that were freely given to us by God. 13 These things, further, we communicate not in speech taught out of mere human cleverness, but in language which the Spirit teaches, interpreting things of the Spirit to people of the Spirit.

14 The person who lives on an entirely human level does not receive the things of the Spirit of God; for they are folly to such a one, and they cannot come to know them because they are discerned spiritually. 15 "Now the spiritual person sifts out everything, but he or she is put on trial by no one." 16 For "Who has come to know the mind of the Lord, that he should instruct him?" But as for us, we have Christ's mind!

In vv. 10-16 Paul expounds a theology of the Holy Spirit that paves the way for coherent themes in his later exposition of "gifts of the Spirit" in chapters 12-14. Jüngel stresses that *divine address* is the very condition of *divine intelligibility*, as through the Holy Spirit "God . . . speaks out of himself," but it is in christological terms that the infinite, transcendent, unsurpassable, otherwise inexpressible mystery of God becomes "think-able" for human beings (*God as the Mystery of the World*, pp. 152-58). In his exposition of these themes Paul first insists that **the Spirit** of God pro-ceeds forth **from God** (v. 12) as the transcendent, holy "Other," who is not merely an immanent human spirit or a divine cosmic spark or "world soul" of Stoic philosophy. **It is not the spirit of the world that we received, but the Spirit who issues from God** (v. 12). I have trans-lated the Greek as **the Spirit who issues** [or *proceeds*] **from God** because the adjectival clause *(to ek tou theou)* is more emphatic and explicit than *Spirit from God* (REB), and because the context demands that we signal a clear-cut contrast in Paul between an immanent "cosmic spirit" and the transcendent Holy Spirit who proceeds from God. We may compare John 15:26, "Spirit of truth, who issues [or *proceeds*] from the Father," and *"proceeds"* in the Niceno-Constantinopolitan Creed.

Paul disengages the activity of **the** Holy **Spirit** from mere innate hu-man "spirituality." "**Spiritual**" is what pertains to the Holy **Spirit** (2:12-13; 3:1-3; 12:1-7; 15:44). It does *not* denote deploying some *"higher" human capac-ity*. The gift of **God's Spirit** transcends the boundaries of the human self. Paul's redefinition of **Spirit** (vv. 10, 11, 12, 13, and 14) and **spiritual** or **spiri-tually** (vv. 13, 14, and 15) dominates and shapes the argument in vv. 10-16 and 3:1-4. Only when readers have noted the intimacy or inter-penetration *(perichoresis)* of the Person of the Holy **Spirit** and the Being of **God** (v. 10) can they fully discern Paul's redefinition of **spiritual**.

The **Spirit** explores the **depths** of God's very Self. Only thereby can the Spirit convey the heart and mind of God-in-Christ authentically. We need not read a dualism of self and spirit into v. 11. Paul's main point is well summed up in the axiom widely associated with Karl Barth: "God is known through God alone" (*Church Dogmatics*, II/1, sect. 27, p. 179). Athanasias made broadly the same point: there is no natural "kinship" between "the Spirit and the creatures. . . . The Spirit is from [Greek *ek*] God" (*Letter to Serapion* 1:22 in J.-P. Migne, *Patrologia Graeca* 26:581).

God's wisdom is "secret," or known only to God (v. 11b) in the sense that talk of "spirituality" and "wisdom" comes to nothing unless

God's Holy Spirit activates the message of the cross and brings it home afresh. Hence Paul employs **language which the Spirit teaches, interpreting things of the Spirit to people of the Spirit** (v. 13).

Commentators have sometimes made heavy weather out of the ambiguous gender and vocabulary of this verse. The Greek verb or participle may mean **interpreting** or *comparing* or *matching*, while the dative plural of the noun *(pneumatikois)* may be either masculine, **to people of the Spirit**, or neuter, *by spiritual faculties* or *in spiritual language*. Yet the general principle is clear, and the translations **interpreting** and **to people of the Spirit** fit the context precisely.

The person who lives on an entirely human level (v. 14) translates *psychikos de anthrōpos*. Such a person lives on the level of mere human life force (Greek *psychē*), not in response to the action of the Holy Spirit *(pneuma)*. Paul's next words corroborate this: such a person **does not receive the things of the Spirit . . . because they are discerned spiritually** (v. 14). The NJB translates the phrase as *the natural person*, and the NIV, also acceptably, as *the man [person] without the Spirit*.

We cannot determine with complete certainty whether v. 15 reflects a Corinthian catchphrase or comes only from Paul himself. Probably self-styled "**spiritual people**" in Corinth claimed, in a self-congratulatory sense, "**The spiritual person judges everything**, *but also stands under no one's judgment*." Paul endorses this only with a decisive twist. In one sense, truly "**The spiritual person** [as you say] **sifts out everything**" — but only in a limited sense is **the spiritual person put on trial by no one**. Since the one, foundational criterion is the cross of Christ (1:18–2:16), if the Holy Spirit gives to the believer genuinely **the mind of Christ** (v. 16), self-evidently there can be no higher criterion. Nevertheless, the Christocentric or Christomorphic criterion must be applied. Only where a cruciform, Christ-like, mind-set is transparent does the provisional thrust of v. 15 remain operative, whether or not the words reflect a Corinthian catchphrase.*

*Technical Note: The absence of quotation marks in a Greek text makes it difficult to be certain when Paul is quoting Corinthian theological slogans. Nevertheless virtually all scholars agree that examples exist: "All things are lawful" (6:12 and 10:23) is clearly a quotation, to which Paul adds the qualifications, "But . . ." The overwhelming majority of commentators regard "All of us possess knowledge" (8:1), "An idol has no real existence" (8:4), and almost certainly "It is well for a man not to touch a woman" (7:1) as making good sense only on the assumption that Paul is quoting a Corinthian catchphrase. By parity of

Sifts out (v. 15), or *discerns* as in v. 14 (with NRSV), is probably a more accurate translation here than *judges* (AV/KJV), although NIV has *makes judgments;* and REB, *can judge the worth of.* In the passive this verb may mean **put on trial** or perhaps *fathomed out.* On the lips of the Corinthians, *judged* becomes more possible, but Paul would not endorse any hint that "people of the Spirit" are invulnerable or infallible. He would agree, however, that their lives reflect dimensions and depths that remain unintelligible to those who do not have **the mind of Christ**. Meanwhile Paul stresses the "otherness" or transcendence of God (v. 16) and that any claim to be "spiritual" has to be measured by the criterion of **having the mind of Christ** (v. 16).

8. SUGGESTIONS FOR POSSIBLE REFLECTION ON 2:10-16

1. *On "spirituality" and the Holy Spirit:* What criteria should be used when applying the word "spiritual" to people or events? How closely is "spiritual" related to what accords with the mind of Christ, at the prompting of the Holy Spirit? Is there a danger in using the word "spirituality" in an overly vague, free-floating sense rather than in a more direct relation to Christ and the Holy Spirit? Or might it be argued that a broader meaning allows a more inclusive and generous understanding even if Paul does not use the term in this way?

2. *On the depths of the wisdom of God:* Contemplation of "the depths" of God requires patience, attention, sensitivity, imagination, openness, understanding, desire for God, and worship. Does God's sharing of revealed understanding through Christ call forth the serious, attentive seeking that it invites?

C. Christians Who Cannot Be Called "Spiritual" (3:1-4)

1 For my part, my Christian friends, I could not address you as people of the Spirit, but as people moved by entirely human drives, as people who in Christian terms are infantile. 2 I gave you milk to drink, not solid food; for you could

---

reasoning, Paul would hardly offer such a hostage to "the spiritual person" unless he had good reason. Even so, whether or not he quotes from his readers, his strong qualification about "the mind of Christ" provides Paul's distinctive proviso to the impact of v. 15.

not take it. Indeed, even now you still cannot manage it. 3 You are still unspiritual. For where jealousy and strife prevail among you, are you not centered on yourselves and behaving like any merely human person? 4 When someone declares, "I, for one, am one of Paul's people," and another asserts, "I, for my part, am for Apollos," are you not all too human?

Paul explains that however much he and they would have liked him to **address you as people of the Spirit**, or *as "spiritual" people*, he **could not** apply this term to them (v. 1). They appear to be moved by **entirely human drives**, with competitive concerns about power and status that demonstrate their *childish* or **infantile** lack of "maturity" (v. 6). The very fact that the application of the word *spiritual* or **of the Spirit** was a bone of contention proves that they reveled in this title and desired it. Yet Paul uses the analogy, well known in literature of the ancient world, of having to feed them baby food: **I gave you milk to drink, not solid food; for you could not take it. Indeed, even now you still cannot manage it** (v. 2).

Almost against the grain Paul flatly declares: **You are still unspiritual** (v. 3a). In Paul's own primary sense of **spiritual** or **of the Spirit** this seems to be a self-contradiction. For in chapters 12–14 he is at pains to assert that *all* Christians have received the Spirit. Indeed, without the action of the Holy Spirit, a person cannot make a Christian profession of belief and a practical commitment to Christ as Lord at all (see 12:3). This receives further proof in Rom. 8:9: "If anyone does not possess the Spirit of Christ, he or she is no Christian." There are no "second class" Christians as far as the gift of the Spirit is concerned.

How, then, can Paul withhold the term **spiritual** from the Christians in Corinth in 3:1-4? In part he is withholding the word *in their sense of the term*, that is, as if it applied to a more "advanced" spiritual elite. But more fundamentally he is pointing out that their competitive, self-seeking **jealousy and strife** undermine and contradict evidence of the Holy Spirit's sanctifying activity in their lives, and their identity as people of the cross. *Since they are self-contradictory*, Paul can describe them *only in self-contradictory language, as if* they did not possess the Spirit at all. They contradict their baptism into the cross and their transformation through the Spirit. They remain **centered on [them]selves and behaving like any merely human person** (v. 3b). They indulge in destructive power play: **"I, for one, am one of Paul's people"; "I, for my part, am for Apollos"** (v. 4).

The term that we translate **people moved by entirely human drives** (Greek *sarkinos*, v. 1) must be distinguished from its parallel in Greek, *psychikos anthrōpos*, which we translated in 2:14 as **the person who lives on an entirely human level**. Both terms stand in contrast to "**of the [Holy] Spirit**" or "**spiritual**." They broadly mean *unspiritual*. But *psychikos* reflects the more neutral associations of the life energy of simply being human, without openness to the saving action of the Holy Spirit. The Greek words *sarkinos* and *sarkikos* (vv. 1 and 3) are traditionally translated *of the flesh* (v. 3, NRSV), and reflect the more strongly rebellious thrust of *the mind of the flesh* that is "hostile to God" (Rom. 8:7, NRSV). When it is used in this way as an explicitly theological term, it denotes "the self in pursuit of its own ends" or "life pursued in independence from God" (Robinson, *The Body*, pp. 19-26; and Bultmann, *Theology*, vol. 1, pp. 239-46).

9. Suggestions for Possible Reflection on 3:1-4

1. *On when lifestyle contradicts Christian identity:* How often does a Christian's daily lifestyle contradict and undermine his or her new identity as a baptized Christian who has received the Holy Spirit? The world will perceive this as an ambivalent, confusing witness that has no cutting edge.

2. *On childishness among Christian people:* Children are often attention seeking and demanding. Why is it that often the least "mature" in the church seem bent on gaining attention, often bidding for positions of leadership? Conversely, deeply spiritual Christians sometimes seem reticent to speak or to accept leadership roles, often through modesty. What kinds of power games in the church or in the world seem to signify a childish or unspiritual mind-set?

IV. Applying These Criteria (Cross and Holy Spirit) to Church and Ministry (3:5–4:21)

A. Paul Rejects Too High a View and Too Low a View of Ministers (3:5-9a)

5 What then is Apollos? What, now, is Paul? Servants through whom you came to faith, even as the Lord assigned the role to each. 6 I planted, Apollos watered, but God went on giving the increase. 7 So then neither the one who plants nor the one who waters is anything, but God who went on giving the increase. 8 Now the one who does the planting and the one who waters are one in the work, and each will receive their reward in accordance with their own labour. 9a For we are fellow labourers who belong to God.

If we take the traditional view of 1:12 and of these verses, Christians in Corinth have been appealing to some link with the "big names" of Paul, Apollos, and perhaps Peter, primarily to gain some status or borrowed prestige for themselves by a bid to share in the reflected glory of those with "names." This ploy would work only in a society like that of Corinth, where much was made of the patron-client relationship. A client could receive a measure of the honor and respect that his or her patron had earned. On the other hand, we noted above the view of David Hall that 1:12 and these verses allude to leaders whom Paul does not name, but for whom he uses the names *Paul, Apollos,* and *Peter* as disguised, substitute names to maintain the anonymity of the teachers concerned, as 4:6 might suggest.

Whichever view is right, the principle remains that a number of Christians in Corinth tried to gain status and wider respect for themselves by hanging on to the coattails of rising or recognized stars. It is also quite likely that the group who declared, "I am of Christ" (1:12), sought spiritual status by claiming a hot line to heaven without resort, they claimed, to recognized ministers and leaders.

Against all this Paul formulates a pastoral strategy that attacks the problems on two fronts. (1) Against those who make too much of the "names" or of local leaders, *Paul attacks too high a view of Christian ministers:* **What** [Greek neuter, not *who*] **is Paul**? Simply **servants** ... (v. 5). (2) Against those who seek to bypass the support of ministers, *Paul attacks too low a view of Christian ministers.* Their work is *indispensable* for growth: **I planted, Apollos watered, but God went on giving the increase** (v. 6).

If the status and persons of ministers are overrated, the church falls victim to the "politics of personalities" that Paul condemns in 1:10-12 and 3:1-4. Yet, by an important inversion of logic and argument, to exalt one minister at the expense of another is thereby to suggest that the less favored minister and ministry is of little or no significance. *Paul attacks both views equally.*

On one side, **neither the one who plants nor the one who waters is anything, but God who went on giving the increase** (v. 7). The tenses or "aspects" of the verbs in v. 6 are significant. Paul and Apollos represent episodes of planting and watering (aorist active tense or aspect); God continuously gives the increase (imperfect tense), while ministers come and go. On the other side, ministers derive their calling not as an optional, self-chosen task, but **as the Lord assigned the role to each** (v. 5). They are not dispensable competitors seeking the church's favor, but **one in the work** (v. 8). Their labor is significant enough for them to be called **fellow laborers who belong to God** (v. 9a). The translation "fellow laborers *with* God" does not quite grasp Paul's point. They are fellow laborers *together,* and as such *belong to,* or *work under,* **God**. Paul will resume these points in 3:18–4:5: "All things are yours, whether Paul or Apollos or Cephas . . ." (v. 22). This means: "Don't cheat yourselves out of resources that God has provided for your good," including the resources of various ministries.

10. Suggestions for Possible Reflection on 3:5-9a

1. *On having too high or too low a view of ministers and ministry:* Some tend to exaggerate the status and importance of Christian ministers and Christian leaders, while others undervalue them and pay them scant respect. Which is more harmful for the church and for its leaders? Is flattery or lack of appreciation the more damaging burden for a minister?

2. *On ministerial "personalities":* What consequences follow when ministers or congregations make "personalities" out of a leader? When might this lead to division? How might it distract from Christ and the gospel? Often people seem to "attach themselves" to the views or cult followings of cer-

tain church leaders, either to gain easier acceptance or to avoid having to think for themselves. What further effects follow for the church?

3. *On workers together under God:* How can we encourage more collaborative examples of ministry? One price may be a readiness to share equally both credit and blame, or, better, to forget altogether about credit and blame, and to leave everything in God's hands (cf. 4:1-5). If all Christian work is "under God," is our main accountability only to God, or does it still matter "what other people think of us"? Is it the case that they should not shape our message, but we should remain sensitive to their perceptions (cf. 8:1-13)? Since all growth comes from God, what looks like "self-constructed" religion or faith could be sterile. Can we expect growth if we lose sight of *God* in a complexity of infrastructures and strategies?

B. The Church as God's Field, God's Building, and God's Holy Temple (3:9b-17)

9b You are the field that belongs to God. You are also a building of God's. 10 According to the gracious privilege which God gave to me, as a skilled master-builder I laid a foundation, and someone else is building on it. But let each person take care how they continue the building. 11 For no one can lay down any other foundation than that which has already been laid down, namely, Jesus Christ. 12 Now if anyone builds upon the foundation with gold, silver, and costly stones, or with wood, hay, and straw, 13 the work of each will become apparent, for the Day shall reveal it, because it is disclosed by fire; the fire will test what kind of work each has done. 14 If anyone's work which that person built abides, he or she will receive a reward; 15 if anyone's work is burnt up, that person will suffer loss, but such persons themselves will be saved, but as if through fire. 16 Do you not know that you are the temple of God, and that the Spirit of God dwells in you? 17 If anyone destroys God's temple, God will destroy that person. For God's temple is holy, and that temple you are!

In 3:6-8 Paul had implicitly begun to employ the metaphor of the field by alluding to "planting" and "watering," although in these verses the emphasis lay on the role of ministers rather than on that of the church as a whole. In v. 9 Paul underlines that the *church* owes its being to God. It belongs to God as **God's field**. This looks back to the initial address in 1:2, where Paul uses the *possessive* genitive: Christian people are **God's** church. Apart from God they would remain a wild or barren piece of land; but God gives the growth and provides the necessary conditions for their care.

Paul makes similar points in a further analogy about the church as **God's building** (v. 9b). **Jesus Christ** is the **foundation** (v. 11). The third analogy is still more explicit: only the Holy **Spirit** can consecrate the church to be **God's** holy **temple**. Only from the Spirit's **dwelling** in the church does the church derive its fit status as a **holy** shrine for God's own presence (v. 17). To damage the church, therefore, would be *sacrilege against the Holy* **Spirit**. It would be more than a merely social sin.

Field (v. 9) may look back to Old Testament allusions to Israel as God's vineyard, but the Greek word simply means **field** in the broad sense of any piece of cultivated land. The key to the metaphor lies in its need for *cultivation*. The main condition for fertility and growth is the sun, rain, and nutrients that **God** alone can give; the subsidiary condition is the oversight of gardeners who "plant" (as Paul does) and "water" (as Apollos does) in accordance with the instructions given by the owner of the field. The **field** itself has a potential either to remain barren (or wild) or to bring forth a harvest.

In vv. 9b-15 Paul moves from the organic metaphor of the **field** to the structural metaphor of the **building**. First a building rests upon a **foundation**, and the church is not the church unless it rests upon the **foundation** of **Jesus Christ** (v. 11). Second, a **building** must hold together with mutual dependency and integration of the component parts. The metaphor excludes individualism and any "autonomy" of individual parts. This anticipates the image of the body in chapter 12. To transfer the metaphor into these present terms: "the roof cannot say to the walls, 'I have no need of you'" (cf. 12:21), and "the door cannot say, 'because I am not a wall, I do not belong to the building'" (cf. 12:15-16). Third, a **building** is the result of a process of *building up*. Building up or *edification* is a major theme in this epistle. "Love builds" (8:1), while glossolalia merely "builds up the self," that is, it does not build the community *as a community* (14:4). Mitchell (*Paul and the Rhetoric*) and Lanci (*A New Temple*) put forward careful arguments to the effect that *building up* is the key theme of the whole epistle.

Paul extends the analogy in vv. 10-15 to include the team of builders that work on the building. In accordance with recent research

(Shanor, "Master Builder") Paul is like a foreman or managing architect (v. 10) who coordinates a small team of working builders to insure a coherent and accurate overview of the work as a whole. In contracts from this first-century era, there could be *penalties* or *fines* for working builders who fell down on their job badly enough to damage the work as a whole: **that person will suffer loss** (v. 15); but they might not be excluded from the team (v. 15).

Paul presses a further analogy *within* this analogy: builders may use combustible or fireproof materials. To the latter category belong gold, silver, and costly stones; but wood, hay, and straw would go up in smoke if the building caught fire. This provides a forceful and unforgettable parable of the pathos of work that cannot stand the test of the **fire** of the last judgment, and of the everlasting significance of what is built of solid quality upon the true **foundation** of **Christ**.

Hence Paul warns Christian workers: **Let each person take care how they continue the building** (v. 10). Just as in the previous analogy, the essential primary condition is **God who gives the increase**, so here the major reference point is **Christ** as the **foundation**, which gives the building its coherence and identity. Just as those who **planted** and **watered** constituted secondary conditions for growth in a field, so here the agents who **build** with selected materials all play a necessary part in the construction and development of the church, but **Christ** alone is its **foundation**.

Bad workmanship does not of itself threaten loss of salvation (v. 15). But the **loss** will be serious enough. At the last day such a builder may become aware that he or she has contributed little or nothing permanent to the kingdom. Such awareness may be an in-built (or logically "internal") penalty, even though in every important sense their ground of "glorying" will remain in the Lord and the Lord's work (cf. 1:31). Such a builder will be **saved, but as if through fire**. This cannot refer to a supposed doctrine of purgatory, not least because Paul alludes to the Day of Judgment, not to some continuing postmortal state. It is clearly a metaphor for escaping "by the skin of one's teeth." Just as it is **God's field** and **God's building**, the church is also **God's** holy **temple**, set apart as holy by virtue of the **indwelling** of the **Spirit of God** (v. 16).* Above all, **God's**

---

*Technical Note: Some have credited Augustine with implying an allusion to purgatory here. But he does not equate "the furnace of affliction" where the work is burnt up with

temple is holy, and that temple are you! (v. 17). The two main emphases in these two verses are the dependence of the corporate community of Christians on the Holy Spirit for their very identity as God's **temple** or *holy sanctuary*, and the sacrilege involved in any attempt **to destroy** God's temple by polluting it or by deconsecrating its holiness.

Paul's opening question, **Do you not know that?** reveals his passionate strength of feeling about this matter and his expectation that they would regard this principle as a foundational or axiomatic truth. In addition, it may reflect Paul's near exasperation that the readers fail to apply what is obvious even in pagan religions: the supposed presence of Aphrodite or Apollo in their temples symbolized by their images within the temple shrine gives the temple its very identity.

In 1:10–2:5 Paul has shown that "splits" undermine the very identity of Christians in Corinth as people of the cross (and, in 2:6–3:3, as people of the Spirit). This competitive rivalry and self-promotion constitutes, now in 3:16-17, a threat to the very profaning of the **temple** sanctuary **of God**, so that it is no longer his **holy** dwelling. If Christians have corporately been made **holy** on the basis of the cross (1:30) through the agency of the Holy **Spirit** (3:16, 17), then to devalue a fellow Christian or to sin against a "saint" (1:2) *is to commit sacrilege against the Spirit who consecrates this human temple.* It is not simply to fail at a social or interpersonal level. The sin of splitting *away from* those whom God has consecrated has profound effects in relation to God, not simply social ones.

The Greek of v. 17 reveals a striking symmetrical wordplay. The Greek word *phtheirei* ("damage," **destroy**, "defile") ends the first clause, and it is used again to begin the second clause: "**If** it is **God's temple** that someone '**destroys,' 'destroy' that person — will God.**" Käsemann's work on this structure is well known ("Sentences of Holy Law"). Without endorsing other claims in this work, we agree that the style marks a serious act of divine judgment. But this judgment is brought upon the self. It is almost as if Paul says, "If someone destroys, . . . such a one is *thereby* destroyed." Without publicly naming and

---

purgatory (*Enchiridion*, 68). He refers to the pain of the realization that true and solid realities lie elsewhere than had been thought. Luther regards purgatory as an un-Pauline notion because it undermines justification by grace alone (*Letters of Spiritual Counsel*, especially his letters to Jerome Weller in 1530 and to V. Hausman in 1532 [London: SCM, 1955], pp. 84-87, and *Lectures on Galatians 1535*, in *Luther's Works* [St. Louis: Concordia, 1963], vol. 23, p. 218 [or Weimar edition, vol. 40, p. 353]).

shaming a culprit, Paul refers to those who feed the splits. Here is perhaps their last warning that the effects (for the church *and* for them) are entirely beyond what they imagined when they began a little, "innocent" power play. They are playing with forces that threaten the holiness of God's own temple, in effect pitting themselves against the Holy Spirit. By their attitude they also despise the humility of the cross and the love of Jesus.

II. Suggestions for Possible Reflection on 3:9b-17

1. *On the church as belonging to God:* If the church is God's property, are churchpeople as *careful* when they attempt to change or improve it as someone should be about anything that belongs to someone else? Extreme care is needed not to inadvertently cause any damage to God's church. The church belongs to *God*, but does it sometimes seem as if it belongs to ministers, congregations, or committees?

2. *On building with noncombustible materials:* Christians have a privileged opportunity to use their lives and gifts for a work that will survive "the fire" of the last judgment and survive forever. Are Christian witness, service, ministry, and love (13:13) seen as having potentially *eternal* significance rather than some short-term good? Members may well pray that their work will be "solid" and endure. Might this be someone's call to ministry?

3. *On building together:* (In addition to the above on 3:5-9). All three metaphors (of field, building, and shrine) project a *communal* vision of the church that discourages individualism. A building cannot be constructed without co-ordination and cohesion. What would result from ramshackle, ad hoc projects by independent individuals? Should God's church be constructed like that? Are some tempted to downgrade "order" and structure within the church, or do they seek to expand "their corner" at the expense of others?

4. *On the holiness of the church:* The imagery of the holy shrine (vv. 16, 17) reminds us of the high stakes involved in being part of the church. What might militate against the holiness of the church? Ancient temples were thought to exhibit the character of the god whose image they contained. Does the temple that is our Christian community exhibit the character of God-in-Christ?

68

C. The Fallibility of Human Wisdom: Self-Deception
and the Verdict of God (3:18–4:5)

18 Let no one be self-deceived. If any among you thinks that he or she is wise in terms of this world order, let that person become a fool in order to become wise. 19 For the wisdom of this world is folly beside God. For it is written, "He catches the clever in their craftiness." 20 And again, "The Lord knows that the reasonings of the clever are futile." 21 So then, let no one glory in human persons. For all things are yours, 22 whether Paul or Apollos or Cephas, or the world or life or death, or things present or things to come; all are yours, 23 and you are Christ's, and Christ is God's.

1 Let a person count us as servants of Christ and estate managers of the mysteries of God. 2 As for the rest, here it is required among estate managers that a person is found trustworthy. 3 It counts for very little with me, however, that I should be judged by you or by any human court of judgment; indeed, I do not even judge myself. 4 I do not have anything on my conscience, but I am not thereby pronounced in the right. The One who judges me is the Lord. 5 So do not pronounce judgments on anything before the proper time, until the Lord comes, who will shed light upon the hidden things of darkness and will disclose the hidden motivations of our lives. Then will recognition come for each from God.

The theme of **self-deception** (v. 18) is fundamental not only as a warning to distrust our own (and other) human judgments (3:18-21) but also as a liberating insight into the freedom and wisdom of appropriating the resources of God (3:22–4:5). First, at minimum Paul endorses the Socratic maxim **become a fool in order to become wise** (v. 18), that is, *admit how little you know in order that you may begin to learn.*

Second, such recognition will correct the misplaced, arrogant self-confidence that led some in Corinth to pick and choose certain "approved" ministers and to reject others. If you see how much you need to learn and to understand, Paul insists, you will not cheat yourself by self-deception *out of the full resources God has provided:* **for all . . . are yours, whether Paul or Apollos or Cephas, or the world . . .** (v. 22).

Third, this recognition of the fallibility of human judgments frees Paul himself from worrying about whether *his own life and ministry* reaches acceptable standards or not (4:3, 4). The key phrase, **I do not even**

judge myself (v. 3b), is one of Paul's greatest assertions of *the freedom of the Christian* and not least of Christian ministers. Paul did *not* live as a man with a tortured conscience. His statement, "what I do is not what I want to do, but what I detest" (Rom 7:15, REB), belongs to an entirely different context of thought and is often misapplied. There "I" is not the "I" of personal identity, but the "I" that describes the people of God under the law. In 4:1-5 Paul rejects the criterion of personal introspection as fallible and inadequate. He leaves any verdict upon his life and work in the hands of **the Lord**, to whom he is primarily responsible (v. 4b).

The repeated contrast between **wise** and **fool** (v. 18) and **wisdom** and **folly** (v. 19) points back to the "reversals" determined by the new world of the cross in 1:18-31. However, the quotation from Job 5:13 probably points forward to Paul's condemnation of manipulative people (see under 6:1-8). "[God] **catches the clever in their craftiness**" (v. 20) replaces *in their understanding* (in the Septuagint version) by **in their craftiness**, to suggest that **God catches** *hold of* the *cunning* ploys of those who seek to use power by strategies of "clever" manipulation. (Some writers argue that **craftiness** derives from the Hebrew version. But this would still reflect Paul's choice of the version to make this point.) God has a firm grip on these slippery operators.

Paul's warning, **Let no one be self-deceived. If any among you thinks that he or she is wise**, such a person must take stock and be humble enough to learn (v. 18), suggests that some Christians inappropriately put themselves forward as teachers or leaders in the church. This is all part and parcel of a miscalculation concerning the role of ministers and teachers (see under 3:5-9). Hence Paul declares, **Let no one glory in human persons** (v. 21); "Let the one who glories, glory in the Lord" (1:31). Barth observes that too many at Corinth "believe not in God but in their own belief in God and in particular human leaders. . . . They confuse belief with specific human experiences" (*Resurrection of the Dead*, pp. 17-18). This, he urges, lies behind the force of 3:23 as well as 4:5: **Recognition will come . . . from God**, which forms the climax of this section.

Once again **glorying in** brings us back to the cross. The Christians in Corinth were tempted to **glory in** a spiritual wealth and kingship (4:8-9), as if they were seated on thrones of glory tiered around the arena, watching the bloodied apostles still struggling like gladiators in the ring below them (see on 4:8-13). By contrast, Paul *takes pride in* the cross, which alone is his ground for glorying (Gal. 6:14). This contrast anticipates

Martin Luther's far-reaching contrast between a "theology of glory" and a "theology of the cross," to which we allude under "Suggestions for Further Reflection" on 4:8-13. Luther's language elucidates Paul's succinct statement that self-glorying and the reasonings of the **clever** are simply **futile** (v. 20). They lack any solid substance. They are a distraction.

Paul compares the narrow individualism of illusory self-glory with the multiform resourcing of the whole Christian community through a variety of agents, agencies, and gifts (vv. 22-23). Self-glory and self-sufficiency can *cheat* or **deceive** a believer out of the richer, wider resources that God has provided in his generosity. By selecting **Apollos**, for example, *rather than* **Paul** or **Cephas**, the Christian has missed out on receiving what "Paul" or "Cephas" might give. In his superabundant grace God can use **all things** for the building up of the believer and of the church. However, as Paul will explain more fully in chapters 12–14, God "orders" the distribution or "apportioning" of his gifts in accordance with an "ordering" that God wills (12:4-7). This "ordering" is not merely pragmatic or "ecclesial." The very relation between **Christ** and **God** (v. 23) is determined by divine "ordering." This confirms the point that for Paul "order" is no mere secondary or "church" issue, but relates to the mode of governance that God wills for his creation and even Christ (see below on 11:2 and 15:28).

In yet further contrast to the aspirations to illusory high status found among the Christians in Corinth, Paul prefers the more solid status of being perceived as **servants** or *subordinates* (REB) **of Christ**, and as **estate-managers** or *stewards* (REB; Greek *oikonomos,* 4:1). The two Greek words are suggestive in emphasizing respectively the menial service that a relatively low-level slave may give to his or her master, and the management role that a slave who may administer a household, an estate, or a business on behalf of his or her master may equally provide. The word *oikonomos* suggests that *management* is not out of place, whether in the church or in the world, as a mode of service to Christ or "ministry" (v. 1). It also paves the way for the key requirements of being **trustworthy** or *faithful* in the "administration" of a range of God-given resources (v. 2). This may vary from truths that have been revealed (**mysteries**) to the general running of a "household." In first-century life, this could include purchasing, keeping accounts, collecting debts, allocating a budget, and so on.

Paul combines the two themes of the genuine honor of *serving* and of the need to be *responsible* and worthy of *trust* in handling the Lord's affairs. This entails a faithful dispensing of what God has *given*, not a self-constructed theology of affirmation or self-glory. A chemist or pharmacist is required to administer whatever medicine is *prescribed*, not to substitute supposed "improvements." Ministry may involve taking delegated responsibility to *execute* a *given* purpose.

In 4:3-5 Paul's insists that such **servants** and **managers** will be held responsible to the **Lord** (vv. 4b and 5b). This gives rise to a marvellous sense of *liberation* that he need not be overly distracted by anxieties about the fallible human judgments of other Christians or even his own self-evaluation. All this **counts very little with** Paul. K. Stendahl has shown in a key article that Paul lived with a robust sense of liberation from a tortured conscience, and that the popular picture of Paul as a troubled and introspective soul is entirely misplaced.*

Whatever verdict is yet to come, **the Lord** alone will declare the definitive verdict (v. 4b), and will declare it when **the Lord comes** (v. 5). Meanwhile the true state of personal failure or achievement remains ambiguous and hidden until **the proper time** (v. 5). What is hidden in the present is not only the value of supposed success or failure, but especially **hidden motivations**. The Greek more strictly states that what will be revealed is the wishes or acts of will that proceed from *the heart*. But *heart* regularly denotes the seat of desires that lie beneath the surface of the mind (*our inward motives*, REB). Hence Theissen sees a parallel here with post-Freudian notions of the *preconscious* (*Psychological Aspects of Pauline Theology*, pp. 59-66).

That God alone judges human secrets constitutes both a reminder of human accountability before God and a liberating release

---

*Technical Note: As long ago as 1963 Krister Stendahl wrote his classic study "Paul and the Introspective Conscience of the West" to show that portraits of Paul as a man with a tortured conscience are simply not true to the epistles (reprinted in Stendahl, *Paul among Jews and Gentiles* [Philadelphia: Fortress, 1967 and London: SCM, 1977], pp. 78-96). "Paul was equipped with . . . a rather robust conscience" (p. 81). He was "'blameless' as to righteousness of the law" (Phil. 3:6; cf. Gal. 1:13). This does not mean, however, that Paul underestimated the reality of human sin and its consequences. The point is that whereas humanism and many religions construe this in *subjective* terms as a troubled conscience in need of *forgiveness*, Paul sees the root problem more as an *objective* one: sin is a turning away from God, and this *disrupted relationship* needs to be *"put right,"* that is, in terms of *justification by grace*, rather than simply "forgiven."

from trying to make interim self-assessments on the basis of fallible judgments from the self and from others.

12. SUGGESTIONS FOR POSSIBLE REFLECTION ON 3:18–4:5

1. *On processes of knowing and learning:* "Thinking that we already know" sets up obstacles to *growing* in knowledge or wisdom. Can *doubt* provide a positive incentive to recommence a serious search for truth? When is doubt healthy, and when is it destructive? Can "thinking that we already know" seduce people into a sense of superiority to others?

2. *On selective attitudes to Christian leaders:* Picking out certain leaders for special admiration and loyalty risks devaluing other leaders as additional sources of wisdom. How does this affect other leaders?

3. *On ministry and management:* Paul compares ministers or apostles to those who administer a household, so is there a danger today of undervaluing the "management" aspect of Christian ministry?

4. *On liberty and responsibility:* Why do we so often try to assess how well we are doing when we know that all human judgments, including our own, are fallible? Other people's judgments are fallible, so why do we take so seriously other people's criticisms or flattery? What hinders our enjoying total release from such worrying? How can a right balance be reached between self-discipline (3:18-23) and "letting go" to leave everything in the hands of God (4:1-5)?

D. All from Grace Alone, Freely Given; but the Struggle Is Not Yet Over (4:6-13)

6 I have allusively applied all this [*or, alternatively, I have alluded in language of disguise*] to myself and to Apollos on your account, dear members of our Christian family, that you may learn through our case what "Not beyond what is written" consists in, so that one of you be not inflated on behalf of one against another. 7 For who sees anything different in you? What do you have that you did not receive? If, however, you received it, why do you boast as if you did not receive it? 8 Already you have become glutted! Already you have been "made rich"! Without us you came to "reign as kings"! If only you did "reign as kings," so that we,

73

too, could reign as kings with you! 9 For it seems to me that God has put us apostles on display as the grand finale, as those doomed to die, because we have been made a spectacle in the eyes of the world, of angels, and of humankind. 10 We are fools on Christ's account, but you are wise in your Christian existence; we are weak, while you are strong. You are honored, we are disgraced. 11 Up to this very hour we go hungry and thirsty and poorly clothed; we are roughly treated and have no fixed abode. 12 We toil until we are weary, laboring with our own hands. When we are abused, we reply with good words; when we are persecuted, we put up with it; 13 when we are slandered, we appeal to them directly. Up to this very moment we have become, as it were, the world's scum, the scrapings from everyone's shoes.

The alternative translation in v. 6 marks one of the very few verses in which the translation depends upon which of *two perhaps equally possible but different* understandings of Paul's meanings we accept. The italic type follows our translation in our larger commentary, which is the more traditional and entirely possible one. However, as we have noted already, David Hall argues forcefully that Paul uses the names of Apollos and himself as "disguised" allusions to anonymous leaders in Corinth whom he does not wish to name and shame, perhaps because they are not responsible for the fact that others invoke their names as "personalities" for their power politics. Although either meaning is possible, the choice does greatly affect the main issue that Paul raises. If pressed, we should still opt for the more traditional view.

The heart of Paul's argument in this section, as in much of this epistle, finds expressions in v. 7b: **What do you have that you did not receive? If, however, you received it, why do you boast as if you did not receive it?** The Epistle to the Romans has been widely associated with the doctrine of justification by grace through faith alone; but *this theme is no less prominent in 1 Corinthians*. The popular impression owes its force largely to the fact that whereas indiscriminate grace and sovereign election occupy the center of the stage in Romans, 1 Corinthians addresses a wide variety of themes, all of which rest *implicitly* upon the doctrine of grace that lies behind them. This very variety of themes may draw attention away from what gives them their basis, unity, and coherence.

The proclamation of the cross is founded upon grace alone (1:18–2:5); revelation and the Spirit are sheer gifts in contrast to discovery and "spirituality" (2:6–3:4); the basis of noncompetitive ministry lies in

God's free gift of apostleship and call to service (3:5–4:5). Later in the epistle respect for "the other" arises from the mutual dependence of all Christians upon the same grace, especially in worship (ch. 11), and on "gifts" bestowed freely by the Spirit (chs. 12–14); finally, the resurrection is an event to which the dead can offer no contribution but that rests solely on God's power as sheer gift (ch. 15).

The phrase "**not beyond what is written**" (v. 6) has caused endless difficulty to commentators. (1) Probably the most widely held view is that **what is written** refers to the Old Testament as the church's scripture (Barrett, *First Epistle,* pp. 106-7; Schrage, *Der erste Brief,* vol. 1, pp. 334-35; Hays, *First Corinthians,* p. 69). (2) Some interpreters specify this more narrowly as scriptures that Paul has already quoted in this epistle (Hooker, "Beyond the Things"; Fee, *First Epistle,* 167-68). (3) Others take it to refer to what Paul has already written in this epistle. (4) The inclusion of the Greek definite article *to* in the best manuscript suggests that the phrase may allude to a saying that has "the character of a maxim" (Welborn, *Politics,* 43-75).*

Far from being "unintelligible" as Conzelmann claims, this verse attacks any notion of a self-generated, "second stage" gospel alongside or subsequent to the proclamation of the cross as this is understood within the framework of Scripture and apostolic doctrine. Our translation, **what "Not beyond what is written" consists in**, conveys Paul's point to this effect, while it also does justice to the inclusion of the unexpected Greek definite article at an otherwise awkward point. Ambrose and Calvin connect this notion of falsely "adding" to the gospel with the next verse (v. 7; Ambrose, *Opera Omnia* 124D, in J.-P. Migne, *Patrologia Latina,* 17:215; Calvin, *First Epistle,* p. 91). How can some of the

---

*Technical Note: In addition to these four main views, a fifth intriguing but speculative alternative is familiar to all who have studied the textual criticism of the New Testament. The original Greek text, it is suggested, omitted "not beyond what is written," and hence ran smoothly "that you may learn from our example not to be puffed up." An early copyist, however, accidentally omitted the word "not" (Greek *mē*), but tried to rectify his error by sandwiching the word *mē* above the *"a"* of the Greek word *hina* that followed. All might have been well, but for the overconscientious zeal of the next copyist. He inserted a gloss (or marginal note) to say, "The *mē* has been written above the alpha; in Greek *to mē hyper a gegraptai,* namely, the Greek of the usual text to which a "rough breathing" over the *"a"* was later added: *to mē hyper ha gegraptai,* [the] **not beyond what is written**. Whether this was originated by J. M. S. Baljon in 1884 or earlier by F. A. Bornemann, Héring regards it "the only explanation at all satisfactory" (*First Epistle,* p. 28).

readers *boast* in what they received as an undeserved gift unless they are trying to add to it? Paul expounds this as an issue of sheer logic in Rom. 11:6. The falsity of such a notion leads to an incisive attack on self-important triumphalism in vv. 8-13.

It is no accident that in vv. 8-10 Paul employs a rhetoric of irony that takes up self-descriptions common to triumphalist, self-congratulatory, religious experience in a number of religious cults of the time. In Hellenistic-oriental cults converts could be overwhelmed by a new sense of power and status: "Many . . . felt that they could do anything: they were **kings** (1 Cor 4:8), they were in the Spirit, they were emancipated" (Nock, *St. Paul,* p. 174). That Paul is in fact using "biting irony" is demonstrated by his parenthesis, **If only you did!**

By contrast, Paul uses material drawn equally from apostolic experience and from philosophical "catalogues of afflictions" when he compares apostolic self-descriptions as **those doomed to die . . . a spectacle . . . fools . . . weak . . . disgraced . . . hungry and thirsty . . . roughly treated . . . of no fixed abode . . . abused** (vv. 9, 10, 11, 12). They are **persecuted, slandered,** and regarded as **scum** and the **scrapings from everyone's shoes** (vv. 12-13). "These Corinthians are lucky. Already they enjoy forms that the apostles dare only hope for. . . . The Messianic kingdom seems to have come to Corinth and these people have been given their thrones, while the apostles dance attendance and are placed with the servants" (Deluz, *Companion,* pp. 46-47). The apostles still struggle like gladiators in the arena, **doomed to die** and a **spectacle,** while the Corinthians "lounge in the best seats and just applaud or even boo" (p. 47).*

The contrast between **wise** and **fool** reminds us that the view of truth and knowledge that is at issue here continues to reflect the criterion of the cross expounded first in 1:18-31. If the cross is "folly" (1:18) and "an affront" (1:23), it is not surprising that the apostles who place it at the center of their value systems are regarded as **scum** (4:13). The Greek for this word denotes what is removed as a result of scouring

---

*Technical Note: A number of studies explore the rhetorical use of "catalogues of affliction," including Karl Plank, *Paul and the Irony of Affliction* (Atlanta: Scholars, 1987), pp. 33-70; John Fitzgerald, *Cracks in an Earthen Vessel* (Atlanta: Scholars, 1988), pp. 117-48; K. T. Kleinknecht, *Der leidende Gerechtfertigte* (Tübingen: Mohr, 1984); and M. S. Ferrari, *Der Sprache des Leids in den paulinischen Peristasenkatologen* (Stuttgart: Katholisches Bibelwerk, 1991).

around a dirty vessel. Likewise **the scrapings from everyone's shoes** or *dirt* translates a word that denotes the unmentionable dirt that people scrape off their shoes when they wipe them clean. For the unbelieving, self-styled "wise," the apostles are a foul smell to be avoided, or filth of which they are ashamed. As "fools" they bear the authentic marks of a cruciform witness, but many Christians in Corinth want no part of this, but to be treated with honor as "somebodies" in the eyes of the world.

13. Suggestions for Possible Reflection on 4:6-13

1. *On what has been freely given:* Pride sometimes stops people from freely *accepting* something they need ("I don't want charity from *anyone*"). Would anyone reject a gift from God on this ground? Christians from Corinth may have feared that this cuts the ground from being "a self-made person." What would it be like to give a gift, and to have gifts criticized, rejected, or treated as entitlements or achievements? What does receiving all we have and are from God suggest about human "boasting"?

2. *On "second stage" faith?* Do some Christians seem to seek a "wisdom" that goes "beyond" what is written in Scripture or in apostolic faith? Do they seek a "second stage" faith that goes beyond the gospel?

3. *On pilgrimage, struggle, and triumphalism:* Do some Christians seem secretly to despise those Christians who seem always to be "up against it," while we or others achieve an illusion of peace by disengaging from struggle? Moltmann writes, "Presumption is a self-willed anticipation of the fulfilment of what we hope for from God. Despair is the premature, arbitrary anticipation of the non-fulfilment of what we hope for from God. Both forms of hopelessness . . . cancel . . . hope" (*Theology of Hope*, p. 23). Luther writes, "God is not to be found except in sufferings and in the cross" (*The Heidelberg Disputation*, sect. 21, p. 291).

E. Pastoral Care in Action: The Heart of Paul's Concern (4:14-21)

14 I do not write all this to bring you into shame, but as a warning to my dearly loved children. 15 For you might have thousands of people in Christ to correct you, but you can hardly have more than one father. For in Christ Jesus it was I who became your father through proclaiming the gospel. 16 I ask you, then,

take your cue from me. 17 It is for this reason that I send to you Timothy, who is my very dear child and trustworthy in the Lord: he will bring to your mind the patterns of life which I live in Christ Jesus, even as I teach them everywhere in every Christian congregation. 18 As though I were not coming to you, however, some have begun to be inflated with arrogance. 19 But I shall come to you soon, if the Lord wills, and I shall discover not the talk of these inflated people, but what they can do. 20 For the kingdom of God is not a matter of talk but of solid efficacy. 21 What do you prefer? Am I to come to you with a stick in my hand or with love and a gentle spirit?

Paul reveals his pastoral care and sensitivity in several ways in these verses. First, although appearances are to the contrary, even his blistering rhetoric of irony (vv. 8-13) was not written **to bring you into shame** (v. 14). To be sure, he uncompromisingly places his readers under the critique and criterion of the cross (cf. 1:18-25). But unlike those preachers who chastise their congregations in part as an ego trip, Paul derives no satisfaction from this. There are other rhetoricians or teachers who enjoy **correcting** them (v. 15), but as a **father** he seeks only their good, and the ultimate flourishing of his Christian **children** who are **dearly loved** (vv. 14b, 16).

Second, other teachers or leaders may be disengaged from heart-to-heart empathy with the readers, but as their **father** Paul identifies with their welfare and sensitivities. His use of the imagery of **father** is *not* to legitimate a *manipulative rhetoric* based upon *paternalism*, as Castelli and Wire claim.*

*Technical Note: These two writers in particular have argued that **father** here reflects a paternalist strategy of power and control. Elizabeth A. Castelli (*Imitating Paul: A Discourse of Power* [Louisville: Westminster/Knox, 1991], pp. 97-115) perceives the metaphor of **father** as "authoritarian" and "political" when it is used in conjunction with the command to be "imitators" (Greek *mimētai,* v. 16 [translated above as **take your cue from me**], Castelli, pp. 107-11). She argues that Paul's combination of authoritarian assertion and apparent self-effacement is a "clever rhetorical strategy" of manipulation (p. 99). It instantiates Michel Foucault's principle that claims to truth serve often if not always as disguised bids for power. The other major exponent of this view is Antoinette C. Wire in *The Corinthian Women Prophets* (Minneapolis: Fortress, 1990), esp. pp. 45-47. Here, she urges, is one of many examples of a manipulative rhetoric of power on Paul's part. He *alone* is the **father** of the Corinthian church (v. 15). Other teachers, including presumably Apollos, are merely "hired tutors" (Wire, p. 46). This rhetoric of the "threatening father" is risky, and "the appeal to the churches at large as a standard for Corinth discred-

If Wire and Castelli are right, this section reflects not pastoral *sensitivity* but pastoral *control*. Castelli's work, however, is more cautious than that of Wire, and she is entirely right about the extent to which *in general* claims to *truth* on the part of Christian leaders may often be partly disguised bids for *power*. Foucault writes persuasively about "the smiling face in the white coat" where such "regimes" as hospitals, prisons, churches, and the armed forces may exert power under the pretext of acting only for the general good. Nietzsche anticipated Foucault in pressing this point (cf. Thiselton, *Interpreting God and the Postmodern Self*).

Nevertheless, Paul's appeal to the unity and catholicity of church order (4:17; 7:17; 14:33) does not rest, as Castelli and Wire appear to suggest, on "sameness" (Castelli, *Imitating Paul*, pp. 97, 111, 119). Paul promotes a powerful dialectic between unity (12:4-13) and *diversity* (12:14-26). It would not be accurate to describe Paul as politically egalitarian in the sense that the term bears in Western modernity or in postmodernity.

"Order" and "orderedness "is built into the very fabric of creation" and "divine" reality (11:3; 15:23-28). The "foundation" of the church is Christ crucified (3:11), not something socially constructed. Was Paul so contemptuous of rationality and logic that he could pursue a strategy of self-interest founded upon the very Christ who utterly renounced self-interest? Would he have sought petty power in Corinth at the price of undermining and betraying the very gospel for which he daily sacrificed life and limb?

Paul places his own ministry under the critique of the cross, no less than the "spirituality" of others. The key criterion of authenticity in 1:1–4:21 is that which "accords with the crucified Christ" (Schrage, *Der erste Brief,* vol. 1, p. 358). Once we argue, with Foucault, that even appeals to *acting as a servant* can be manipulative, virtually any altruistic action can be construed in this way, not least the political strategies of Foucault himself. It is Paul's gentleness that is to be copied, not a self-assertion that demands freedom from constraints. Against Wire the criterion of Christlikeness pinpoints *acceptance of constraints* as a mark of authenticity in Christ's messianic temptations. Paul does not impose upon the Christians in Corinth criteria that he does not accept for himself.

---

its their unique gifts" (p. 46: v. 17). By calling the readers **children** (v. 14b) Paul demotes them to subadult apprentices. "Here he is a father because his focus is on control," and he seeks "compliance" (p. 47).

We have identified two ways in which Paul exhibits pastoral care: his desire for the readers' good and his personal involvement or empathy with them. The "father" image necessitated a wider exegetical discussion. Now we identify a third way. As pastor and father, Paul expresses his care not only through his *talk* but also through his *walk* (in rabbinic terms, not only *haggadah* but also *halakhah*); not only through his *words* but also through his *life and actions*. He sends (or has sent) Timothy in his place until he himself can return to them in person (vv. 17-19), and they may witness not only his beliefs but also his "ways" (NRSV) or **patterns of life** (v. 17), which are consistently taught **in every Christian congregation** (v. 17b).

These "ways" or **patterns of life** have already emerged in the "catalogue of afflictions" of vv. 8-13. Paul regularly alludes in ascending order to his writings, his sending of an emissary, and his own arrival (Phil. 2:25-30; 1 Thess. 2:2-3) in a way that reflects the *consistency* of his apostolic witness. When he arrives, Paul will expose what those who **have begun to be inflated with arrogance can do** rather than their mere **talk**. The clause **what they can do** translates the Greek word for *power (dynamis)* and is one of many examples that demonstrate that *power* often denotes *what is effective* rather than what is spectacular.

Calvin (*First Epistle*, p. 262) and Barth (*Resurrection*, pp. 18, 24, 26, 49, 52, 75, 79-82) endorse this meaning, and we thus translate v. 20: **The kingdom of God is not a matter of talk but of solid efficacy**. Paul is concerned with the contrast, so relevant today in relation to rhetorical "spin" and to postmodernity, between *rhetoric* and *reality*. The reign of God manifests *solid reality* in and through the cross of Christ (cf. 1:18-25; 3:18–4:5).

Paul uses a deliberative subjunctive in the final verse to express the longing of his pastoral heart: **Am I to come to you with a stick in my hand or with love and a gentle spirit?** (v. 21). Paul as pastor does not seek confrontation, even if he cannot rule it out. **Love** may require firmness; it "never gives up; never falls apart" (13:7-8). Nevertheless, it "builds" (8:1); "waits patiently . . . shows kindness . . . never tires of [giving] support" (13:4-7). Paul's pastoral care leaves no room for moral cowardice: he will have matters out if he has no other choice. But his pastoral sensitivity leaves him reluctant to risk tearing anything down when his aim is *to build up*. The theme of *building up* runs through every section of this epistle, as Margaret Mitchell claims. This is the goal of pastoral care.

14. SUGGESTIONS FOR POSSIBLE REFLECTION ON 4:14-21

1. *On the pastoral or parental heart:* Might genuine concern for other people sometimes slide into a desire to take some control over them? The opposite of love is not wrath but indifference. Should it surprise us if mistakes or willfulness provokes God to sorrow or grieve him? Parental love that is wise seeks to avoid equally both smothering the child with overly protective, tight reins and giving enough freedom to make mistakes that are *fatal*. Should pastoral care seek to tread a similar middle path?

2. *On the "imitation" of Christ and the holy "walk" with God:* To imitate Christ and to imitate holy Christians does not mean mechanically replicating their routines or minutiae of beliefs. How can believers "take their cue" from holy Christians more creatively? How can churches avoid exercising too much control over their members, while also providing guidelines and models of holy living? Holiness is not only Christian talk but also a Christian walk (cf. rabbinic *haggadah*, "story," and *halakhah*, "walk," 4:20).

V. Moral Issues That Require Clear-Cut Challenge and Change (5:1–6:20)

Introduction: Paul's Moral Reasoning in 1 Corinthians (especially in chapters 5–10)

Contrary to many superficial impressions of his thought, Paul often readily acknowledges moral grey areas and complexities, in which differing circumstances may contribute to differing evaluations. This aspect of his thought finds expression especially in chapters 7–10, and in part in 12-14. But in chapters 5 and 6 no such complexities and circumstantial factors affect clear-cut moral judgments. In 5:1-13 the case of incest provokes sheer outrage: **It is actually reported that** . . . (v. 1), **and you remain complacent!** . . . (v. 2). **We are to consign this man . . . to Satan** (v. 5). This outright condemnation matches the mood of 6:1-11: **How dare such a person . . . ?** (v. 1). **Do you not know that** . . . ? (v. 9).

In chapter 7 Paul acknowledges complex issues in which what is "good" may not serve as well as what is "better" (7:9), *given certain circumstances*. Whereas 5:3 formulates an act of "solemn judgment," 7:25

expresses an "opinion." If an inflexible adherence to some principle risks the "destruction" of the "weak" or "insecure" Christian brother or sister, there must be room for second thoughts (8:7-12).

That Paul appears sometimes as a moral absolutist and at other times as one who respects the importance of variable situations does not arise from inconsistency, nor from prejudices about "worse" sins. Chapters 5-6 derive their moral force from *theology;* in particular from the contrast between the newness of the new creation wrought by the work of Christ as **Passover lamb** (5:7-8) and as *Redeemer* (6:20), and the old mode of life associated with the order prior to faith. Chapters 7-10 derive their moral force largely from *pastoral concerns,* in particular from the contrast between what "destroys" and what "builds up" (8:1). Clear-cut issues arise if or when the integrity of the Christian as a *new creation* is compromised (2 Cor. 5:17). But in pastoral terms, *what constitutes genuine love for "the other"* may take more than one form. Here the concern is *building up,* as Margaret Mitchell argues *(Paul and Rhetoric).*

A. An Extreme Case of Conduct "beyond the Boundaries" (5:1-13)

1 It is actually reported that there is an illicit sexual relationship among you: immorality of a kind which is not tolerated even among the Gentiles. Someone is having relations with his stepmother. 2 And you remain complacent! Ought you not rather to have entered into a state of mourning, that the man who has committed this practice be removed from your community?

3 For my part, as physically absent but nevertheless present in the Spirit, I have already pronounced judgment on the man who has perpetrated this act under such circumstances, as also effectively present. 4 When you are assembled together in the name of our Lord Jesus, with my spiritual presence, and with the effective power of our Lord Jesus, 5 we are to consign this man, such as he is, to Satan with a view to the destruction of the fleshly, in order that the spirit may be saved at the day of the Lord.

6 Your self-satisfaction is ill placed. Do you not know that a little leaven leavens all of the dough? 7 Clean out the old leaven, so that you may be a newly begun batch of dough, even as you are indeed without old leaven. For our Passover lamb, Christ, has been sacrificed. 8 So let us celebrate the Passover festival not with old leaven, not with leaven that ferments wickedness and evil, but with the unleavened bread which is purity and truth.

9 I wrote to you in my letter not to mix indiscriminately with immoral people. 10 In no way did this refer to people in secular society who are immoral or grasping or who practice extortion or idolatry, since you would then be obliged to withdraw from the world. 11 As matters stand, however, I am writing to you not to mix indiscriminately with someone who accepts the name of Christian and remains immoral or grasping in their stance or is involved in idolatry or is characterized as a person of verbal abuse or a drunkard or someone who gains by extortionate dealing. With such a person you should not even share your table. 12 For what business of mine is it to formulate verdicts about outsiders? Is it not those inside to whom your verdicts apply? 13 Those outside have God as their judge. "Banish the evil man."

In accordance with the first of the two principles outlined above, Paul perceives the particular case of outrageous immoral behavior that has been **reported** to him (v. 1) as threatening the very identity of the "Christian" community. It promotes a public self-contradiction. How can the church lend support to, or show indifference about, the situation? How can it be that **you remain complacent** (v. 2) and show **self-satisfaction** (v. 6)? The reported habits of life flagrantly contradict the values and lifestyle that in part define and characterize the "Christian" church.

The direction to expel the man concerned (vv. 4-5) has a twofold aim. One purpose is that **the spirit** of the offender **may be saved at the day of the Lord** (v. 5). A second purpose is to **clean out the old leaven** (v. 7) so that the Christian community may regain the newness of the **newly begun batch of dough** that reflects the identity of God's new creation. To **celebrate the Passover festival** while leaving aside the injunction to purge out **the old** leaven is a self-contradiction. How can any **celebrate the Passover** with **old leaven**? How can the church in Corinth celebrate **new** life in **Christ** their **Passover lamb** while publicly flaunting (v. 2) their incorporation of **old leaven**?

These are the main contours of 5:1-11. A number of details, however, shed further light on particular verses. Some scholars claim that the **complacent** (v. 2) acceptance of so gross a scandal by the church may perhaps suggest that they have found ways of accommodating *a wealthy patron* among their number. A special version of this explanation is that the relation between the offender and his **stepmother** (v. 1) may have had the effect of manipulating laws of *inheritance*, with the effect of keeping substantial wealth or property within the membership of the church.

In favor of these views we may note the close connection that this situation would then have with the issues of greed and manipulation that lie at the heart of going to law and other ethical matters in chapter 6. There is indeed a broad unity of content between chapters 5 and 6. But there may be a simpler and less speculative reason for this **complacent** attitude and the church's failure to enter into a **state of mourning** (v. 2). Some at Corinth seem bent on exaggerating Paul's own theology to the point of distortion. Thus the **complacent** rejection of regret might well be due to a misplaced assertion of Christian *freedom* as this emerges clearly in the quotation from Corinth in 6:12 and 10:23, "Liberty to do all things." Even the sinful Christian, they argue, cannot be condemned by the law; here this bold "gospel" is put into practice! Whichever explanation is accepted, however, the church in Corinth has placed a mistaken or at best secondary consideration above its own integrity as a witness to Christian identity as founded upon the way of the cross (1:18-31; 2:1-5).

Mistaken or secondary concerns have seduced the church into accepting and condoning an **illicit sexual relationship** of a kind **not tolerated even among the Gentiles** (v. 1). The Roman jurist Gaius wrote in the second century: "It is illegal to marry a father's or mother's sister . . . nor can I marry her who was at one time [Latin *quondam*] my mother-in-law or stepmother" (*Institutes* 1.63). In the century prior to Paul, Cicero expressed disgust when "mother-in-law marries son-in-law"; it is "unbelievable" (*Pro Cluentio* 5.27). Even the sexually liberal poet Catullus draws the line here, speaking of it as abhorrent (*Poems* 74 and 88-90). Paul's expression of outrage expresses precisely the evidence of the times. The perceptions of those outside the church *do* matter in relation to Christian witness and integrity.

Yet Paul is also endorsing a biblical provision. The general purpose of the Levitical "prohibited kinship and affinity relations" traditionally included in the English *Book of Common Prayer* (1662) does not depend on anthropological theory about tribal kinship. Within the framework of an extended family, they place the pull of certain possible attractions "off limits" for the security and the protection of prior marriage loyalties. These Levitical laws were to nurture security and trust rather than to impose arbitrary curtailments of freedom.

All the same, for those in Corinth who were obsessed with "autonomy" and "freedom," to sweep all this aside seemed a sign of boldness rather than an occasion for grief. Hence Paul formally declares both the church and the offender to be at fault. A *judicial verdict* and *formal sentence* are solemnly *pronounced* (vv. 3-5).

As is the case with declarations of this kind (technically called "performative" language), certain *conditions* have to apply for it to be effective. Paul specifies four such conditions: first, he is a personal *participant* in the action through the work of the Holy **Spirit** (v. 3a); second, his apostolic agency counts as *apostolic presence* (vv. 3b, 4, discussed above); third, the church is **together** solemnly **assembled** as a corporate entity; and fourth, **together** they invoke the **power** of **Jesus** as **our Lord.**

Given these four conditions, a *sentence* is *pronounced.* This entails more than one stage and more than one purpose. First, they **consign** the offender to **Satan**; second, the intermediate purpose is the **destruction of the fleshly**; third, the ultimate, positive, purpose is that the **spirit** [Greek *pneuma*] **may be saved at the day of the Lord** (v. 5). Each word, however, is a minefield for exegetical difficulty.*

Many interpret **the destruction of the fleshly** (Greek *sarx*) to denote physical illness and death. But if it denotes death, how does this sentence aim at the offender's final salvation? This would assume that Paul refers to some postmortal period for repentance. In Rom. 8:5-9 and in numerous other passages Paul uses *sarx* ("flesh") to denote not physical being but a *mode of life lived in pursuit of its own ends,* in an attitude of self-sufficiency, *without reliance upon God* (cf. Rom. 8:5-9). Paul envisages that the offender, bereft of the approval and support of the community, will find his self-sufficiency and self-reliance eroded until he comes to reach a change of heart.

To be consigned **to Satan** may also suggest illness and death, especially in Judaism (Job 2:5-6; *Jubilees* 11:11-12; 48:2-3; *Testament of Benjamin* 3:3). But Paul refers infrequently to the agency of Satan. Further, when he does so, examples more readily include deception, accusation, or the crushing of pride. In 2 Cor. 12:7-10 "the messenger of Satan" brings not

---

*Technical Note: In 1973 I produced a twenty-page study of these verses ("The Meaning of *Sarx* in 1 Cor. 5.5: A Fresh Approach in the Light of Logical and Semantic Factors," *Scottish Journal of Theology* 26 (1973): 204-28; considered further in *First Epistle,* pp. 390-400).

death but a challenge to self-glory. Satan is also associated with punishment or with being cut off from the kingdom of God. The only clear difficulty with the above interpretation is the use of *pneuma* to denote the human **spirit**, since this use occurs infrequently in Paul. This usage is not characteristic of Paul; nevertheless, it does occur.

Paul's **Do you not know that . . . ?** (v. 6) occurs ten times in this epistle. The words generally introduce a principle that should have been self-evident to the Corinthians. This self-evident axiom is the contrast between the old and the new, which Paul expounds in terms of the imagery of the **new leaven** used at the **Passover** (vv. 6-8). **Leaven** has *unstoppable effects out of all proportion to its size* (Matt. 13:33). Hence Paul's imagery operates on two levels. First, it addresses a counterargument from Corinth: How can the sin of a single offender affect the whole church? Second, it underlines the "newness" of the new creation in Christ.

At the Passover every scrap of "old" leaven was swept out of the house to underline the radical nature of the new beginning. Here the ethical injunction, **clean out**, comes into play because the theological statement **you are indeed without old leaven** is true (vv. 7-8). This principle is often expressed by some such formulation as "the imperative is spoken because the indicative is true." Its logic is rooted in biblical theology, where the imperative is addressed to Joshua to "*go in* and *possess* the land," on the ground that *God has given* the land (Josh. 1:6-13). The new is "dynamic" and "crowds out" the old; the old has a tendency to remain merely what it is (Harrisville, *Newness,* pp. 69-79). The theology of "becoming what you are" sometimes finds expression as "possessing your possessions" (as in traditions of the Keswick Convention).

To Christians well grounded in their Old Testament scriptures, this radical disengagement with the "old" and preoccupation with the "new" would call to mind the decisive model of "redemption" as experienced corporately in the Exodus and Passover. Israel was redeemed *from* Egypt *through* God's mighty acts *to* a new status, identity, and lifestyle as God's people. This is the backcloth to warnings against **mixing indiscriminately** with those Christians who habitually resume the "old" ways.

Paul sets aside a "misunderstanding" that might have been manipulative or malicious. Of course he never meant that the church should withdraw from the world to look inward as a ghetto community (vv. 10-11). Neither did he necessarily mean that they were "not to associate with" (NRSV, NIV) Christians who retained habitual vices of the world of unbelievers. The Greek may mean *associate with* in rare passive uses, but it has the force of a double compound with *mix:* "mixing up *(ana)* together *(syn),*" that is, without discretion. Paul is warning the church against an overly easy blurring of Christian witness. What will the outside world make of this? The readers are to use their sense about maintaining boundary markers without becoming a "pure" church withdrawn as a ghetto community from the everyday world.

Some suggest that where "catalogues of vices" occur in Paul (as in Rom. 1:29-31, where Paul lists twenty-one, or in Gal. 5:19-21) the whole has been constructed for rhetorical effect without specific reference to each individual moral "vice." Conzelmann follows this approach (*1 Corinthians*, pp. 100-101). However, Brian Rosner shows how deeply the specific examples chosen for mention by Paul reflect the ethics of the Old Testament, especially Deuteronomy (*Paul, Scripture, and Ethics,* pp. 61-93). Several of these moral features allude to an attitude of **grasping**, or always wanting more than they have. This not only reflects an aspect of Corinthian society as a whole but also provides a bridge between 5:1-5 and 6:1-11. Similarly, the allusion to **extortion** refers to the exploitation of people, whether through business practice or general aims in life. **Idolatry** points forward to 8:1–11:1. Paul is not simply using traditional material for rhetorical effect (see further in 6:9-11).

15. Suggestions for Possible Reflection on 5:1-13

1. *On complacency:* Complacency may come from two opposite tendencies in a church. It may derive from being a "pure" church from which all dissenting opinion has been driven out, or it may come from an overly tolerant church where anything goes without the raising of an eyebrow. If judgmentalism breeds one type of complacency, and overtolerance breeds another, how do we try to steer a safe course between the two? When does a church become a social club for mutual entertainment and self-affirmation? Sometimes lack of suffering breeds complacency: "God whispers to us in our pleasures and shouts in our pains" (C. S. Lewis).

2. *On giving undue attention to the wealthy and influential:* Was a desire to retain the financial benefits from the immoral man part of the problem in Corinth? Might churches today give undue deference to wealthy or influential Christians?

87

3. *On transparency in administration in church or at work:* Paul enjoins transparent action and the implementation of agreed procedures. Do some prefer arrangements "behind closed doors" in order to be less accountable, or to avoid a need for moral courage?

B. A Warning against Manipulative and Grasping Behavior (6:1-11)

1 If one of you has a case against another, dare that one seek judgment at a court where there is questionable justice, rather than arbitration before God's people? 2 Or do you not know that "the saints will judge the world"? Well, if it is among you that the world is judged, are you unfit to hold a tribunal for small claims? 3 Do you not know that we shall judge angels; need I add, then, matters of everyday life? 4 If, rather, you hold tribunals concerning matters of everyday life, do you set upon judgment seats those who are viewed in the church as "people of no esteem"? 5 It is to make you feel ashamed that I say this to you. Has it come to this, that there is found not a single one among you who is sufficiently "a wise person" to be competent to arbitrate between two fellow believers? 6 But must a Christian go to law with a fellow believer, and this before unbelievers! 7 In fact, already it is a total moral defeat for you that you have cases for judgment with one another. Why do you not rather let yourselves be deprived of your rights? Why do you not rather let yourselves be defrauded? 8 But you, as it is, deprive people of justice, and you defraud, and fellow Christians at that.

9 Or do you not know that people who practice evil cannot inherit God's kingdom? Stop being misled: neither those who practice immoral sexual relations, nor those who pursue practices bound up with idolatry, nor people who practice adultery, nor perverts [or *those involved in pederastic practices*], nor men who practice sexual relations with men, 10 nor those who practice thievery, nor those who always grasp for more, nor drunkards, nor those who practice verbal abuse, nor people who exploit others in their own interests shall inherit the kingdom. 11 And this some of you used to be. But you were washed clean, you were set apart as holy, you were put right in your standing in the name of the Lord Jesus Christ and by the Spirit of our God.

At first sight chapter 6 may appear to address three separate issues that have little in common: supposedly "going to law" (6:1-8), immoral behavior (6:9-11), and freedom and discipline (6:12-20). But these conventional headings are misleading. 6:1-8 is not primarily about going to law as such. The legal background suggests that these first eight verses constitute a warning against manipulating fellow Christians for personal advantage. A Christian who has more economic and social standing takes advantage of his or her position. This reflects an attitude of "grasping" what is not one's own, and this prompts Paul to reflect on a cluster of "grasping" attitudes and actions, some of which are sexual actions that overstep the mark. The Christian should leave all such grasping practices behind, as no longer compatible with being part of God's new creation (v. 11).

The background to legal action in civil lawsuits in a Roman colony in the mid-first century makes a difference. It arises from the explicitly *Roman* character of the administration in Corinth. Roman *criminal* law in this period was relatively fair and objective. But this was not the case in *civil* law. Here judges and even juries expected to receive some *quid pro quo* for a favorable verdict. This might come in terms of a straight financial gift with strings; a promised payment; or a debt to be paid by using economic or social influence or by providing new business opportunities or openings.

Against this background Paul saw **seek**ing **judgment at a court where there is questionable justice** (v. 1) as audacious (**How dare you?** v. 1). It amounted to an attempt on the part of a Christian to use superior economic or social power to manipulate a more vulnerable fellow believer into losing the dispute (vv. 6-8). Unlike his earlier, gentler remonstration in 4:14-21, Paul wants that person to **feel ashamed** (v. 5).

We should not be too distracted by the extravagant language about Christians **judging the world** (v. 2) or **angels** (v. 3). Paul again uses irony and parody. He earlier parodied claims in Corinth about their "reigning as kings" (4:8-13); here he presses this further to shame the person who prefers to place even a small-claims case (v. 2b) before those who are viewed in the church as **unbelievers** or **of no esteem** (vv. 4, 6) while making grandiose claims about believers' "judging" and "reigning" in the tradition of Daniel and apocalyptic (cf. Matt. 19:28 and Rev. 2:26; 20:4).

Several Church Fathers point out that allusions to Christians "judging" others at the end of the world do not denote "judging" as independent individuals, but as derivatively and corporately sharing in Christ's own glory as Judge. But Paul allows his readers to glimpse the cosmic drama that ends in world judgment partly through parody: it throws into relief concerns that appear relatively petty and even self-contradictory. His ironic remonstration, **Has it come to this, that there is not found among you . . . a sufficiently "wise person"?** looks back to the reversals of the cross in 1:18-28. Has not Christ turned the "nothings" into *"wise"* people? The same Greek word is used in 1:28 *(exouthenēmena)* as in 6:4. Paul then resumes his exposé of manipulative, grasping conduct, which he regards as downright wicked. It would be better to yield up one's **rights** (v. 7) than **to deprive people of justice and defraud fellow Christians** (v. 8).

Paul's sense of outrage at the situation now spills over into a broader warning against "grasping" qualities that remain incompatible with the Christian's status as part of God's new creation. It is important to note that the list in vv. 9-10 denotes *habits* and *practices, not isolated acts.* Paul does not suggest that a Christian who was once tempted into a single act of adultery, theft, verbal abuse, or exploitation of others remains forever excluded from the kingdom of God.

The introductory clause **do you not know?** may suggest that the "list" formed a catechism, or less formal basic instruction, on the nature of the Christian life. This may have been standard teaching prior to baptism. The new life is no longer characterized by the practice of **evil**, habitual **drunkenness**, the **practice of verbal abuse**, or the **exploitation** of others, perhaps in business or social relations or in the employment of services. These are patterns of life, not isolated sins.

While we cannot allow other passages wholly to determine exegesis, the parallel in 1 John sheds light on this issue. Those who pursue such practices, Paul asserts, will **not inherit the kingdom of God** (v. 9a). 1 John 3:6 declares, "The person who abides in him [Christ] does not practice sin." But John has already acknowledged that every Christian *sins:* "If we say that we have no sin, we deceive ourselves" (1:8). Hence many versions insert the word "cannot" before "sin" to indicate a *logical* rather than a *causal* statement. Neither Paul nor John suggests that moral failure disinherits a Christian from salvation; otherwise the themes of forgiveness and justification by grace alone would lose their currency. Paul, like John, warns his readers that willfully to practice evil without resolve to change casts suspicion on the genuineness of a professed commitment to follow Christ. The Christian will look ahead to the new creation and God's kingdom; not behind, to the sins from which deliverance has in principle been granted. Paul anticipated this point in 5:7-9, where Christ as the Passover sacrifice opens the gate to the new life.

The translation of v. 9 raises difficulties. The first word (Greek *pornoi*) denotes any kind of **immoral sexual relation** that is "outside the line" in nonspecific terms. The third term (Greek *moichoi*) denotes this practice specifically with reference to those who are married, and thus means **people who practice adultery.** The next two terms are the most controversial (Greek *malakoi* and *arsenokoitai*). They may well denote respective roles within a homosexual partnership (Barrett, *First Corinthians,* p. 140). Alternatively the first of the two terms may denote *either* **those involved in pederastic practices**, that is, male prostitution, *or* **perverts**. Whichever is more probable, the second denotes **those** [men] **who practice sexual relations with men.** It is possible that the terms apply to men who have relations with call boys since the general emphasis is on *exploiting,* or taking advantage of people for self-desire. But the Greek term does not specify this, and it would be an "overtranslation" of the words. There is a mass of research literature that supports various views, and I include an extended note both on the literature and the text in my larger commentary (*First Epistle,* pp. 438-55).

The last of these verses brings welcome relief to this somber catalogue: **And this** [is what] **some of you used to be** (a continuous imperfect indicative, rightly so rendered by NRSV and NJB, against the more insipid and general *such were some of you* [REB; AV/KJV]). Paul now expresses an emphatic contrast with a compound verb in the aorist indicative middle: **you were washed clean** (v. 11). The middle voice may carry a nuance of "you had your sins washed away." We need not interpret this too narrowly as a "baptismal" aorist, although it is certainly the decisive moment of new beginnings that once-for-all baptism represents and signifies.

Paul now continues: **you were set apart as holy, you were put right in your standing.** Justification by grace through faith alone is no less important in 1 Corinthians than it is in Romans. For everything comes from God as a freely given gift *(charisma)* of divine grace to which humankind is in no position to contribute. God puts believers and other situations "right with him," and it is this new "put right" relationship that determines all other relationships. Paul expounds this new Christian identity further in terms of union with Christ (vv. 12-20).

16. Suggestions for Possible Reflection on 6:1-11

1. *On manipulation:* To maneuver someone into a situation where they have little freedom of choice for action is like using a kind of "indirect force" upon them. Are some too fond of using levers of power over a friend, husband, wife, parent, or child? Are people always aware when they are being manipulative?

2. *On mediation versus confrontation:* Jesus left us an example of his unique work as Mediator. Moses was also "one who stands between," representing God to Israel and Israel to God, even though at times this made him "a man torn in two." Do people think of mediation before confrontation when personal or professional relationships are at loggerheads? In disputes concerning relationships, should we regard law courts as a last resort?

3. *On grasping what is not rightfully ours:* A common thread of "grasping" what is out of bounds runs through the list of sins or vices in vv. 9-10. Are some more serious than others, or are they all expressions of the same self-centered, grasping attitude expressed in different ways in different spheres of life?

4. *On newness of life:* Christians still sin, but we are called to a radical newness of life. This has been compared to coming out of the cold into a warm room. The heat is the decisive force, but pockets of cold have yet to thaw out.

C. Union with Christ Lived Out in the Body or "Public World" (6:12-20)

12 "Liberty to do all things"; but not everything is helpful. "Liberty to do anything"; but I will not let anything take liberties with me. 13 "Food for the stomach, and the stomach for food; and God will do away with the one and the other." 14 But the body is not for immorality; on the contrary, it is for the Lord, and the Lord for the body. God raised the Lord, and he will raise us up through his power. 15 Do you not know that your bodies are Christ's limbs and organs? Shall I, then, take away Christ's limbs and organs and make them the limbs and organs of a prostitute? Perish the thought! 16 Do you not know that a person who is united in intimacy with a prostitute is one body with her? For as it is said, "The two shall become one flesh." But the person who is intimately united with the Lord is one Spirit. 18 Keep away from sexual immorality. Every other sin

which a person may commit is done outside the body. But the person who sins sexually sins against his or her own body. 19 Or do you not know that your body is a temple of the Holy Spirit who indwells you, whom you received from God, and that you do not belong to yourselves? 20 For you were bought with a price. Show forth God's glory, then, in how you live your bodily life.

This section begins with a counterreply (either already used in Corinth or anticipated by Paul) to the effect that Christians have received *liberty* through the gospel. If the gospel has done away with the law, is not this "liberty" absolute and unqualified? Is it not *liberty to do all things?* Paul, the counterreply from Corinth runs, is backing down from the gospel into a stuffy moralism.

The Greek used in the first century did not employ quotation marks, and the convention used in modern printed Greek texts of introducing direct speech by means of a capital letter postdates the period when all Greek letters were capitals or uncials. So the reader has to judge when a phrase or sentence is a quotation. In 6:12 and 10:23 most commentators rightly agree that "**Liberty to do all things**" is a slogan or a catchphrase used in Corinth. These are not the only examples: "It is a good thing for a man not to have sexual intimacy with a woman" (7:1) is a quotation that Paul proceeds to contradict. "All of us possess 'knowledge'" (8:1) is a quotation to which Paul responds with "Yes, but. . . ." (See Murphy-O'Connor, "Corinthian Slogans.")

It is difficult to convey in English Paul's wordplay in Greek between *exesti* ("it is lawful"; **liberty** . . .) and *exousiazō*, "I have control over"; but in the passive, "I came under the power of" (cf. Danker, *A Greek-English Lexicon,* pp. 353-54). I try to convey the flavor of the pun by translating: **"Liberty to do anything"; but I will not let anything take liberties with me.** This second clause (v. 12b) repeats and amplifies the thrust of v. 12a, **"Liberty to do all things"; but not everything is helpful**.

Surprisingly, Fee declares that how this section relates to the previous one "is not at all certain." But Paul chooses to elaborate on how freedom and self-discipline relate to each other to anticipate how his readers might seek to sidestep his warnings about manipulative and immoral conduct: "We are free from the law, Paul!" But, he insists, such license contradicts what it is to be "in Christ." "Freedom" is not unqualified license to gratify the desires of the self, not least because the new Christian self has a new identity as a new creation "in Christ."

Still more clearly the issue of manipulation by means of "using" civil law-courts (vv. 1-8) and the cluster of inappropriate habits and practices that Paul has cited (vv. 9-11) *all concern what it is to be a Christian in the public domain.* Paul uses the word "**body**" *(sōma)* to denote this *interpersonal, social, public mode of being a Christian.* Hence, in technical theological terms, he introduces a theology of the **body**. The Christian lifestyle is *more than a private "inner" state;* it manifests itself in "bodily" action and behavior *in the public domain.* Christian faith finds there *visible, tangible, communicable, observable, recognizable expression.* In this respect the Christian remains part of God's created order.*

The **body**, therefore, is more than some transient, physical "shell" for the soul. It is to be distinguished, for example, from **the stomach** (v. 13). In my view, v. 13 also extends the quotation used in Corinth: "**Food for the stomach, and the stomach for food; and God will do away with the one and the other.**" This slogan could be used to promote the news that it did not matter what Christians did with their "physical" bodies since these were merely transient houses of the soul. Seemingly paradoxically, but on reflection quite consistently, those of a cast of mind later called "gnostic" could argue on this basis equally for extreme abstinence (7:1), on the ground that the vehicle of salvation was only "the soul."

In vv. 13c-16 Paul stands this argument on its head and utterly rejects it. First, **the body is for the Lord**, and **the Lord for the body** (v. 13c). **The body** provides the public domain of *visible, concrete obedience* to the Lord in everyday terms. It enables discipleship to count. Second, if Christ's resurrection provides the model for the future resurrection of believers, this event demonstrates that some kind of *embodied* mode of existence characterizes life after death. The "**body**," in the

---

*Technical Note: It is worth quoting what one New Testament specialist observes about Paul's use of the word "body." Ernst Käsemann writes that it is "That piece of the world that we ourselves are and for which we bear responsibility because it was the earliest gift of our Creator to us. . . . It signifies man in his 'worldliness' [i.e., in his worldhood, or his being-part-of-the-world] and therefore in his ability to communicate [i.e., his relationality, visibility, recognizable identity]" (Käsemann, *New Testament Questions of Today* [London: SCM, 1969], p. 135). Although we must avoid imposing modern philosophical notions onto Paul, we may say that Paul recognizes that the human self is what it is only in terms of how we relate to others. In philosophical language, the New Testament does not speak of an isolated, individualistic, autonomous self in the sense implied by Descartes, but of an interdependent, accountable, stable self in the sense implied by Paul Ricoeur.

sense outlined above, is not merely transcendent, although merely *physical* organs, such as the stomach, *are* indeed transient. (Paul will elaborate on this in chapter 15.) Third, the **bodies** of believers are **limbs and organs of Christ** (v. 15). Robinson long ago observed that "members" no longer conveys Paul's idea. For in modern parlance the metaphysical use of the word has become dominant, so that we speak of "members" of a club or of a society without the serious prior meaning of beings' **limbs and organs**, which cannot be torn apart without destroying the entity of which they are "members." Paul's notion of being **limbs and organs of Christ** would have seemed to verge on the offensive, but, Robinson urges, today "the language of 'membership' of a body corporate has become so trite that the idea that the individual can be a 'member' has ceased to be offensive" (Robinson, *The Body*, pp. 51-55).

Do you not know that . . . ? (v. 15) repeats the rebuke of 6:2, 3, and 9 that the church in Corinth has forgotten basic teaching that is axiomatic. It is the sixth occurrence of the rhetorical question in this epistle. It is not only that Paul had taught them that their bodies were **limbs and organs of Christ** (v. 15a). He had also urged that bodily conduct was important; that salvation was no merely "inner" and private affair. Dale Martin suggests that Paul deliberately reverses the Greek "religious" and philosophical assumption that "spirit" took precedence over "body" in importance for the human self (Martin, *The Corinthian Body*, pp. 174-78).

The second half of v. 15 now confronts readers with a sharp alternative: **Shall I, then, take away Christ's limbs and organs and make them the limbs and organs of a prostitute? Perish the thought!** The emphatic negative in Greek, "May it not happen!" represents some such exclamation as "Unthinkable!" ("Never!" NIV; "God forbid!" AV/ KJV). The explanation for this otherwise difficult rhetorical question comes in v. 16, which is introduced by a seventh **Do you not know that . . . ?** This declares an axiomatic or basic Christian truth. To be **united in sexual intimacy** with another person, whether with a prostitute (**one body**, v. 16a) or in marriage (**one flesh**, v. 17b), is to become "one." The Greek word denotes a method of *bonding together,* for example, in woodwork by *glue,* or in metallurgy by *welding.* In Matt. 19:5 a man becomes *intimately united* with a wife in marriage when he "leaves (behind)" his father and mother. The couple become "**one flesh**"; Greek uses the same prepositional phrase *(eis sarka mian)* as that of

6:16. (Cf. Mark 10:8 and Eph. 5:31.) This reproduces the Greek of Gen. 2:24, which translates the Hebrew *wĕhāyû lĕbāśār 'echād.*

Does **one body** (Greek *hen sōma,* v. 16a) or **one flesh** (Greek *sarx mia,* v. 16b) mean *one person?* As Levinas stresses, to be "one" with another ceases to be life-enhancing and becomes potentially destructive if the one merely *assimilates and absorbs* the other into itself, as if to "gobble it up." Hence Paul adds further precision by adding a third parallel, **one Spirit** (v. 17). Union with Christ (v. 17) finds expression in the same Greek verb that we have translated **united in intimacy** in v. 16. Union with Christ determines the believer's mode of being and mode of life, but Christ does not "assimilate" the Christian as if the self of the Christian were submerged, lost, or "gobbled up." By parity of reasoning Paul insists that it would be self-contradictory to be committed to union with a prostitute and to union with Christ. Hence v. 18 begins: **Keep away from sexual immorality** (also NJB).

Commentators have wrestled with the meaning of the rest of v. 18. In what sense is inappropriate sexual union more clearly **a sin against one's own body** than, for example, drunkenness, gluttony, or suicide? At first sight this appears to corroborate suspicions that the Christian and Pauline traditions are harsher about sex than other aspects of life. But this is not the case.

First, the comment that **every other sin . . . is done outside the body** might well pick up the misleading theological slogan used, as we have noted, in Corinth to suggest that Christian conduct is really a "private" and "inner" affair relating to the soul or spirit, not to **the body**. This verse addresses and rejects this suggestion.

Second, **body** *(sōma),* unlike the term **flesh**, denotes the human self *in its wholeness and its relation to other selves.* So it is arguable that in sexual acts the mind, body, and whole person are involved, and the self shapes its identity not in isolation but in relation to another self with which it interacts in mutuality. In twenty-first-century idiom, we might say that this area involves higher stakes at a more "personal" level than many other examples from the list involve.

Third, William Loader has recently explained this difficult phrase on the basis of the tradition of the Septuagint (the Greek translation of the Old Testament) that sexual intercourse "brings into being a new reality" (i.e., that of *one flesh*). "Sexual intercourse actually changes people by creating a new reality: oneness with another person, as Gen. 2:23 is understood" (*The Septuagint, Sexuality, and the New Testament,* pp. 90-92). This LXX text, he observes, forms the basis of Paul's argument in vv. 12-20.

Paul's eighth use of **Do you not know . . . ?** (v. 19) introduces his explicit teaching about the **body** prior to his further development of the subject in chapters 12 and 15, and this leads on to the reality of *redemption* (v. 20). **The body** is a **temple** [Greek, strictly inner sanctuary or shrine] **of the Holy Spirit who indwells you.** On this temple theme, see on 3:16, although here the theme has a more *individual* application in contrast to the more *communal* emphases in 3:16. Greco-Roman readers would readily recall that the images of pagan deities "dwell in" pagan temples, dominating both their impact and their character as temples. Dare anyone set up another image as a rival?

A *fellow* believer, however, is no less **a temple of the Holy Spirit who indwells [them]** than those immediately addressed. Hence the thought probably points back also to 6:1-8, 9-11: to try to manipulate a fellow Christian for selfish gain is like committing sacrilege against the holy **temple** indwelt by the **Holy Spirit.**

The final master-stroke comes in v. 20: **For you were bought with a price.** This verse alone would question the conventional notion of being redeemed as a slave in order to be *free.* Deissmann commended and popularized this unduly influential view for too long. Dale Martin and others rightly argue that *purchase by another,* or being **bought with a price**, signifies *transference of ownership from one master or "lord" to another.* The Christian is not purchased out of slavery simply to gain some new autonomous "freedom" in which he or she faces the world on their own. In such a situation they face every hazard alone, and might even face becoming enslaved again to a worse master. Christ purchases or redeems men and women as *his.* Henceforth it is he who has them in his care. They *belong* to Christ.

Recent research on slavery in the Greco-Roman world of the first century demonstrates that what it meant to be a slave depended first and foremost on the character and attitude of the new "Lord" *(kyrios)* who purchased the slave. In the second place, it depended on the status and function that the Lord assigned to the slave. To be sure, the situation of some slaves was dire: they would be exploited, humiliated, and violated without redress; they were the "property" (Latin *res,* "thing") of their lord. But some slaves with appreciative masters enjoyed high responsibilities, even privileges, such as managing an estate, household, or business affairs. Paul states that this change of ownership leaves no room for serving their previous master. Christians have been purchased to enter a new world and to serve a new master.

Price indicates the *costliness* of redemption: Christ shed his blood, submitting himself to the humiliation and contempt of death by crucifixion (1:23-25). It is misleading to try to extrapolate *to whom* the price was paid since this takes us beyond the immediate purpose for which the word *price* is introduced. The phrase corroborates Christ's entitlement to be "rightful Lord" of those whom he has redeemed. The concept of **body** resonates closely with the notion of a slave redeemed *to belong* and *to serve*. The public, everyday life of the redeemed Christian is to **show forth** the **glory of God**.

17. Suggestions for Possible Reflection on 6:12-20

1. *On Christian freedom:* In what sense are Christians *free* from the law? Can we not say, "All things are lawful" (v. 12)? Luther writes: "A Christian is the most free lord of all and subject to none; a Christian is the most dutiful servant of all and subject to all" (Luther, *Concerning Christian Liberty*). How can the Christian hold together this coexistence of freedom and belonging to Christ as his purchased slave?

2. *On bodily obedience and public, credible discipleship:* Bodily, visible obedience in the public world relates closely to what people call an "incarnational" theology. Is there any truth in the critical jibe "The Word became flesh, but we have made it 'word' again"? Christians cannot avoid the *vulnerability and costliness* of everyday discipleship in the public domain because this gives discipleship its visibility and credibility. "The body is for the Lord" (v. 14) points to the *credibility* of Christian discipleship in the eyes of others as being visible and public rather than inner and private.

3. *On being "Christ's limbs and organs"* (v. 15): Our privileged status is that we are "members" or *limbs and organs* of Christ. Might this suggest that "Christ has no hands but our hands"? This is true only in certain limited ways, for it is not the case that Christ cannot act without us. But God *chooses* to let the world see Christ through the church. What does the world see?

4. *Belonging to Jesus Christ as Lord:* As those purchased by Christ's blood (v. 20), Christ takes responsibility for us. Belonging to a gracious Lord puts

us in a better position than that of an independent person trying to do everything alone. But are Christians sometimes tempted to try to take back what belongs to Christ?

5. *On being a temple of the Holy Spirit* (v. 19): Since all Christians are God's temples, how we treat them becomes a matter of how well we respect God's consecrating presence in them. Is a sin against a fellow believer more like sacrilege (profaning what is holy) than a social failure?

6. *On the cost of our redemption* (v. 20): What does this infinite cost tell us about Christ and about ourselves?

VI. Paul's Replies to Questions from Corinth about a Series of Practical Issues (7:1–11:1)

Introduction to 7:1–11:1

This next section (7:1–11:1) signals a clear change of mood and of pastoral strategy from 1:10–6:20. It addresses two broadly different types of issues. Chapter 7 mainly concerns marriage, celibacy, and a person's role or status within a household. Chapters 8-10 concern the extent to which a Christian should (or need not) withdraw from aspects of general social and business life that would involve either implicitly or explicitly certain practices associated with pagan idol worship. The sensitive issue is that of eating food that had (usually at an earlier stage) been dedicated to a pagan deity in a pagan temple. Within the framework of this debate chapter 9 elaborates Paul's personal example of forbearing to claim certain "rights" where practice might suggest a different application from abstract theory alone.

There are three ways in which this change of pastoral approach can most readily be described and explained. First, *Paul is about to reply to issues raised by the church.* In chapters 1-6 Paul confronts the church with failures and unchristian attitudes that give deep cause for concern, or in some cases deep shame, but the Christians in Corinth seem unaware of their seriousness. In those earlier chapters Paul has to create such awareness and to correct unwarranted complacency. In 7:1–11:1, by contrast, the *Christians in Corinth had already voiced concern* about the issues, and they were *seeking Paul's advice and direction.*

99

Hence, second, in 7:1–11:2 *Paul is able to leave the past behind to focus on the future.* As long as the Christians in Corinth need still to be made aware of what is wrong, Paul has less need as pastor than he had in 1:10–6:20 to dwell upon past failure, but redirects the debate to *deliberation* about the future.

Third, *this allows Paul to engage more flexibly with what we might term grey areas.* Whereas the contrast between right and wrong seems clear-cut in chapters 1–6, Paul can respond in 7:1–11:1 in ways that clearly consider merits on both sides of a debate. Thus his advice for people who have not yet married and are considering the future is far from absolute (7:25-38). He concludes that those who appeal to the monotheist creed that one God exists as grounds for viewing pagan deities as "nothing" indeed have a strong point; but he adds that there is much more to be said than this (8:1-13). He pleads for the adaptability and flexibility that can minister to Jew and Gentile and to the weak and to the strong as is appropriate for each (9:19-23). Here Paul combines *pastoral sensitivity with pastoral flexibility.* We touched on these issues in the main Introduction (pp. 13-14 and 26-27).

A. Marriage, Singleness, and Those Who Have Been Widowed (7:1-40)

1. Implications of the Married State (7:1-7)

1 Now for the matters about which you wrote: "It is a good thing for a man not to have physical intimacy with a woman." 2 On the contrary, on account of cases of irregular physical intimacy, let each man hold to his own wife, and let each woman hold to her own husband. 3 Let the husband give to his wife what is due to her, and similarly the wife what is due to her husband. 4 The wife does not have exclusive rights over her own body, but the husband; similarly also the husband does not have exclusive rights over his own body, but the wife. 5 Stop depriving each other of what is due in marriage, except perhaps by mutual agreement for a specific span of time, that you may find unhurried time for prayer, and then come back together again. The goal would be nullified if Satan went on putting you through trials beyond your self-control. 6 I say this by way of concession, not as a command. 7 To be sure, I should like everybody to be as I myself am too. But each person has his or her own gift freely bestowed from God: one person, this kind; another, that kind.

Paul's view of marriage has been widely misunderstood over the centuries. One major cause of misunderstanding has been a general failure to recognize until relatively modern times that v. 1b, "**It is a good thing for a man not to have physical intimacy with a woman** [or *with his wife?*]" does not stem from Paul, but represents a quotation or a maxim used by some in Corinth, perhaps cited from the letter they sent to Paul. As we observed in connection with 6:12, the Greek of Paul's day did not use quotation marks, and readers had to judge what passages embodied quotations.

The first two words in the Greek of v. 1a *(peri de,* sometimes translated *now concerning)* often function to mark the introduction of a new topic, and probably also to signal the opening of passages drawn from questions raised by the letter from Corinth, as here: **Now for the matters about which you wrote**. Thus "**It is a good thing for a man . . .**" is most naturally understood as part of the content of the letter. This receives further confirmation from the adversative **but** (Greek *de*) at the beginning of v. 2. (Some argue that v. 1b can still be understood as Pauline if "**good**" is viewed as denoting one acceptable option among others, but the logic is against this, in spite of vv. 7-8.) Even by 1965 Hurd had identified twenty-five modern scholars who treat v. 1b as a quotation from Corinth, and since that time this has become the overwhelming majority view (*The Origin of 1 Corinthians*, p. 58).

What kind of people in Corinth would advocate total abstinence from sexual union, either as a constraint upon those already married (especially if we translate the Greek *gynē* as *wife* rather than **woman**) or as advice not to marry at all? We may recall the point of the argument about "the body" in 6:12-16. Some tried to argue that "spirituality" had nothing to do with bodily actions, but was an inner, private state of mind or "knowledge" *(gnōsis)*. Such "gnostics" either disdained the body as a domain of no consequence or disdained it as unworthy of concern for "spiritual" people. The former led to license; the latter to ascetic self-denial. Paul utterly rejects both as unchristian. "The body is the temple of the Holy Spirit" (6:19) and is "for the Lord" (6:13). Some in Corinth, however, insisted that "the spiritual" should avoid sex.

This disastrous heresy has had negative consequences, but also provoked Paul to formulate a positive and sensitive Christian view of marriage far ahead of its times (vv. 2-6). In the ancient world sexual intimacy was regarded either (in some cases) as a duty for the sake of procreation or (in other cases) as a pleasurable experience for men that women provided. Paul appears to be the first writer to suggest that such "pleasure" could be *mutual.* Otherwise it remains unintelligible that he urges *both men and women* equally to **stop depriving each other** (Greek continuous present) of what is the *rightful due* of the *other.*

Research into the nature of marriage in the Greco-Roman world of Paul's day shows how distinctive and innovative was Paul's own positive approach.* In Stoic traditions marriage promoted the full responsibilities of a husband as a householder, father, and citizen and stability in society. Thus in effect most Stoics regarded marriage as a duty for the majority, although some, for example, Epictetus, allowed the more intellectual to avoid its "distractions" to focus upon philosophy.

Admittedly there is a practical similarity between Paul's approach and some strands of Hellenistic philosophical thought insofar as both consider the role of "special circumstances" in assessing whether marriage is right or wrong for some (cf. affinities with vv. 7-9 and esp. vv. 26-31). However, apart from this, Paul's concern for mutuality, reciprocity, and most especially the presupposition that sexual intimacy provides *mutual* pleasure remains distinctive and far ahead of its times. Paul declares that prolonged or permanent sexual abstinence, in effect, robs the spouse of his or her *"rights"*: **Let the husband give the wife what is due to her** [Greek *tēn opheilēn apodidotō*], **and similarly the wife . . . to her husband** (v. 3).

Paul also asserts that neither partner has **exclusive rights** over his or her own body (v. 4). The Greek verb *exousiazō,* "to have the [exclusive] right of control," also occurs in the passive in 6:12, where we noted the wordplay between *having liberty (exesti)* and taking control or (passive) *taking liberties.* Against the notion of sexual politics as power play, perhaps Paul's observations of a transformed, new tenderness in Christian marriage lay behind his new insight that sexual union, far from being a matter of manipulation or control, constituted a mutual giving and receiving as an expression of love, not to be denied to either partner. Such speculation might seem farfetched until we place alongside

*Technical Note: To select only one or two examples, W. Deming compares the background in Stoic philosophical thought in *Paul on Marriage and Celibacy: The Hellenistic Background of 1 Cor. 7* (Cambridge: Cambridge University Press, 1995); O. Larry Yarborough compares both the Hellenistic and rabbinic backgrounds in *Not like the Gentiles: Marriage Rules in the Letters of Paul* (Atlanta: Scholars, 1985).

each other the "bodily" theology of chapter 6 and the profound insight into the nature of love in chapter 13.

The implications of 7:2-6 are groundbreaking against the background of the times. They may also serve to question Antoinette Wire's radical feminist reading that Paul wants to manipulate Christian women in Corinth into retaining more "home-based," less public roles (*The Corinthian Women Prophets;* also questioned by Witherington, *Women in the Earliest Churches,* pp. 24-42). Every clause in 7:2-6 breathes the spirit of mutuality. If the couple decides to refrain from sexual intimacy to facilitate more time for prayer **for a specific span of time**, this must be **by mutual agreement** (v. 5; Greek *ek symphōnou*).

I should like everyone to be as I myself am (v. 7) has raised speculation over the centuries about whether Paul is widowed or has never married. It would have been usual for a leader in Pharisaic circles to be married (cf. Phil. 3:5-6). Paul does not place celibacy *above* marriage; he honors both. Yet the very complexities of the issues that he has to handle in this chapter remind him of how much "easier," in certain respects, a total preoccupation with gospel mission might be for the unmarried person. However, *contentment* is important, as his allusions to experiencing **trials** and battling for *self-control* (vv. 5b and 9) suggest. He declares that ultimately the two states of marriage and singleness require different and respective **gifts freely bestowed by God** (v. 7b).

The Greek for a freely bestowed gift here is *charisma.* Its occurrences as a necessary gift for a celibate or married life should exclude the mistaken notion that every charismatic "gift" must of necessity be "spontaneous" and have little to do with sustained discipline, reflection, and training. In chapters 12-14 Paul changes the Corinthian preferred word *pneumatika,* spiritual (gifts), to *charismata, freely given gifts, gifts without strings,* gifts generously given.

18. SUGGESTIONS FOR POSSIBLE REFLECTION ON 7:1-7

1. *On honoring both marriage and celibacy:* Marriage and celibacy are both gifts and callings of God. Does our generation accord sufficient honor both to celibacy and to marriage? Whether people experience strains in the single state or strains in the married state, ultimately it is God's sovereign gift that will maximize the benefits of each state and sustain Christians on

their life journey. Would "living together" in neither marriage nor celibacy detract from honoring both states?

2. *Mutuality in the married state:* Paul places an entirely new emphasis (absent from Greek and Roman writings of the day) upon mutuality, reciprocity, and mutual agreement in marriage. Sexual union is "for" the other (rather than simply "for" a husband's pleasure). It is not to be used for power or control. How does this relate to the importance of the body in chapter 6, and to the courteous tenderness of love that respects "the other" and the other's needs in chapter 13? In that chapter love is seeking the best for "the other." There is a clear unity of concern through these chapters.

2. A Case for Getting Married? A Case for Separating? (7:8-11)

8 To those who are not married and to widows I say that it is a good thing for them if they remain unmarried, as I am. 9 But if they do not have power over their passions, let them get married; for it is better to marry than for their passions to burn. 10 To those who are married I give this charge, which is not mine but the Lord's: a wife should not separate from her husband 11 (but if a separation occurs, she is to remain unmarried or else be reconciled to her husband); and a husband is not to divorce his wife.

Paul now addresses a different set of readers and a different situation, although every situation remains relevant to the life of the church, in which each cares for the other (12:12–13:13). He now addresses **those who are not married and . . . widows**. Some suggest that **those who are not married** denotes those who are *widowed*. The Greek used here *(tois agamois)* can denote not only those who have not *yet* married, but also those who are *now* unmarried, whose spouse has died. Hence Paul probably means especially *widowers* and *widows,* but he may also be including those not yet married and those who have been divorced.

The sentence **it is a good thing for them if they remain unmarried** requires extreme care in understanding Paul's point. First, the expected age for marriage, especially among girls, was very young, often about twelve years old. Widows were often expected to remarry within a year. Paul may be urging Christian resistance to pressures from the conventions of society that were unhelpful. If so, this means "**good . . . for a time.**" Second, **good** does not suggest a negative alternative. A pastor might say, "It is good to be ordained as a Christian minister" without in any way suggesting that laypeople are second class, or that everyone should be ordained.

With respect to **as I am**, we noted that Paul may well have been a widower, although we cannot exclude his being permanently single. Even more care is needed over the words **if they do not have power over their passions** (v. 9a) and **for their passions to burn** (v. 9b). Paul does not suggest that marriage is a second-class, fallback arrangement for those who cannot otherwise control their sexual desires. He has already stated that sexual intimacy in marriage is God-given (7:2-6). He simply paints a scenario of a couple whose desire for each other is so strong that it constantly distracts them from the centrality of the gospel. *For some,* the service of the gospel is better achieved by concentrating all their energies on gospel matters without the "distraction" of duties to a married partner and a household. *For others,* the desire for each other is so strong that this causes more distraction from gospel priorities than the actual commitments of the married state.

In vv. 10-11 Paul considers the issue of possible **separation** between married Christians. He explores the different situation of "mixed" marriages in vv. 12-16. It is essential to bear in mind that divorce was frequent and very easily executed in Roman society of the day, especially when a man wanted to divorce a woman. The very utterance of the Latin expression *tuas res tibi habeto* could execute an act of divorcing a wife. Seneca grieves that in this era (contemporary with Paul) many women "reckon their years . . . by the number of their husbands. They leave home to marry; and they marry in order to divorce" (*De Beneficiis* 3.16.2).

In rabbinic Judaism, although the school of Shammai permitted divorce only in cases of unfaithfulness, "the School of Hillel say, 'He may divorce her even if she has spoiled a dish for him . . .'" (*Mishnah, Gittin* [or *Bills of Divorce*] 9:10). This rabbinic difference of view probably formed the background to the pronouncements of Jesus on divorce in Mark 10:11-12. The context of 7:10-11 may include this.

Since at least the 1930s scholars have spoken of a "feminist party in the local church" that claimed "freedom to desert or to divorce a husband." Some women sought this because of "an ultra-spiritual" outlook (Moffatt, *First Epistle,* p. 78). More recently Wire urges that Christian women prophets sought a liberated lifestyle while Paul sought to restrict their "power" by confining them to the sphere of the home (noted above, *Corinthian Women Prophets*, pp. 82-97, with Witherington's critique).

Paul probably appeals here not to his own apostolic authority but to the tradition of the words of Jesus that later found expression in Mark 10:11-12 (cf. Matt. 19:9). Some argue that here the women wanted a divorce in order to remarry (Dungan, *Sayings*, pp. 83-99). Paul appears to endorse the axiom that in principle marriage is lifelong (vv. 10-11, 39; cf. Rom. 7:1-3). But he would be aware that Deut. 24:1-4 provides for a husband to initiate divorce, provided that he certifies the freedom of the divorced wife to remarry; otherwise she would remain without protection. What remains open to debate is whether it is possible to distinguish between God's will for a lifelong commitment and the possibility of "particular circumstances" permitted by Deuteronomy 24 and by the language of Jesus about "the hardness of your heart." Do these give grounds for a parallel distinction in Paul? In my longer, detailed commentary I include two additional notes on this issue (*First Epistle*, pp. 521-25 and 540-43). Whether in the Jesus tradition "hardness of heart" may allude to what today we call "irretrievable breakdown" remains, once again, a matter of debate.

19. Suggestions for Possible Reflection on 7:8-11

1. *On more than one possible "good"*: Can more than one possible alternative for future action be *good*? Is it the case that *only* one path forward can please God, or may more than one please God? Does it matter *how* we respond to a chosen path? Are marriage, celibacy, and celibate singleness all "*good*"?

2. *On the relevance of particular circumstances*: Might such issues as undue pressure from others to marry (or not to marry) color Paul's definition of what is "good" for the person concerned? To what extent do individual gifts and circumstances determine which course of action will allow a more central place for Christian service?

3. *On pastoral guidance and a "middle" path*: Sometimes one will say, "It all depends on the situation," while others say, "It is a matter of principle." How can we observe the ideal while paying adequate attention to the real in specific situations? Does Paul's example imply that responsible pastoral judgments arise from recognizing both considerations?

4. On whether there are ever grounds for divorce: Divorce and separation fall short of God's will. But does Paul suggest that if "reconciliation" proves to be utterly impossible (v. 11), the alternative of separation might be less mutually destructive than a bitter, recriminatory relationship? (See, however, vv. 12-16; do these suggest otherwise?) Paul urges a sensitive and tender realism about the need for Christians to be delivered from situations of inner conflict, frustration, and turmoil. But how can this be found, given the human need for love, companionship, and "bodily" life? Even among Christians, Paul implies, marriage may either provide a joyful mutuality or degenerate into frustration and recrimination. He constantly keeps in view God's free gift *(charisma)* for all situations.

3. What about Those Married to Unbelievers? (7:12-16)

12 But to the rest I say (not a saying of the Lord): if any Christian brother has a wife who is an unbeliever and she consents to continue to live with him, he is not to divorce her. 13 And if any woman has a husband who is an unbeliever, and he consents to go on living with her, she is not to divorce her husband. 14 For the husband who is not a believer is made holy through his [Christian] wife, and the wife who is not a believer is made holy through her Christian husband. Otherwise, it follows, your children would not be cleansed; but now in fact they are holy. 15 If, on the other hand, the unbelieving partner takes the step of separation, let the separation take place. The Christian husband or the Christian wife does not remain in slavery in such circumstances. No, God has called you to live in peace. 16 For how far do you know, you who are the wife, whether you will bring your husband to salvation? Or how can you know — you who are the husband — whether you will save your wife?

The Christian husband who is married to an unbeliever is not to initiate separation or divorce if the wife **consents to continue to live with him**. Typically Paul makes this a mutual and reciprocal principle: if the husband **consents to go on living with her**, the wife **is not to divorce her husband** (v. 13). **The rest** (v. 12) means the remaining category of married readers, that is, those married to spouses who have not yet come to faith. The Greek word *aphiēmi* has its regular meaning of **divorce** in this context, although in previous verses the distinction between separation (Greek *chōrizō*) and divorce *(aphiēmi)* is less clear-cut.

Presumably Paul's main reasons for advising that the couple stay together are two: first, that divorce in principle falls short of God's will (see above); second, that the Christian's lifestyle, love, and witness may play a part in leading the other to faith (vv. 14, 16). All the same, Paul does not advise the use of pressure if the unbeliever insists that they have now become incompatible.

Paul's declaration that the unbelieving spouse and even the child are made **holy** through their intimate tie with the Christian (v. 14) has understandably given rise to debate. Whatever the finer points, Paul's main point is to allay any anxiety on the part of the Christian spouse that to remain with the non-Christian spouse might somehow imperil their status as Christians or their walk with God. Such anxiety is not at all unreasonable, for in 6:12-20 Paul has stated that sexual union with a prostitute can rip apart the limbs and organs of Christ with damaging effect.

In response to such a concern, Paul insists that the purity of Christians and their holy standing as set apart for God will not be compromised by remaining with the unbelieving spouse. Indeed, he asserts, the solidarity of the family works in the other direction: the consecration, lifestyle, values, and influence of the Christian spouse and parent has a wholesome and salutary effect on the unbeliever, and on the child also.

If the Christian spouse lives in faith, prayer, and a gospel lifestyle, this will permeate the home and in effect amount to a consecrating influence on spouse and child. The allusion to the child, who would more readily be influenced than the adult, provides an *a fortiori* argument: you know that Christians influence their children for good; so why doubt that you can influence your husband or wife, or that God will bless the family? If we recall that the Greek *hagios*, "holy," reflects here the Hebrew *qadōsh*, the latter denotes *holiness* often in the sense of being separate or different. One Christian in the family makes it a *different* family from wholly unbelieving families.

Paul does not license a Christian's deliberately marrying an unbeliever on this basis. He simply describes a situation where the Christian is *already* married to a partner who has not (yet) come to faith. Among the Church Fathers, Tertullian emphasizes this, citing 7:39 (*To His Wife*, 2:2). Chrysostom stresses that these verses are "to deliver the woman from fear" if she is already married to a man who does not respond to the gospel (*Homily on 1 Corinthians*, 19:4). Calvin succinctly observes: "The godliness of the one does more to 'sanctify' the marriage than the ungodliness of the other to make it unclean," though adding: "not in the *contracting* of marriage but in *maintaining* those already entered into" (*First Epistle*, p. 148).

In v. 15 Paul underlines the different point that if the unbelieving partner wants to renounce the marriage, the believer should not exert pressure to prevent this. A recalcitrant partner who is hostile to the new life of the Christian might indeed disrupt the marriage. In such a case, the dynamic described in the previous verse might be compromised, and **peace** dissipated.

Interestingly, v. 16, **how do you know . . . whether you will bring your husband to salvation? Or how can you know . . . whether you will save your wife?** has been understood in either of two opposite ways, sometimes called *optimistic* or *pessimistic*. If v. 16 belongs with v. 15, it means: "Do not try to keep your partner at any cost, for you cannot be sure that you will succeed in your Christian witness" *(pessimistic)*. If v. 16 refers back to vv. 13-14, it may mean: "Of course you sanctify the other; for you may well win them for Christ by your witness" *(optimistic)*. Commentators have been divided since the Middle Ages. Our translation excludes neither view, for Paul may well be addressing *both sides, with the encouragement "you never know . . . ," and the warning "you cannot assume. . . ."* In our view the double meaning makes perfect sense, and fits the Greek.

20. Suggestions for Possible Reflection on 7:12-16

1. *On the Christian home:* Are we encouraged to think that Christian husbands or Christian wives can have decisive influence on the home, *whatever* its nature and circumstances? Even *one* Christian spouse or parent, it seems, can maintain unilaterally an ethos that makes that home "different" or *holy*. What does this say about the distinctive ethos of a Christian home? Wherein might this distinction lie?

2. *On one-way or two-way influence:* Can the effect of the Christian partner's prayer, faith, witness, and love have more effect than the supposedly more "neutral" values of a non-Christian spouse? How might this affect the nurture and upbringing of children? (Note: the current fashion of disparaging the nuclear family as unknown in biblical times is often overstated. Even within a larger Greco-Roman "household," many, including slaves, could

maintain close relationships at the "nuclear" level with spouse and children, as many funeral inscriptions testify.)

3. *On "irretrievable breakdown"*: Does Paul's insistence that the Christian should not try to force a reluctant unbelieving partner to remain against his or her will suggest a realistic recognition that conflicting values may lead to "irretrievable breakdown"? Whether this leaves the abandoned partner free to remarry remains a matter of debate among biblical specialists and theologians and in church doctrine. (This matter is discussed further in Thiselton, *First Corinthians*, pp. 521-25 and 540-43.)

4. God's Call Is More Fundamental Than Seeking "Better" Circumstances (7:17-24)

17 At all events, let each person conduct his or her life as the Lord has apportioned it, and as God has called each. So, too, I lay down this charge in all the churches. 18 If anyone was circumcised already when he was called to faith, let him not cover over his circumcision. If anyone was uncircumcised at the time of his call, he should not be circumcised. 19 Circumcision is nothing, and uncircumcision is nothing; what matters is keeping God's commandments. 20 Each person should remain in the situation in which he or she was when God called them. 21 If, when God called you, you were a slave, do not let it worry you. Even if there is a possibility that you might come to be free, rather, start to make positive use of the present. 22 For the slave who was called in the Lord is a freedperson to the Lord; likewise the free person who was called is a slave of Christ. 23 You were purchased with a price. Do not become slaves to human persons. 24 Dear Christian brothers and sisters, let each person remain in whatever his or her situation was when they were called, with God at their side.

Paul and his readers continue their dialogue about the varied circumstances in which Christians serve Christ as Lord in "bodily," everyday experience. Some situations lie beyond the control of human agency to change; others may invite a degree of human choice and action. Paul considers marriage, celibacy, widowhood, and the single state. In addition, as in Gal. 3:28, he includes the respective situations of Jew and Gentile, slave and free person, alongside those of men and women.

On the basis of v. 20, many older commentaries see the theme in this section as "Stay as you were when you became a believer." However, the issues are more complex. The key point is not "staying as you were" but that Christians can fully serve Christ as Lord *in whatever situation they find themselves.* Nevertheless, every Christian must remain open to the question: *Does the call of God direct us to be here or elsewhere in a new situation?*

One clear point of contact emerges between the culture of Corinth and that of the modern or postmodern consumerist West. "Secular" questions about jobs, careers, and positions usually find expression *in terms of self-fulfillment, self-advantage, status, and self-promotion; more "Christian" attitudes explore vocation.* Issues of *vocation* need to be restored to Christian reflection.

Let each person conduct his or her life as the Lord has apportioned it, and as God has called each (v. 17a) strikes the keynote. These verses are not a digression. Paul regularly urges this axiom, whether on the subject of ministerial tasks (3:5) or that of duly apportioned gifts of the Spirit (12:7-11, 14-18). The Greek word translated **apportioned** *(merizō)* means *to separate into parts* and *to distribute what has been allotted.* Paul presses this principle not only on the competitive Corinthians but also **in all the churches** as a deliberate **charge** to all Christians (v. 17b). Although there is some debate about whether **called** refers to being called as *a believer* or called *to a particular job,* this does not change the weight placed on the theme of God's **apportioning** the Christian's gifts or situation for service.

In vv. 18-19 Paul addresses the situation of Christians who had been born and raised as Jews, or who had become converts to Judaism at an earlier stage. Paul insists that such people do not become "better" Christians by seeking to **cover over** [their] **circumcision** (v. 18). The Greek term is a medical one that occurs only here in the New Testament and reflects the Hebrew *moshek* to denote a surgical procedure designed to hide the evidence of circumcision as far as possible. Those Jews who wished to maintain their social and business contacts with Gentiles in such contexts as the gymnasium sometimes took this step to hide their Jewish identity (cf. 1 Maccabees 1:15; Josephus, *Antiquities* 12.5.1 and *Against Apion* 2.13.137). Circumcision could be an occasion of ridicule in some Gentile circles.

Paul is evenhanded. Neither becoming circumcised nor hiding the marks of circumcision makes any difference to being a "better" Christian: **what matters is keeping God's commandments** (v. 19). When he speaks of circumcision as **nothing** (v. 19), Paul means that it is "nothing" in this specific context of seeking to improve the circumstances surrounding Christian service. He does not devalue what was a divine ordinance for the Jewish people as such. Paul does not sit light to the Old Testament.

Significantly in view of the constant assumption in Corinth that their culture and church are somehow "special," Paul asserts what becomes a repeated theme: **I lay down this charge in all the churches** (v. 17b). Paul emphasizes "catholicity": the church is holy, apostolic, "catholic," and one. Much of its ordering is universal among all local churches. The contextual has a place, but only within the framework of certain universal characteristics of what it means to have Christian identity, and of what it means to be a Christian church.

Much debate surrounds the meaning of vv. 20-24, especially v. 21: **make use of it**. Many commentators understand Paul to be saying that if a Christian is a **slave** in a household, **each person should remain** in this situation (v. 20), and **not let it worry you** (v. 21). An equally large number of commentators apply the words **make positive use** (v. 21) to the possibility of becoming **free** (v. 21) from slavery. The truth is that the Greek grammar and syntax allow for either possibility. Whole books have been written about the meaning of the small Greek phrase at the heart of the debate.* The English versions are as divided as the commentators.† In my larger commentary I have assessed the arguments on both sides in detail, and have added an extended Note on slavery in the first century (*First Epistle*, pp. 552-65). Some literate slaves might well hold responsible positions of household management, business accounting, or other kinds of influence, and this lends plausibility to the more positive, second view.

All the same, the two views might suggest similar conclusions: freedom is not essential for acceptable Christian service. For *slavery might entail opportunities for Christian service; but so might the chance of becoming a free person. Whatever the circumstances,* slave or free the Christian

---

*Technical Note: Notably S. S. Bartchy, *Mallon Chrēsai: First-Century Slavery and the Interpretation of 1 Cor. 7:21* (Missoula: Scholars, 1973); see also more broadly Dale B. Martin, *Slavery as Salvation* (New Haven: Yale University Press, 1990), esp. pp. 63-68.

†A Note on the Translations: the AV/KJV, RSV (but not the NRSV), TEV, and NIV translate in such words as "if you can gain your freedom . . . do so" (NIV), where the REB offers a more subtle version of this. On the other hand, the NRSV and NJB translate the words in such terms as "make use of your condition as a slave" (NJB).

may equally well serve the Lord, as the one who belongs to the Lord. Our proposed translation, **Even if there is a possibility . . . start to make positive use of the present** (v. 21), brings home the fruitlessness of merely waiting for supposedly better opportunities for service rather than starting to get on with the job (Greek aorist imperative) of service to the Lord whatever the circumstances.

The closing verses of this section (vv. 22-24) recall the theology of purchase, or redemption, in 6:19-20. Paul now applies this to each of the two possible situations of slavery and freedom. Since the Christian has been **purchased with a price** (6:20; 7:23), he or she who remains a slave in socioeconomic terms has been *freed* from the powers of darkness and destruction. Yet the "purchase" of redemption also means that the Christian *belongs to* Christ as Redeemer: **You are not your own** (6:19). A freedperson belongs **to the Lord** (v. 22). In relation to 6:19-20, we noted that the redeemed Christian is not "free" in the sense of being his or her own master; but he or she is "free" in the sense that Christ has taken responsibility for them as his or her own Lord. In *this* sense the Christian is **a slave of Christ**, under Christ's care and protection (7:22).

Whatever happens in earthly, social terms, the Christian can rejoice in being **freed** from the powers of evil, but rejoice no less in *belonging to* a new Lord as Christ's **slave**. In the light of all this, the Christian should not **worry** (v. 21) about his earthly situation. *Any* situation offers opportunities to serve Christ as Lord.

21. Suggestions for Possible Reflection on 7:17-24

1. *On vocation versus self-fulfillment: a second consideration (cf. 1:1-3):* Do we consider future careers or jobs in terms of what God calls us to do for him, or in terms of what we think we shall find fulfilling and satisfying? Has Christian talk of vocation in the mid-twentieth century given place today to language about self-fulfillment? Do Christians lose something by thinking first of self-fulfillment?

2. *On making the best of things versus pining for what might have been:* How often have we been tempted to cry, "If only . . . !" especially "If only my situation was different"? Is it easy to imagine that Christians can give of their best only if circumstances suit them? Paul does not minimize the hardships that may face the Christian, but he robustly urges his readers to make the

best of each set of constraints or opportunities. How can we best redirect our energy into making the best of the situation rather than in "worrying" about whether things could be different (cf. v. 21)?

3. *On temptation to envy others:* How does this relate to being tempted to envy another Christian? Did menial slaves envy free people? Even if a person is a "slave" (v. 22), Paul insists, a Christian may rejoice because at a profound level he or she has been "purchased" by the Lord, and "belongs" to Christ (v. 23). Conversely, if one has been freed, it is foolish to indulge in self-congratulation, for the Christian is still not "autonomous," but pledged to the service of Christ as one "purchased" (6:20). This bears on the pull of envy or contentment.

4. *On yet another call to look beyond the "local":* Do we try to measure everything in terms of local situations and local stories? Paul gives a charge to "all the churches" (v. 17). Christians cannot make up local rules regardless of Scripture, tradition, and wider Christian practice.

5. To Marry — or to Remain Single, Separated, or Widowed? Four More Case Studies (7:25-40)

25 Concerning those who have not yet married, I have no charge from the Lord. But I give my opinion as someone whom the Lord's bestowal of mercy has made worthy of trust. 26 Accordingly I think that it is well on account of the impending severe pressures for a person to remain as he or she is, as a good course. 27 If you have become bound to a woman, do not seek to loose the tie; if the tie has been dissolved, stop seeking to marry. 28 But if you do get married, you have done no sin. If, too, a woman who has not yet married becomes married, she has done no sin. But such married couples will have pressures in everyday life, and I would spare you that.

29 I affirm this point, dear brothers and sisters: limits have been placed on the critical time. 30 For what remains of this time those who are married should be as if they had no married ties, those who weep as if they were not weeping, those who rejoice as if they were not rejoicing, and those who have transacted commerce as though they did not hold possessions. 31 And those who deal with the world must not be as though they were engrossed in it. For the external structures of this world are slipping away. 32 Now I want you to be free from anxieties. The unmarried man devotes his concern to the things of the Lord, how he is to please the Lord. 33 But the man who has married has anxieties about the af-

fairs of the world, how he is to please his wife. 34 And he is pulled in two directions. Both the woman who is currently free of wedlock and the woman who has never married devote their concern to the things of the Lord, in order to be holy both publicly and in the Spirit. But the woman who has become married is anxious about the affairs of the world, how she is to please her husband. 35 I am saying this entirely for your own help, not to throw a tight rein over you, but with a view to what is proper and well suited to undistracted devotion to the Lord.

36 If anyone thinks that he is not behaving in a proper way toward his betrothed, if it is a matter of undue strain and it seems the right thing, he should do what he wishes. There is no sin: let them get married. 37 Nevertheless, a person who stands firm, steadfast in his conviction and not because persons or situations are forcing him, has a full right to make his own decision, and has reached the decision by independent personal conviction to respect her virginity, he will do well. 38 So, then, he who marries his betrothed does well, and he who does not marry will do better.

39 A wife is bound in marriage for as long as her husband lives. But if her husband dies, she is free to get married to whom she wishes — only in the Lord. 40 But in my opinion she is happier if she stays as she is, and I, for one, also think that I have the Spirit of God.

Paul now addresses four further case studies (or perhaps five, if vv. 36-38 refer to another). All broadly raise the question "to marry or not to marry?" but with different variations because the situations of those in question differ. (1) Paul begins with a question from **those who are not married** (the Greek genitive is not gender-specific, *tōn parthenōn*, "virgins" in NRSV, v. 25). (2) He then addresses *married men* (**If you have become bound to a woman . . .**) who are wondering whether **to loose the tie** (v. 27). (3) Next, Paul turns to couples **seeking to marry** (vv. 28-35). Depending on how we understand v. 36, Paul addresses *either* fathers about the situation of a daughter of marriageable age, *or* couples whose desires for each other have become strongly passionate (vv. 36-38). (4) Paul lastly addresses *widows* about whether to marry again.

a. Those Who Are Not Married (7:25-26)

Paul begins by affirming Christian *freedom*. Both marriage and the single state are equally honorable. This should not be taken for granted. Some Greco-Roman philosophers perceived marriage as a "higher" duty that befitted the full responsibilities of a stable citizen of the state. On the other hand, some of a more ascetic or self-styled "spiritual" cast of mind exalted singleness or celibacy above the "distractions" of having to perform marital obligations. Part parallels with both views persist today. In view of Paul's language about **pressures** (v. 26) and distracting **anxieties** (v. 32), it is important to note that *Paul freely honors both states*, commending one over the other only on the basis of different callings and **gifts** (7:7), and sometimes on pragmatic **opinion** (v. 25) about what may be a better alternative for a specific situation or time (vv. 26, 29).

The most controversial issue of interpretation (but not the only controversial issue) in this section concerns the meaning of **on account of the impending severe pressures** (v. 26). The Greek *anankē* denotes a hardship or *necessity that pinches* or *constrains*. Today we might think most readily of **pressures**, or those forces that close in upon us, tighten their grip, and force us into unchosen paths. The adjacent term *enestōsan* has more than one meaning. It may mean *present* or **impending**. (1) Many have understood the two words together to denote an eschatological question mark that hangs over the stability or permanence of the world. (2) Some think that it refers to the time of distress that comes immediately before the last day in apocalyptic literature. (3) However, the phrase need not denote this. Bruce Winter urges that the "specific circumstances" to which Paul alludes concern the imminence of serious famine ("Secular and Christian Responses," pp. 86-106).

These two views need not be exclusive alternatives since famine may be one possible indication among others of an eschatological question mark over the permanence of the present world order. The tone of v. 31 is distinctly eschatological (**the external structures of this world are slipping away**) and, together with the coming event of the fall of Jerusalem in A.D. 70, famine, and other large-scale disasters, is seen as pointing beyond the present to realities that will confront the world in the final coming of Christ and the last judgment. Luther holds these together: we must reckon with hardship but also with the fact that "all Christians [are] . . . like guests on the earth" (Luther, *Commentary*, pp. 49 and 52).

b. Considering Ending a Committed Relationship? (7:27)

A second notorious problem concerns whether the couple to whom v. 27 refers are *married* (with REB, NRSV, NIV, NJB) or a betrothed couple who have pledged their commitment to each other (with most modern commentators). Again the Greek terms can be understood in both ways: *gynē* may mean "wife" and "woman"; *lysis* may mean divorce, separation, or revoking an agreed commitment. At all events, Paul offers a recommendation but not an absolute moral prohibition, as v. 28 underlines. He enjoins *responsible rational reflection* upon the situation and the circumstances that pertain. Unless these dictate an opposite conclusion, the commitment should be honored and maintained.

c. Again, to Marry or Not to Marry?
Freedom from Anxiety (7:28-38)

The Greek aorist tense behind v. 28 is best understood as "ingressive," that is, to be translated **But if you do get married**. The aorist in the next clause is "gnomic" or "timeless": "you do no sin" (NRSV) or **you have done no sin** (cf. REB, "you are not doing anything wrong"; NJB, "this is not a sin"). This raises a huge question, however, about v. 27: if v. 27 refers to *married couples,* v. 28 appears *to permit remarriage after divorce or separation* from the first partner; if v. 27 refers to *betrothed couples,* v. 28 permits their *fulfilling their betrothal in marriage.*

The former would appear to conflict with 7:10-11, as well as with the tradition of the sayings of Jesus formulated in due course in Mark 10:9-12 (although cf. Matt. 19:8-9). I have included two extended Notes on divorce and remarriage in my larger commentary (*First Epistle,* pp. 521-25 and 540-43). If v. 28 belongs with vv. 29-38, the whole theme appears to concern betrothed couples moving forward to marriage. But v. 28 *may* refer to remarriage after separation, provided that due consideration is given to Paul's emphasis upon "circumstances."

It is just arguable that while he endorsed the indissolubility of marriage as God's will for all (Mark 10:9-12), even Jesus allowed for the Old Testament permission for divorce and remarriage "for the hardness of your hearts" (Matt. 19:8, *sklērokardia*), that is, either unchastity (Matt. 19:9, *porneia*) or what we nowadays call "irretrievable breakdown." Paul's careful endorsement of the noun (indissolubility), qualified by possible circumstances that might offer exceptions, would cohere with this. On the other hand, these verses alone are hardly clear enough to provide an adequate basis for a decisive answer to this question. (David Instone-Brewer, *Divorce and Remarriage in the Bible* [Grand Rapids: Eerdmans, 2002], sets out the case for the possibility that both Jesus and Paul envisaged remarriage as a less-than-ideal but permitted exception.)

The seven verses that follow (vv. 29-35) focus on the single theme of the need to avoid whatever distracts the Christian from single-minded service of the Lord. This may take the form of preoccupations about **possessions**, *property, business,* and all that married responsibilities entail for maintaining the household in decent living conditions (vv. 30-31); or general anxieties about relationships, including **anxiety about . . . how to please his wife** (vv. 32-33); and anything that causes the Christian to be **pulled in two directions** (v. 34). Paul applies this mutually: **the woman who has become married is anxious about the affairs of the world, how she is to please her husband** (v. 34b).

Paul's outlook and language become all the more readily understandable when we recall how marriage was viewed in the Greco-Roman world of Paul's day. We must note four lines of approach, which all draw attention to the "distractions" involved in marriage.

First, in *Stoic and Cynic* traditions of philosophy and ethics "marriage involved a man in weighty responsibilities" (Deming, *Paul on Marriage,* p. 52). This background reminds us that societal responsibilities were regarded more seriously than our more individualistic Western value systems often imply. It is not simply a matter of one man and one woman deciding to live together. Marriage in Paul's world entailed obligations to the two families of the couple, and in particular the commitment of a father, householder, citizen, and breadwinner, with obligations in the social, political, and economic dimensions of life. The husband and wife gained in public status, but not without strings attached. Paul appears to presuppose this background as he compares the advantages and disadvantages of marriage and singleness for Christian people.

Second, some focus upon Paul's language, repeated five times, four in v. 30: **"as if they were not": married as if they had no married ties . . . weep as if they were not weeping, . . . rejoice as if they were not rejoicing, . . . transact commerce . . . as if they did not hold possessions**. On this basis it can be argued that Paul pursues a "middle way" in praising equally disengagement from "worldly" concerns to devote attention to the things of God, and no less on the other side (in the case of married Christians) fully entering into their "worldly" responsibilities. Paul acknowledges that married people *cannot* and should not escape responsibilities as financial providers, citizens, and those committed to their families (Wimbush, *Paul: The Worldly Ascetic*).

Third, a division between "private" and "public" spheres laid certain constraints upon women in the Roman world. Paul gives Christian women freedom either to gain the measure of security that marriage brings, or to abstain from marriage. Paul thus brings a new dimension of mutuality and reciprocity to the male-female relationship (Witherington, *Women in the Earliest Churches,* pp. 24-42; and *Conflict,* pp. 170-85).

Fourth, on the arguments about "eschatological imminence" we may note one further comment from Caird. He asks, "Does Paul mean that world history is about to come to an end, or simply that . . . Christians must expect to live under hard social pressure? . . . The one governing principle is: 'I want you to be free from anxiety' (7:32)" (*Language and Imagery,* pp. 270-71). Paul uses "end-of-the-world language metaphorically" to refer to what they well knew was "not the end of the world" (p. 256). He invokes an eschatological dimension, but in the sense of *relativizing* worldly things. He wants all Christians to keep their eye on the goal: single-minded service of Christ as Lord (6:20; 7:22-24, 33-35). He urges: go for what will best empower you to serve Christ without anxiety and distraction.

The tailpiece in vv. 36-38 simply spells this out. The one major problem is whether Paul continues to address the concerns of a betrothed man about his fiancée, or whether he now addresses the concerns of a father about a daughter of at least marriageable age. In either case, the practical outcome looks back to the previous verse, to **undistracted devotion to the Lord** (v. 35).

Each of these meanings is possible. This is because (1) Paul's use of the pronoun **anyone** does not specify whom Paul addresses at this point. (2) The phrase that we translate **his betrothed** *may* simply mean "unmarried woman," while **his** could denote either the "betrothed man" or her "father." (3) The Greek that we have translated **as a matter of undue strain** *(hyperakmos)* may denote either "the pull of passion beyond due limits," or "beyond the prime of life." Finally, (4) the Greek word *akmē* may denote *either* a peak of maturity (hence NIV, "if she is getting on in years"), or a peak of *emotion,* or a peak of *passion* (hence NRSV, "if his passions are strong"). In this latter case the Greek *hyperakmos* denotes an intensity of passion *beyond* which it is not easy to live. Whichever view we take (and most scholars adopt the latter with NRSV, REB, and NJB) Paul wants Christians to avoid distraction and anxiety.

A genuine concern for the welfare of the person or persons concerned decides the issue. In chapter 13 this is described as love that seeks the welfare of the other. Yet no decision must be imposed upon the one responsible for making it. Paul insists that the issue must **not** be resolved **because persons or situations are forcing him** (v. 37). This may well imply a rebuke for those Christian communities that try to impose the corporate preferences of the local church upon individuals when no moral principle or gospel principle is involved. Above all, Paul insists, Christians are not to be manipulated into needless **pressures** or into needless **anxieties** (vv. 26, 34, 37). In many situations, the decision is *not* one of right *versus* wrong, but of *good versus even better* (v. 38). In such cases even if the merely "good" is chosen, **there is no sin** (v. 36).

d. Widows: To Marry Again? (7:39-40)

Chapter 7 underlines the pastoral principle that the apostle or pastor addresses the full range of situations and persons who need support or advice. Paul does not merely address the young, or the married, or the single, but also the separated and the bereaved. In v. 39 he reaffirms the general principle of marriage as lifelong: **as long as her husband lives**, or until "death us do part" (cf. Rom. 7:1-3). Yet if her husband has died, **she is free to get married**.

The widow may marry **whom she wishes**, with the single proviso that this is **in the Lord** (v. 39). The NIV translation *he must belong to the Lord* goes further than the Greek text, but without doubt it makes explicit what Paul implies: she must marry a Christian. The only "mixed" marriages that Paul contemplates are *existing* marriages in which one partner, but not the other, comes to Christian faith. Deliberately to marry someone who did not endorse or understand a Christian's relationship with Christ would indeed be to exacerbate **being pulled in two directions** (v. 34).

At the same time Paul registers his **opinion** (as REB, NRSV), or "way of thinking" (NJB), that a widow might well be better advised **to stay as she is** (v. 40). Again, in Paul's view, both options are "good," but the latter is "better." Perhaps unexpectedly, he bases his view not on the proverbial "holiness" of Christian widows but on a prognosis that she may well be **happier** (Greek *makariōtera*) as she is.

Paul may well be strengthening the resolve of widows in the church (especially if they had status and property) not to succumb to the opposite pressures of being pressed into marrying some supposed "suitable" man, who may have been widowed and looking for a wife for his household. To see the force of this we must recall how many women in Paul's day died in childbirth and the shorter life expectancy of the first century. The **pressures** would be from fellow Christians, probably egged on by a man whose wife had died, thereby leaving a gap in his household arrangements. If you belong to the Lord and have an income and property, Paul suggests, you may be happier serving God in your own way. This would explain his linking the suggestion with an allusion to the **Holy Spirit's** guidance.

22. Suggestions for Possible Reflection on 7:25-40

1. *On trying to hold together two complementary principles:* How can we hold together the two principles that (a) we can effectively serve God *whatever* our particular circumstances in life, and that (b) we should endeavor to place ourselves in whatever situation involves least distraction from serving God with relative peace and singleness of mind? Paul is concerned that varying situations and desires should not be a source of undue *anxiety:* "I want you to be free from anxieties" (v. 32). Does this reflect the teaching of Jesus on freedom from anxious care (Matt. 6:25-34) and single-minded trust and obedience (Matt. 5:20-24; 1 Cor. 7:31-34)?

2. *On moral courage to take responsibility for decisions:* As Christians do we have the moral courage to take responsibility for our own actions (v. 37), and not to be pressured into decisions and actions that we cannot own as ours, merely in response to manipulative pressures in the church? A Christian must reach a decision "not because persons or situations are forcing him" (v. 37). Paul gives pastoral advice in ways that are neither manipulative nor heavy-handed: "I am saying this entirely for your own help, not to throw a tight rein over you" (v. 35).

3. *On overanxiety to do "the right thing" (once again):* Are we sometimes overanxious about identifying a single "right" course of action as God's will when several paths may be "good"? (See above also.) Might not the "good" remain "good," whether or not an even better might turn out to be a less distracting path? One path *might* be "happier" (v. 40); but the other need not be "sin" (v. 36).

4. On "dealing with" the world: What immediate practical considerations are invited by Paul's allusions to "impending severe pressures" (v. 25) and to "structures of the world slipping away" (v. 31)? Does this commend escape from the world? Or is it a down-to-earth reminder that to enter a situation in which we have to depend more heavily on economic, social, and political stability brings its own risks and anxieties? Paul does not advocate retreat from the world, but he does warn his readers against undue *reliance upon* the world: Christians "deal with the world," but they do not become "engrossed in it." They "belong" to the Lord (6:20; 7:22-24).

5. On the multiform obligations of the married state: Do we think of marriage as merely a relation between two individuals, or as also entailing obligations to families, to children, and to society, with financial and economic responsibilities? Might Paul imply that while marriage is good, if the Christian wishes to withdraw from these responsibilities, singleness and celibacy would be a more appropriate option? Whichever path is followed, the Christian is to follow it with "conviction" (v. 37a), "free from anxieties" (v. 32).

6. On Paul's pastoral concern: Contrary to the undeserved mythologies about him, might we conclude that Paul treats every category within the church with gentleness, sensitivity, and love? Is it only when moral or doctrinal principles come into the picture that a different, firmer side appears? For example, might the moral support for widows not to remarry (vv. 39-40) be less likely to reflect Paul's seeking to impose a view on them than to provide support and backing for those widows who feel "expected" to remarry against their personal wishes? From this chapter of case studies onward chapter 13 on love is never far from view.

B. Love for the Other or "My Rights"?
Meat Associated with Idols (8:1–11:1)

1. Does a Decision Rest Solely on "Knowledge" and "Rights"? (8:1-6)

1 Now on the subject of meat associated with offerings to pagan deities: we are fully aware that "All of us possess 'knowledge.'" This "knowledge" inflates; love, on the other hand, builds. 2 If anyone thinks that he or she has achieved [some piece of] this "knowledge," they have not yet come to know as they ought to

know. 3 But if anyone loves [God], he or she has experienced true "knowing" [or *is known by him*].*

4 To return to the topic of eating meat associated with idols, then, we share your knowledge that "An idol has no real existence," and that "There is no God but One." 5 For even if there really exist, for the sake of argument, so-called gods whether in heaven or on earth, as indeed there are many "gods" and many "lords," 6 yet for us there is one God, the Father, from whom all things take their origin, and the goal of our existence, and one Lord Jesus Christ, through whom all things come and the means of our existence.

In chapters 8–10 Paul appears to side first with one group and then with another. Chapter 8 appears to offer a "lenient" view of eating meat associated with the offerings to idols in pagan temples. Chapter 10 appears to equate it with a nearly blasphemous betrayal of the Christian pledges made at the Lord's Table. So strong is this difference that some scholars attribute chapters 8 and 10 respectively to different letters. Nevertheless, the difference in tone is readily explained by taking account of the different circumstances that Paul has in view when he writes.

The issues in chapters 8–10 are complex. Hence to see what is at issue we need to distinguish between two (or more) groups in the church in Corinth, to see what eating meat associated with false gods might mean and entail, and to consider several related themes, rather than comment verse by verse on vv. 1-6, which shed light on the whole section. We enumerate these issues and themes as follows.

a. Those Who "Possess Knowledge" (8:1) and the Insecure or "Weak" (8:10)

A significant group in the church were relatively unconcerned about the problem that Paul addresses, except insofar as the "insecure" group criticized them for their lack of sensitivity or even Christian loyalty. Their logic, it seemed, was faultless. Their Christian creed affirmed, **"There is no God but One"** (8:5), and the immediate deduction is that

---

*Technical Note on MSS Readings: The inclusion of [*God*] and [*is known by him*] in square brackets (v. 3) indicates a difference of manuscript readings. The oldest (p46) and Clement of Alexandria (late second century) omit what is in brackets, and this makes sense. Two more (Sinaiticus2 and 33) also omit *by him*. The bracketed words are included by some important but slightly later MSS (p15, A, B, and D). Experts are divided on which readings to follow, but Paul seldom speaks of love *to God*.

"An idol has no real existence" (v. 5). They applied this axiom to the question of eating meat that had originated from a pagan temple as the main supplier of the meat market. What did it matter if meat had on some earlier occasion been offered or dedicated to some pagan deity, such as Zeus or Aphrodite? These "deities" are "nothings," and a "nothing" cannot affect meat! Those who criticize this practice are "weak." They failed to work out the implications of the falsity of idols robustly and confidently.

The "weak," as the others called them, remain troubled in their hearts. The Christian should not touch anything that has had pagan, godless prayers or blessings spoken over it. The meat is defiled. Yet some of the "weak" find themselves pulled in two directions. Meat was a luxury in the world of the first century, not lightly to be refused, and some social occasions and dinner invitations provoked tantalizing moments of inner debate and self-doubt. Probably the "strong" were not only those who appealed to "knowledge," but also among the socially influential and financially better off. The "weak" were vulnerable both in terms of self-doubt and in social and economic status. In both senses they were *insecure*.

b. Meat Associated with Offerings to Pagan Deities? (8:1)

This is our translation in the larger commentary of the Greek word *eidōlothyta,* but there are other possible translations as well. The Greek does not specify whether the substance in question is **meat** or simply *food* in general. Here AV/KJV and RV are accurate in translating *"things* offered. . . ."* This provides one of many debates among biblical specialists. The components of the Greek word also suggest what is *sacrificed (-thyta,* from *thyō)* to *idols (eidōlo-),* which is the regular word for false or pagan deities in the Greek (Septuagint) version of the Old Testament. NRSV/NIV proposes "food sacrificed to idols," which is entirely defensible, while REB has "consecrated to heathen deities," and NJB "dedicated to false gods." The first readers would know precisely how to understand Paul's word. However, the more traditional translations do not allow sufficiently clearly for the variety of situations and scenarios that were involved. Hence we use the broader, vaguer phrase, **associated with offerings to pagan deities**. **Meat** reflects a judgment based on historical re-construction. "False gods" (NJB) well reflects the logic applied by "the strong."

c. The Viewpoint and Arguments of "the Strong"

The strong would have argued as follows. (1) The best-quality meat sold in the marketplace usually came through the temples as wholesale suppliers, and it would be difficult or pedantic to avoid using these sources. (2) Second, influential non-Christian friends, business contacts, and political officials (whom Christians want to win for Christ) often invite Christians to dinners or banquets in the temple precincts. It would be churlish and needlessly defensive to refuse such invitations, and would isolate believers from their Gentile friends.

Further, (3) these meals are not really "liturgical" acts of worship; the temples simply have the most suitable premises for entertaining guests even if, admittedly, the invitations often say (to cite a known example), "The Lord Serapis invites you . . ." (or another god). This is no more than a courtesy nod to the false god of that temple as supposed "president" of the meal. (4) Above all, these are *false* gods. So if these gods are "nothings," how can it "do" anything to what we eat if we eat meat in the name of a "nothing," or blessed by a "no one"? (5) Those who make such a fuss about all this are "weak" Christians. They forget that we have pledged loyalty to a creed that gives us the basis for our action: "**There is no God but One**" (8:4), so "**An idol has no real existence**" (v. 4). The "strong" have reflected on this: "**All of us possess 'knowledge'** *(gnōsis)*"; and we act on the basis of "**knowledge**" (v. 1).*

d. The Viewpoint and Arguments of "the Weak"

(1) The so-called weak do not know what to think because Christians of knowledge, influence, and education or wealth seem to know what

---

*Technical Note on "Knowledge": Knowledge involves more than rational reflection alone. In v. 3 Paul uses **knowing** not in the largely Greek context of the noun *gnōsis,* but in the largely Old Testament context of *knowing* persons. Here, as in the use of the Hebrew "know" for sexual intimacy, authentic knowing entails a dimension of loving attention, care, and focus on "the other." In philosophy, this involves changing the traditional model of knowledge as I-it "mastery of an object" in favor of a deeper, reciprocal, multidimensional, mutual self-involvement, which Martin Buber calls an I-Thou relation, and which Hans-Georg Gadamer and Paul Ricoeur call hermeneutical understanding. Self-involving knowledge also receives attention in Bernard Lonergan and Michael Polanyi. For Bernard Lonergan knowledge entails being attentive, intelligent, reasonable, and responsible (*Method in Theology;* London: D.L.T., 1972). **If anyone loves . . . he or she has experienced true knowing** (v. 3). A Christian "theory of knowledge" begins here.

they are talking about. But (2) believers have been redeemed from the power of the deities whom they used to worship. Hence to have any truck with their temples, festivals, or social gatherings in their honor seems like a return to the old life and brings deep discomfort and distress. It goes against the grain of everything that Christians have become as a new identity.

Further, (3) when believers pledge themselves to Christ as *sole* Lord at the Lord's Table, it seems as if some fellow churchpeople come straight to the Lord's Table from "offering sacrifices to demons" (10:20). How can other Christians share with them in the Lord's Supper? On top of this, might half of their motives reflect a desire to retain former business contacts? (4) Many have become Christians at great personal cost; are often ridiculed; and former friends turn against them as narrow-minded. Is this all worthwhile if some can carry on just as before? Some are ready to give up; many remain confused about what it means to be a Christian. How is our church any more a "holy" people?

e. Paul's Pastoral Strategy in This Section

(1) Paul assures "the strong" that he is **fully aware** (v. 1) that they base their argument on their possession of "**knowledge**" (v. 1). He does not dispute this. But he reminds them at once that mere knowledge alone can make people overconfident and seem to offer an illusory self-affirmation: **"knowledge" inflates; love, on the other hand, builds** (v. 1). Paul distinguishes between *knowing* (using the *verb*) as a process that is continuous and ever learning, and **knowledge** (the noun *gnōsis*) as denoting a *static, completed* state. The latter (but not the former) leads to a cast of mind that regards everything as *"buttoned up," mastered,* and fully *processed* (v. 1a). Step 1 of his pastoral strategy is a critique of the *adequacy* of knowledge-as-mastery, as if anyone could know *everything* that needs to be known. **If anyone thinks that he or she has achieved this "knowledge," they have not yet come to know as they ought to know** (v. 2). The humble processes of **coming to know** and of **knowing** as part of a journey are commended rather than criticized.

(2) The second step of Paul's pastoral strategy is to commend love for the other person as that which **builds** (v. 1b). **Building**, as Margaret Mitchell *(Paul and the Rhetoric)* insists, constitutes a major theme of this epistle. **Knowledge** "puffs up" or **inflates**, like pumping mere air into

bellows or, in modern times, a balloon. The Greek word for **inflates** occurs six times (4:6, 18, 19; 5:2; 8:1; 13:4). Paul Gardner rightly suggests that while **love** reaches its climax in chapter 13, *inflation* is not unrelated to certain claims for certain kinds of "gifts" of the Spirit in chapters 12 and 14 (*The Gifts of God*, pp. 23-27). **To inflate** suggests the illusory self-importance of the frog in Aesop's *Fables*.

(3) Third, Paul introduces a series of qualifications into what "the strong" had thought was a simple, conclusive argument. One such qualification is that "it is not everyone who possesses this 'knowledge'" (v. 7). Paul *reasons* with his readers with both realism and diplomacy: not everyone, he advises the strong, has your perceptions and advantages. They remain in the grip of habitual ways of thought that die hard: they are subject to "force of habit" (v. 7). The "weak" never did share the sense of "being at home" in the banquet held by the influential. Paul makes a sensitive pastoral distinction between the *ontological nonexistence* of the false gods and the *existential reality* of their influence on the sensitivities of the vulnerable.

(4) Finally, Paul exposes *the damage* that the cocksure approach of "the strong" can do. They can "cause my brother's or sister's downfall" (v. 13). Paul will expound this statement further in chapter 10. We need only note at this point that in chapter 10 Paul also accepts the right of "the strong" to eat meat that may have come from the temple, provided that the situation excludes the possibility of "the weak" being involved in what would cause them damage (10:23-32).

f. The Creedal Formulation (8:6; cf. 8:5)

In v. 6 the *Christian* creed goes further. As Paul and other New Testament writers declare elsewhere, God, **the Father**, is *"originating"* Creator, **from whom** [Greek *ex hou*] **all things take their origin**, and also **the goal** (Greek *eis auton*, "to him") of everything (Greek *panta*). The **one Lord Jesus Christ** is *"mediate"* Creator, **through whom** [Greek *di' hou*] **all things come**, and **the means** [Greek *dia*] **of our existence**. Paul will repeat these same three perceptions in Rom. 11:36, "from him, through him, and to him are all things"; while the Gospel of John and the Epistle to the Hebrews also use "through" (Greek *dia*) of Christ's role in creation (John 1:3; Heb. 1:2). All of these implicitly suggest Christ's role as mediating agent. The literature on this is too vast to cite.

The first part of v. 5 introduces a hypothesis: **even if there really exist, for the sake of the argument, so-called gods....** It is likely that Paul is beginning to introduce a distinction between an "ontological"-level existence (whether they really do exist in every sense) and an "existential" or more subjective, psychological sense (whether they exist in the consciousness of their former worshipers). Clearly a residual or misplaced sense of guilt or anxiety "exists" as a crippling and debilitating force, even if the existence of pagan deities *as deities* or *as "realities"* is illusory.

23. SUGGESTIONS FOR POSSIBLE REFLECTION ON 8:1-6

1. *On the problem that "being right" may not be the only criterion for right action:* Why is "being right" not always the be-all of everything? Paul does not deny that the logic of "the strong" is faultless as far as it goes, but is this enough? Would it go too far to suggest that without a caring, loving concern for others who may see things differently, "being right" can bring confusion, minister to moralism and judgmentalism, and even perhaps destroy fellow believers? (This is explicated further in vv. 12-13.)

2. *On the false security sometimes conveyed by "knowledge":* When might "knowledge" merely inflate the self? How does this relate to thinking of "knowing" as a state of "mastering" all the data set before us? For Paul, the only authentic knowledge is *coming to know* and *continuing to learn:* "If anyone thinks that he or she has achieved this 'knowledge,' they have not come to know as they ought to know" (v. 2).

3. *On the importance of how some people perceive things, and the effects of habits of perceptions:* How can forces that have no basis in reality exercise power over people as "real" forces? Is part of "coming to know" not only coming to perceive illusions in ourselves but also acquiring sensitivity about the power of such forces over others? *Habits of mind* may place us under a bondage from which we need liberation. In the end, however, no pseudo-power need be an object of fear or anxiety, for the Lordship of Christ and the sovereignty of God the Father are cosmic and universal. *One God* alone "exists" as the only sovereign and the focus of grace, worship, trust, and obedience.

4. *On perceiving the same things in different ways, or on seeing them as parts of "different stories":* The case of "meat associated with offerings to pagan deities"

shows how readily fellow Christians perceive the same phenomenon in utterly different ways. Should this surprise us? Is it good or bad that each believes that some justification exists for the view held? Are there parallels to such different perceptions of the same situations or phenomena in the church today?

5. *On pastoral reconciliation:* How does Paul achieve pastoral reconciliation? Can this entail anything less than sensitive mediation and patient, explanatory clarification and argument? How can we prevent fellow Christians from "talking past" one another? If *love* for the other becomes the key to so much, how may we insure that particular regard is given to the most vulnerable and most readily damaged? (This section looks ahead to 12:12-26 as well as to chapter 13.)

2. Problems That Face the "Insecure" or "Weak" (8:7-13)

7 But it is not everyone who possesses this "knowledge." Some are still gripped by the idol through force of habit even now, and they eat meat as an actual idol sacrifice. Hence their self-awareness, being insecure, is tainted. 8 "Food will not bring us to God's judgment": neither if we abstain from food do we lose any advantage, nor if we eat do we gain any advantage. 9 Only see that this "right to choose" of yours does not become a cause of stumbling to the less secure.

10 Suppose someone sees you seated at table in the actual place of an idol, you who "possess knowledge": will the insecure person's self-awareness not be "built" into eating meat sacrificed to the actual idol? 11 Then, to be sure, the insecure person finds destruction by being drawn into your "knowledge" — the brother or sister for whom Christ died. 12 But in such a way as this, in sinning against your brothers and sisters by inflicting damaging blows on their self-awareness while it is still insecure, you are sinning against Christ. 13 Therefore, if food so affronts my brother or sister as to trip them up, I will certainly never in any event eat meat in any form lest I cause my brother's or sister's downfall.

The opening verse (v. 7) stands in contradiction to the claims of "the strong" voiced in the opening verse of the previous section (v. 1). Paul *rejects* the catchphrase of the strong, "All of us possess 'knowledge'" (v. 1): **But it is not everyone who possesses this "knowledge"** (v. 7). Yet did not Paul appear to endorse the claim up to a point, qualifying it rather than rejecting it in vv. 1-6? The issue turns on the use of "all" or

everyone. The "strong" use the word "all" to mean: "all in my local, like-minded circle."

Paul diagnoses a first source of difficulty for those who are vulnerable, "weak," or **insecure** (v. 7; Greek *asthenēs,* as also in vv. 10-11). They are **still gripped by the idol through force of habit even now** (v. 7). (The Greek manuscript evidence for **force of habit** or *habituation* is very strong, even if some later MSS have a different reading.) This replicated experience is so powerful that if they participate alongside the strong in "eating meat associated with offerings to pagan deities," they experience such an act as **eating meat as an** *actual idol sacrifice*. Clearly this comes under the heading of betraying and denying their very identity as Christians, for they have turned their back on such former cultic practices. It is unthinkable, Paul insists, to place them in such a contradictory position.

The effect of this generates a further problem. **Their self-awareness, being insecure, is tainted** (v. 7b). There is no difficulty about the meaning of the word translated **tainted**. The word (Greek *molynō*) denotes "to stain, to defile, to render unclean, to pollute." Paul Ricoeur expounds the power of such symbolic dimensions in *The Symbolism of Evil*. On the other hand, the translation of the word that we have rendered **self-awareness** (Greek *syneidēsis*) is contested and has generated an extensive literature. Does it mean **self-awareness** (or *consciousness*), or *conscience?* NRSV translates the phrase "and their conscience, being weak, is defiled," while NIV likewise uses "conscience" and "defiled" (cf. Thiselton, *First Epistle,* pp. 640-46).

The word usually means *conscience* in classical and in Hellenistic Greek. Like the Latin *con-scientia,* the Greek denotes "knowing" *(-eidēsis)* "with" or "alongside" *(syn-)*. Yet even in Latin *conscientia* means either "consciousness or joint witness," or "conscience." In both languages a *knowing with* denotes the activity of a part of the mind that is *self-aware* or *self-conscious,* that is, able to observe the mind's responses and activities. It is specifically in *Stoic* philosophy that the word takes on a regular and explicit *moral* meaning as a kind of internal *judge* of good and evil. In the Stoic traditions *conscience* becomes, in effect, the voice of God expressed internally. But it is doubtful whether Paul viewed "conscience" in this way. Certainly conscience usually reacts to evil actions with remorse, or discomfort, or pain. But Paul does not regard it as an infallible guide.

In biblical scholarship the view that Paul holds a "Stoic" under-standing of conscience was widely assumed during the late-nineteenth century to the mid-twentieth. In 1955 C. A. Pierce argued that Paul saw conscience rather differently. "Conscience" inflicted pain when an action *had* occurred (in the past) that was believed to be wrong. He rightly argued that Paul did not view conscience as an infallible guide to *future* conduct (*Conscience*, pp. 13-20 and 111-30). It is not for Paul the "divine voice." In 1 Cor. 8:1-13 Paul does not want *the weak* to be exposed to its *pain*. In 1978 Horsley ("Consciousness") proposed the translation **self-awareness**, and subsequent studies take full account of this (e.g., Eckstein, *Syneidēsis;* Willis, *Idol-Meat;* and Gardner, *Gifts*).

What difference does this newer translation make? First, it disso-ciates Paul's language from widespread assumptions about the role of conscience that owe more to Stoic thought than to the New Testament. The Old Testament has no word for conscience, but the nearest is the broader word "heart" (Hebrew *lēbh*). This denotes the *inner depths* of one's being, or the human self in its capacities for emotional intensity, reflection, or self-deception. Eckstein sees this as the key background to the use of the word translated *conscience* or **self-awareness** (*Syn-eidēsis*, pp. 35-135).

Second, this approach exactly fits the contrast between *strong* and **weak** in this context. The strong have a robust **self-awareness**: their self-perception and perception of themselves as Christians is strength-ened by their "**knowledge**" about the nonexistence of **the idol** (vv. 7 and 10). But the weak have an **insecure self-awareness** (v. 7b). Gardner paraphrases this as "a lack of knowledge of oneself in relation to oth-ers.... [This] would provide ample motivation to do something known to be wrong" (*Gifts*, p. 45).

Such yielding to the pressure imposed by the practices of the "knowledgeable" group, however, **taints** their confused sense of Chris-tian identity (v. 7b), **and then, to be sure, the insecure person finds destruction by being drawn into your "knowledge"** (v. 11). This is not primarily a *moral* lapse of sinning against *conscience;* it is a *Christian* or *theological* lapse of doing what seems to compromise one's Christian identity, causing *confusion about one's awareness of oneself as a committed Christian*. The divided heart is drawn on to act in ways that **inflict dam-aging blows on their self-awareness while it is still insecure**. By in-sisting on these destructive and damaging practices the "strong" **dam-**

age (v. 12) **the brother or sister for whom Christ died** (v. 11), thereby **sinning against Christ** (v. 12b).

The quotation in v. 8, "**Food will not bring us to God's judgment,**" probably reflects a counterreply on behalf of the strong that Paul has heard, or about which he has been informed, or perhaps that he anticipates. Food is value neutral, they say, so what we eat is of no spiritual or moral significance.

It is more difficult to decide whether the quotation continues to the end of v. 8: **Neither if we abstain from food do we lose any advantage, nor if we eat do we gain any advantage.** If it continues the quotation of the strong, it may well mean, in effect, "Food is neither here nor there," with the implication "don't make a fuss about it." But it may well represent Paul's response to the slogan of v. 8a. If so, Paul uses the deliberative rhetoric of "advantage," namely, that if they abstain they will not be the losers, while if they eat the "advantage" is more illusory than they think. Both possibilities make sense.

The logic of vv. 9-11 is crystal clear and straightforward by comparison. The strong promote this "**right to choose**" (v. 9a). The Greek has simply **this right of yours.** We explicate **right** as relating to *choice* because **right** *(exousia)* has already gained a currency of this kind in 6:12; will reappear in 9:4, 5, 6, 12, 18; and will feature especially in 10:23. AV/KJV, NRSV, and REB translate the word as "liberty," and NIV/NJB as "freedom." But this erodes away Paul's deliberate questioning of **rights** here, which the other translations recognize in 9:4-18. Chapter 9 precisely concerns **the right to choose**, and Paul's voluntary renunciation of such a **right** for the sake of the gospel.

In sum, "the strong" adopt an aggressive attitude about their **rights** without regard to whether it constitutes **a cause of stumbling** to the vulnerable, anxious, or **less secure** (v. 9b). Paul now illustrates the principle with a concrete example: **Suppose someone sees you . . . in the actual place of an idol, you who "possess knowledge,"** . . . what will result? (v. 10). The net effect is that **the insecure finds destruction** (v. 11).

How and why does this come about? Paul uses an ironic wordplay that centers on *building up* (Greek *oikodomeō*, v. 10). Repeatedly Paul explains that "love builds" (8:1), and that "building up" is the goal of the church and its ministry. In 8:1 Paul has placed "knowledge" in contrast to love as potential "building" modes, and rejected "knowledge" as an illusory substitute that merely pumps air into a structure to inflate its size. The "strong" appeal constantly to *knowledge,* and Paul alludes to it again and again in these verses as a key catchword (vv. 1, 2, 7, 10, and 11). No doubt, then, the influential, confident group urged the others that this knowledge would *build them up* into maturity.

Many of the less secure are drawn into this seduction, leading Paul to exclaim with due irony, **will the insecure person's self-awareness not be "built" into eating meat sacrificed to the actual idol?** (v. 10b). Here is a fine kind of "building," if they end up convinced that they have slipped back into **offering sacrifices** to pagan deities; that they have compromised their Christian identity and have betrayed their Lord!

All this self-contradiction and needless confusion constitutes **the damaging** blows that strike them (Greek *typtō,* "to hit," usually "to hit hard enough to leave a mark"). The high point of Paul's argument is that this is tantamount to attacking **Christ.** Paul never forgot that when he persecuted Christians in his former life as a pharisaic zealot, Christ declared, "Why are you persecuting *me* . . . ? I am Jesus whom you are persecuting . . ." (Acts 26:14-15; also 9:4-5; 22:7-8).

This is no isolated statement. In 1 Cor. 3:15-17 Christians are shrines of God's Spirit; in 12:12-30 they are the limbs and organs of Christ's own body. Christ identifies himself with the "weak" or **insecure** on the basis of Christ's concern for the weak or "little ones" in Matthew's Gospel: "If any of you put a stumbling block [Greek *skandalizō*] before one of these little ones who believe in me, it were better for you if a millstone were fastened around your neck and you were drowned in the depths of the sea" (18:6). "Take care that you do not despise one of these little ones" (18:10).

Paul uses the same Greek word as that of Matthew 18 in his final sentence: **If food so affronts [*skandalizō*] my brother or sister as to trip them up, I will certainly never in any event eat meat in any form lest I cause my brother's or sister's downfall** (v. 13). Paul uses the most emphatic Greek idiom at his disposal: double negative *ou mē* (like "not! — no way!") and *eis ton aiōna* (negation of "forever," i.e., "never, never"; or qualitatively, *not* **in any event**; "no way!"). Such selfish disregard for the effects of one's actions upon a fellow Christian is *unthinkable.*

24. SUGGESTIONS FOR POSSIBLE REFLECTION ON 8:7-13

1. *On attitudes toward fellow Christians and the possible seduction of a "local" postmodernity today:* Do "influential" or "confident" people in the church tend to discount other "weaker" or less prominent fellow Christians? Does the very catchphrase *"all of us* possess 'knowledge'"* (v. 1), used when Paul contradicts it ("it is *not* everyone who possesses this 'knowledge'"), betray their estimate of who "counts" as *"all of us"*? Does a self-selected group impose *their* values onto other Christians by viewing itself as *"all of us"* or *everyone?* How much does this damage our twenty-first-century church? Is it also a by-product of a "local relativism" that reflects radical postmodern thought? Does the critique of the cross (1:18-25) make us more aware of the "catholicity" of the church, in which all groups, all temperaments, rich and poor, black and white, find a place of respect and welcome?

2. *On what counts as "worldly" in the light of earlier habits of mind or action:* How much do earlier habits of mind or action condition us to think and to act in certain ways now? Rather than dismiss habituated attitudes, Paul takes them into account. How readily do earlier, preconversion attitudes toward what in retrospect seems to smack of "the world" make their impact on different Christians in different ways? Do some Christians overreact against such earlier activities, while others too easily accommodate them and assimilate them as "Christian"? Being reinvolved in them may have different effects on different Christians.

3. *On conscience, knowledge, and love:* Paul does *not* say that "conscience" is an infallible guide to appropriate future conduct. But what does he put in its place? If whatever leads to actual damage among more vulnerable Christians is unthinkable, does love for the other person or persons always take precedence over "knowledge"?

4. *On attitudes toward knowledge:* Knowledge is a steady process. Should we think positively or negatively about "knowledge," and do we distinguish between knowledge and *wisdom?* (Cf. 1 Cor. 2:6-16.) To acquire knowledge entails a long process of listening. If we think we have "got it," might we need to think again? (Some "have not yet come to know as they ought to know," v. 2.)

5. *On the right to choose:* Is to regard "the 'right to choose'" (v. 9) as absolute a Christian view? Does respectful love for the other take priority over

"rights" and "freedom" as well as "knowledge"? Paul drives home the warning that any self-interest that results in damaging vulnerable fellow Christians is "sin against Christ" (v. 12). How does this relate to the warning of Jesus not to *despise* "the little ones" or the vulnerable (Matt. 18:10)? Does this further resonate with Paul's redefinition of what it is to be "spiritual" (2:16; 3:1-4)? To be "spiritual" is to have "the mind of Christ" (2:16); to be "unspiritual" is to be "centered on yourselves" (3:3).

6. *On habits of life and growth in holiness:* Although in the example of these verses the impact of habit tends to be negative and unhelpful, can we draw a positive inference about good habits? To what extent does growth in holiness concern the nurture and formation of *habituated* attitudes and action? For parents, godparents, pastors or ministers, and teachers of children, is the goal of Christian nurture *neither* merely "knowledge" *nor* simply "right acts," but the *spiritual formation of* processes of *habituated* prayer, study of Scripture, right decisions, and attitudes of love? Are these what produce habits of respect, care, courtesy, and kindness? Good habits nurture stability of Christian character, no less than bad habits generate problems.

3. Paul's Personal Example of Foregoing a "Right" (9:1-18)

1 Am I not "free"? Am I not an apostle? Have I not seen Jesus our Lord? Is it not you who are my work in the Lord? 2 If to others I am no apostle, at any rate I am to you. For you yourselves constitute my certificate of apostleship in the Lord.

3 This is my statement of defense to those who investigate me. 4 Surely it cannot be that we have no "right" to eat or to drink? 5 Can it be that we have no "right" to take about with us a Christian who is our wife, as the rest of the apostles also have, as well as the brothers of the Lord and Peter? 6 Or do Barnabas and I alone have no right to stop working for our living? 7 Who has ever been known to serve in the army bringing all his own provisions? Who plants a vineyard and eats none of its fruit? Or who tends a flock without using the product of its milk?

8 You cannot think, can you, that I am urging this on the level of purely human example! Or does not the law also say this? 9 For in the law of Moses it is written, "You shall not muzzle an ox while it is treading out the grain." Is it perhaps about oxen that God is concerned? Or is he not certainly speaking in our interest? 10 It was indeed on our account that it was written: "It should be in

hope that the one who plows does the plowing; and in hope of a share of the crop that the thresher does the threshing." 11 If we ourselves have sown the things of the Spirit for you, is it a big issue if we reap material benefits from you? 12a If other people share what you grant them as a right, do not we deserve our due all the more?

12b By contrast we did not make use of this right, but put up with everything, in order not to make any cut across a path for the gospel of Christ. 13 Do you not know that those who are employed in sacred duties gain their subsistence from the temple offerings, and those who officiate at the altar have a share of what is sacrificed on the altar? 14 In the same way the Lord commanded that those who proclaim the gospel should derive their living from the gospel.

15 For my part, I have never availed myself of any of these rights. Nor am I writing all this in order that they may be thus applied in my case. I would rather die than — Well, no one shall invalidate my ground for glorying! 16 For simply to proclaim the gospel does not constitute my ground for boasting. For compulsion presses upon me; it is agony for me if I do not proclaim the gospel. 17 If I do this entirely by personal choice, I am in the realm of reward. But if it does not arise from my own initiative, I accept it as one entrusted with a task. 18 What counts, then as my "reward"? — That when I proclaim the gospel I make the good news free of charge, with a view to gratuitously foregoing my right in the gospel.

It is astonishing that many regard chapter 9 as a "digression" on the subject of apostleship, or even as a separate writing on a different subject. It is in fact an integral part of the argument from 8:1 through to 11:1, as our heading for this section indicates. Paul has appealed to "the strong" to give up something to which they are arguably entitled in theory or in the abstract, but which practical circumstances clearly throw into question. He now explains that a parallel issue has faced him in the shape of a "right" to financial support for his ministry, where practical circumstances force him to decline.

Paul's so-called *apostolic defense* (mainly vv. 1-6) serves not to defend his apostleship as such (although this is true in an incidental sense), but more fundamentally to establish the point that he has as much "right" to apostolic financial support and maintenance as any other apostle. Only when it is fully agreed that he possesses this right can he then point out that *he voluntarily chooses to forego that to which he is otherwise entitled.* As he exclaims with some irony in vv. 4-6, **Surely it**

cannot be that we have no "right" to eat or to drink . . . as the rest of the apostles also have? Or do Barnabas and I alone have no right to stop working for our living? He clinches the argument by a series of parallels or analogies. Does someone who **serves in the army** have to provide **all his own provisions** (v. 7)? Paul sets out his argument in the following stages.

a. Paul Fulfills the Qualifications for Apostleship (9:1-3)

Four rhetorical questions in v. 1, beginning **Am I not "free"? Am I not an apostle? Have I not seen Jesus our Lord?** indicate Paul's strength of feeling here. But is this indignant reaction primarily, as many claim, about those who cast doubt on his apostleship? Or is it a continuation of his indignation against those who "sin against Christ" (in 8:12), and cause a "brother's or sister's downfall" (8:13) by claiming to act on the basis of "rights," "freedom," and "knowledge" (8:1, 2, 4, 7, 9, 10, 11)? Paul is about to apply the same set of issues to himself. He establishes these rights, only to renounce them. It is as if he parodies the impatient, self-confident self-affirmation of the strong in a string of questions of the kind that they no doubt fired at *"the weak"* or "insecure."

This is confirmed by an important shift of emphasis in recent research on the meaning of **apostle** (v. 1). As we briefly observed on 1:1, the older, more traditional view was that the term functioned in this epistle to appeal to *authority*. While this aspect is not lacking, it is not quite the main point of emphasis. (There is an extended Note on this in my larger commentary, *First Epistle*, pp. 663-75; cf. also 64-68.) Chrysostom among others rejected the notion of self-presentation here. The term underlines that "Here, of him that calls is everything; of his that is called, nothing" (*Homilies*, 1:1 and 2:3).

The essence of apostleship is *witness to* the raised Christ (**Have I not seen Jesus our Lord?** v. 1) and to the gospel. *Apostleship thus points away from the self to Christ.* Crafton rightly states that it places the emphasis *upon agency, not upon agent.* He writes, "Divine presence is perceived not *in* but *through* agency. . . . Apostles are windows on God's design. . . . An agent is intentionally visible; an agency is inherently transparent" (*Agency*, pp. 62-63).

Because this witness or agency is above all focused upon Christ, it is also a cruciform agency; it points to Christ's self-emptying and death, and does so not only in word but also in deed and in life. Hence "the signs of the apostle," as Barrett points out, entail visibly sharing in the suffering and death of Christ, not in exhibiting miracles (*Signs,* pp. 11-84). Paul made this clear in 4:7-13.

Two specific explanations follow. First, as Paul also implies in 12:28, there is something "foundational" about the witness of apostles. Hence one qualification is to be among the witnesses of the resurrection or of the raised Christ during the forty days. **Have I not seen Jesus our Lord?** (v. 1) addresses this point, together with 15:3-9. Second, apostleship has effective or operative currency in its outcome: **You yourselves constitute my certificate of apostleship in the Lord** (v. 2). **Certificate** here denotes *an attestation of genuineness* or *a confirmation* of what has been claimed.

This is my statement of defense (v. 3) may either point back to vv. 1-2, or point forward to what follows. Paul's defense of the weak and his renunciation of "rights" give substance to his claim to embody the Christ-like, cruciform character of apostolic witness to Christ in word and deed. **Am I not "free"?** confirms that Paul's renunciation of "rights" is voluntary.

b. Arguments and Examples That Confirm These Rights
(9:4-12a)

Paul does not want "the strong" to be able to argue that Paul's case is less convincing than they claim about their "**rights**" on the basis of *"knowledge"* and *freedom.* So he fills every possible gap in his argument.

(1) First, are he **and Barnabas** (v. 6) in any different a situation from that of such unimpeachably accepted apostles as **Peter** (v. 5)? The introductory syntax in v. 4 is an emphatic negative rhetorical question: **Surely it cannot be** [the case] **that we have no "right" to eat or to drink** [can it]? (Greek *mē ouk,* double negative, repeated in v. 5). It appears that the churches fully expected to support apostles and their wives as married couples, presumably traveling together in most cases. There is little to support the view that the Greek means "female assistant."

This is the only reference in the New Testament to the rights of **the brothers of the Lord** to receive financial support (v. 5). The Gospels allude to **the brothers** of Jesus as James, Joses (Joseph), Judas, and Simon (Mark 6:3; parallel, Matt. 13:56; cf. also Mark 3:32). Paul refers to James as the Lord's **brother** in Gal. 1:19. Speculative legends about them abound in the second century, but these cannot be substantiated. Paul brackets **Barnabas** with himself here (v. 6; cf. Acts 4:36-37; 11:22-26; 13 and 14) because they choose to pay their own way in spite of their apostolic status.

(2) The second stage of the argument is to cite analogies from everyday life in which people expect financial support to go with their work (v. 7). No soldier in the Roman legions or in the auxiliary troops would be expected to provide food, lodging, or equipment for his work (v. 7a). The Greek word *opsōnia* includes *rations* and *expenses,* so **provisions** offers a useful inclusive translation. Similarly, one who **plants a vineyard** expects to benefit from its **fruit**, just as one who **tends a flock** expects to benefit from its **produce**, including cheese.

(3) The third step is to look to Scripture to provide endorsement of the general principle. This is more than a matter of **purely human example** or social convention (v. 8). If someone produces something, it is humane to allow them a share of the product. So universal is this axiom that it applies even to animals: "**You shall not muzzle an ox while it is treading out the grain**" (v. 9, citing Deut. 25:4).

We need not make heavy weather of Paul's comment, **Is it perhaps about oxen that God is concerned?** (v. 9b). Contrary to popular misunderstanding, Paul seldom grabs isolated "proof-texts" out of the air, but knows full well as a trained student of Scripture the context that surrounds his citations. In the context surrounding Deut. 25:4, the laws in the main "all serve to promote dignity and justice for human beings" (Hays, *First Corinthians,* p. 151). Since it is in Christ that humankind finds what it is to be "human" as God purposed humanity to be, these ideals for humanity relate to God's **speaking in our interest** (Greek *di' hēmas,* v. 9b) or **on our account** (v. 10) in this Deuteronomy passage.

This is not an example of "allegorical interpretation." Paul conceives of Old Testament revelation as a *historical* unfolding of God's will for his people. This has immediate application to Israel, but ultimately it also applies to the "true" Israel of the people of God in Christ (who include many Jews who have come to Christian faith). Paul now explains this expression of God's will for his people's well-being. Work conditions are not to crush the human spirit, but to lift and to encourage it with thoughts of the benefits of the goal of labor. Hence **plowing** should take place **in hope** (v. 10).

(4) The arguments of vv. 4-10 have prepared the way for the con-

clusion of the main argument: **If we ourselves have sown the things of the Spirit for you, is it a big issue if we reap material benefits from you?** (v. 11). The use of the metaphor of **sowing** and **reaping** picks up the examples and analogies of the earlier verses. The argument is so cogent that it almost takes on the status of deductive logic. This is no doubt to persuade "the strong" that it affords a very close parallel with their claims to "achieved" *knowledge* on the basis of the non-existence of idols. The final step is to draw the inference that this is tantamount to establishing **a right** (v. 12a). Others claim this financial **provision** as a **right**; so why should Paul not also claim it as **our due**, or even **more** (v. 12)?

All of this cogent, rigorous, logical argument is to establish **a right** on the basis of *freedom* and of *"knowledge,"* which Paul chooses *voluntarily to forego!* The turn in the argument in the next part of the verse is crucial.

c. Paul Chooses Voluntarily Not to Make Use of This Right (9:12b-18)

Paul immediately declares his renunciation of these rights: **we did not make use of this right** (v. 12b): **I have never availed myself of any of these rights** (v. 15).

It is important to note that in the culture of Paul's day to reject a gift or to turn one's back on a right was often construed as a serious *affront*. On reflection, this point does not feature adequately in my larger commentary. *It requires something of overriding importance to justify such a decision.* Paul provides this overriding reason: to do otherwise would make a **cut across a path** that would block the progress of **the gospel of Christ** (v. 12b). This is precisely the reason or motivation that he has held before the strong in 8:7-13 for them to take to heart. They are to avoid *tripping up* Christians, and bringing about their *downfall* (8:13). In both cases (Paul's and theirs), influential people would be upset at any refusal to take up a **right**; but in both cases Paul insists that it is a matter of **putting up with everything** (v. 12b). At all costs, the level pathway for the word of God (Isa. 40:3-4) cannot be disrupted to divert the good news of **the gospel of Christ**.

For a moment Paul returns to reemphasizing the legitimacy of the right to financial maintenance. Perhaps he is concerned lest his words about renunciation and forbearance should be taken as an implied criticism of the other apostles. In v. 13 he explicitly cites the *labor* or *toil* of **those who are employed in sacred duties**. Like the plowman and the plodding oxen, priestly duties entail real "work," and hence they are entitled to sustenance from the materials in which they deal. In v. 14 Paul turns to the case of Christian ministers as **those who proclaim the gospel**. He quotes a saying of Jesus that circulated orally among the churches and found its way into the written text of Matt. 10:10 as what **the Lord commanded** (v. 14). The context in the Gospels is that the Twelve in Matthew (or the Seventy in Luke) take neither money nor provisions with them because they may expect support from those to whom they minister. Jesus explains: "For the laborer deserves his pay" (Matt. 10:10; cf. Luke 9:58; 10:3-9).

In vv. 15-18 Paul becomes increasingly passionate about his decision not to accept the "right" of financial maintenance. The earliest and most reliable Greek manuscripts reproduce Paul's passionate breaking off of a construction and recommencing his words differently. In grammar and syntax this is known as *aposiopesis:* **I would rather die than — Well, no one shall invalidate my ground for glorying!** (v. 15). We may imagine Paul dictating the letter, reaching a peak of white-hot fervor with **I would rather die than —** , and realizing midflow that he must keep to the subject. Most English versions smooth the syntax away into something blander and less passionate.

Behind these verses stand two distinct issues. First, Paul is aware that if he accepts financial provision from Christians in Corinth, this will come mainly, if not entirely, from the wealthier members of the church, who constitute, or are linked with, "the strong." They will become, in effect, his *patrons,* and he, their *client.* In the Greco-Roman culture of the day, "favors" are regarded as implying some *reciprocal* obligation. Hence, if Paul accepts their financial provision, they will expect "favored terms" from Paul in their claims about their position in the church, their relation with the weak, and their role in the "ordering" of the church, perhaps in terms of a hierarchy of status within the church. Such hostages to pastoral pressures would be unthinkable. Paul insists on being evenhanded or, when necessary, on giving particular attention and respect to the most vulnerable and fragile (cf. 12:22-24).

Second, Paul has his own special reason for wanting to pay his way. Overwhelmed by the generosity of God's grace personally to him for his salvation and apostolic call (15:8-10), he longs to give to God some *voluntary* thank offering. But this cannot be his apostolic labor. For, in Paul's personal perspective, this has been pressed upon him *as a commission and obligation*. God in Christ set Paul apart or "marked him out" (Greek *aphorizō*) from before birth, and "called" him to preach the gospel among the Gentiles (Gal. 1:15-16). Paul could no longer "kick against the goads" (Acts 9:5). Like one of the prophets constrained by "the burden of the LORD" and "appointed" to fulfill a commission (cf. Jer. 1:5, 10), he declares, **Compulsion** [Greek *anankē*] **presses upon me; it is agony for me** [Greek *ouai gar moi estin*, "woe to me") **if I do not proclaim the gospel** (v. 16b).

How, then, could Paul choose to offer this service of proclamation as a freely given thank offering? In his own heart Paul cannot **glory** in his commission unless there is some way in which he can live out the *"giving freely."* Hence to live by the labor of his own hands allows him that one point of Christ-like giving, in which he can **glory**. His own labor permits him to proclaim the gospel *gratis*, which is akin to going "the second mile."

Paul's "**reward**" (vv. 17-18) is *not* some *external return* that he receives in consequence of a personal sacrifice; it is the joy that this renunciation of rights gives him in and for its own sake. The act and its "reward" are linked by "internal grammar" like the delight of giving a gift to a loved one, not by external cause and effect. This "internal" grammar has a parallel in Isaiah, where "His reward is with him" means not that God brings an external reward, but that *his very coming* is itself "reward" (Isa. 40:10).

25. SUGGESTIONS FOR POSSIBLE REFLECTION ON 9:1-18

1. *On the voluntary foregoing of "rights" as such:* How might the notion of voluntarily foregoing *rights* revolutionize attitudes? If enforced loss of "rights" causes resentments, would voluntarily foregoing them eliminate and heal such resentments? Often resentment comes when we have to forfeit time or resources to which we feel we have a *right*. C. S. Lewis warns us of the seduction of the word "my," as in "my shoes," "my wife," "my God" (in *Screwtape Letters*). If Christians were as overwhelmed as Paul was about the need to give something of one's own in free, voluntary response to God's generous grace, would such resentments be transposed into occasions for delight and glory?

2. On the effect of foregoing "rights" that relate to property or money: In particular might this principle revolutionize attitudes toward money and property? (Some think that private transport, for example, is a gift from God rather than a right, and such people are transparently more ready to use such resources for the benefit of others than those who see themselves as owners of "my" vehicle.) Might the entire culture of "making sacrifices" for God assume a different shape if there were no assumption that Christians who live in the prosperous West have a right to "Western" standards of income, provision, and comfort, and were willing to forego some of them? Are those who sit loose to "rights" better equipped to regard the twists and turns of life as opportunities to make sacrifices a source of *glorying* (vv. 15-16)?

3. On seeing the validity of service or ministry in its effects or "certificate of apostleship": Does our Christian service result in a parallel with Paul's certificate of apostleship (v. 2)? Gregory of Nyssa argues that just as one does not put someone in charge of a ship who has never brought a ship into a harbor, the church should not entrust its leadership to those who have never brought living persons into the haven of salvation. Can we offer some evidence of authentic witness, service, or agency in terms of its effects?

4. On perceiving "reward" as "internal" to the joy of giving and service: Are we too often tempted to look for *external* "rewards" (vv. 17-18), when the "reward" has an *internal* relation to what we offer? Is it "more blessed to give than to receive" because to give is a joyous blessing in itself? To learn to play a Bach organ fugue or a Beethoven piano sonata "brings" a reward in the very joy of playing it. Does it not degrade the task to look beyond it for a *further* reward? Those who *cannot afford to give,* or are *too incapacitated to serve* actively, might well long for the "reward" of the very act itself.

5. On possible guidelines for employment or management: How can we insure that those who labor long and hard will labor in *hope* (v. 10) that they will share in the benefits of the very process of production? Do we take full account of the **hope** that such residual benefits generate?

4. Using Many Strategies, but Keeping One's Eye on the Goal (9:19-27)

19 Free is what I am — no slave to any human person — yet I put myself into slavery to every human person, in order to win all the more of them. 20 To the Jews I

made myself as a Jew to win the Jews; to those under the law as one under the law, although I myself am not under the law, in order to win those under the law. 21 To those outside the law, as one outside the law, even though I am not outside God's law but subject to the law of Christ, in order to win those who are outside the law. 22 To the "weak" I made myself weak in order to win the weak. To them all I have become everything in turn so that through every possible means I may bring some to salvation. 23 Now all this I do on account of the nature of the gospel in order that I may have a jointly shared part in it.

24 Are you not aware that while all of the runners in a stadium take part in a race, it is only one of them who receives the prize? Run with this approach, to make the prize yours. 25 Everyone who enters as a combatant exercises self-control in everything: athletes, however, do it in order to win a crown that fades and disintegrates; but we, in our case, to win that which will never fade away. 26 I, on my part, therefore, am so running, as one not distracted from keeping an eye clearly on the goal. I am not like one who shadowboxes into empty air. 27 My day-to-day life as a whole I treat roughly, and make it strictly serve my purposes, lest after preaching to others, I find myself not proven to stand the test.

In vv. 1-18 Paul focused mainly on the "strong," providing a personal example of foregoing rights with an eye to their responding in kind. Now in vv. 19-27 Paul looks at the other side of the coin, namely, the "weak": *he will do anything and everything to care for, and to win, "the other,"* standing in loving solidarity with them. He wants the strong to do the same.

Each of the groups cited in vv. 19-23 is an "outsider" from the point of view of the opposite group. The **free** (v. 19) may not view those in **slavery** as "one of us." Gentiles regard **the Jews** as "other" (v. 20). Jesus regarded **those outside the law** as "other" (v. 21). The strong regard "**the weak**" as "other" (v. 22). Hence, to stand in solidarity with all these outsiders and to show them practical love, care, and respect, Paul declares: **To them all I have become everything in turn**, in order to **bring some to salvation** (v. 22). This, he concludes, is **the nature of the gospel**, as he seeks to live it out (v. 23). But this is not easy and demands costly effort and sacrifice. Hence Paul concludes in vv. 24-27 with the analogy of the disciplined, trained **runner**, who makes sacrifices and shares hardship for the sake of **the goal** (v. 26).

This as a strategy of *flexibility* and *adaptability*, and Glad devotes a large volume to this theme (*Paul and Philodemus*, esp. pp. 43-45 and 240-77). But this is not "adaptability" in the abstract, or for its own sake. It emerges entirely as *a pastoral demand,* as Paul seeks to enter the respective "worlds" of **slave** and **free**, **Jew** and Gentile, vulnerable and confident. It by no means suggests any "inconsistency" on Paul's part (Carson, "Pauline Inconsistency," pp. 6-45). The principle of coherence emerges in the single goal that these various strategies serve: **All this I do on account of the nature of the gospel** and to **bring some to salvation** (vv. 22-23). Nothing must hinder the gospel.

If this approach accords with **the nature of the gospel** (v. 23), we may expect that the principle will be instantiated in the person and ministry of Jesus Christ. This is what we find. Jesus enters into every kind of situation and uses every kind of method of communication. Some parables entice "outsiders" into a narrative world, where often prior expectations are unexpectedly reversed (e.g., Matt. 20:1-16). Sometimes Jesus teaches by gnomic aphorisms, or wisdom sayings (Matt. 5:1-16). Jesus rejoices with those who rejoice and weeps with those who weep (Mark 2:18-20; Luke 14:1-6). The messianic temptations are temptations to throw off the constraints of the way of suffering, hardship, and self-emptying (Matt. 4:3-11). Paul, likewise, voluntarily accepts certain constraints of a **slave** in **freedom** of choice. He does not simply please himself.

In all cases the strategy embodies sensitivity to where "the other" stands. Paul avoids both snobbery and inverted snobbery. He understands and respects the scrupulousness of the "weak" and their sense of insecurity in relation to the self-confidence of the strong. But his conduct and mode of communication take all this into account. He despises neither the inhibited and overly cautious nor the outgoing and overconfident. The most pregnant expression of all this in relation to 8:1-13 is: **To the "weak" I made myself weak in order to win the weak** (v. 22).

In vv. 24-27 Paul explains that this comes not merely from a series of spontaneous, warmhearted gestures, but from a *settled strategy* that involves personal cost, *"doing without"* and keeping one's eyes on the **goal** (v. 26). He draws on the analogy of **runners in a stadium** who **take part in a race** (v. 24). A runner who has the will to win will do anything and everything necessary to **receive the prize**. The same applies to any **combatant** or **athlete** (v. 25a). Whether the context is boxing, wrestling, weaponry, or some other kind of competitive activity, the struggle will involve rigorous **self-control** (v. 25). Athletes will resolve to do without excess food or luxuries that they might in other circumstances have the "right" to enjoy.

The Christians in Corinth would know full well all about competitive **races** and the **stadium**, and such other competitions as boxing, wrestling, weaponry, and even music and poetry. The Isthmian Games were held every two years on the very doorstep of Corinth, within a short walking distance, and they provided a major tourist attraction and a huge source of external revenue and employment for all types of trade and business for the city. The Games were held in A.D. 49, shortly before Paul's arrival in Corinth, again in A.D. 51 while he was ministering there, and again in A.D. 53 and 55, around the period of the arrival of this letter. We discuss the huge impact of the Games upon daily life and thought in Corinth in our Introduction above (pp. 4 and 11).

Competitors did everything **to win a crown**, even **a crown that fades and disintegrates** (v. 25b). The winner received a *garland* traditionally made from pine leaves, although some Greek writers allude to other kinds of leaves. The metaphor of competitive **races** appears in several Greek and Roman writers, also to emphasize the need for self-discipline and **self-control**. Paul, however, adds that Christians aim to receive not a mere garland of leaves that **fades and disintegrates** but a crown **which will never fade away** (v. 25b). The two contrasting Greek words that have to do with **fades** and **never fades** (*phtharton* and its opposite, *aphtharton*, v. 25) are similar to those that respectively describe the preresurrection body that suffers *decay* (*phthora*, 15:42) and *decay's reversal* in the resurrection. **Runners** and **athletes** will go to extreme lengths for a transitory prize and a reputation that lasts only momentarily. Christians are invited to exercise restraint and **self-control** on the journey that leads to lasting glory (cf. 15:43-44).

Paul hammers home the point in the last two verses of the chapter. He keeps his eye **clearly on the goal**. He will **not** be **distracted** (v. 26). The last phrase of the verse may allude to **empty air** to denote an undisciplined boxer whose blows miss the target. But more probably the allusion is to **shadowboxing**, which is alien to the "game" played by the strong in Corinth in contrast to real-life concern for the vulnerable and genuine engagement with issues of life and death. The use of self-restraint or self-influence may bring life or downfall to a fellow Christian (8:13).

Paul is "serious" about what is at stake. In his **day-to-day life** he does not indulge himself, or handle his life with kid gloves; he **treats his life roughly** (v. 27). The Greek verb suggests bearing the hardships and lack of luxury usually experienced by slaves. He wants his life **to stand the test**, and to be **proved** to do so (v. 27). He puts daily action where his mouth is, and he will not be "shown up" as merely playing games with words.

26. Suggestions for Possible Reflection on 9:19-27

1. *On the maxim "all for the sake of the gospel" (v. 23, NRSV):* To what lengths are we prepared to go to further the gospel? Do we try to stand in the skin of *every possible kind of person* to win them for Christ (vv. 19-23)? Do we try to exercise sustained restraint and self-discipline, including "going without," to make all this credible and effective?

2. *On projecting ourselves into the "world" of those whom we seek to reach:* Paul exercises such solidarity with the vulnerable as to declare "I made myself weak" (vv. 20-22). How do we show a solidarity with "the other" that calls for sensitivity and the projection of imagination into the other's "world"? Bishop George Ridding of Southwell composed a litany embodying the petition that we may enter into the concerns of others *as our own,* yet patiently considering "their likenesses to us and differences from us." Does Paul's use of *as* (three times in vv. 20-21) make this point? If we cannot replicate others, how far can imagination and sensitivity carry us into their "worlds"? How far does this reflect the incarnation, in which Jesus Christ took the *likeness* of humankind and the *form* of a human being (Phil. 2:7-8)?

3. *On investing time and energy for Christian service:* The impact of the Isthmian Games on Corinth was inescapable everywhere. The Games revealed the extraordinary stakes that athletes and spectators invested where the winner gained a pine or "laurel" wreath that soon "faded" and "fell apart." Great sacrifices were made; but for what? How do the "high stakes" of salvation and gospel outreach compare with this? Is our respective investment of energy, time, and commitment appropriate to the goal of serving the gospel?

4. *On the perspective of future glory:* The adjectives that describe a garland of leaves as *fading and falling apart* bring home the mortality of human life and the transitoriness of much human endeavor. By contrast, in the resurrec-

tion chapter Paul will elaborate further on the "reversal of decay" and "glory" (15:42-43) that awaits the transformation of the Christian at the resurrection of the dead. This is the "crown" that "never fades" (v. 25b).

5. A Broader Perspective: Models Drawn from the History of God's People in the Old Testament (10:1-13)

1 For I do not want you to fail to recognize, my dear fellow Christians, that our spiritual ancestors were all under the cloud and all passed through the sea. 2 All of them had themselves baptized into Moses in the cloud and in the sea. 3 All of them also ate the same spiritual food, and all of them drank the same spiritual drink; 4 for they used to drink from a spiritual rock which went with them. Now the Rock was Christ. 5 Nevertheless, on the far greater part of their number God visited his displeasure, for their corpses were strewn over the wilderness.

6 Now these events occurred as formative models for us, with a view to our not craving for evil things, even as those people craved for them. 7 Do not take part in idol worship like some of them, as it is written, "The people sat down to eat and drink and rose up to virtual orgy." 8 Neither should we indulge in sexual immorality, as some of them did, and in a single day twenty-three thousand fell. 9 Nor should we continue to put Christ to the test, even as some of them tested him and suffered the process of destruction by the snakes. 10 Also stop your querulous moaning, just as some of them muttered with complaints and suffered destruction at the hands of the Destroyer. 11 [All] these things happened in succession to them as formative models of broader patterns. They were written also to serve as warnings for us, upon whom the ends of the ages have come. 12 So, then, whoever thinks that he or she is standing fast, watch out lest you fall. No temptation has fastened upon you except what is part and parcel of being human. 13 Now God is faithful: he will not allow you to be tempted beyond your powers, but he will make an exit path alongside the temptation. His purpose in this is for you to bear up under it.

Paul is not one of those pastors who are content to base everything on personal anecdotes. He points out that the Christians in Corinth stand in continuity with a long history of God's dealings with his people. Recurring patterns or **formative models** emerge (v. 6) that offer parallels from the past with the present situation in Corinth.

Rather than letting everything hinge on the experiences, persons, and communities of the present moment, Paul provides a sense of historical perspective as well as of scriptural authority. In our own day, the tendency of "postmodern" attitudes is to make the present moment the arbiter of everything, rather than to permit the "grand narrative" of the people of God from the past through the present to the purposive future goal to mold thought and practice. The Old Testament witness to the experiences of ancient Israel tells Christians about **our spiritual ancestors** (v. 1, Greek, strictly, *our fathers*).

a. The Contrast of "All" versus "the Greater Part" (10:1-5)

The logic of vv. 1-3 is crystal clear. Paul reminds the church that the blessings and benefits of belonging to the people of God were experienced by **all** (vv. 1a, 1b, 2, 3, and 4; no fewer than five times). **All** experienced the covering shelter and leading of the presence of God represented by **the cloud** (v. 1, alluding to Exod. 13:21; 14:19-20); **all** experienced God's redemptive act of deliverance from bondage in Egypt to the new life when they **passed through the sea**, that is, the Sea of Reeds (Exod. 14:19-22). **All** shared in the corporate solidarity of the redeemed community led by **Moses. Baptized into Moses** indicates their being initiated into a new status of loyalty to his leadership as those who share in the blessings and also the renunciations of the group *as a whole.*

The fifth and final use of **all** in this section recalls the shared blessings of eating **the same spiritual food** and drinking **the same spiritual drink** (v. 4). The allusion is to eating the manna that God provided by direct providence, and to drinking the water that gushed forth when Moses struck the rock. Paul underlines both the privilege of these blessings and the solidarity of all Christians with the **all** by pointing beyond the immediate reference of the manna and **the rock** to the further realities of which they constitute visible signs.

Two phrases raise difficult questions: a **rock which went with them**; and **Now the Rock was Christ** (v. 4). A rabbinic legend seems to have been in currency that **the rock** that Moses struck actually followed the people of Israel as they journeyed in order to provide a constant water supply. It is conceivable, but surely unlikely, that Paul alludes to this legend when he uses the phrase **which went with them**. A. T. Hanson understands the two difficult phrases as belonging together, and argues that Paul assumes "the real presence of Christ in Israel's history" accompanying, and providing for, Israel (*Paul's Technique*, p. 100).

This view is not to be dismissed, for Paul would have been one of many who believed that God's *wisdom* guided and sustained the people of Israel, and in the epistle he has already expounded the person and work of Christ as God's wisdom (1:30; 2:6, 16; cf. Wisdom 7:25 and 11:20–12:18). James Dunn concludes, "Paul was attributing to *Christ* the role previously attributed to Divine Wisdom" (his italics, *Theology of the Apostle Paul,* p. 270). At the very least Paul is consciously using symbolic resonances that permit a legitimate wordplay. We should also note in passing that it is unhelpful to describe this as "allegorical interpretation" since *typology* (which is a better term here) draws parallels between *events,* while allegory (in general) rests on parallels between *ideas* and can become too often self-generated and arbitrary.

In v. 5 we reach the climax of the buildup of five uses of **all** in a sharp contrast. In contrast to five sets of "blessings," a discordant note is struck with the contrast, **Nevertheless, on the far greater part of their number God visited his displeasure.** Divine displeasure led to their **corpses** being **strewn over the wilderness,** where **strewn** or *scattered* accurately reflects the Septuagint (Greek version) of Num. 14:16, which recounts the episode.

b. Formative Models Drawn from Scripture
and Israel's Experience (10:6)

What incurred **God's displeasure** was the **craving** (Greek *epithymeō,* v. 6) of those who were not satisfied with what God provided. **Craving** is the root attitude that vv. 7-13 will spell out in terms of concrete attitude. The key to this section (vv. 1-6) is that this episode provides **formative models** (Greek *typoi,* v. 6) for Christians, especially for "the strong" in Corinth, to note by way of warning. The **craving** for what lies on the other side of a permitted line brings divine judgment and disaster.

The Greek word *typos* may in many contexts mean no more than *example,* or a *mark* or *imprint.* But in certain contexts it denotes an *example taken as a* **model** or *norm,* almost akin to Thomas Kuhn's notion of *paradigm* in the philosophy of science. However, it goes further: it may denote a classical norm or example that plays a special role in the *formation* of those to whom it is presented as a paradigm. Hence our translation follows the suggestion of G. Schunack, that the word here denotes **formative models** ("Typos," in H. Balz and G. Schneider, *Exe-*

getical Dictionary, vol. 3, p. 374). The appeal to the **formative** models points to the root attitude of **craving**, *yearning for* or *intensely desiring* what God has placed out of bounds.

c. Four Instances of Destructive "Craving" (10:7-13)

G. D. Collins argues convincingly that 10:1-13 is an almost self-contained explication of (or Midrash on) the theme of craving in Numbers 11, especially in the light of Exod. 32:6 and other Old Testament passages ("That We Might Not Crave Evil . . . ," pp. 55-75). Sin is related to *misdirected desire,* as Paul and Augustine make clear (*Augustine on Free Will,* 1:3-4; 3:17-19; *Confessions,* 2:5). In W. Pannenberg's words, sin is "an autonomy of the will that puts the self in the center and uses everything else as a means to the self as an end" (*Systematic Theology,* vol. 2, p. 243). This misdirected desire of the will leads in these verses to (a) idolatry, (b) immorality, (c) doubt that puts God to the test, and (d) despair, complaint, or "murmuring."

(1) The allusion to **idol worship** describes the activity of the "strong" in Corinth as seen through eyes of the "insecure." But Paul may also be making a broader point about the connection between undue license in frequenting pagan temples and the moral laxity that he had to address in chapters 5-6. The parallel, or part parallel, in Exod. 32:1-6 is that the idolatrous worship of the golden calf led to unrestrained **eating and drinking** and to a **virtual orgy** (v. 7b). Unrestrained "letting one's hair down" led to a spiral of self-indulgence in contrast to the "self-control" for which Paul pleads in 9:25. The translations "amuse themselves" (NJB) and "play" (NRSV) fail to convey the point for today's readers.

(2) We cannot be certain how closely Paul is simultaneously referring to social banquets in the temple precincts, but Greco-Roman literature suggests that the link is more than a distant one. The explicit allusion to the second example of **craving** is that of **sexual immorality** (v. 8), which probably carried a double allusion to the history of Israel and the other cults of Dionysus (Bacchus), Apollo, Aphrodite, Isis, and Serapis. In spite of its earlier date, Euripides' play *The Bacchae* provides an explicit model in which unrestrained pagan frenzy spirals into self-destruction and sinister evil.

Paul's reference to the **twenty-three thousand** who **fell in a single day** (v. 8b) draws on Num. 25:1-9. Since Numbers appears to speak of twenty-four thousand, this verse has been an endless source of debate about biblical "inerrancy." The Church Fathers seem untroubled by the difference, and it is speculative to follow Calvin's suggestion that Numbers rounded the number up, while Paul rounded it down (predictably followed by Charles Hodge). Paul wants to give an idea of the magnitude of the sum.

(3) The third example consists in **putting Christ to the test** (v. 9). The common factor between Israel in Exodus and in Numbers and "the strong" in Corinth appears to be the presumptuous attitude of provoking God to the very limit in the confident, complacent assumption that God will protect his people and not let them go. Their overconfident attempt to play off God's protective love against their willful **craving** failed to work. They found **destruction by the snakes** (v. 9b).

(4) Similarly, **querulous moaning** (the Greek uses onomatopoeia with the word *gongyzō*) also brought **destruction at the hands of the Destroyer.** The Greek word and the context in Exodus and Numbers suggest a constant grumbling, griping, groaning, murmuring, whispering, and complaining that expresses discontent with what God had provided. Thus this was in part a sin of ingratitude, in part a disloyal sowing of seeds of discontentment among others. In 1 Corinthians 8–10 it pinpoints, first, an ungrateful discontent with the generosity of God's grace; and, second, a behind-the-back unsettling of those who would otherwise have accepted what God's grace has assigned. In all probability *the insecure* in the church in Corinth felt, with good reason, that some of the "strong" whispered about their confusions and doubts behind their hands.

All these events, Paul declares, are **formative models of broader patterns** (v. 11a). In other words, they serve as warnings and examples that point beyond their immediate context in the experience of Israel. Exodus and Numbers are more than a biblical "history of Israel." **They were written also to serve as warnings for us** (v. 11b). There are similarities and differences between the history and experience of Israel and that of the Christian church. All the same, the Old Testament remains a "Christian Scripture" (as well as the "Hebrew Bible"). J. W. Aageson entitles his book on this subject *Written Also for Our Sake* (cited above), and rightly reflects the inclusion of the word **also** in the Greek *(egraphē de . . .)*.

If Scripture is written to nurture, to instruct, and to provide *for-*

mation of life and thought for the people of God, the broader readership includes both Israel and the church, and transcends the specific "local" target audience or readership that an individual writer consciously addressed. However, this does not detach the biblical texts from their original interpersonal historical grounding and anchorage. For what gives initial currency of meaning is what constitutes the meaning of the text as a communicative act, shaped by the directness of the text usually (although not always) to a specific situation. On the other hand, this specific situation *does not exhaust* authentic potentialities of further meaning. Meanings become "actualized" in additional ways as new situations arise, as long as these do not contradict or violate the primary communicative event that remains a "control" for evaluating subsequent actualizations of meaning.

Thus Paul's application of the Old Testament narrative of Num. 25:1-9 to the readers in Corinth respects the integrity of the text but also enlarges its scope. Further, in the light of the definitive revelation of God *in Christ,* Paul Gardner observes that a "Christian" or christological context is not merely a matter of "spiritual" extension, but, on the contrary, in this new context "God revealed more about how things actually were" (*The Gifts of God,* p. 113).

Paul's appeal to the "eschatological" situation of Christians clinches this. Christians are those **upon whom the ends of the ages have come.** The traditional understanding of this is that Christians live "in the last days." But Paul is more precise than this. He refers to "the two ages" of both Jewish apocalyptic and Pauline thought. Christians stand on the borderline between the continuing "age" of the present world order and the new age of the last days and new creation. These "intersect" where "the close of the old coincides with the beginning of the new" (Weiss, *Der erste Korintherbrief,* p. 254).

The practical point, therefore, is twofold: (1) because Christians still live within the continuing world order, they must guard against presumption and heed moral exhortation; but (2) because they belong to the new age, they have access to a definitive disclosure of God's will and access to divine grace in Christ. Their relation to the *old* underlines the need to take **warnings** seriously (v. 11b); their relation to the *new* addresses *doubt and anxiety* on the journey of pilgrimage, self-discipline, and growth.

This double perspective paves the way for the two complementary halves of vv. 12-13. (1) To the complacent, overconfident, and cocksure, Paul gives the warning, **Whoever thinks that he or she is standing fast, watch out lest you fall** (v. 12a). Christians are still on the journey of the pilgrim where temptation and danger still lurk. (2) On the other hand, whatever **temptations** come, these are no more than what arise as **part and parcel of being human**, and **God**, who is **faithful, will not allow you to be tempted beyond your powers** (vv. 12b-13a). Furthermore, since God's purpose in such experience is for Christians to attain maturity by **bearing up** under temptation rather than suffering destruction, God **will make an exit path alongside the temptation** (v. 13).

Again, as Moltmann urges in *Theology of Hope* (p. 21), the two "sins" to resist are those of *presumption* and *despair*. Each respectively relates to the problems of the "strong" and the "weak" in Corinth. (1) No doubt some appealed to claims that they suffered "special" temptations. Paul replies that their experience is simply part of being human, alongside all misplaced desires, misdirected passions, self-deceptions, and illusions. (2) Paul also insists that we can never say, "There is no way out." God would **not allow** a temptation that is in principle irresistible, without their being some way of skirting around it or escaping it.

27. Suggestions for Possible Reflection on 10:1-13

1. *On lifting our eyes to wider horizons:* When we are under pressure, it may help to lift our eyes to wider horizons. Paul does not rely upon anecdotes about "local" or contemporary situations, but sets his readers' thoughts on common patterns of experience to be found in Scripture and in the regular experiences of the people of God from ancient to more recent times. Can we apprehend a proper perspective on our situations and temptations without such a broader biblical, historical, and global view (vv. 1-6)?

2. *On misplaced or misdirected desire:* Too often human sin is portrayed more as a matter of committing wrong acts, or of failing to live up to some standard, than of misdirected *desires* that then find expression in these wrong acts and in wrong *attitudes*. Augustine speaks of the folly of seeking satisfaction in created objects rather than in the God who created that which attracts us. Why do misdirected desires often lead to seeking *idolatrous substi-*

tutes for God rather than God himself? If restraint is discarded, where does it all end? Does a spiral of self-indulgence lead to self-destruction (vv. 7-9)?

3. *On the culture of blame:* As soon as matters become out of hand, we often seek someone else to blame. Sometimes self-recrimination emerges in the form of "transferred anger" against God or others. People will claim that God should have intervened (when they had sought to be free of God) as if God were on trial or "put to the test" (v. 9). We may sometimes "mutter with complaints" (v. 10) about situations that we have largely brought upon ourselves. Has the early-twenty-first-century culture of the Western world come to mirror all this largely as a culture of *blame?* Do we make everything the fault of someone else? Arguably it was ever thus (Gen. 3:12-13), but does our culture of increasingly obsessive litigation make it even worse? The gospel speaks of mediation and reconciliation.

4. *On presumption, despair, and humble trust:* We cited Moltmann's axiom that the promises of God exclude human presumption and human despair, but invite trust. Does the first attitude characterize the "strong" in Corinth, and the second threaten the weak? God's purpose in permitting temptation is in part to enable Christians to grow in trust, maturity, and resilience, rather than presumption, by "bearing up under" temptation (v. 13b). "God" promises that he "will not allow" an unbearable degree of pressure to build up without also providing an "exit path alongside the temptation" (v. 13).

5. *On Scripture, including the Old Testament, as a God-given resource for "formation."* In what ways do the Scriptures exercise formative power over life, thought, and character? Do we too often seek simply "teaching" to inform us, or do we also seek a transforming engagement with Scripture that makes a formative impact? God's word is inseparable from God's active presence and sanctifying power. God often speaks through "formative models" in narratives as well as through promises and commands. Scripture speaks in many ways.

6. Sharing in the Lord's Supper: A Paradigm of Covenant Loyalty (10:14-22)

14 So then, my very dear friends, flee from idolatry. 15 I appeal to your common sense. Judge for yourselves what I declare. 16 The cup of blessing over which we

offer a blessing, is it not a communal participation in the blood of Christ? The bread which we break, is it not a communal participation in the body of Christ? 17 Because there is one bread, many as we are, we are one body; for it is the one bread that we all share. 18 Consider Israel of earthly descent: are not those who eat the sacrifices communal participants in the altar of sacrifice? 19 What, then, do I mean to affirm? That the offering of what is sacrificed to idols amounts to anything, or that an idol is anything? 20 Not that! — But that when they sacrifice, "they offer sacrifices to demons and not to God." I do not want you to become communal participants in demonic forces. 21 You cannot drink from the cup of the Lord and the cup of devilish powers: you cannot participate in the table of the Lord and the table of demons. 22 What! Are we in process of arousing the Lord's jealousy? Surely it cannot be that we are "stronger" than he, can it?

The scriptural examples drawn from Num. 25:1-9 and related passages has underlined the clear-cut contrast between sharing the privileges and responsibilities of the people of God under the old covenant and risking forfeiture of those privileges by illegitimate cravings and idolatry. Now the central focus shifts to the climactic example of faithfulness or unfaithfulness under the new covenant and its covenantal institutions. The Lord's Supper presents a key model or paradigm case of **communal participation** [Greek *koinōnia*] **in the blood of Christ** and **in the body of Christ** (v. 16).

Once again the unity of thought in this epistle is apparent. Paul develops the argument of 6:12-20 even more incisively here that a lifestyle that makes commitments that are incompatible with those of the gospel tears apart or "**takes away Christ's limbs and organs**" (6:5). Christians are "**bought with a price**" to belong *to the Lord* (6:20). In a deeper parallel here, **You cannot drink the cup of the Lord and the cup of devilish powers** (v. 21a). Because **the Lord** has purchased Christians to be *his*, and Christians in turn have pledged themselves to him in sharing in **the cup of blessing** and the broken **bread** (v. 16), duplicitous Christians who retain a parallel involvement in **idolatry** (v. 14) risk **arousing the Lord's jealousy** (v. 22).

Fleeing from idolatry (v. 14) suggests in part the need for urgent and prompt action. Chrysostom paraphrases it, "Be rid of this sin with all speed." But it also suggests the folly of *delaying to debate* whether eating meat in idolatrous liturgical events really constitutes "idolatry" on the ground that "**we know** [that] **an idol has no real existence**" (8:4).

Clearly Paul is addressing "the strong" in the larger context of 8:1–11:1, for he appeals to them as those capable of exercising *intelligence* or **common sense** (Greek *hōs phronimois,* v. 15a). They are to **judge for yourselves what I declare** (v. 15b). The Greek construction emphasizes the word *you* or **yourselves**: they cannot pass the buck; Paul has told them enough for them to draw rational inferences on their own part. Their appeal to what they "know" has become subtly redefined. They had thought that *knowledge* mainly concerned the nonexistence of idols and liberty to act in a robust, libertarian way; it turns out that *knowledge* more profoundly concerns solidarity with the whole covenant people of God, who include the *vulnerable,* and the risk of incurring divine displeasure. At all events, Paul now trusts them to make a genuine reappraisal. He does not bludgeon them with bare appeals to authority, for this is not necessary. He wants them to see the point.

The cup of blessing (v. 16a) is the Passover cup over which "grace" would have been said. This is a *prayer of thanks* in which *the speaker blesses God.* In a Jewish household the standard form would often be "Blessed be You, Lord God, King of the Universe, who created the fruit of the vine" (*Mishnah Berakōth* 6:1). There were other variant forms. (I include an extended Note on this in my larger commentary, *First Epistle,* pp. 756-61). In the celebration of the Passover in the Passover meal, four cups of wine were used, and the phrase may perhaps identify the third of these cups. Whatever theory of dating for the Last Supper is adopted, without question Jesus intended it to be *his* (and the disciples') Passover meal, and in this context a *benediction* was offered to *God* initially over the first cup.

Robin Routledge has provided a helpful placing of the Lord's Supper in the context of the words and actions of the Passover *Seder* of the first century ("Passover and Last Supper," pp. 203-21). His headings include "Retelling the Story of Salvation" (*Maggid*) (p. 213) and "Reliving the Exodus" (p. 219). Unleavened bread (cf. 1 Cor 5:2) and a paste of nuts and fruit (*the haroseth*) are brought before the host, the head of the household. Then in response to the question about its meaning, he recites the saving events of the Passover (Exod. 12:37-39; Deut. 26:5ff.; also *Mishnah Pesharim* 10:1-7).

"Why do we eat bitter herbs?" "[We eat] because the Egyptians embittered the lives of our fathers" (*Pesharim* 10:5). In place of "this is the bread of affliction . . . ," Jesus declared, "This is my body. . . ." Israel's recital of the Passover *Seder* (the semiliturgical sequence of events) *actively involved* those who *participated* in the ritual; they were *"there."* The church's recital of the events of the new Passover of the body and blood of Christ *actively involved* Christians as no less *"there"* in the very events of the Passion. The Black spiritual "Were you there when they crucified my Lord . . . ?" reflects this dynamic accurately and poignantly. Thus it was a **communal participation in the blood of Christ** (v. 16b) and in **the one bread that we all share** (v. 17b).

We use **communal participation** to translate the Greek word *koinōnia* because the conventional translation, "fellowship," is simply too bland. Numerous writers rightly argue that the "vertical" dimension of the relation between believers and God is the fundamental basis for the "horizontal" dimension of interrelationship between fellow believers. The term denotes more than mere social bonding, as if in a society or club, even though some writers stress this social aspect (Hainz, *Koinonia;* Panikulam, *Koinonia in the New Testament*). Thornton *(Common Life)* underlines the aspect of "being a shareholder" or "stakeholder" in Christ, in the cross and resurrection, and in the divine reality of the church as God's people. Paul uses the word in 1:9 above, and reinforces the point by using the Greek word *metechein* (v. 17), **to share,** *to participate in.*

In v. 17 Paul repeats the word **one** three times: **one bread . . . one body . . . one bread.** There is *a single, common ground of unity, a single basis of salvation,* namely, the *"broken"* **body of Christ,** represented by **the bread which we break** (v. 16b), and . . . the shared **blood of Christ** (v. 16a). The giving and receiving of the **bread** and the **cup** constitute *covenant pledges of loyalty and of solidarity:* God pledges himself to his people; God's people pledge themselves to their God.

Although we should not read *into* Paul an oversacramentalist theology of later years, Paul without doubt reinforces his earlier language about "bodiliness" against those in Corinth who suppose that everything that relates to salvation is merely "inner" and private. The physical pledges of giving on one side and of eating and drinking on the other are "sacramental" in the sense of constituting effective signs of the realities that they convey. They are "tangible" and "visible" pledges of God's redemptive love and of Christians' reception and pledges to be faithful. They are more, but not less, than "visible words." As Paul Ricoeur insists, symbol may resonate with creative and productive power in the recesses of the human heart and mind where merely cognitive discourse does not fully operate as conscious thought (*Interpretation Theory,* pp. 45-60; further, Thiselton, *First Epistle,* pp. 761-71).

The function of v. 18 as both a recapitulation and further development of the argument continues in vv. 19-20. Paul recalls that his arguments in no way contradict the agreed, common, Christian axiom that **an idol** is not **anything** (as in 8:4-6). However, he also **affirms** that the *perceptions* of some Christians about what occurs in this action differ. Paul makes both a *pastoral* point and a *philosophical* or *theological* one. The profound *pastoral* point is that *people's perceptions matter,* even if they may be mistaken. They cannot be ignored. The *philosophical* or *theological* point is that there is a difference between *metaphysical, ontological, or divinely "given"* truth and what is interpreted or perceived as "true" by *human social construction.* (Ideally it is best to avoid the catchall term "objective"; but we might have said that "objective" or "given" truth differs from intersubjective or constructed truth.) Some further questions about MSS readings and syntax arise, but these do not substantially affect the force of these verses (discussed in Thiselton, *First Epistle,* pp. 772-75).

Some in Corinth perceive the idol sacrifices as offered to **demons**, and perceive those who **offer** them (or have them offered on their behalf) as **participants in demonic forces** (v. 20). Paul's concern to do justice *both* to the absolute nonexistence of idols and false deities *and* to the perceived experience of becoming dominated by them as "powers" reflects a double tradition in the Old Testament and in Judaism. Isaiah 40–55, for example, represents the robust prophetic tradition that idols are "nothings"; God alone is the sovereign Creator. The later Jewish traditions of apocalyptic, however, also perceive the world as in the grip of evil powers, even though God will defeat them in due time.

In pastoral terms both traditions insist that God's sovereignty is absolute, and Paul likewise declares that no "power" (whether angels or "powers" [Greek *archai*] or height or depth [perhaps perceived as forces of astrology or fate]) "can separate us from the love of God in Christ Jesus our Lord" (Rom. 8:38-39). Jesus Christ has purchased believers from the claims of any other master to belong to him alone (1 Cor. 6:20). Paul does not hold a "dualist" notion of the world order as dominated by two sets of powers, demonic and divine.

However, Paul also recognizes the destructive effects that idolatry and belief in **demonic forces** have played and still can play in people's lives (vv. 20-21). These effects have still to be addressed. This may remind us of Jesus' acts of casting out "demons" (Matt. 9:33-34; Mark 7:26; Luke 9:49; 11:15-19). On the other hand, Paul uses the word **demons** only here (10:20-21; Greek *daimoniōn*, used four times) in all of his epistles together. Collins observes, "Only in 1 Cor. 10:20-21 does Paul speak about demons. . . . All reality belongs to the one God who has entrusted sovereignty over all things to the one Lord" (8:6; 15:27; *First Corinthians,* pp. 380-81). The victory of the resurrection of Jesus Christ has supervened between the ministry of Jesus and the epistles of Paul, which accounts for some difference of emphasis.

Paul refrains from characterizing **demons** explicitly as "personal" agents. Yet he acknowledges that the world, especially the world of Gentile religion and culture, embodies pockets of evil power that serve as foci for evil forces in relation to God and to God's people. This power is in process of crumbling, but still retains the *impact and effect* of **devilish powers** that operate more forcefully in their *corporate, structural, or institutional effects* than any evil generated by any individual human person as such. *Evil systems* have such power. Sometimes the net effect of corporate or structural evil is greater than the sum of the individuals who promote it.

Paul views the liturgical events of pagan temples and idol worship as part of such structural forces (at the very least in terms of their practical *effects*), and this leads him to intensify his warnings to Christians not to be involved in this **communal participation** (v. 20). In more specific terms, **you cannot drink from the cup of the Lord and the cup of devilish powers; you cannot participate in the table of the Lord and the table of demons** (v. 21). **Cup** and **table** have double meanings. In the context of sharing in the Lord's Supper, they denote the **cup** and **table** of the Lord's Supper, or Eucharist. But Jesus also spoke of sharing the **cup** and **table** of his "baptism" as a suffering, redeeming Messiah, in whose messianic task his disciples are called to share or **participate** (Mark 10:38-39). To receive **the cup of the Lord** is *both* to participate in the Lord's Supper with its covenant solidarity *and* to participate in the redemptive death and resurrection of Christ. The corresponding implication is that more than one level of involvement operates in **drinking from . . . the cup of devilish powers.**

Such a breach of covenant loyalty and love would risk **arousing the Lord's jealousy** (v. 22). The thrust of Paul's rhetorical question is: Do you really want to risk doing *that*? NJB's translation, "Do we really want to arouse the Lord's jealousy?" captures the force well, but our translation **What! Are we in process of arousing the Lord's jealousy?** does better justice to the present tense of the Greek verb. The final rhetorical question (v. 22b) is a hesitant or ironic question introduced by the Greek word *mē:* **Surely it cannot be that we are "stronger" than he, can it?** (even though we are the "strong" and not "the weak" in the church!). If, as Mitchell argues, Paul often uses in this epistle a rhetoric that appeals to practical advantage, he suggests here that none of the supposed advantages of retaining all their Gentile contacts and sharing in the rites of pagan temples is worth a candle compared with risking **arousing the Lord's jealousy**.

This section may seem at first sight to imply that Paul retracts the softer or more balanced view that appeared to emerge in 8:1-13 and in much of chapter 9. But Paul has yet to summarize both sides of the issue in the remaining verses of this chapter (vv. 23-33 and 11:1).

28. SUGGESTIONS FOR POSSIBLE REFLECTION ON 10:14-22

1. *On the responsible, biblically informed use of rational reflection among Christians:* Paul asks his Christian readers to use their *common sense, intelligence,* and *judgment:* "Judge for yourselves" (v. 15). This implies that in the light (1) of Scripture (10:1-13, esp. 10:6, where Scripture provides *formative models*), and (2) of Paul's further instruction, Christians are expected to use their *rational reflection* to arrive at decisions that they can "own" as theirs. But their *knowledge* must be informed by Scripture, apostolic teaching, and the Holy Spirit. Paul criticized a reliance upon "knowledge" that supposedly assumed a *prior* grasp of all the necessary factors for understanding (8:1-3, 7-8). *Coming to know* is a *process* in which love for the other, Scripture, openness to God's Spirit, and apostolic testimony remain essential elements. Some in Corinth had confused "knowledge" as an achieved state with what turned out to be *partial* knowledge. But once their eyes had been lifted to less self-centered concerns, Paul does not question the capacity of Christians to draw valid inferences and to make constructive judgments. *Always* to appeal *only* to "authority" is not Paul's pastoral strategy at all.

2. *On participation in the Lord's Supper as a covenant pledge:* Paul urges the seriousness of involvement in *the Lord's Supper,* or the Eucharist. Concerns to avoid imposing onto the text some post-Pauline doctrine of the *Lord's Supper* should not blind us to this robust language about "communal participation in the blood of Christ" and "in the body of Christ" (v. 16). In 11:26 Paul will warn the readers that participants are like those who enter the witness box *to proclaim* their absolute involvement in, and dependence upon, the "broken body" and shed "blood" of Christ as the basis of salvation, and indeed of *their* salvation. The giving of the broken *body* and shed *blood,* on the one side, and the receiving of the *cup* and the *bread,* on the other, ratify a twofold covenant pledge of union with Christ. Thus those who are "in Christ" are not free to retract their allegiance and to offer it elsewhere, any more than God will retract his promise of covenant blessing. Such a hypothesis would entail a self-contradiction of identity. Double or duplicitous expressions of "belonging" undermine and contradict the very basis of who and what a Christian is or has become.

3. *On steering clear of whatever causes damage to Christian faith and life:* Paul never retracts the common basis of the argument that "an idol has no real existence" (8:4-6). In principle this applies to all supposed "entities" that threaten the well-being of the world and of God's people. Christians have nothing to fear because they have become the purchased possessions of Christ (6:20) and because God in Christ alone is sovereign (8:4-6). Yet some "powers," whether or not they are "personal," remain damaging *in their effects.* Some or all of these may be social constructs of human belief systems, or of socioeconomic or pseudo-national interest. Even after the victory of the cross and resurrection, the created order remains disturbed by specific "foci" that serve as magnets of attraction for evil structures or forces. Christians must insure that they do not actively "participate in" these in the sense of pledging loyalty to them or solidarity with them. Yet neither should they fear them. In the language of 2:6, they are "doomed to pass away"; their power is *crumbling.* For God alone is sovereign.

4. *On the relative importance of people's perceptions, whether right or wrong:* Sometimes the "power" or effect of evil rests on mistaken perceptions. There is a difference between *reality* and *perception.* Nevertheless, Paul refuses to agree with the more "robust" or confident Christians that these are "only" perceptions that we can sweep aside as neither here nor there. Perceptions matter, even when they are not grounded on truth. Pastoral

strategies and Christian actions must heed what effects perceptions have, and adjust their strategies and actions accordingly. This is part of the dominant theme of respect and love for "the other" that runs through from 8:1 to 14:40, whether the context is food offered to idols, Christian worship, the Lord's Supper, or the exercise of gifts of the Holy Spirit.

7. Drawing the Argument Together: Liberty and Love (10:23–11:1)

23 "Liberty to do all things" — but not everything is helpful. "The right to do anything" — but not everything builds up [the church]. 24 No one should seek his or her own interests, but the well-being of the other. 25 Eat whatever is sold in the meat market without asking about it to reach a judgment because of your self-awareness [or, just possibly, *conscience*]. 26 For "The earth is the Lord's, and all that is in it." 27 If someone who is an unbeliever invites some of you to a meal and you want to go, make a practice of eating anything that is put before you without asking about it to reach a judgment because of your self-awareness. 28 If, however, someone should say to you, "This has been offered in sacrifice," make a practice of not eating it, out of regard for the person who informed you and their self-awareness: 29 the self-awareness, I mean, not of one's own, but that of the other person. 30 For why [you ask] is my freedom being subjected to another person's self-awareness? Well, if I take part in a meal with thanksgiving, why should I suffer defamation of character over that for which I, at least, give thanks? 31 Whether, then, you eat or drink, or whether you do anything different, do it all for the glory of God. 32 Avoid doing damage both to Jews and to Gentiles, as well as to God's church. 33 In just the same way, I, on my part, strive to take account of all the interests of everyone, not seeking any advantage of my own, but the good of the many, with a view to their salvation. 11:1 Take me as your pattern, as I take Christ for mine.

Much of this section summarizes and recapitulates the argument from 8:1 through to 10:22, except that Paul includes two further distinctions raised by case studies. One case study concerns buying meat from the shops; the other arises when a Christian is invited to a Gentile household for a meal, and is offered meat that has probably been resold in the market after it had first passed through a pagan temple. Some argue that almost all the meat sold in the meat market would have followed this route. Often the best quality meats and best cuts would become available this way. In effect, much would have been involved in the liturgical processes of sacrifice, but it would also be of a quality suitable for hospitality to guests.

Paul repeats the guiding axiom that he formulated in response to the same Corinthian slogan in 6:12. Against the slogan, "**Liberty to do all things**" (10:23a and 6:12a), he responds, "**But not everything is helpful**" (10:23a and 6:12a). Against the slogan "**The right to do anything**" (10:23b), or "liberty to do anything" (6:12b), Paul replies, "**But not everything builds up**" (Greek *oikodomeō*, 10:23b), or *"But I will not let anything take liberties with me"* (6:12b). The plea to ask what is helpful (Greek *sympherei*) is an appeal to *advantage,* which is the hallmark of deliberative rhetoric in Paul's era (discussed more fully in Mitchell, *Rhetoric*). However, whereas in 6:12 the basic axiom explicates the language of "liberty" and "rights" in terms of putting the self into bondage to illegitimate "rights" or power (Greek *exousia*), here Paul anticipates the key theme of **building up** the Christian community, which becomes dominant in chapters 12-14.

A responsible, caring Christian will not exploit his or her **liberty** or **rights** if to do this damages or inhibits the **building up** of fellow Christians. The whole argument spells out what is implicit in 8:1: "knowledge inflates [the self]; love builds up [the other]." The next verse carries this further: **No one should seek his or her own interests but the well-being of the other** (v. 24). In English idiom we would well translate the Greek singular, **the** [interest] **of the other**, *to tou heterou,* as a plural, *of the others.* In philosophical and ethical discourse, as well as hermeneutics, this becomes almost a technical term, as in the phrase "respect for the other" (in Emilio Betti), or even respect "for the otherness of the other" (in Paul Ricoeur). Paul implies such language when he speaks of Christ's dying not for those like him (the "good" or "righteous"), but for "the other," or "the ungodly" (Rom. 5:6-8).

Nevertheless, **liberty** retains a serious currency when its lack of constraint does not cause damage. In normal circumstances the Christian need not and should not be overly scrupulous, overly earnest, or hair splitting about buying meat on the open market. It is foolish to initiate awkward questions about how the meat reached the market stall and came to the host's table.

Whether or not sacrificial meat was openly distinguished from that which came from other sources remains a matter of debate. Murphy-O'Connor insists that in effect virtually all meat came from the temples, but Gill warns us that the situation may have varied from year to year ("The Meat Market at Corinth," pp. 389-93). Paul instructs his readers not to make a fuss. Whether we translate the Greek term *syneidēsis* here as **self-awareness** or as *conscience,* this issue relating to the *self* should not determine the matter. It is better to recall Ps. 24:1: "**The earth is the Lord's.** . . ." Every good gift from God can be received with thanksgiving. In metaphorical terms, look upward rather than inward!

Does this matter become more complicated if a Christian accepts an invitation to a meal in the home of a Gentile friend or colleague? Since the host would normally serve good-quality meat to a guest, the probable source of supply would be a temple. Even so, normally: **eat anything that is put before you without asking** fussy or overly scrupulous questions (v. 27). Yet there is more to be said.

The next two or three verses raise difficulties of interpretation. All the same, whichever view is accepted, the broad criterion for a decision about what to eat rests *not with "my" worries or "my" overconfidence, but with factors that relate entirely to the "other" person.* Many early commentators suggested that the warning "This has been offered in sacrifice" was uttered by a thoughtful Gentile host, or by one of the Gentile guests, probably out of respect for Christian sensitivities that they may already have encountered. In this case, it would be a thoughtless rebuff to such courtesy to eat, as well as needlessly making the other scrupulous Christians look overly earnest. More recently many have argued that the warning came from a fellow Christian who would be uncomfortable about eating food sacrificed to idols. In this case, the second of the two considerations identified above would still apply. They are not to be shown up or demeaned by some supposedly more "liberal" behavior on the part of the Christian whom Paul is addressing. Hence, however we view the details, the guiding principle remains: **not . . . one's own** scruples or emancipation, but **that of the other person.** *The criterion for action depends on concern for* **the other,** *not for one's self* (v. 29a).

The question, **Why is my freedom being subjected to another person's self-awareness** [*or concerns*]? (v. 29b), is probably *rhetorical,* reflecting "deliberation" in the manner of deliberative rhetoric (argued by Watson, "I Cor. 10:23–11:1," pp. 1-18). The question thus expresses the hypothetical or actual view that Paul has shown to be untenable for the reasons cited in the context. In essence, this is *not loss* of freedom, but a *proper use* of freedom to do what is best "for the other" in a given situation. "What is best" is made clear in chapter 13 as *love* for "the other."

Defamation of character (v. 30; Greek *blasphēmoumai*) is thought to be at risk on the basis of inconsistent action, namely, eating meat on one occasion and not on another. Hence while the second rhetorical question might suggest that it would be simplest to follow the path that causes least difficulties for the self, Paul's reply substitutes what causes least difficulty for **the other**.

The final verses of this section (vv. 31-33; 11:1) set out the criteria for decision and action in an aphoristic, succinct, summarizing form. (1) The *highest positive* criterion is to **do it all for the glory of God** (v. 31b). (2) The *highest negative* criterion is to avoid doing damage (NIV, *"do not cause anyone to stumble"*), whether those under consideration include non-Christians (**both Jews** and **Gentiles**, v. 32a), or fellow Christians (**God's church**, v. 32b). (3) The *second positive* criterion is **to take account of all the interests of everyone** (v. 33a), having universal respect for the concerns and well-being of "others." (4) The second negative corollary is **not seeking any advantage of my own** (v. 33b). (5) The specific goal, or *final cause*, is **the good of the many, with a view to their salvation** (10:33c). (6) The *formal cause* arises from following the example of Paul, which he, in turn, derives from the way of **Christ** (11:1).

Take me as your pattern, as I take Christ for mine (v. 1) follows the NJB translation. However, the word **pattern** does not occur explicitly in the Greek. We use it because the Greek phrase *mimētai ginesthe* does not mean "be imitators" in the sense of *replication*. The phrase suggests that Paul's apostolic witness to Christ and to apostolic lifestyle should offer a **pattern** or broad *model* in terms of what he has just specified, namely, aiming at glorifying God, at avoiding damaging anyone, and at putting the interest of others before one's own. This is an acceptable model not because it is Paul's (cf. "Were you baptized into the name of Paul?" 1:13), but because Paul perceives it as Christ-like and therefore part of the apostolic witness *to Christ*.

This provides a major criticism of Elizabeth Castelli's suggestion that Paul is using, in effect, a paternalistic and manipulative strategy to impose his own ideals and interests onto his opponents in Corinth. She describes these verses as "presumptuous" (*Imitating Paul*, p. 113; also 89-138). Such a view turns Paul's argument upside down. For Paul does not force a single stereotypical strategy of action onto the church, but advocates what builds up the "other" and the whole church without regard to self-interest. Castelli's argument would violate the logic of 1:12-17, where she does not press the stance of the "Paul" group, but the very reverse. It would violate Paul's understanding of apostleship that Best and Crafton perceive as transparent "agency," not one of an authoritarian "agent." It would attribute to Paul a lifestyle and motivation wholly at variance with the proclamation of a crucified Christ (1:18-25). On the contrary, Paul can appeal to a publicly observable personal integrity that allows him to appeal to deeds that give backing to his words.

29. SUGGESTIONS FOR POSSIBLE REFLECTION ON 10:23–11:1

1. *On love for the other as a common theme in Jesus and Paul that demands our response:* A widespread but mistaken mythology seeks to drive a false wedge between Jesus and Paul. This ascribes a simple "love" ethics to Jesus and complex "doctrine" to Paul. In this section, however, Paul formulates a key axiom, "No one should seek his or her interests, but the well-being of the other" (v. 24). The whole argument of 8:1–14:40 revolves around this. It closely parallels the "golden rule" of Jesus that many take as summarizing the Sermon on the Mount: "Always treat others as you would like them to treat you" (AV/KJV, "Whatever ye would that other men should do to you . . . ," Matt. 7:12). Ways of reading of the New Testament that attempt to find a "second" or different gospel in Paul from that of Jesus are superficial and shallow. Does driving a wedge between Jesus and Paul provide a way of evading hearing God's voice through Scripture? Love for the other is at the heart of the gospel.

2. *On using the right criterion in reaching certain Christian judgments:* The goal of much Christian prayer and service is to "build up" (v. 23b) fellow Christians. Is the criterion that governs the answer to much Christian heart searching about decisions and conduct the same? Will this be "helpful" (v. 23a) to others? Paul gives this "objective" criterion priority over "inner" feelings about whether a course of action is that with which we may feel "comfortable." Do we too often rely on the more "subjective" criterion of feelings when these may be more fallible and individualistic? Do we rank more highly the well-being of others and the good of the whole?

3. *On whether a Christian can be overly scrupulous or overly earnest:* A fussy over-scrupulousness can sometimes raise needless complications, doubts, and

questionings that may become inward-looking distractions. When does a right sensitivity and moral integrity begin to degenerate into an obsessive overconcern to be "right" in every detail? Can such a concern become an obsession about the self? How does this relate to justification by grace? Paul invites a more relaxed freedom to rejoice in God's good gifts of creation (v. 26), rather than an inward-looking overearnestness that mars a more healthy outward-looking witness to Christ. Nietzsche and Foucault perceived Christians as obsessed with negation, "docility," and fussy mediocrity. Might we sometimes provide people with grounds for such a perception? Against this, Luther, Bonhoeffer, and Moltmann remind us of the importance of boldness, robustness, and saying "yes" to life (see Moltmann, *The Spirit of Life*).

4. *On grace at meals as one hallmark of a Christian home:* Christians eat "a meal with thanksgiving" (v. 30). The New Testament church continued the Jewish tradition of saying grace at meals. This might take the form of "blessing God" for the meal, often, although not always, with an allusion to Ps. 24:1, "The earth is the Lord's. . . ." This act of thanksgiving or blessing (usually blessing *God*) invoked God's presence at the family table and gave expression to thanksgiving for God's gifts. If this signals part of the identity of Christian institutions and Christian households, what part does this play for us? Does it provide a backbone for handing on the gospel to the next generation?

5. *On seeking not to overreact, and to respect two sides of a case:* Paul sets out case studies that illustrate his pastoral practice. He does *not* simply *confront* "the strong" in Corinth. He does not overreact. He concedes that they have a point with a "Yes, but. . . ." Those who are secure in themselves and in their theology have no need to thump the table and denounce all dissent. Paul *qualifies and redirects* their points by adding key tests for the applicability of their claims: Would it be "helpful" to apply what they advocate? Would it *build* others, or might it have *destructive* effects? In some situations what "the strong" advocate is acceptable: "Eat whatever is sold in the meat market without asking about it. . . ." For "the earth is the Lord's . . ." (vv. 25-26). *All* food is part of God's good creation. However, Paul adds, there is more to be said, and he leads his readers forward to appreciate both sides of the case.

6. *On integrity of life, thought, teaching, and lifestyle:* Perhaps the greatest challenge for Christian leaders and Christian ministers comes in 11:1 on Paul as

a model. Paul has integrity of life and thought, of word and deed. This enables him to offer not only his words but his life as a model for the church. However, this would be presumptuous if he were not able to add, in effect, *to the extent that I model Christ* (11:1). True, authentic, Christian and apostolic *witness* is to point to Christ not only through words but also through *life* and *lifestyle*. Christ is the model or paradigm case of living and dying *for others* (cf. v. 24). It is understandable and sometimes wise that often Christians hesitate to rush in with *words* about Christ (e.g., in their workplace) until they have been able to establish enough of their *lifestyle and lived-out values* through how they *act and relate to others* day by day. To "take Christ as my pattern" (v. 1b) involves the whole of life. What does all this suggest for our strategy of witness and our lifestyle?

VII. Mutual Respect in Matters of Public Worship (11:2–14:40)

A. *Mutual Respect and Self-Respect in Matters of Gender (11:2-16)*

2 I give you full credit for keeping me in mind unfailingly, and for continuing to hold fast to the traditions which I, in turn, handed on to you. 3 However, I want you to understand that while Christ is preeminent [or *head?* or *source?*] for man, man is foremost [or *head? source?*] in relation to woman, and God is preeminent [or *head? source?*] in relation to Christ. 4 Every man who prays or who utters prophetic speech with his head covered [possibly, *with long hair*] shames his head. 5 Every woman who prays or who utters prophetic speech with her head uncovered [less probably, *with long, loose, unbound hair*] shames her head, for it is one and the same thing as a woman whose head had been shaved. 6 For if a woman will not retain her head covering, let her have it cropped close to the head. If, however, to have it cropped close or to have it shaved off brings shame, let her retain her head covering. 7 For a man, for his part, ought not to have his head covered up since man is constituted in the image of God and [manifests] his glory. Woman, on the other hand, is the glory of a man. 8 For it is not the case that man came from woman, but woman was made out of man. 9 Further, man was not created on woman's account, but woman was created on account of man. 10 Because of this a woman ought to keep control of her head, on account of the angels. 11 Nevertheless, as those in the Lord, although woman is nothing apart from man; man is nothing apart from woman. 12 For just as woman had her origin from man, even so man derives his existence through woman; and

the source of everything is God. 13 Come to a decision for yourselves. Is it appropriate for a woman to conduct prayer to God without wearing a hood? [Just possibly, *with her hair unbound?*] 14 Does not even the very ordering of how things are teach you that long hair degrades a man, 15 while long hair is a woman's glory, because long hair is given as a covering? 16 If anyone is minded to be contentious, we ourselves have no such custom, nor do the churches of God.

This passage is not merely relative to a dated context in the ancient world, as if it had no further relevance. Throughout history the choice of attire and dress codes has carried a symbolic as well as a literal significance. In Roman society the wearing of hoods (or veils, or some parallel symbolic expression) marked a married woman as both "respectable" and deserving of respect. In this passage, moreover, Paul addresses *both* man *and* woman, not simply woman alone, in terms of a mutual and reciprocal respect each for the other gender, for the self (self-respect), and also for God, the focus of public worship. Nothing should distract worshipers from God or from holding others in respect on the basis of one group's intrusive social agenda. This theme of respect for those who are "other" featured in 8:1-13, continued to 11:1, and will continue to 14:40, especially in 13:1-13. It is a travesty of this serious passage to reduce it to a matter of "wearing hats," or to construe Paul's evenhanded theology of mutuality into supposed misogyny or patriarchalism.

In v. 2 Paul commends the church in Corinth for **continuing to hold fast to the traditions which I, in turn, handed on to you**. The English **continuing to hold** translates a continuous present in the Greek. It is not easy to decide whether the aspect of the tradition that Paul commends alludes to the shape of public worship in general, or more specifically to the role of women in speaking prophetic discourse in public. The contrast in v. 17, "I cannot continue my commendation," may suggest the latter.

Paul speaks of **every woman who prays or utters prophetic speech** . . . (v. 5). The setting is clearly that of *public* worship, where the two verbs *proseuchomai*, to *pray*, and *prophēteuō*, to *utter prophetic speech*, must mean respectively in this context *to lead in prayer* and *to articulate an applied pastoral message*, or *to preach* (on the meaning of **prophesy** [verb] and **"prophecy"** [noun] see below).

On the other hand, we cannot be certain to which aspect of **hold-**

ing the tradition Paul refers. The important point is that maintaining the common apostolic tradition *does matter.* The churches are not to wander off into "do it yourself" styles of doctrine and polity. This is a regular theme in this epistle, where Corinth was tempted to try to be "better" than the run-of-the-mill congregations in self-styled "spiritual" maturity. Paul does not oppose "contextual" theology (cf. 9:19-23), but he subordinates it to faithfulness to common apostolic tradition.

The adversative Greek *de,* translated **however,** at the beginning of v. 3, may reinforce the point that while men and women may pray and preach, this does *not* imply a uniform *sameness* between the genders. Men and women are equal, just as the Christian church worships God as Father, Son, and Holy Spirit without differentiation of status. Nevertheless, the characteristics, or qualities, and "position" ascribed to God the Father are not "the same" as those attributed to the Son: **God is preeminent** (or *head?* or *source?*) even **in relation to Christ** (v. 3c). There are analogous differentiations between man and woman: **man is foremost** [or *head? source?*] **in relation to woman** (v. 3b). Man's position also becomes relativized: **Christ is preeminent for man** (v. 3a).

The Greek word for which we retain three possible translations is *kephalē* (used three times in v. 3a, 3b, and 3c). I retain "source" as an alternative out of respect for those who have argued for this meaning. However, after a period when it was a fashionable and often favored translation (mainly the last quarter of the twentieth century), the weight of research today puts it in question, even in spite of the fact that Barrett, Fee, and Schrage advocate this view. The arguments are too complex to rehearse with fairness here, but I have expressed my doubts in *First Epistle,* pp. 811-23, with a special extended note on "source," "topmost," and "head." *Head* might be nearer, but this has unfortunate associations with domination and mastery in the modern world that fail to fit Paul's precise meaning. There is little doubt that the word is used *as a metaphor.* It transfers the notion of *"head" in physiology* not as the location of the brain, but as *"topmost"* or (by *synecdoche*) what *represents* the whole, as in *head of cattle.* The *kephalē* of a family is the one who represents its *"public face,"* the *representative contact person* who *focuses* its identity, but it does *not absorb or assimilate* its identity. It remains clear that love within the Godhead and love between man and woman exclude any competitiveness that might lead one to "impose" upon the other by sheer weight of authority. Only if or when there are divided interests would this notion come into play. If "otherness" (on *either* side) ever hints at difference of interest, then mutuality and reciprocity of respect for the "other" need to come to the fore (vv. 11-12).

The first two verses of the section (vv. 2-3) have set the stage for the main point. In vv. 4-5 Paul states his thesis: **Every man who prays or utters prophetic speech with his head covered** [or perhaps *with long, unbound hair*] **shames his head; every woman who prays or who utters prophetic speech with her head uncovered** [just conceivably, but much less likely, *with long, unbound hair*] **shames her head**. The two verses are symmetrical, addressing both **men** *and* **women**, except that Paul makes an addition in the second case: **it is one and the same thing as a woman whose head had been shaved.... To have it shaved off brings shame** (v. 6).

Paul uses the word **shames** (Greek *kataischynō*) or **brings shame** in three verses (vv. 4-6). The whole issue turns on *respect* or *lack of respect*. First, this respect, or its opposite, **shame**, includes *respect for God,* for the subject is public worship. Even **the angels** (v. 10) show awe, reverence, and respect in the presence of God, using their "wings" as a covering (Isa. 6:2). Second, what is worn or not worn serves as a mark of *respect to one's husband or wife* and to other members of the Christian congregation at worship. The verses on *mutuality* (vv. 7-12) underline this. Third, the choice of appropriate attire is no less a matter of *self-respect*. It is quite possible that in vv. 4-5 the phrases **shames his head** and **shames her head** reflect a deliberate wordplay: **head** is the physiological "topmost," the *representative feature of the self,* but it also alludes, in the case of a **man**, to **Christ**, and, in the case of a **woman**, to her **husband**.

It is often suggested that whereas the modern West may be more concerned with personal *guilt,* and freedom from guilt, both the Mediterranean world of the first century and perhaps many Eastern cultures today were (and are) more concerned with the contrast between public **shame** and public **honor** (see Malina, *The New Testament World,* pp. 28-62). Paul insists that **man** as well as **woman** can appear in public worship in a mode of attire that will reduce his self-respect and also (perhaps thereby) appear to demean **Christ** as his Lord and Head. Barrett argues that **head** refers here (v. 4) exclusively to Christ (*Commentary,* p. 250). But most writers perceive a wordplay: to demean the self is thereby to dishonor Christ. One writer compares attending an important formal dinner wearing a baseball cap. This is not simply a breach of good manners (see on 13:5, "love" is not "ill mannered . . ."); it is also attention seeking when all eyes should be elsewhere, not least on the glory of God.

With evenhandedness Paul now turns to the (married) **woman**. It is beyond doubt that in Roman society a **hood** (or perhaps a *veil*) was what a married woman was expected to wear *in public* as a mark of *respectability*. In the context of *public worship*, a married woman *without* a hood or veil was, in effect, inviting men to "size her up" as a woman who *might* be willing to be propositioned and "available." In an era in which marriages were usually for financial, social business or other advantage, and seldom for love, promiscuous relations were (unsurprisingly) relatively common (see the comments on 7:10-16). There can be little doubt that "free," gender-neutral attire would have attracted some Corinthian Christian women who wanted to break free from more conventional roles or constraints on the basis of gospel "freedom" and gender equality. To throw off gender restraints on the ground that both genders were equally free seemed legitimate from the viewpoint of women who had leadership qualities. Apparently Paul approved of their new freedom to lead in prayer, to utter prophetic speech, or to preach longer "prophetic" reflections in public worship. Such women understandably no longer wished to be categorized as "modest violets" among the more forceful married women of Roman society. So they showed off their "freedom" publicly (cf. Wire, *Corinthian Women Prophets*).

Paul does not criticize their exercising a leadership role. He is happy about their public praying and giving a prophetic message or discourse. But he is deeply unhappy about any assumption that gender equality means gender sameness or gender interchangeability, and even more unhappy about their indifference to the principle of respect and respectability. Most seriously of all, indifference to whether questionable dress code might *distract* others from attending to the things of God in public worship cannot be accepted among Christians.

On the contrary, Paul urges, this substitutes **shame** for respect, and attention seeking for mutuality. Aline Rousselle has shown convincingly that head coverings, veils, and hoods were significant symbolic expressions of self-awareness and attitudes toward others. She

173

writes, "Respectable women did nothing to draw attention to themselves. . . . A veil or hood constituted a warning: it signified that the wearer was a respectable woman . . ." ("Body Politics in Ancient Rome," p. 315; cf. pp. 296-337; similarly, Martin, *The Corinthian Body*, pp. 229-49). As Roland Barthes has well argued, we are entirely familiar with uses of dress codes and choices or format of furniture to signify moods, attitudes, and aspirations to perceptions of social class, rather than comfort or utility as such. In certain eras in the twentieth century beards and blue jeans have had a significance far beyond their more superficial functions (*Elements of Semiology* and *Mythologies*).

Thus in v. 6 Paul presses his point as a *reductio ad absurdum*, to call the bluff of the "liberated" addressees. If you really do not care about respect, self-respect, gender mutuality, and good manners, why not go the whole hog? Why not appear in public **shaved**? This would be an ultimate way of showing one's indifference to femininity, womanliness, or perceived respectability, for this symbolic abrogation of the feminine was often the lot of slaves or prostitutes. A number of cultural anthropologists argue that (1) *covered* hair (hair covered, e.g., with a veil or hood) was symbolic of *controlled* sexuality, in contrast to (2) *uncovered* hair as symbolic of *uncontrolled* sexuality and (3) a *shaven* head as symbolic of the *sexless*. But Paul's rhetoric may be rather more moderate: if you are indifferent to gender, why not adopt a cropped, boy-like style? At least this might answer the problem of appearing as an "available" woman.

Paul affirms the difference, complementarity, and mutuality of gender in vv. 7-12. Against some postmodern trends today, Paul insists that *gender difference* is more than a matter of mere physiology, and that this "more" is not merely the result of social construction or social convention. God *created* humankind male and female. The relation between the genders is neither one of domination and subservience, nor one of sameness and interchangeability. Judith Gundry-Volf makes some excellent comments on this passage. She observes, "Paul's main point is that men and women are both the *glory of another* and therefore both have an obligation not to cause shame to their 'heads.' . . . Since they are the glory of different persons . . . they must use different means to avoid shaming their 'heads'" ("Gender and Creation in 1 Cor. 11:2-16," p. 157).

For Paul, the "orderedness" of creation is important, just as "order" in the church is important (12:1–14:40). Even v. 10, **on account of the angels**, serves to underline this. Every "order" of created being has its way of showing reverence to God and of performing its God-given role, and **the angels** play their part in this. If **angels** are not to step over their boundaries, who are we to throw off such constraints? The principle of mutuality and reciprocity is well expressed in v. 11: **woman is nothing apart from man; man is nothing apart from woman.** In other words, **man** can be truly *man* only if he can be so in relation to woman *as truly "woman"*; **woman** can be truly *woman* only if she can be so in relation to man as truly *"man."*

This sheds light on Paul's appeal to the parallel or analogy between **man** and **woman**, and **God** and **Christ** (vv. 3, 7, 12). It is as if God is more "God" in relation to *Christ;* Christ is more "Christ" in relation to *God. The* very notion of *self-identity depends upon* how *we relate to* others. But this is a *theological* truth derived from how God has created humankind to reflect his own nature as his "**image**." It is not merely a matter of human sociology. Stanley Grenz explores this "relational" condition for selfhood and for self-identity further in *The Social God and the Relational Self.* He writes, "Mutual help is an essential part of human existence. . . . Sexuality is the dynamic that forms the basis of the uniquely human drive toward bonding. . . . [It reflects] incompleteness . . . and wholeness" (pp. 277-80).

The gender differentiation that is a condition for human identity as **man** and **woman** therefore finds different visible, public, symbolic expression in different ways of exhibiting *respect* for God, for "the other," and for the self (as self-respect or respectability) in public worship. Yet Paul insists no less that gender difference nurtures *mutual* respect, not domination on one side or manipulation on the other. *Difference* undermines competitiveness and serves mutuality. The relationship is "ordered" and "controlled."

Traditionally most interpreters have agreed from the third or fourth century until today that the outward expressing of the self constitutes, in v. 10, a *mark, sign, or symbol* of *authority* or *control*. But is the "authority" of v. 10 that which a **woman** possesses, or that which someone else (usually her husband) has over her? In 1964 Morna Hooker proposed the former, namely, that to wear a *veil* or *hood* constituted a sign of her empowerment or authority to prophesy. She writes, "The head covering . . . also serves as a sign of the *exousia* [Greek for authority, right, or control] which is given . . . — authority in prayer and prophecy" ("Authority on Her Head").

The plausibility of this proposal relates in part to the following phrase, **on account of the angels**. It is conceivable that the flow of thought alludes to the status of angels as beings commissioned to serve with authority and to speak on behalf of God. In this case the connection may also be with Isa. 6:2, that these empowered messengers "covered" themselves in God's presence with something like "wings." In the early church the opposite view was broadly held. Chrysostom insisted that "covering" is a mark of subjection. On the other hand, T. C. Edwards anticipated Morna Hooker's proposal in the nineteenth century (*Commentary*, p. 277), followed by Ramsey (1907) and by Allo (1956). Allo views the "authority" as the authority of the woman prophets *against* evil angels. This in part reflects Tertullian's view in the third century (*Against Marcion* 5.8). Nevertheless, the context is governed by the need for reverence and respect, as demonstrated by the awe and reverence of the angels in Isaiah 6. Paul approved of women leading in prayer and pastorally applied discourse, but only with the proviso that it has nothing to do with an agenda of self-assertive "liberalism" and does not violate established norms of courtesy, respect, reverence, respectability, and recognition of gender differentiation. One recent writer, Jorunn Økland, adopts an entirely different interpretation from that proposed here. Against any notion of mutuality she urges that "Paul veers between . . . gender hierarchies . . . and the silent subsumption of female under all-male categories" (p. 222). Paul uses "body of Christ" to denote a same-sex, all-male "church." In my view this misses the continuous thread that runs through from 7:2 to 14:40 on respect for "the other," which reaches its peak in chater 13.

Once again Paul invites the addressees to **come to a decision for yourselves** (v. 13a), as he did in 10:15, **judge for yourselves**. The use of the aorist in Greek confirms the use of the Greek verb *krinō* to mean *to reach a decision* and not to go on vacillating. Paul throws the ball into their court in order to avoid their drawing the mistaken inference that after rehearsing axioms drawn from creation and the will of God it all turns on a dubious appeal to "conscience" with an even more dubious appeal to "nature" (Greek *physis*, v. 14). Paul has already declared that *conscience* or *self-awareness* can be fallible, even if it cannot be ignored. The Greek *physis* need not always denote *nature*. In my larger commentary on the Greek text I have argued that the nearest English parallel is probably **the ordering of how things are** (Thiselton, *First Epistle,* pp. 844-48).

Different understandings of the word persist. Chrysostom, Calvin, and Schrage think that it refers chiefly to the prevailing customs of society. Hofius views it as denoting a physical reality behind the ordering of the world. Bengel and Meyer believe that it denotes an intuitive sense of what is fitting. The Old Testament does not speak of "nature" in the sense in which Stoic philosophers use the term. Without doubt, respectable, thoughtful Roman society *did* believe in gender differentiation, for whatever reason. Here, it seems, after Paul has laid proper foundations for his argument, he ends with a commonsense, practical appeal: Do you want the church to appear as those who have no respect at all for norms that invite respect in society at large? It is one thing for a woman to share with men in the ministry of prayer and preaching. It is quite another thing to substitute "sameness" for mutuality, reciprocity, and an ethos for respect and respectability. Judith Gundry-Volf helpfully identifies no fewer than three distinct foci of Paul's concerns: (1) the order of creation, (2) custom and propriety, and (3) eschatology or the gospel ("Gender and Creation").

30. Suggestions for Possible Reflection on 11:2-16

1. *On whether or when accepted dress codes matter:* It might be reasonable to think that choice of attire is entirely a matter of personal preference. This may often be the case, but not when a person is fulfilling a key role in public worship such as leading in prayer or prophetic preaching (vv. 4-5). Our choice of clothes or dress code often says something about how we wish others to perceive us. It serves unavoidably to indicate an aspect of our self-identity in public contexts. In public worship it may help or hinder the gospel, and 11:2-16 anticipates the principle expounded in chapter 13: "Love does not behave with ill-mannered impropriety, is not preoccupied with the interests of the self" (13:5).

2. *On the apostolic traditions of the church and the relativity of local variations: Holding fast* to apostolic and scriptural traditions remains part of the identity of a local church, as it is of the wider church as a whole. When are local churches free to make up their own rules? What happens if they do this in such a way as to become seriously out of step with mainline apostolic tra-

dition, even though traditions develop (11:2)? What is the difference between legitimate innovation or sensitivity to local context, and illegitimate deviation?

3. *On the difference between gender equality and gender sameness:* In matters of gender, equality is arguably one thing; *sameness* is arguably another. But can this argument become manipulative, to erode away "equality" on one side, or on the other side to compromise "difference"? Mutual respect may be enhanced by an acceptance of difference in the light of God's way of *ordering* creation, that is, giving it a structure with boundaries. Paul calls the bluff of extremists: if you view gender as a handicap or source of resentment, why not have your hair "cropped close" like a boy, or "shaved off" like a slave?

4. *On not distracting attention from God in public worship:* Today many attention-seeking forms of behavior or thoughtless obtrusions of speech or manner may distract others from attending to God. What examples come to mind? Are long domestic notices a help or a distraction? How can infants be warmly welcomed without their becoming causes of distraction for some? Can a style of attire distract others from focusing upon God in public worship today? Just as in 8:1–11:2, Paul insists that Christians should be concerned about the effect of our actions on the thought processes and even possible temptations *of others* rather than about the status of *one's own*.

5. *On the role of gender and sexuality as part of "being human" in God's created order:* Authentic gender characteristics help "the other" to be more "themselves." "Woman is nothing apart from man; man is nothing apart from woman" (v. 11). Can we *be* what God has made us and wills us to be if we cannot relate to a genuine "other"? Paul implies that this principle applies even to *God* in relation to *Christ*, and to *Christ* in relation to *God*. Christ's ministry involves witness *to God*; God's work involves the empowerment and vindication *of the Son*. Hence complementarity and mutuality in relationships is not an optional or marginal issue. It belongs to the very fabric of reality as God wills it to be. Do we sufficiently value the "otherness" of others (including the other sex) to make us more *ourselves*? Or do we diminish ourselves by trying to make everyone else like us?

6. *On whether we are fair about Paul's attitude to women:* Do we perceive Paul as a misogynist? For Paul, from chapter 7 onward everything turns on mutuality. He addresses *both men and women* in this chapter about attire; he says that while "woman was made out of man" (i.e., in the Genesis accounts of

the "ordering" of creation, v. 9), all the same "man derives his existence through woman" (i.e., through his being born into the world v. 12). F. F. Bruce observes that his alleged misogyny is "incredible. . . . He treated women as persons: we recall his commendation of Phoebe . . . his appreciation of Euodia and Syntyche, who worked side by side with him in the gospel. . . . Priscilla and Aquila risked their lives for him" (Rom. 16:1-2, 4; Phil. 4:2-3; Bruce, *Paul,* p. 457). Why would Priscilla risk her life for him if he consistently demeaned women? His view of intimacy in marriage as involving *mutual* pleasure (1 Cor. 7:4-5) is in advance of his times.

7. On respect as a key feature of love for "the other" in Jesus and Paul: Respect for the "other" is the keynote of this passage: for God, for fellow Christians at worship, for the Roman world as it perceives Christians, and not least for the self in terms of self-respect. What aspects of the ministry of Jesus does this reflect? How did Jesus treat outcasts and the despised? The Prodigal Son in the world of the parable (Luke 15:22) receives back a robe, sandals, and a ring as marks of dignity and respect. Genuine respect nurtures and supports *love* (13:4-7), which is the desire for the well-being of "the other." Why does love not despise "respectability"? This positive effect of mutual respect is not only common to Jesus and Paul; it is also a matter of commonsense reflection: "Come to a decision for yourselves" (v. 13).

B. The Focus of the Lord's Supper Not to Be Undermined (11:17-34)

17 Now in giving these directives I cannot continue my commendation because the meetings you hold as a church do more harm than good. 18 First of all, I am given to understand that when you meet together as an assembled church splits occur among you, and to some extent I believe it. 19 For "dissensions are unavoidable," some of you claim, in order that those who are tried and true among you may be visibly revealed. 20 Accordingly, when you meet together in the same place, your meeting does not amount to an eating of the Lord's Supper; 21 for at the time of eating each individual devours his or her own meal: one *actually* goes hungry; another is *even* drunk! 22 Surely it cannot be that you have no homes of your own for your eating and drinking, can it? Or do you show contempt for the church which is God's, and put to shame those who have nothing? What am I to say to you? Am I to congratulate you? On this matter I cannot give my approval. 23 For, as for me, I received a tradition from the Lord which I have handed on to

you, namely, that the Lord Jesus, in the night on which he was handed over, 24 took bread and gave thanks; he broke the loaf and said, "This is my body, which is for you. Do this in remembrance of me." 25 In the same way, with reference to the cup after supper, he said, "This cup is the new covenant in my blood. Whenever you drink it, do this in remembrance of me." 26 For as many times as you eat this bread and drink the cup, it is the death of the Lord that you are proclaiming, until he comes. 27 Consequently, whoever eats the bread or drinks the cup of the Lord in a way that is not fitting will be held accountable for so treating the body and blood of the Lord. 28 On the contrary, a person should examine his or her own genuineness, and only in this way eat from the loaf and drink from the cup. 29 For all who eat and drink eat and drink judgment on themselves if they do not recognize what characterizes the body as different. 30 It is for this reason that many among you are suffering weakness and ill health, and a good number have died. 31 If, however, we recognize what characterizes us as Christian believers, we should not fall under judgment; but if we are judged by the Lord, we are disciplined by the Lord so that we do not become condemned along with the world. 33 So then, dear fellow Christians, when you gather together for the meal, wait for one another. 34 If any of you is hungry, let that person eat at home, so that when you gather together it will not be to fall under judgment. With regard to the remaining matters, I will set them in order when I come.

In contrast to the general ordering of public worship in which women as well as men play a role (11:2-16) Paul **cannot continue** [his] **commendation** of the conduct and ordering of the Lord's Supper in Corinth (v. 17a). The major cause of concern parallels the problem of the **splits** in 1:10-12, where Paul uses the same Greek word *(schisma)*. These have the effect of so undermining the very focus and purpose of the Lord's Supper that **the meetings you hold as a church do more harm than good** (v. 17b).

In the following five verses (vv. 18-22) Paul unfolds the nature of these **splits** (v. 18). It emerges that these **splits** owe their origins largely to factors arising from wealth, the use of houses for worship, and social status (vv. 20-22). This may well reflect differences from the splits of 1:10-12, since those in 1:10-12 are clearly not doctrinal ones (see on 1:10-12). The same social division lay behind the manipulative strategy of the Christian who had enough wealth and social or business influence to take a fellow Christian to a civil tribunal with the expectation of winning (6:1-8).

Clearly those who owned houses large enough to enable them to "host" meetings of the church for the Lord's Supper were among the wealthy and influential. They virtually assumed the role of "patrons," and other church members could hardly avoid being put into the position of "guests," whom the style of arrangements sometimes risked categorizing into different classes of guests who might dine in different areas of the house.

The phrase "**dissensions are unavoidable**" (v. 19) is a source of difficulty. Does Paul say this seriously or ironically, or is it a citation from a saying that circulated in Corinth to justify divisions? It may be that Paul acknowledges the inevitability of different groups of like-minded people within the church, but adds that this can also provide a redemptive dimension by way of sifting out the **tried and true** within the church, namely, those who refuse to take sides or promote division. Gordon Fee calls this "one of the true puzzles in the letter" (*First Epistle*, p. 538). Richard Hays understands Paul to say that it is "presumably necessary in the divine plan" (*First Corinthians*, p. 195). R. A. Horsley applies the term directly to social categorization: there must be "discrimination" between more distinguished guests (*1 Corinthians*, p. 159). It seems most probable that the phrase expresses an *excuse* or pretext made by householders in Corinth for the way in which the Lord's Supper was conducted, for it is likely that complaints had been made by the poor about the outrageous effects described in vv. 20-22, and corroborated in v. 33.

Paul's position reveals the difficulties that face any minister, pastor, or church leader. On gender in 11:2-16 he has argued that equality is not sameness, but does involve *difference*. But almost any argument of this kind can be turned back onto the speaker: "Oh well," someone might reply, "our differences of arrangements do not signify lack of 'equality' either; merely differences!" Hence Paul portrays in detail what the "Supper" experience would feel like for Christians of different social class and status (vv. 20-22). It *does* involve being made to feel "second class."

For readers today it is essential to understand the background of Roman dining conventions, as well as the effects caused by the size and arrangement of rooms within a large Roman villa of the day. Archaeologists have demonstrated the latter with reference to a Corinthian villa at Anaploga on the outskirts of the city, dated between A.D. 50 and A.D. 75. (For a description of the villa see J. Wiseman, "Corinth and Rome I; 228 B.C.-A.D. 267," pp. 438-548; also described in J. Murphy-O'Connor, *St. Paul's Corinth*, 154-55, which includes a plan of the villa.)

The *triclinium* used by the host and favored guests covered an area of about 7.5 × 5.5 meters, or roughly 24 × 18 feet. This room would be furnished with couches at which these guests would recline. Hence up to nine or ten guests could normally be accommodated. However, a courtyard-hallway, or *atrium,* also served to accommodate "lesser" guests. It included at its center a pool for the collection of water, but with the absence of couches up to thirty guests might be accommodated here in an area of about 6 × 5 meters, or 20 × 16 feet. The less esteemed guests, who often include servants or younger relatives of the special guests, would either sit or stand in what amounted to an "overflow" room. In the situation that Paul describes, latecomers and less-well-connected Christians would be likely to find that more highly honored guests already reclined in the *triclinium,* while the *atrium* felt like the place for second-class guests.*

Those who "hosted" the Lord's Supper in Corinth might well argue that they merely followed the accepted dining conventions of upper-middle-class Roman society. But Paul sees this as turning the **Lord's Supper** upside down. **The Supper of the Lord** (v. 20) is not simply a meal hosted by a wealthy Christian that could become an occasion for the host to determine who was more welcome and more honored than another. Paul declares indignantly, **Your meeting does not amount to an eating of the Lord's Supper** (v. 20), and earlier, **the meetings you hold as a church do more harm than good** (v. 17b). The conventional Roman dining arrangements help to explain what otherwise seems almost incredible: **one *actually* goes hungry; another is *even* drunk!** (v. 21).

Paul insists that **the supper of the Lord** is more than a mere

---

*Technical Note: David R. Hall (*The Unity of the Corinthian Correspondence* [London and New York: T&T Clark, 2003], pp. 64-74) agrees that the "have nots" arrive later than the "haves," but dissents from Theissen's view that the division was based mainly on difference of social class. He denies that v. 22 describes the cause of the division (p. 69). He questions the theory of different menus, even though Roman historians allude to the social qualifications required for "reclining" in some households. Some record that often hosts provided different qualities of food and wine for the *triclinium* and the *atrium.* Pliny the Younger records that the "the best dishes" were served in the *triclinium* to the "top" guests, while "the rest of the company" might receive only "cheap scraps." Sometimes there were up to three "grades" of wine that corresponded to the social standing of the guests. It is difficult, however, to conclude that this background is not entirely relevant.

"meal together"; **Surely it cannot be that you have no homes of your own for eating and drinking, can it?** (v. 22a). The present "ordering" of the so-called **Lord's Supper** is a travesty that **puts to shame those who have nothing** (v. 22b), that is, makes them experience public **shame** in contrast to *honor* (on the role of honor and shame in Roman and Corinthian culture, see above). Traditionally commentators have associated **those who have nothing** with slaves who arrive at the meal after some "go ahead" (v. 21b) with their own meal, although Bruce Winter argues that the word translated "goes ahead" in NRSV, NIV and NJB (variant) should be understood to mean *"greedily devours"* (cf. REB, *takes his own supper;* Winter, "The Lord's Supper at Corinth," pp. 73-82).

The word translated **supper** (Greek *deipnon*) primarily denotes the main meal of the day, without any necessary reference to timing. In this respect, like the English *dinner* it usually refers to evening dinner where the term is used in its traditional sense, but it can denote a different timing in such contexts as "Christmas dinner," "Sunday dinner," or "school dinner." In other words, it denotes the importance of the occasion rather than a time. Paul insists that when it is **the Lord's Supper**, the dynamics of this meal are determined *not* by the household, the host, or favored guests, but by *apostolic tradition* and by *scriptural and ecclesial* arrangements (v. 22b).

The tone moves from negative to positive in vv. 23-26. The *positive* way forward is to heed the *dominical* and *apostolic tradition* concerning **the Lord's Supper** that Paul **received from the Lord** and **handed on** to the church. The words translated **received** and **handed on** found together in this way (Greek *paralambanō . . . paradidōmi*) denote the transmission of a living *tradition.* Hence the phrase **from the Lord** refers to the origins of this tradition as coming from Christ himself through the earliest apostles as a pre-Pauline tradition that Paul then **received** and **handed on**. The content of this tradition (cf. Latin *traditio*, a handing over, handing on) begins "**the Lord Jesus, in the night on which he was handed over, took bread. . . .**" There is almost a wordplay on the Greek for **handed on** *(paredidoto)* with *handed over.* The Greek here means either *betrayed* (in a narrower, more specific sense) or **handed over** *(to death)* in a broader sense.

The *historical anchorage* of the words of the institution of the Lord's Supper remains central to the apostolic pre-Pauline and Pauline tradition. This historical context, together with the actual words of Jesus cited in the tradition, places the institution firmly in the context of the Last Supper as a new Passover meal. Whatever the technicalities of holding together the dating to the Last Supper in the first three Gospels with a date in John, it was clearly a *Passover meal* for Jesus and his disciples, and the words of Institution should be understood in this context.

The central act of the institution is the breaking of bread. . . . Jesus **took bread . . . he broke the loaf** . . . (vv. 23b-24). The Greek translated **gave thanks** *(eucharistēsas)* gives rise to the widely used term *the Eucharist* although Paul uses the term **the Lord's Supper** here, and in 10:16 he calls it *Communion* (Greek *koinōnia*). Arguably, all three titles are "biblical," although strictly **Lord's Supper** seems to be the most usual term in Corinth and for Paul.

Giving thanks reflects both the custom of Jesus and Christians in thanking God for a meal in the sense of "saying grace," and also of *blessing God* for the cups of wine in the Passover liturgy in early Judaism. Versions that insert *it* after "blessed" in the Gospel accounts are misleading, for even where the object of blessing is absent from the Greek, the *blessing* in this context blesses **God**, not the food, as an act of **thanksgiving**.

If breaking the bread is the central *act* of the Lord's Supper (also cited in 10:16-17), the central *words* are: "**This is my body, which is for you. Do this in remembrance of me. . . . This cup is the new covenant in my blood . . . do this in remembrance of me**" (vv. 24-25). Almost as important in this context and for Christian theology are Paul's explanatory words, **As many times as you eat this bread and drink the cup, it is the death of the Lord that you are proclaiming, until he comes** (v. 26).

The connection between the words of Jesus and the Pauline explanation of their meaning emerges most clearly within the framework of the Passover and the Passover meal. In first-century and second-century Jewish practice, each action held highly symbolic meaning as a "memory" and almost a reenactment of the redemptive experience of the Passover, as described in Exodus 12. The *Mishnah* sets out an "order" or liturgy (the Passover *Seder*) in which the participants, in effect, "relive" the drama of redemption from bondage in Egypt. They recite and celebrate the history of God's saving acts (Deut. 26:5), focusing on the living, symbolic meaning of the unleavened bread as representing the event of redemption. The bitter herbs represented embittered lives in bondage awaiting divine deliverance. Thus, in every generation a man must so regard himself as if he in person came forth out of Egypt (*Mishnah Pesharim* 10:5). In other words, as the Passover meal focused on the redemptive events of the Passover, the words of recital and symbolic action projected a "world" in which participants traveled as it were in time, to be "there" in the redemptive events that took place.

In place of "This is the bread of affliction that your fathers ate . . . ," Jesus declared, "**This is my body, which is for you**" (v. 24). This "meal" was to be repeated, not to celebrate and to relive the events of the Exodus Passover, but "**in remembrance of me**" (v. 24b). The cup taken after supper (v. 25a) represented "**the new covenant in my blood**" (v. 25b). The logical force of "**this is my body**" is determined by the parallel *"reliving" and sharing in* the event in which "this *is* the bread of affliction. . . ." It is not an "**is**" of total identity, but denotes a "living through" that entails more than mere semantic representation. The words of the Black spiritual, "Were you *'there'* when they crucified my Lord?" well conveys these dynamics of *participatory involvement.*

Paul brings this to an incisive focus in his own explanation of the meaning of these words and actions: **For as many times as you eat this bread and drink the cup, it is the death of the Lord that you are proclaiming, until he comes** (v. 26). Each participant declares, proclaims, or preaches in the breaking of bread that *"Christ died,"* and in eating the bread and drinking from the cup that "Christ died *for me*"; I *appropriate* his death *for me;* I "take" Christ as "mine," even as I take and receive broken bread and wine poured out.

There are some variant manuscript readings in the Greek text, but these need not detain us here. I address these and certain differences of interpretation in *First Epistle,* pp. 846-55 and 866-94. These pages include an extended note on **in remembrance of me** (pp. 878-82). **Remembrance of me** (vv. 24-25) denotes more than merely mental recollection, but less than any notion of "repeating" the once-for-all death of Christ. Some scholars (e.g., J. Jeremias) claim that the phrase alludes to *God's* "remembering." But while there are examples in the Old Testament and in Christian prayers today that concern God's "remembering," this is not what the context and syntax suggest. For Christian believers who participate in appropriating the bread and the cup **in remembrance** of Christ's covenantal death and shed blood, the

remembrance is a dramatic *involvement* or *actualization* of placing ourselves *"there"* at the foot of the cross, just as to eat the Passover was not simply to think about it but to be *"there"* as one who *took part in* the remembered events. In this sense Christian believers **proclaim** the death of Christ as (a) an *event*; and (b) an event *"for me"* that involves *me*.

The phrase "**This cup is the new covenant in my blood**" (v. 25) underlines all of this. In Old Testament enactments of the covenant-making ceremony, blood might be sprinkled or splashed on each party of the covenant. Each covenant participant *pledges* an involvement in, and commitment to, the covenant terms and promises. Hence, while Israel's neighbors in the ancient world perceived themselves as always at the mercy of unpredictable divine actions (as Eichrodt expresses it), with the covenant God of Israel believers or worshipers *knew where they stood*. God in sovereign generosity pledges himself freely to limit his range of actions by committing himself to known promises of grace to Israel; likewise Israel was required to respond with commitments and pledges of her own. The explicit description of the shed blood of Jesus Christ in this context as **the new covenant in my blood** demands, on one side, a serious pledge to all that the cross involves, but on the other side a full assurance of faith that follows from taking God at his word and appropriating his promises.

Until he comes looks forward to the final coming of Christ in glory. Some (again, e.g., J. Jeremias) have argued that the very observance of the Lord's Supper somehow "brings forward" the time of this coming. But this is not Paul's thought. Pledges, promises, and covenantal *signs* give assurance of faith precisely for the period when believers live *by faith* and are in need of such assurances and tokens. When the *reality* comes to pass, *signs* of this reality become redundant and obsolete. Heaven itself becomes the fulfillment of language about "the messianic banquet" to which the Lord's Supper points forward.

In vv. 27-34 Paul leaves the central exposition of the meaning and theology of the Lord's Supper (vv. 23-26) to resume his specific pastoral commentary on the mode of its observance in Corinth. The eating and drinking in Corinth have, at least on the part of many, become *unworthy* or **not fitting** (Greek *anaxiōs*) as a so-called sharing in the Lord's Supper. The divisiveness of the meal and the eating and drinking that verge on revelry for some and hunger for others are an offense against **the body and blood of the Lord** (v. 27)

Those who participate with this wrong attitude **will be held accountable for so treating the body and blood of the Lord**. Hence Paul urgently demands that **a person should examine his or her own genuineness** (v. 28). *Self-examination* is an appropriate way of testing whether a Christian approaches the Lord's Supper with a right attitude. The REB and NIV translate the word that is rendered here as **accountable** with the English word "guilty" (also AV/KJV, RV, and Barrett). NRSV and NJB, however (also with R. F. Collins), translate "answerable for." In a legal context the Greek word *(enochos)* denotes "liability," or (with the genitive, as here) "liable for." It is followed by the noun denoting the person against whom the offense has been committed. The issue is that of *answerability*.

This clearly coheres with the second half of the verse: some will **eat and drink judgment on themselves if they do not recognize what characterizes the body as different** (v. 29b). The Greek phrase at the end of the sentence is difficult to translate. *Mē diakrinōn to sōma* is often translated "not discerning the Lord's body." But without explanation this may have the effect of changing the nature of Paul's point.

(1) He does not appear to be saying that the sin in Corinth is failing to appreciate a sacramental change of substance from bread to the body of Christ here. The "discernment" is not of this nature, even though this view reflects a venerable tradition, including Augustine, Thomas Aquinas, and Peter Lombard.

(2) Others argue, on the contrary, that Paul's complaint concerns a failure to discern or to recognize *the church* as the body of Christ since, in effect, the "second-class citizens" at the Lord's Supper are treated with a degree of disrespect or even contempt. Bornkamm and Schweizer hold this view (Bornkamm, "Lord's Supper and Church in Paul," pp. 123-60). This might be supported with reference to 12:12-27, but this still lies ahead, and the **body** *(sōma)* to which Paul has hitherto referred in these verses (vv. 17-28) is the **body** of Christ of the words of the Institution (vv. 23-26). Neither of these two proposed interpretations adequately fits the context of the words that Paul has used up to this point.

(3) While he does not speak of some change in substance, Paul does indeed speak of the body of Christ "broken" upon the cross as of a different order of being and meaning from bread used merely to provide a meal for revelry or to satisfy physical hunger. What the participants **do not recognize** is what it means *to share in the death of Jesus "for*

you." W. Schrage, C. Wolff, and O. Hofius express some version of this view. In other words, they **do not recognize what characterizes the body as different.** This translation captures the mood of Paul's concern without seeking to specify any more narrowly than Paul does in which respect **the body** is **different** except in the general context of the death of Christ upon the cross, which is different from bread eaten for a dinner party in a social context. It is not recognizable as a proclamation of **the Lord's death** (v. 26).

Eating and drinking judgment (v. 29) appears to be explicated in terms of **suffering weakness and ill health,** and the fact that a **good number have died** (v. 30). Only one or two commentators try to claim that this language is metaphorical. Many ancient writers use the analogy of medicine, which, as Dale Martin observes, may equally cure or poison depending on its dosage and the situation (*The Corinthian Body,* p. 191). Most writers regard this as a judgment upon participating in the Lord's Supper that is not **genuine** or, in other words, unconnected with any witness to sharing in the cross of Christ and appropriating God's covenant promises. To pretend to be **proclaiming the death of the Lord** (v. 26) while merely wanting to secure a good meal in a wealthy household sinks to the level of *perjury.* The person concerned makes a solemn oath through sharing in these pledges and promises, while having no serious involvement in them.

The text describes what has occurred rather than specifying any particular means by which the effects were brought about. A guilty realization of claiming to "belong" while not belonging may have been a contributory factor to an inner malaise, but it is hardly an exhaustive explanation. Paul portrays the effects as those of **judgment,** although sometimes this may be self-imposed. Moule brings this judgment into a wider context of conviction of sin by the Holy Spirit and the *anathema* language of 12:3 and 16:22 ("The Judgment Theme in the Sacraments," pp. 464-81).

The positive, constructive corollary finds expression in vv. 31-32. **If we recognize what characterizes us as Christian believers** reflects the translation of the last clause of v. 29, except that whereas v. 29b concerns **recognizing** or *discerning* **the body** (Greek *to sōma*), the present verse (v. 31) concerns **recognizing** or *discerning* **ourselves.** The verb remains the same *(diakrinō).* The repetition of the same semantic force and logic suggests that **recognizing what characterizes us as Christians** is parallel with **recognizing what is different about the body**. Both distinguish what gives something or someone its (or their) proper identity as what they are. Moule explains that it depends on a person's response to the situation whether the **judgment** proves to be remedial or "plunges him [or her] further into a condition of fatal self-concern" (p. 481). Moule and Alan Richardson perceive association with the death of Christ in baptism and in the Lord's Supper as a "pleading guilty," which is followed by being placed in a right relation with God through Christ.

It is difficult to reproduce in English the wordplay conveyed by the Greek. The Greek verb *krinein*, "to judge," is interdispersed with *diakrinein*, "to differentiate, to distinguish a difference." Paul says something like: *We judge ourselves aright . . . and will not be judged* (at the last judgment). Such judgment performs part of the role of *being trained*, or being **disciplined** (v. 32). An awareness of Christian "difference" or distinctiveness now prepares the way for the ultimate declaring of "differences" at the last judgment, whereby Christian believers are **not . . . condemned along with the world** (v. 32b).

Unfortunately, even the last two verses of the chapter, by way of summary, contain the possibility of two different translations. The major English versions (NRSV, REB, NIV, NJB, with Collins and AV/KJV) translate the Greek verb *ekdechesthe* as **wait for one another**. But in Rom. 15:7 Paul uses the same verb to mean "welcome one another." The former translation, which fits the context better and is more likely, refers specifically to the wealthier or more favored "haves" beginning the meal before the arrival of the "have nots" who receive only the leavings. Nevertheless, the second alternative also applies. Each believer must receive the same unqualified welcome, as Paul enjoins in Rom. 15:7 of Jewish and Gentile Christians.

Paul anticipates the lame counterreply: But why cannot we start if we are hungry? He indignantly responds: If the "meal" is to satisfy physical hunger, eat at home! That is not the purpose of the Lord's Supper. The final verse (v. 34) hints that other respects also require attention. But Paul does not want to obscure the main issue by details that can wait until later. The verb that he uses is important in an era when even some Christians favor the postmodern preference for chaos as a sign of rejecting form and structure. Paul will **set in order** the liturgical practices of Corinth. This "orderedness" reflects the first half of the chapter (cf. 11:2, 3, and 16).

31. SUGGESTIONS FOR POSSIBLE REFLECTION ON 11:17-34

1. *On whether an act of Christian worship can defeat its own purpose:* This section holds out the unsettling example of a Christian worship event that so deviates from its true nature that it no longer counts as the act of worship that goes by its name. Might there be Bible studies, prayer meetings, expositions, or even celebrations of the Lord's Supper in which self-centered or manipulative purposes arise to *betray* or to *undermine* the very event that it claims to be? Paul exclaims: "Your meetings do more harm than good!" (NIV, v. 17b). "It is not the Lord's Supper you eat" (v. 20). Can prayer or Holy Communion ever become so formal and hollow that merely "going through the motions" becomes a routine causing more harm than good? Can "saying prayers" become a substitute for truly praying?

2. *On letting certain Christians feel second class:* The world of the twenty-first century may not replicate Roman dining conventions, with first-class and second-class locations for food and drink. But what more subtle ways might there be of making some Christians feel second class? Any grouping that invites some Christians to feel that a segment *within* the community of believers divides the church between "us" and "them" starts down the slope that damaged Corinth. Are there physical, geographical, sociological, or educational factors that, while innocent in themselves, unwittingly minister to a Christian class system? Might this lead supposedly "second class" Christians to say, "I do not belong here" (12:15)?

3. *On the need for both rich and poor within the church:* The church needs both its wealthier members (sometimes for such facilities as houses large enough for church meetings) and poorer members to remind Christians of their lack of self-sufficiency (12:12-27). But are there dangers for both if a Christian believer becomes a "host" to others in the church, with consequent temptations to assume a leadership role "above" others? Patronage was a characteristic of Roman society. But does the patron-client relation have any place within the Christian church?

4. *On worship as celebration:* Two opposite extremes or deviations sometimes damage the church. On one side it is easy to forget that worship in the Bible, especially in the Psalms, is often a celebration. On the other side we can let celebration of God sink to self-congratulation and mutual entertainment, forgetting *whom and what* we celebrate. Paul exclaims: Have you

not houses to eat and drink in? (v. 22). Which of these two extremes is a greater threat to churches we know?

5. *On the dangers of empty or false witness:* Unworthy or inappropriate participation is not merely a mistake in church order; such action may result in "**eating and drinking judgment**" for the one who participates. It is a terrible mistake to regard the Lord's Supper simply as a "welcome" service, thereby encouraging less-than-serious, committed participation in it. The admission of young children poses a difficult dilemma: to turn away young children may seem to make them "second class"; to encourage too readily those who are not ready for serious commitment may risk possible damage.

6. *On the whole congregation's vocation to preach and to proclaim:* The Lord's Supper provides an opportunity for every committed Christian to bear witness and to preach a short sermon. "As many times as you eat this bread and drink the cup, you proclaim the Lord's death" (v. 26). Bread broken speaks of the reality of Christ's death; wine poured out, of his shed blood. To take and to eat, and to drink, proclaims, "Christ died *for me;* I am his, and he is mine." Do we see participation in the Lord's Supper as a confession of faith (like saying the creed), a proclamation (like preaching the sermon), and a witness (like giving our personal testimony)?

C. A Unity and Variety of Gifts for Building Up the Church (12:1-31)

1. Christ-Centered Criteria for "What Comes from the Spirit" (12:1-3)

1 Now about "what comes from the Spirit," my dear Christian family, I do not want you to remain without knowledge. 2 You know that when you were pagans, you used to be carried away to idols that were incapable of speech. 3 Therefore I am imparting to you this "knowledge," that no one who is speaking through the agency of the Spirit of God says, "Jesus grants a curse [or *is cursed*]." And no one is able to declare, "Jesus is Lord," except through the agency of the Holy Spirit.

Paul continues to redefine "spiritual" as "**what comes from the Spirit**" (v. 1). He had begun the process in 2:6-16 and especially in 3:1-4. To many of the Christians in Corinth, to be regarded as "spiritual" constituted a claim to high status within the community (see Martin, *Corinthian Body*, pp. 87-105, and Hall, *Unity*, pp. 163-70). Hall speaks of "two gospels" and "a different Spirit" (p. 163). In 3:1 Paul had declared that where there was competitive jealousy and strife, those involved could not be called "spiritual." This forms the background to the meaning of 12:1-3.

Should the opening phrase of this chapter (12:1) be translated *concerning spiritual persons* (Weiss, Blomberg, Ellis, and Wire) or *concerning spiritual gifts* (Conzelmann, Senft, REB, NRSV, NIV, NJB)? The Greek uses an adjective with the definite article: *spiritual, tōn pneumatikōn* (in the form of a genitive plural), so this could strictly be either masculine (persons) or neuter (things). Most grammarians and commentators argue that neuter is more probable, but Barrett insists that there is no "objective ground for a decision" (*First Epistle*, p. 278). Early and medieval commentators remain divided on this question.

The important point to make is that while *spiritual* (people) or *spiritual* (gifts) represents the preferred term of the *Corinthians, Paul* decisively changes it to the Greek word *charismata*, "freely given gifts, given without merit and without strings." *Charismata cannot be a "high status" term*, he insists, since it comes as sheer *gift, without qualifications or deserving*. Yet Paul takes the term *tōn pneumatikōn* seriously enough to specify criteria for its application, first of all in 12:1-3. So, again, what does *Paul* mean by the term?

Paul uses it to denote **what comes from the Spirit**, for his own use of *pneumatikos* denotes *what pertains to the Holy Spirit, not "human spirituality."* This is decisive in 15:44, where he speaks of a "spiritual body" *(sōma pneumatikon)* as a mode of being characterized by the presence and activity of the Holy Spirit (Thiselton, *First Epistle*, pp. 1275-81, and Wright, *The Resurrection of the Son of God*, pp. 342-56, esp. p. 354). Hence the capacity to confess Jesus as Lord of life and thought (12:3) is a criterion of the activity of the Holy Spirit (by the Holy Spirit, v. 3b), not the criterion of human "spirituality" or the elitist status of "spiritual persons." Hall considers that here Corinth and Paul are so far apart that they each appeal "to a different Spirit" (p. 183).

Paul has already laid the groundwork for this argument in 2:10–3:4. The Holy Spirit *proceeds from God* (*to pneuma to ek tou Theou*, 2:12). "Spirituality" is not an immanent principle in humankind. Christlikeness (2:16) is the criterion of whether the Holy Spirit is actively at work in the Christian. In 12:1-3 Paul alludes by implication to pagan religions where claims to be "spiritual" differ from this in two radical ways. First, "spirituality" may be *self-induced.* Idols cannot be the source of "spirituality"; they are **incapable of speech** and cannot inspire (v. 2). Some writers view 14:4 as corroborating an allusion to self-induced spirituality: such spirituality merely produced narcissistic self-edification. This brings us to the second criterion. Second, where the Spirit is active, believers will confess Jesus as Lord and live out this Lordship of Jesus in ways that lead to constructive *building up* of others, not to their destruction or competitive denigration.

This prepares the way for Bruce Winter's exploration of the otherwise extremely difficult v. 3: **No one who speaking through the agency of the Spirit of God says, "Jesus [*is*] *cursed*,"** or (more probably) **"Jesus grants a curse."** This verse has attracted many attempts at an explanation. In my larger commentary I discussed twelve possibilities (*First Epistle,* pp. 917-27). The key to Winter's new interpretation is twofold. First, because the Greek contains no verb but simply has "Jesus-anathema" *(Anathema Iēsous),* the translation *need* not be (as in the twelve suggestions) "Jesus *is* a curse," or "*is* accursed"; it may be "Jesus *grants* a curse." Second, in recent years some twenty-seven ancient curse tablets made of lead have been unearthed in or around Corinth (fourteen on the slopes of Acrocorinth in the precincts of pagan temples), and these witness to the practice of appealing to pagan deities to "curse" rivals or competitors in business, love, litigation, or sport (Winter, "Religious Curses and Christian Vindictiveness, 1 Cor. 12–14").

Winter argues that the allusion to **when you were pagans, you used to be carried away to idols** (v. 2) refers not to some bogus "spirituality" of pagan religious frenzy or ecstasy, but to the religious world in which pagan worshipers sought the aid of their deities to gain advantage over rivals and competitors in various areas of life. This would offer a parallel to manipulative advantages in 6:1-8. Many years ago A. D. Nock drew attention to this practice in the so-called "Magical" Papyri.

Winter argues that within the setting of Corinth attitudes of jealousy and strife (cf. 3:1-3) might manifest themselves in explicit requests for the deity to set in motion a curse imposed upon those over whom the pagan worshiper sought to gain advantage. In the light of 3:1-3, 6:1-8, and other passages, it is plausible that some Christians claimed to be "spiritual people" at the same time as asking Jesus to impose some "curse" of this order against those who had earned their disfavor. Paul declares that this *contradicts* any claim that the Holy Spirit is manifest in their life. This cannot *build* or manifest Christ's *Lordship.*

This may well be the best explanation of 12:2-3, but it remains a strong hypothesis rather than an established fact. Hence we cannot simply write off more traditional approaches. Among these, (1) Oscar Cullmann argues for the importance of the confession of Jesus as Lord in a *persecution* setting. Jesus, rather than Caesar, is Lord. Christians may have suffered pressure to blaspheme the name of Jesus *as a sign of their renouncing their faith* (as the reference in *Martyrdom of Polycarp* 9:3 may indicate). (2) Some suggest that "Jesus is accursed" might have been uttered in a trancelike frenzy of *ecstatic "spirituality"* (M. Thrall, W. Schmithals, J. Weiss). This might appear farfetched except for psychiatric research on the effects of removing the "censor" in certain states of heightened consciousness. On the other hand, C. Forbes and others strongly reject this interpretation. (3) A variant of this view suggests that "spiritual" people rejected any reference to the *historical, earthly Jesus* in contrast to the risen, "spiritual" Christ. They had moved "beyond" the earthly Jesus. (4) W. C. van Unnik suggests that the allusion is to the atonement theology according to which Jesus bore the *"curse"* for human sin (Deut. 21:23; Gal. 3:13). The confession translated "Jesus is accursed" may on this basis express a belief that Christ's death was a sacrificial atonement, but it is significant here for what it omits, namely, it fails to extend such a faith to trust in the living Jesus Christ of the resurrection. Such a reduced, partial, truncated faith does not, this verse suggests, come from the Holy Spirit.

We have considered the four most plausible explanations of twelve or more that have been put forward, alongside Bruce Winter's recent illuminating restructuring of the sentence to make what is probably more convincing sense of these obscure words.

The second half of v. 3 expresses what many call the earliest Christian creed in clear terms: **No one is able to declare, "Jesus is Lord" except through the agency of the Holy Spirit.** If, as many claim, Paul regards this as a litmus test for what identifies or constitutes being a Christian, clearly this expresses more than a purely intellectual belief about the status of Jesus Christ as Lord. To confess Jesus as Lord *(kyrios)* involves the whole self in an *attitude* of trust, obedience, commitment, loyalty, and reverence to Jesus as the Lord who has the care of one's life.

What most clearly exhibits the cash currency of confessing Jesus as **Lord** is the speaker's acknowledgment that he or she is the *slave* of Jesus Christ. The Christian believer has been "bought with a price" (1 Cor. 6:20) in order to *belong* to Jesus. In the world of Paul's day, to acknowledge someone as Lord was either, in the case of the confession "Caesar is Lord," to express total allegiance, loyalty, and obedience, or, as in the case of allegiance to the "lord" of the household, to express the unqualified trust, dependence, and obedience of a slave who is *at the disposal of* the one *to whom he or she belongs.*

In the case of an insensitive or unscrupulous slave owner or "lord," this could bring disaster and misery. The slave was a mere "object" or "thing" (Latin *res*), the *property* of the master. Paul uses this language to depict slavery to sin and the law. However, sensitive, caring "lords" took *responsibility* for the *welfare* and *protection* of their slaves. *Belonging* to a "good" lord brought security and invited confident trust as the slave ceased to bear personal anxiety for that which his or her lord had taken into his own hands. The popular Christian song "Now I belong to Jesus; Jesus belongs to me" captures some of the daring boldness and trust that goes along with ceasing to carry the burden of self-care.

This freedom of "letting go of the self" in trust lies at the center of Paul's theology of grace and justification through faith, and relates closely to this dimension of confessing Jesus as Lord. Hence the heart of the gospel is "to preach Christ as Lord" (2 Cor. 4:5). Paul applies the word *kyrios,* **Lord,** some 220 times in his letters. The confession of Jesus as Lord occurs at the climax of some key arguments or reflections, for example, in Rom. 10:9; 14:9; 1 Cor. 8:5-6; Eph. 4:5; and Phil. 2:11. The acknowledgment of Jesus Christ as Lord does carry with it a belief about a state of affairs. God has enthroned him as Lord at the resurrection (Rom. 1:4) or his exaltation (Phil. 2:9-11). Nevertheless, the confession remains above all a *practical* and trustful expression of allegiance and "belonging" on the part of the Christian, who hands over to Jesus all anxieties about his or her sins, calling, assignment of tasks, failures, successes, and destiny. "If we live, we live *to the Lord;* if we die, we die *to the Lord;* so, whether we live or die we belong *to the Lord*" (Rom. 14:7). Bultmann rightly regards this verse as the one of the greatest affirmations of Christian freedom.

32. Suggestions for Possible Reflection on 12:1-3

1. *On claims to be regarded as a "person of the Spirit" and the criterion of Christ-likeness.* Many at Corinth too readily liked to be regarded by others as "spiritual." Paul has doubts about whether this reveals something less than genuine about them. The test case is whether their thought and life exhibit Christ as Lord. What does it mean to call Christ "Lord," or to call him "our" or "my" Lord? Why did the early church (and we today) regard the confession of faith "Jesus is Lord" the most succinct test of the claims to be a Christian in whom the Spirit of God is at work?

2. *On the difference between faith in Christ and magic:* If Winter's view of the "curse" verse is right, to use "prayer" to Jesus to put another person at a disadvantage exposes those who do this as being far from "spiritual," or even Christian. This reveals the key difference between faith and magic. Magic seeks *to control supernatural forces for the benefit of the self.* Faith places the self in the hands of God for *God's* will. Might we ever demean faith into a means for self-advantage? Can we conceive of examples when this occurs in religious contexts? In his resistance to his messianic temptations Jesus *accepted* the constraints and path of obedience that faith requires, placing himself in God's hands. Do Christians ever seek to usurp "control" from God?

3. *On confessing Jesus as Lord:* If we place ourselves wholly and without reserve in the hands of Jesus Christ, in what sense does this constrain us, and in what sense does it liberate us? From what does it liberate us? In this confession of faith, can we distinguish between (a) a state of affairs that is true whether the world believes it or not; and (b) a practical attitude on the part of ourselves as believers that some describe as "building him a throne"? Is it helpful to distinguish between a fact-stating aspect and a commitment or attitude aspect in confessing "Jesus is Lord"? Is "Jesus is [my] Lord" the same as saying "I am his slave"?

2. Varieties of Gifts for Building Up the Whole Church (12:4-11)

4 There are different apportionings of gifts, but the same Spirit. There are varieties of ways of serving, but the same Lord. 6 And there are different apportionings of what activates effects, but the same God who brings about everything in everyone. 7 To each is given the public manifestation of the Spirit for common advantage.

8 To one person, for his or her part, God bestows through the Spirit utterance relating to "wisdom"; to another, in accordance with the same Spirit, discourse relating to "knowledge." 9 To a different person faith by the same Spirit; to another, gifts for various kinds of healing by the one Spirit. 10 To another, actively effective deeds of power; to another, prophecy; to another, discernment of what is "of the Spirit"; to another, species of tongues; and to another, intelligible articulation of what is spoken in tongues. 11 All these things one and the same Spirit activates, apportioning as he wills to each person individually.

Verses 4-7 have a double importance. First, they provide a kind of "ground plan" of *trinitarian theology*. Second, they expound a dialectic of unity and diversity: there are varieties of **gifts** (v. 4), **ways of serving** (v. 5), and **apportionings** (v. 6), but all derive respectively from **the same Spirit** (v. 4), **the same Lord** (v. 5), and **the same God** (v. 6). The use of **the same** affirms two axioms or principles: (1) God is *one* (1 Cor. 8:4-6); and the common source of the **gifts, ways of serving**, and (2) **apportionings** or *assigning of effective working* are not competitive or mutually undermining, but serve the same overall purposes of the one God, namely, the **common advantage** or *common good* of the whole church. They are not for the benefit of one section of the church, nor (least of all) simply for the person who exercises the gift or performs the service (cf. 14:4). Paul's emphasis upon unity-in-diversity is grounded in the nature of the one God, who is holy Trinity. Paul underlines the coherence of the gifts that God assigns as a unity-in-diversity. This excludes rivalry or competition.

Paul expounds this principle in the second main part of the chapter (12:12-26, with vv. 27-30) in terms of the mutually supportive structure of the limbs of a body. Competitive claims for the hands or the feet against the importance of the eye or the ear are absurd. The whole body needs every limb.

Nevertheless, **different apportionings** of gifts and their respective roles remain essential for the well-being of the body. It is not up to members of the church to select or to rank these diverse gifts; God gives them **to each** as the Spirit wills **for common advantage** (v. 7). The list of gifts is not comprehensive. On the other hand, Paul implies that no single individual alone is likely to receive the full range of possible gifts. The *full* range of gifts can be found only in Christ or in the church *as a whole*. This is *one reason among others why the individual needs the church*.

(1) The phrase **utterance relating to "wisdom"** (v. 8a) is too often seen through a lens constructed from the assumptions of a particular Christian tradition or culture. This may read into the phrase more than Paul says. REB's translation, "the gift of wise speech," is thoroughly acceptable not least because the Greek word *logos* often denotes "speech," "discourse," or "utterance" rather than simply "word." The genitive **of wisdom** may well be descriptive (as REB, "can put the deepest knowledge into words"). But if it is an "objective" genitive (derived from wisdom), it may mean "speech derived from [God's] wisdom." This would accord with 1:18-25 and 2:1-16.

In Isa. 11:2-3 the Spirit of God gives wisdom and knowledge to the messianic figure, and Christians see these gifts of the Spirit as derived from the Spirit's anointing of Christ. *Wisdom* was a catchword in the church of Corinth (cf. 1:17; 2:1, 5, 6; 3:19), and Paul may be distinguishing the wise speech that derives from openness to the Holy Spirit from merely "clever" speech that is a human construction. To restrict the phrase to ad hoc messages to individuals about their condition would be to diminish the gospel-centered and contextually determined content, and to overlay them with a specific tradition of modern thought. It would both narrow the verse and go beyond the text.

(2) **"Knowledge"** (v. 8b) is another Corinthian catchphrase (cf. 1:5; 8:1, 7, 10, 11; 13:2, 8; 14:6). Paul uses it in a different sense from that favored in Corinth. For him knowledge is never an attribute fully possessed or fully achieved, prior to the last judgment. It is a process of *coming-to-know* (Greek *ginōskō*, verb, rather than *gnōsis*, noun), and begins with a recognition of one's need to listen and to learn (3:18-21; 13:12).

Commentators since the earliest Church Fathers have strained to identify some clear difference between the gift of "wise" speech and the gift of "knowledge," but most recognize that we cannot be certain about any difference. In many *other* contexts the difference *is* clear: *wisdom* (in theological and philosophical traditions, *phronēsis* rather than *sophia*) involves *the whole mind,* including rational assessment, intuitive perception, and especially *practical understanding.* By contrast, *knowledge* may relate to grasping technical data (often *technē* rather than *gnōsis*). Some commentators view both of the gifts as gifts of theological reflection (Senft, *Première Épître,* p. 158). This is more likely than assumptions about messages conveyed to individuals, but it is still less than certain.

If there is a difference between the two gifts, the best clue to it may lie in associating *wisdom* with *prophetic* application of truth, and *knowledge* with the gift of *teaching*.

(3) **Faith** (v. 9a) appears strictly in this context as a gift given to **a different person**, and thus is clearly different from the trustful faith that *every* Christian has as part of their very identity as a Christian. Justification by grace through faith is the gift of every Christian, and Christians are regularly defined as "believers" or the faithful. This trustful faith is an attitude of *appropriation*. Tillich sees the faith of justification as *accepting* being *accepted*. The gift in v. 9 is clearly *not this*.

Probably this gift promotes an ebullient, robust, optimistic acceptance of God's sovereign love and mercy in such a way as to put heart into a troubled church in times of uncertainty. Such a gift would "build" the whole church in moments of trial when stability or progress seems under threat. It may also denote a settled disposition of robust confidence in God that raises the spirit and morale of fellow Christians. As such it serves **common advantage** (v. 7).

(4) **Gifts for various kinds of healing** come next (v. 9b). The use of a *plural* form for *both healings and gifts* (Greek *charismata iamatōn*) is important. Most versions render the plural of *one* of these words, but not the other (NRSV, REB, "gifts of healing"). But does the plural *healings* denote *more than one* healing (healings on more than one occasion or for more than one individual) or, more probably, *more than one kind of healing* (in a generic sense)? In modern English we often reserve plurals for an indeterminate entity to indicate *kinds* of, or *varieties* of, that entity (as in *cheeses* or *fruits*). Edwards (*First Epistle*, p. 316) and Zodhiates (*1 Corinthians 12*, vol. 1, p. 152) adopt this understanding of *healings*.

Although a number of writers believe that this gift necessarily involves "supernatural" healing, this must be questioned. One of the founders of the modern Pentecostal movement, Donald Gee, states that whatever the verse denotes, we should "not preclude . . . the merciful and manifold work of medical healing" from this gift (1963 [1928], pp. 47-62). Bengel also insists that it does not exclude "natural" means of healing (*Gnomon*, p. 652). Paul does not appear to refer to gifts of healing anywhere else in his epistles, although implicit allusions may occur. (On the work of Pentecostal writers here, see Thiselton, *First Epistle*, pp. 947-51.) As Barth insists, Paul's aim is to underline the *source* rather than the *means* of healing: this is a free, "unearned" gift from the *one* Holy Spirit for the benefit and building up of the *whole* church.

It is tragic that a gift that should unify the church in thankfulness to God sometimes becomes divisive. This might happen less frequently if full account were taken of the sovereignty of the Spirit to determine *whether, when, and in what way* healing might or might not occur through the Spirit's *distribution* of this *gift*. If, *against* the meaning of this passage, healing is perceived as a *universal* gift for healers or healed, the problem of suffering or "incompleteness" for some rather than others becomes severe and debilitating. Paul prayed no fewer than "three times" for God to remove the "thorn in [his] flesh" (2 Cor. 12:7), but God gave him "sufficient grace" to be content with "weakness" (vv. 6-10). Whatever the **variety** of the Holy Spirit's **apportioning** of gifts (vv. 4-5), these are "sufficient" for the church as expressions of divine presence and love.

(5) **Actively effective deeds of power** (v. 10a) are given **to another**. The NRSV and AV/KJB translate the phrase "the working of miracles" (REB and NIV, "miraculous powers"). But the words "miracle" or "miraculous" are not in the Greek. The Greek phrase is simply "workings of power" *(energēmata dynameōn).* Hence the RV margin, "has the working of powers." The most recent standard scholarly Greek lexicon (Danker-Bauer, known as *BDAG, Lexicon,* 3rd edn. 2000) translates the first of these two words as "activity" or "expression of capability," although it concedes that in 1 Cor. 12:10 this might denote "activities that express themselves in miracles," or "miraculous powers," as an inference from the context (p. 335).

The second Greek word, *dynamis,* occurs in the genitive plural *(dynameōn).** My translation, **actively effective deeds of power**, leaves open whether the "miraculous" is implied without excluding it. When

---

*Technical Note: BDAG renders the Greek word as "potential for functioning in some way," or "power, might, strength, force, capability" (p. 262). It may sometimes more narrowly denote "a power that works wonders" (Mark 6:14; Acts 10:38; 1 Cor. 12:28-29; Gal. 3:5; Col. 1:29), but in 1 Cor. 4:19-20 and 1 Thess. 1:5 it denotes "effectiveness" in contrast to mere word or appearance (p. 263). Under a second main classification it describes "ability to carry out something, ability, capability." In a third category, *which includes our present passage,* it denotes "ability to function powerfully." This may range from "a deed of power," or "miracle," to a more general "power" or "resource" (p. 263). *Effectiveness* and *resource* are the minimal meanings of the two words together.

we place it alongside the other gifts, we cannot help asking: is it *miracles* or *effective leadership* that Paul perceives as more vital for the building up of the body of Christ? Moreover, the very concept of "miracle" implies a division of divine action into the two levels of "natural" and "supernatural," and this may owe more to a reaction against the materialism of the eighteenth-century Enlightenment than to the biblical conviction that God acts in any way that God chooses. To mark off a special level of divine action as "miraculous" may sometimes have the unintended effect of reducing rather than expanding our understanding of the scope of God's action within the world. Paul's argument in this epistle concerns more especially *authentic effectiveness* for the gospel in contrast to human pretensions. Karl Barth urges this point very well (*Resurrection,* p. 18; also pp. 24-26, 79-82; and Thiselton, *First Epistle,* pp. 952-56).

(6) **Prophecy** (v. 10) offers no problem of translation, but the meaning of the Greek and English remains notoriously controversial. One recent writer, as we noted, believes that behind virtually all the differences between Paul and many Christians in Corinth stands "a clash between two different understandings of prophetic inspiration" (Hall, *Unity,* p. 71). If this is correct, extreme care is needed to determine whether our understanding of "New Testament prophecy" is more akin to that current in Corinth or nearer to the apostle's view. On the level of vocabulary alone, *prophecy* may denote a gift or activity as broad and general as declaring or telling forth the revealed will of God.

Moses remains a prophet in this broad sense of the term. He mediates the word of God to Israel, just as in the role of "ascending mediator" he mediates the prayers of Israel to God. The canonical prophets of the eighth and seventh centuries B.C. (Amos, Hosea, Isaiah, and Jeremiah) also "tell forth" the divine word, sometimes distancing themselves from the ecstasies or "inspiration" associated with earlier "prophets," including the prophets of the Baalim in the ninth century. (See 1 Kings 18:26-29 in contrast to 1 Kings 19:36-38; Amos 1:3, 6; 2:1, 4, 6; 3:1, 11; 5:1, 2; and especially in this context 7:14-16.) Amos views prophetic speech as synonymous with proclamation or preaching (7:16, "do not prophesy against Israel," is in synonymous parallelism with "and stop preaching against the house of Isaac," NIV).

The near equivalence between prophecy and "pastoral preaching" in Paul has been urged by the following writers: Hill, *New Testament*

Prophecy, pp. 110-40; Héring, *First Epistle,* p. 127; Müller, *Prophetie und Predigt,* pp. 47-108; Gillespie, *First Theologian,* pp. 130-50; and Thiselton, *First Epistle,* pp. 956-65 and 1087-94. Since Paul explicitly defines the aim of prophetic speech as "to edify, exhort, and encourage, it coincides therefore to a large extent with what we call a sermon today" (Héring, *First Epistle,* p. 127; see also Garland, *1 Corinthians,* pp. 582-83). It would be as misleading to "read back" from modern times a stereotyped fifteen-minute monologue as it would be to stereotype Pauline prophecy as a series of unprepared one-sentence staccato "messages," especially if these turn out to concern individuals rather than the gospel. Three further factors remain helpful for understanding Paul's own view.

(a) Paul regarded his personal calling to apostleship as also, in effect, a call to prophetic ministry, akin to the call of Jeremiah, whose call is described in similar terms (Gal. 1:15; and Jer. 1:5; Sandnes, *Paul — One of the Prophets?).*

(b) This approach in the tradition of the Old Testament stands in contrast with many examples of "prophecy" in the Greco-Roman world. The "prophecies" of the Sibyl and other Greco-Roman oracles were often uttered in an ecstatic or trancelike state of the kind that Amos and the canonical prophets of the Old Testament would despise. The most notorious example is the frenzied cries of the Bacchae (disciples of Bacchus or Dionysius) depicted by Euripides. It is not far-fetched to ask whether, in the absence of closer instruction, some in Corinth might have simply assumed that prophecy meant this even within the Christian church. This would account for Paul's vehement emphasis on "controlled" speech (1 Cor. 14:29-33). Eugene Boring (as well as Hall) insists that notions of prophecy *in Corinth* were more "oracular," ecstatic, and individualistic than *Paul's* view.

(c) Prophetic speech "built up" the church, both by convincing "outsiders" of the truth of the gospel (1 Cor. 14:24-25) and by the nurturing believers' faith. In the Reformation era Zwingli and Bullinger were nearer to the view outlined here than some today. They identified prophetic discourse with scriptural reflection leading to pastoral application and nurture.

(7) The seventh of these gifts is **discernment of what is "of the Spirit"** (v. 10). The Greek uses the plural, *"spirits" (diakriseis pneumatōn).* But a number of writers urge that Paul very seldom alludes to "evil spirits" (e.g., Robertson and Plummer, *First Epistle,* p. 267), and Fuchs

argues that the contrast addresses the difference between what is only generated by the human spirit and what is prompted by the Holy Spirit (genuine revelatory discourse [*Christus und der Geist*, pp. 36-48]). If these writers are correct, Paul is describing a gift that enables its recipient to discern whether a claim to speak at the prompting of the Holy Spirit is genuine. This fits the argument that this gift is for the testing of prophecy (Dautzenberg, *Urchristliche Prophetie*, pp. 93-104).

The interpretation of this phrase (REB, "the ability to distinguish true spirits from false"), however, remains controversial. Complex arguments from all sides are discussed in *First Epistle*, pp. 965-70. Most views hold that this gift involves *discernment*, and in particular the gift to discern when the Holy Spirit is at work.

(8) **Species of tongues**. Whatever may or may not be claimed about *glossolalia*, or speaking in tongues, it is imperative to note that Paul uses the generic phrase "**species** or *kinds* of tongues" (Greek *genē glōssōn*). Many theories may fall short because they do not allow for the fact that within the New Testament and even in Paul's epistles there is more *than one unitary phenomenon that may be called a tongue*. Hence the general question "What is speaking in tongues?" hardly helps anyone until we specify what the term denotes *in this or that context of Scripture*. Thus it is a huge leap to suggest that because the term might allude to "angelic language" in 13:1 this is necessarily what it denotes throughout chapters 12 to 14.

Two key contrasts help to explain Paul's definition of "tongues" here. Whereas *prophetic discourse* is *articulate* and understandable, *"tongues"* remain *inarticulate* and unintelligible unless this utterance is transposed into articulate speech. Second, tongues are addressed *by* or *through* human persons *to God* (14:2); prophecy is addressed *to* human persons *from God* (14:3).

At least five distinct views about speaking in tongues find a place in scholarly literature. These include tongues as: (1) angelic speech, (2) miraculous power to speak foreign languages, (3) liturgical or archaic utterances, (4) ecstatic speech, (5) mechanisms of release, especially in releasing longings or praise. (On 5, see Thiselton, *First Epistle*, pp. 970-88.) I have long held this last view, first publishing it in 1979. I agree with the Pentecostal writer F. D. Macchia, who, together with E. Käsemann, K. Stendahl, and G. Theissen, sees a very close parallel with the Spirit's speaking in or through a Christian "with sighs too deep for words" in Rom. 8:26-27 (Macchia, "Groans Too Deep for Words," pp. 149-73, and "Tongues and Prophecy," pp. 63-69; Theissen, *Psychological Aspects,* pp. 276-341, esp. pp. 304-41). This "sighing" or "groaning" in Romans is a longing for eschatological fulfillment and completion in the light of a glimpse of what God's glory can and one day will be. It combines praise and yearnings that go beyond words.

Insight, feeling, or longing, at the deepest level of the heart, however, needs an outlet; it needs to be "released." Here Stendahl and, in a fuller way, Theissen help us. The Holy Spirit gives the capacity to plumb the depths of the unconscious as the Spirit's *gift.* This is where the Holy Spirit sheds abroad the love of God ("God's love has flooded our hearts," Rom. 5:5, REB). *Heart* frequently includes what nowadays we call the unconscious (1 Cor. 4:4-5). Hence, as Theissen expresses it, "Glossolalia is language of the unconscious — language capable of consciousness," which makes "unconscious depth dimensions of life accessible" (cf. Stendahl, "Glossolalia," in *Paul,* p. 111; and Theissen, *Psychological Aspects,* 306; cf. pp. 59-114 and 276-341).

Paul expresses his approval of the use of this gift but qualifies it in three ways. First, in genuine form it comes from the Spirit of God; it must not be self-generated as a counterfeit (14:4, especially as discussed by Vielhauer, *Oikodomē,* pp. 91-98). Second, it must not be exercised in public, but strictly only in private (14:5-25). Third, the only way in which the gift of tongues may be used for public benefit is for the speaker (the Greek text does not refer to a *second* person called an "interpreter") to receive the further gift of being enabled to communicate the content in articulate speech (14:13, "Anyone who speaks in tongues should pray for the ability to interpret," REB).

(9) **Intelligible articulation of tongues speech** (v. 10c). Many regard this gift as separate from the gift of speaking in tongues. They suggest that whereas one person speaks in tongues, another receives the gift "to interpret" what the tongue speaker has said in intelligible speech. In favor of this long-standing view, they point out that Paul introduces each gift with the contrasting formula, to *another:* to yet another *(allō de)* the interpretation *(hermeneia)* of tongues. But the final "another" may refer to a contrast between *one* person who has *only* the gift of expressing released praise, while *another* person may have the gift of such release *together with* a subsequent capacity to share the experience with others in words.

In favor of translating *hermeneia* as **articulation** rather than *interpretation* is the fact that this meaning is well attested among writers contemporary with Paul. Josephus writes to his Roman readership that he longs to convey the indescribable wonders of Herod's temple, but he cannot quite *"hermeneuō"* (or *"di-ermeneuō"*) them, that is, cannot quite fully put them into words (Jewish *War* 5.176, 178, and 182). More examples can be found in Thiselton, "The Interpretation of Tongues?" pp. 15-36.

Second, the major contrast between prophetic speech and tongues speech turns on "articulate and intelligible" versus "inarticulate and unintelligible" (especially in ch. 14). This provides the context with reference to which we have to decide whether *hermeneuō* and *hermeneia* allude to "interpretation" or to "producing articulate speech."

Third, a pivotal verse is 14:13, which, as we have noted, REB translates, "Anyone who speaks in tongues should pray for the ability to interpret," that is, the *tongues speaker* should do this. Unfortunately, the NRSV uses the phrase "unless *someone* interprets," but it has introduced *"someone"* into a Greek text from which the word (Greek *tis*) is absent.

Whichever view we take of these last two gifts, Paul implies that it is not good to repress deep emotions, longings, and experiences that need to be *released*. Further, concern for the public impact of "private" conduct must also be held in balance. *Communication* in intelligible, rational terms to others of insights revealed through a gift should not be hugged to ourselves as "private" possessions of benefit only to the self. They are given for the "building up" of others.

Paul concludes this section on gifts of the Spirit (12:8-11) with a summary: **All these things one and the same Spirit activates, apportioning as he wills to each person individually** (v. 11). To envy someone else's gift, or, conversely, to question its value, is to question the sovereign and gracious will of God's Holy Spirit in determining to whom he apportions what gifts.

33. Suggestions for Possible Reflection on 12:4-11

1. *On God the Holy Trinity as a model of unity-in-diversity (vv. 4-7):* The doctrine of the Trinity is no merely theoretical construction. It reflects God's na-

ture as interpersonal, outgoing, and a God of order who delights in both singleness of purpose and variety of expression. How might God's varied modes of self-expression and action nurture an acceptance of diversity within a single divine will in relation to fellow Christians?

2. *On a trinitarian framework for Christian thought and life (vv. 4-7):* Do some Christians focus their devotion too narrowly or exclusively on God as Father alone (God without Christ), or on Jesus Christ alone ("Jesusology"), or on the Holy Spirit alone (Spirit-centered renewal)? Paul sees *all* Persons of the Trinity as involved fully in creation, redemption, and salvation. All gifts come ultimately *from* God the originating and loving Father, but God gives them *through* Jesus Christ as Mediator, and they are appropriated *by* the enabling work of the Holy Spirit. Conversely, prayer in the New Testament is usually addressed *to* God *through* Christ, and prompted and initiated *by* the Holy Spirit (Rom. 8:15-17). Would prayer come to us more readily if we regarded it in these terms?

3. *On speech relating to wisdom and knowledge (v. 8):* Can we distinguish in practice between utterances relating to wisdom and those relating to knowledge without imposing "modern" traditions of spirituality onto Paul? Or may we see a difference here between pastoral application and teaching? Why does Proverbs extol wisdom so highly while Paul warns us that knowledge may inflate the self (8:1)? Does information technology throw into sharper relief the difference between a huge mass of information and wisdom to evaluate and apply it rightly for life?

4. *On the capacity of robust faith to build the church (v. 9):* Granted that this gift cannot be that of saving faith that appropriates Christ, do we value those who are given a robust, buoyant, trustful faith that celebrates the promises of God? Or do we dismiss them as credulous and naïve? How can Christians remain soberly self-critical, yet open to learn from a buoyant faith that lifts the heart and builds confidence in God?

5. *On gratitude for "various kinds of healings" that also honors God's "when, where, how, and for whom":* God's gift of healing is not restricted to one type. If this gift is narrowed to the "supernatural" only, or universalized into "for all times and places," this exacerbates the problem of suffering for many. People ask: Why does God not heal *me* (or him or her)? Just because God does not *declare* a reason, this does not mean that God *has* no reason. Gifts (and their time and place) belong to the inscrutable will of God. These verses do

not describe general ideas, but actions that God wills. What are the most helpful (and least helpful) ways of understanding "gifts for various kinds of healings"?

6. *On carrying plans or initiatives through and implementing them (v. 10a):* Power in Paul and elsewhere in the New Testament often denotes *effectiveness.* Why do Christians often seem ineffective if God gives this power of effectiveness? Can we see God's gift in the ordinary-but-effective as well as in the miraculous?

7. *On the gift of speech in the tradition of the prophets (v. 10b):* Do we have the courage, like the prophets of old, to apply what God reveals for everyday life or for critical situations? Must prophecy be in brief, staccato "messages," or may it take the form of a prepared discourse or sermon inspired by God for a specific occasion and pastoral purpose? Is its relation to the gospel part of its test?

8. *On the gifts of discerning the Spirit (v. 10c):* If "what comes from the Spirit" needs to be discerned, what part is played by patience in such a process of listening to God? Do we need careful reflection under the Spirit's leading, or a sudden flash of insight, or both in due proportion? "Discernment" carefully seeks criteria of Christ-likeness in this epistle (2:6-16; 3:1-3; 12:1-3). At the level of the wider church it may require a longer process of "reception" by other congregations, pastors, and bishops.

9. *On the release of praise and yearning, and on its intelligible communication to others (v. 10d):* If Paul associates speaking in tongues with address *to* God (14:2), how does speaking in tongues relate to Rom. 8:26-27? How do we come to share this experience with others?

3. The Body of Christ: Its Diversity Includes All of Its Limbs (12:12-26)

12 For just as the body is one, and has many limbs and organs, and all the limbs and organs of the body, although they are many, constitute a single body, even so this is the case with Christ. 13 For we were all baptized by one Spirit into one body, whether Jews or Gentiles, whether slaves or free people. Of one Spirit were we all given to drink our fill. 14 For the body is not a single entity but many. 15 If the foot should say, "Because I am not a hand, I do not belong to the body," just because of this does it not belong to the body? 16 And if the ear should say, "Because I am not an eye, I do not belong to the body." On that score does it any

the less belong to the body? 17 If the whole body were an eye, where would be the hearing? If the whole were an ear, where would the nose be?

18 But as it is, God placed the members, each single one of them, in the body as it seemed good to him. 19 But if all were a single organ, in what would the body consist? 20 As it is, on the contrary, many limbs and organs, on one side, constitute a single body. 21 The eye cannot say to the hand, "I do not need you," or, again, the head cannot say to the feet, "I have no need of you." 22 On the contrary, even more to the point, those limbs and organs of the body which seem to be less endowed with power or status than others are essential. 23 And on what we deem to be less honorable parts of the body we invest with greater honor, and our unpresentable private parts have greater adornment to make them presentable. 24 Our presentable parts do not need this. But God composed the body, giving to that which feels inferior greater honor. 25 He purposed that there should be no split within the body, but that its limbs and organs might share the same concern for one another. 26 So if one limb or organ suffers, all the parts of the body suffer with it; or, if one limb or organ is praised, all the members of the body share in the congratulations.

A strict translation of the Greek in v. 12 would render **limbs and organs** simply as "members." But "members" has effectively lost all of its realism in the sense of actual body parts, not least in view of such thinned-down metaphors as "members of a club" or "member of an association." Hence we need a different English rendering to describe the *body parts* **of Christ**. We translate **limbs and organs** (cf. "organs," REB). Paul regards the church as in a specific sense (but not in every sense) Christ's own body. This reflects the voice of the Lord on the road to Damascus: "Saul, Saul, why are you persecuting *me?*" (Acts 9:4; 22:7).

There are several implications of this. One is that it is an affront to Christ if a self-effacing or vulnerable Christian is made to feel second class or alienated, perhaps because he or she does not have what others see as the "right" gifts. It is a betrayal if such a person reaches the point of saying, "I do not *belong* to the body" (12:15).

To drive home this principle Paul borrows, *but also then reverses,* an application of the imagery of the body long known and used in Greco-Roman politics and rhetoric. From the fourth and fifth centuries B.C. through the first century up to the second, Plato, Plutarch, and Epictetus (contemporary with Paul) used the image of the body to promote the need for harmony where there was diversity of status. The Roman historian Livy narrates an appeal by the Senator Menenius Agrippa to rebel workers on strike to resume work (*Ab Urbe Conditu* 2.32). He appeals to the interdependence of the "body" of the city to urge that the workers or slaves must provide food for the governing classes. Paul reverses the thrust of this appeal, *transposing it into an appeal to "the strong" to value "the weak" or despised* (12:20-23; see further Martin, *The Corinthian Body,* pp. 94-105). All Christian believers **constitute a single body** (v. 12); to suggest otherwise is to denigrate or tear apart the very limbs of **Christ** (v. 12b).

For we were all baptized by one Spirit into one body, whether Jews or Gentiles, whether slaves or free people (v. 13). The context is decisive for the meaning of this verse. Entry into the communal reality of being "in Christ" through the agency of the Holy Spirit (cf. 12:3) is what makes Christians Christian, and *all stand on the same footing* as "members" incorporated in Christ. The two allusions to **the Spirit** in v. 12 both relate to **all** Christians: "**all" baptized by one Spirit . . . "all" given to drink of one Spirit**. While the *experience* that is sometimes described in modern times as "baptism in the Holy Spirit" may itself often be valid, the *terminology* often used to describe it is questionable. To cite this verse to justify the notion that "baptism in the Spirit" is an experience reserved for some but not others turns the meaning of the verse on its head. It suggests the very opposite of Paul's point. Paul stresses the word **all**. The baptism of the Spirit is initiation into being-in-Christ, whether or not we view *baptism* as a specific rite of water baptism or as the broader metaphor for being incorporated in Christ's death, which is the *basis* for Christian water baptism.

The contrast here is between *baptism into Moses* (1 Cor. 10:2) under the old covenant and incorporation into Christ through the Holy Spirit under the new covenant (cf. 2 Cor. 3:12-18). Dunn argues convincingly that baptism in the Spirit in this verse is not an experience *subsequent* to that of becoming a Christian (*Baptism in the Holy Spirit,* throughout), while Holland points out that the language of v. 13 alludes not primarily "to the individual believer" but to "the major redemptive event that happened historically" as an antitype to "being baptized into Moses" for Israel (*Contours of Pauline Theology,* pp. 142-47).

Verses 14-20 introduce Paul's appeal to those who feel "inferior" to recognize that they genuinely belong to Christ's body no less than the self-confident and supposedly spiritual elite. They are not to say, **"Because I am not a hand, I do not belong to the body"** (v. 15). Conversely, vv. 21-25 address those who feel "superior": **The eye cannot say to the hand, "I do not need you"** (v. 21). Indeed, if we press the metaphor or analogy of **the body**, in the first place it would not be *a body* if all its parts were replications of a single organ. **If all were a single organ, in what would the body consist** (v. 19; cf. v. 14)? In the second place, the **limbs and organs of the body which seem to be less endowed with power or status . . . are essential** (v. 22). So-called **unpresentable parts** play an even more indispensable role in sustaining the life of the body than, for example, an **eye** or an **ear**, which on the surface may appear more important (vv. 23-24).

The application to Corinth and to church life today is clear. Those who may appear to flaunt supposedly more spectacular gifts (or perhaps those whose social status appears to confer prestige on the church) may turn out to be less indispensable than the faithful, humble, hard-praying, or hard-working "members" whose value may be overlooked by the power seekers. Jürgen Moltmann argues that Christian believers who bring with them disabilities, privations, or experiences of suffering may be the most precious and "charismatic" part of the body, because every church stands in genuine need of such to live out and to teach the character of the gospel (*The Spirit of Life,* pp. 192-93).

The last two verses (vv. 25-26) before Paul returns to recapitulate his point place the emphasis upon interdependence and upon corporate solidarity, in contrast to any hypothetical "ranking" of gifts. This exercise begins to look still more foolish and irrelevant. Gifts depend upon what *the Spirit wills,* or on what **seems good to God** (v. 18). Any competitive comparison between gifts defeats the very purpose of the gifts because this attitude risks causing a **split within the body** (v. 25a). On the contrary, since they share together the very life of Christ, God wills that the **limbs and organs might share the same concern for one another** (v. 25b). **So if one limb or organ suffers, all the parts of the body suffer with it; or, if one limb or organ is praised, all the members of the body share in the congratulations** (v. 26). We do not say to a victorious runner, "I congratulate your legs"; congratulations go to *the person.* "Success" results from the conjoint coordination of *all* the limbs of the body. Conversely, pain or damage in a specific body part can drag down the health of the whole psychological system. The *person* becomes unwell.

In the ancient world the Greek medical writers Hippocrates and Galen both made this axiomatic point that pain or disability on the part of a specific organ or limb had debilitating effects on the whole body. Chrysostom notes that even a thorn on the foot can affect the well-being of the entire person. Thornton observes, "In the Body of Christ there are, strictly speaking, no private sufferings. All are shared because there is one life of the whole. Accordingly wrong done to one member is wrong done to the whole Church, and therefore to Christ himself" (*Common Life*, p. 36). This principle also demands the utmost sympathy and sensitivity between fellow Christians, to share in the joys and sorrows of each. In Latin American liberation theology Boff speaks of *"com-passion"* or fellow suffering among members of Christ's body as a key demand of the gospel.

34. Suggestions for Possible Reflection on 12:12-26

1. *On respect for Christians as the very limbs of Christ:* If Christians are limbs of Christ, sin against a fellow Christian is not merely a social matter. To sin against a fellow believer is in one sense to sin against Christ himself. This matches Paul's earlier language about Christ's regarding as under his care and protection all who call him Lord.

2. *On Paul's subversion of conventions about mutual interdependence:* The Romans used the analogy of the body and limbs to persuade those of less status to serve the elite who depended on their labor. How often do we use this model (as Paul does) to stress that the vulnerable and less favored need the support and service of the strong? Do we stress strongly enough that the weak are honorable and respected parts of the body?

3. *On the two-way logic of Paul's analogy of the body:* Do we apply *both* directions of Paul's analogy? In one direction: "You may not have spectacular gifts, but you *are* part of the body and you are needed." In the other direction: "You may have special gifts, but don't think that you are the be-all and end-all of what the body needs!"

4. *On the shared status of baptism.* Baptism is a sign of Christian unity. By the Spirit Christians are initiated into a common allegiance to Christ as Lord.

Why does the phrase "baptized by (or in)" the Holy Spirit (v. 13) become so divisive at times? How can we avoid this?

4. Fullness of Gifts Not the Possession of Any One Individual (12:27-31)

27 Now you yourselves are Christ's body, and each of you, for his or her part, limbs or organs of it. 28 And God has placed in the church, first, some who are apostles; second, prophets; third, teachers; then effective deeds of power, then gifts of healing, various kinds of administrative support, ability to formulate strategies, various kinds of tongues. 29 All are not apostles, are they? Surely all are not prophets? Could all be teachers? Do all perform effective deeds of power? 30 Does everyone have gifts to heal in various ways? Surely all do not speak in tongues, do they? Do all put the deepest secret things into articulate speech? 31 Continue to be zealously concerned about the "greatest" gifts. Yes, an even greater way still I am going to show you.

The last five verses of the chapter press home the argument by way of summary. If these "gifts" are "different apportionings" in accordance with the will and the generosity of God (vv. 4-6), and if they are given "for common advantage" on the part of the whole church (v. 4) to "one . . . [or] to another . . . ," at least two consequences follow. First, they cannot be a source of *competitive* comparisons in the stakes for status. Second, the full range of gifts (even granted that no "list" of gifts is comprehensive) transcends the capacity of any *individual* Christian alone to possess them. *Only in the church* as a community of diverse individuals who bring diverse gifts for the mutual building up of all can anyone witness and experience the rich fullness of the many gifts of the Holy Spirit.

This challenges any self-styled leader who may imagine that he or she alone is the church's "answer" without reference to the complementary and needed gifts of others. It also challenges those who (in 1:10-12) select certain leaders as "their" models of chosen spiritual attributes in contrast to other leaders. Christians need *all* the resources of God's gifts that are spread throughout the church, and encountered through different individuals and in different forms. This reinforces Paul's argument in 3:5-23, which he brings to a focus in 3:22: "All things are yours, whether Paul or Apollos or Cephas, or the world or life or death. . . . All are yours, and you are Christ's."

In terms of self-promotion, the individual Christian is *not* important. But in terms of value to the whole body of Christians, every individual *is* important. Hence Paul uses a Greek idiom in v. 27 *(ek merous),* which usually means separately or *part by part,* in the sense of **for his part** or **for her part**. These five verses make up a unit of the longer text that begins and ends with an emphatic second person plural to apply the argument personally: **you yourselves, for your part.** "Individually" (NRSV), or "each of you" (REB), does not quite catch the self-involving aspect of the idiom.

In v. 28 Paul takes up five "gifts" that we have already examined: **apostles, prophets, effective deeds of power, gifts of healing** . . . and **various kinds of tongues** (see above under vv. 8-10). We have yet to consider three further gifts that we have translated as **teachers . . . , various kinds of administrative support,** and **ability to formulate strategies**.

This verse raises two major questions: First, does Paul's language **first . . . second . . . third . . . then . . .** denote gradations of hierarchy or importance in the church, or simply an enumeration used to check off a list? Second, does Paul intentionally move in some cases from "gifts" *(charismata)* to roles or offices in the church?

Many regard the enumeration **first . . . second . . . third** as marking "the three most important ministries" of *apostolic* witness, *prophetic proclamation,* and *teaching* the faith, which is also reflected in Eph. 4:11 (Bruce, *1 and 2 Corinthians,* p. 122). Some (but not all) relate this to the later threefold order of bishops, presbyters, and deacons.

(1) The church does not create **apostles,** but is founded upon the truth to which the **apostles** have been witness. In Crafton's terminology, as we noted earlier, it is not primarily as *agents* in themselves that apostles are **first**; but they are **first** through the **agency** by means of which their witness makes the gospel of the crucified and raised Christ transparent *(Agency,* pp. 53-103). This historic witness is a bedrock.

(2) The placing of **prophets** as **second** might arguably add force to our interpretation of prophetic speech often as *pastoral preaching* (above, under 12:10). Prophetic speech is the proclamation of revealed truth in relation to a pastoral context. We lack clear evidence for distinguishing "revelation" from reflecting on Scripture.

(3) **Teachers** exercise rational reflection on goals, content, and methods of communication. In accordance with Dunn (but against Fee), "passing on the tradition" would be a natural part of the work of

teachers in the Pauline churches (Fee, *First Epistle*, p. 621; Dunn, *Jesus and the Spirit*, pp. 236-38). In technical terms, **prophets** typically perform the speech actions of *proclaiming, challenging, encouraging,* and *announcing,* while teachers more typically perform speech acts of *transmitting* or *handing on* and *explaining.* But clearly the two overlap. An imaginative teacher will also provoke and challenge, and a prophet will also transmit and expound. In the light of J. N. Collins's work, there is a case for the view that deacons (or those who exercise *diakonia*) do not simply "serve," but act as deputies to apostles, bishops, or senior presbyters for the teaching of gospel truth (*Diakonia,* throughout).

(4), (5) We have discussed **effective deeds of power** and various **gifts of healing** above (see 12:9-10).

(6) **Kinds of administrative support**. This phrase strictly represents no more than the Greek term *helps* (*antilēmpseis,* plural). The plural may denote *acts of help* carried out on more than one occasion. Dunn takes it to mean "helpful deeds" (*Theology of Paul,* p. 556). However, a careful survey of the many different *institutional* contexts, especially in the non-literary papyri (court documents, government memos, and letters), suggests that in the plural the word conveys the notion of *technical support* of a kind determined by its particular institutional context. In the area of medicine, for example, the term sometimes denotes giving support by *supplying bandages;* in several governmental or political contexts, it denotes offering *the support of administrative assistance;* in business and commerce it often denotes *undertaking an area of responsibility.*

The papyri seem to offer more assistance for understanding Paul's meaning in the context of gifts and roles within a growing church than the literary examples of the standard lexicons (Thiselton, *First Epistle,* pp. 1019-20). However "charismatic" a church is, very soon it requires an infrastructure for notes, records, decisions, policies, implementations, and so forth. Hence, given that the church in Corinth had existed for around three years prior to the writing of 1 Corinthians, no doubt **apostles, prophets, teachers,** and others felt a need for some **kinds of administrative support**. Those who keep financial accounts, send letters, monitor decisions, issue receipts, or whatever always provide needed support.

On the other hand, we need not *exclude* "helpful deeds" of a general kind. If we prefer a compromise with less specificity, Robertson and Plummer propose "general management" (*First Epistle,* p. 280). These proposals assume that this *charisma* requires rational reflection and planned actions over time. Spontaneous administration is a contradiction in terms.

(7) **The ability to formulate strategies** translates the Greek behind the English more accurately than "governments" (AV/KJV, RV) or even "forms of leadership" (NRSV). The Greek *kybernēseis* (plural) may denote "leadership" in a general sense, but the cognate noun *kybernētēs* means "pilot of a ship" or "steersman." As a metaphor for a person who has a special gift for the whole church, it marks out one who has the capacity to steer or guide the ship of the church through crosscurrents, contrary winds, and hidden dangers. In positive terms, a pilot not only preserves the ship from disaster but also steers it toward a goal. When pictured in imagination, a perplexed or uncertain church seeking to perceive the direction in which they ought to go in God's purpose needs as the person of the hour one who has **the ability to formulate strategies**: someone who can perceive what opportunities or dangers lie in this or that direction.

The climax of the argument comes in vv. 29-30. These gifts have been "apportioned out" (v. 4) among the *whole* church. No single individual receives *every* gift; hence each Christian needs the other, and the whole church is interdependent in mutual need and reciprocal respect. It is unfortunate that the NRSV, NIV, AV/KJV, and RV all render the Greek as if these verses merely posed "open" questions: "Are all apostles? Are all prophets? Are all teachers?" The REB and NJB give a gentle (but overly gentle) hint that these are slanted rhetorical questions by translating "Are all apostles? All prophets? All teachers?" The Greek negative *mē* ("Surely not! It cannot be, can it?") needs to be made explicit. Idiomatic English will also avoid stylistic replication, which is monotonous and loses attention. Hence we translate: **All are not apostles, are they? Surely all are not prophets? Could all be teachers? Do all perform effective deeds of power? Does everyone have gifts to heal in various ways? Surely all do not speak in tongues, do they? Do all put the deepest secret things into articulate speech?**

Verse 31 is a transitional verse that belongs equally to 12:1-30 and to 13:1-13. **Continue to be zealously concerned** reflects a continuous imperative with the force of *go on doing it*. But what the readers are to *go on doing* can be understood in either of two ways. Paul might be rebuking their competitive *envy* of other people's gifts (Greek *zēloute can* mean *envy*). He would then be redirecting this to the one gift that *every-*

one can possess, namely, the gift of love, which is noncompetitive by its very nature. Alternatively, and more probably, Paul urges with irony, tongue-in-cheek, that their **zealous concern** (verging on obsessive concern) to receive "spiritual gifts" needs *actually to be extended* to the "**greatest**" of these, namely, **love.**

This also reinforces Paul's redefinition of "spiritual" in 3:1-3. If you are really after more "spirituality," Paul says, this is seen not only in living out Christ's Lordship (12:3) but also in a life given over to the stable formation of those qualities that he is about to unfold as the nature and action of **love** (13:1-13).

35. SUGGESTIONS FOR POSSIBLE REFLECTION ON 12:27-31

(1) *On the self-deprivation of the "loner" Christian (vv. 29-30):* Some say, "I can be a Christian without going to church." This is like saying, "I can stay alive on a diet of bread and water." Only through interaction with fellow Christians in a community (in some form) can the fullness of the gifts of the Holy Spirit be expressed. What causes a Christian to want to be a loner? Is this often the fault of the church as much as disenchantment or fear on the part of the person concerned?

(2) *On building on the foundation of the apostles, prophets, and teachers (v. 28):* Would a self-constructed, do-it-yourself church cease to be a "church"? Various answers are given by different Christian traditions or denominations, but there is general agreement that church identity must rest upon apostolic witness as evidenced in the Scriptures and be in communion with other churches. Without pastoral application of biblical truth, or without teaching, for how long would a community remain a "church"?

(3) *On the spiritual gift of administrative support (v. 28b):* Does the church at large (or our local church) suffer more from too much or too little administrative support? A vision needs to be implemented by stable structures (secretarial, financial, legal, social), but can the infrastructures become so "top-heavy" that they become ends in themselves and hinder the vision that they are to serve?

(4) *On the noncompetitive, complementary character of God's gifts:* Why does this passage so readily lead into the chapter on love? How closely are these two chapters connected?

D. Love and Mutual Respect: The Criterion of Christ-like "Spirituality" (13:1-13)

1. The Nature and Dynamic Effects of Love (13:1-7)

1 If I were to speak with human or angelic tongues, but if I had not love, I would have become only a resonating jar or a reverberating cymbal. 2 And if I should have the gift of prophecy, and if I penetrate all the depths too profound for mere human discovery, and have all "knowledge," and if I possess the gifts of every kind of faith sufficient to remove mountains — but, after all, may lack love, I am nothing. 3 Even if I should divide up all my possessions to feed the needy, and if I hand over my body that I may glory, but have not love, it counts for nothing.

4 Love waits patiently; love shows kindness. Love does not burn with envy; does not brag — is not inflated with its own importance. 5 It does not behave with ill-mannered impropriety; is not preoccupied with the interests of the self; does not become exasperated into pique; does not keep a reckoning up of evil. 6 Love does not take pleasure at wrongdoing, but joyfully celebrates truth. 7 It never tires of support, never loses faith, never exhausts hope, never gives up.

a. Love's Nature: The Fruitlessness of Gifts or Sacrifices without Love (13:1-3)

At first sight neither Christ nor the Holy Spirit features in this chapter on love. Some regard it as a self-contained poem or hymn that originally had nothing to do with chapters 12 and 14. But C. T. Craig rightly declares, "On closer examination it is seen that almost every word in the chapter has been chosen with this particular situation in mind" ("First Epistle," p. 165). **Love . . . is not inflated with its own importance** (13:4; cf. 4:6; 8:1); **love does not burn with envy** (13:4; cf. 3:1-3); **it does not behave with ill-mannered impropriety** (13:5; cf. 1:12; 4:10, 18; 5:1-2, 6; 11:17-22; 12:21; 14:4, 11, 27-33).

The qualities that Paul ascribes to **love**, however, are those that throughout the epistle he views as "spiritual" in the sense of being animated and activated by the Holy Spirit in accordance with the wisdom of God and "the mind of Christ" (2:6-16; 3:1-4). The key to the nature of love is concern and respect for "the other," which is also the connecting thread that runs throughout the epistle.

Why, then, are chapters 12 and 14 so different in tone and content from chapter 13? In 12 and 14 Paul addresses an agenda already outlined, in effect, by the problems, assumptions, and concerns of Corinth. In chapter 13 Paul interposes a proactive agenda of his own. He initiates it. To be sure, the chapter is written with well-matched, rhythmic, polished, poetic phrases. But I have argued (since 1964, proposed in an unpublished Tyndale Lecture in Cambridge) that Paul may well have composed this chapter over several days or more as he reflected upon the situation in Corinth, and subsequently inserted it into the flow of his letter after he had formulated it. Such a view was earlier propounded by Moffatt. Paul, Moffatt argues, did not compose such a "lyric" in the midst of hurried dictation, but "this hymn was written out of a close and trying experience . . . wrung from long intercourse with ordinary Christians, especially those at Corinth" (*First Epistle,* p. 182). Schrage likewise regards it as a "criterion" for 12:1–14:40 (*Der erste Brief,* vol. 3, pp. 276-77). "Love builds up" (8:1) further constitutes a connecting thread throughout the epistle, while chapter 13 "manifests the same interest" as chapter 14 (Hurd, *Origin,* p. 189; also Mitchell, *Rhetoric,* p. 270).

Verses 1-3 allude to "the gifts" as the point of departure, but only *to urge the fruitlessness of all gifts without love.* **If I were to speak in human or in angelic tongues** (v. 1) is an indefinite hypothesis. The NIV and NRSV miss this by treating it as an open or contingent hypothesis, "if I speak . . . ," just as AV/KJV and NJB miss this with "though I speak." Paul paints a *hypothetical* scenario without praise or blame: *suppose it were the case that I spoke with . . . angelic tongues* **but had not love, I would have become** — like what? Paul uses for his analogy a piece of bronze that was constructed *not* to produce a musical note with a definite tone and pitch but only *to amplify sound or noise.* Without love I would merely be an ancient megaphone, **an acoustic resonator** or a **resonating,** *reverberating* **acoustic jar.** The Greek word involved *(ēchōn)* denotes not a pitched note, but what transmits sound, usually through resonating. Coupled with the Greek *alalazon,* it denotes *endlessly reverberating noise that produces no melody.* (See Harris, "'Sounding Brass'"; and Klein, "Noisy Gong or Acoustic Vase?")

On the other hand, the **cymbal** that reverberates is a shallow, metallic, rounded dish struck against its partner to produce a *crash* or *clang.* The ancient *crotal* was thicker than a modern orchestral cymbal, and was hit head-on rather than one across the other. The whole combined metaphor depicts a tongues speaker who may have little love for others as producing self-important, sonorous, intrusive decibels, which amount to little more than that. In the English County of Yorkshire, people often dismiss someone who is "all noise" as "Now't but rattle."

Are we to read any special significance into Paul's choices of the Greek word *agapē* to denote **love** in 13:1-13, rather than other possible Greek words? We should not read too much into *the term itself*, not least because it is the usual word for *love* in the Greek translation of the Hebrew (the LXX, or Septuagint) where the Hebrew uses the regular word *'ahabhah.* Nevertheless, Paul declines to use the word *erōs* for *love,* since this characteristically denotes passionate but also sensual, emotive, often erotic love, which is not Paul's focus here. Paul's use of *agapē* here is rooted in the notion of *care, regard, and respect* for the other and for the well-being of the other. This emerges in his *use* of the word rather than its lexicographical scope in a dictionary. **Love shows kindness. . . . It does not behave with ill-mannered impropriety, is not pre-occupied with the interests of the self** (vv. 4-5) captures the hint of Paul's concern for the growth of love as an *attitude and habitual practice* for everyday life in Corinth.

Of the three most important classic works on love in this chapter and in the New Testament (i.e., Spicq's *Agapē in the New Testament,* Nygren's *Agapē and Eros,* and Wischmeyer's *Der höchste Weg*) Nygren's calls for most necessary comment here. Nygren argues that *agapē* denotes a love that is spontaneous, unmotivated, creative, and free. Christians are not to love only those whom they find attractive, or who share their values, social status, or theology. What motivates Christian love is a prior experience of the love of Christ, not a reciprocal return to those who are kind to us.

This should be understood, however, not as a comment on the word itself since the word does not always carry this meaning, but an accurate account of *Paul's use* of this word. Nygren is right to suggest that *agapē* (in Paul's uses) *creates* value rather than responds to value. The love of God is essentially God's free, sovereign grace that *sets* value upon his people. This use, Nygren rightly suggests, places the word in contrast to the most characteristic uses of *erōs,* which typically denotes a love "drawn out" by desire for the loved one. This spills over into the pastoral application of this word for Corinth and for today. Christians are to respect and care for those who may not seem attractive or like us in their culture, gender, race, or concerns, but are fellow believers or human beings on whom God has set his love. Chapters 8-14 are about respect for "the other," of which this chapter is the peak.

The contrast between **love**, on one side, and the gifts of **prophecy**, **"knowledge,"** and **faith**, each without **love**, on the other side (v. 2), recalls the earlier contrast **"Knowledge" inflates . . . love builds** (8:1). **Prophecy** or supposed **"knowledge"** received or exercised without love merely ministers to an illusory self-importance. In point of fact, without **love, I am nothing**. Paul uses the word **all** to build up the notion of a pretentious and impressive claim (**all "knowledge"** — "I know it all" — **all the depths too profound for mere human discovery**), and then brings us down to the anticlimax: *after all that* **I am nothing** *at all!* Mystery (the Greek word here) denotes what lies beyond human discovery (Bockmühl, *Revelation and Mystery*).

Moving mountains (v. 2b) was a recognized metaphor for surmounting difficulties (cf. Matt. 17:20; Mark 11:23-24). **Every kind of faith sufficient to remove mountains** still cannot compensate for lack of love. Even one who has the gift of such outstanding, robust confidence in the ways of God, without love, is also **nothing**.

The next verse (v. 3) is one of the few that imposes the task of textual criticism (the evaluation of manuscript readings and the traditions of manuscript copyists), even on the shortest commentary. Did Paul and the oldest, most "pure" text say **to be burned** (REB, NJB, NIV) or *to glory* (NRSV, "boast")? The United Bible Societies *Greek New Testament* (1993) acknowledges the difficulty of reaching any firm decision. The only difference in dictation would have been the closely similar sounds in Greek of "th" and "ch" (see note).* Hence some argue that plausibility of meaning is more decisive than the earlier date of "purer" manuscripts. *Giving my body to be burned,* they argue, would have been the natural way of expressing voluntary martyrdom under persecution. Yet, on the contrary view, martyrdom *without love* could well be seen as an act of self-**glory**, and a preference for this reading is justifiable. I discuss the arguments in *First Epistle*, pp. 1042-44, with a tentative preference for **to be burned**.

---

*Technical Note: The earliest manuscripts (including 𝔓⁴⁶ [c. A.D. 200], Sinaiticus [4th cent.], and Vaticanus [4th cent.]), i.e., 𝔓⁴⁶, ℵ, B, A, read and transmit **that I may glory** (Greek *hina kauchēsomai*). However, in general the "Western" texts (C and D, probably fifth cent.) read and transmit *that I should be burned* (Greek *hina kauthēsomai*).

Whatever the reading, the logic of v. 3 is precisely parallel to that of v. 2. Where the previous verse states that however "gifted" a Christian may be, without love he or she is utterly **nothing**, v. 3 states that whatever personal sacrifices a Christian makes, even self-sacrifice in death, if all this is without love, **it counts for nothing**. Paul knows this better than anyone. He cannot "boast"; but if he is forced to boast, he will "boast" only in his "weakness," which enables him all the more to rely solely upon God's grace (2 Cor. 12:5, 9, 10).

Even parting with one's possessions to feed the poor may be done without love, whether as a half-resented duty or to gain approval from God or from humankind. Unless this springs from love, that is, from genuine concern, its value, Paul insists, is precisely *nil*. Most translations render the Greek "I gain nothing" (NRSV, REB, NIV), but in the *passive* the Greek probably means **it counts for nothing**.

b. The Dynamic Action of Love (13:4-7)

Paul uses grammar, syntax, and verbs to bring out the dynamic, active, and effective nature of love. Hence we translate not: "is patient, is kind, is not envious or boastful . . ." (NRSV), but: "*waits* **patiently, *shows* kindness, does not burn with envy, *does not brag*. . .**" (v. 4).

To wait patiently is what we might call a "temporal virtue" (as in the Church of England Doctrine Commission Report of 2003, *Being Human*, pp. 121-23). Patience, like faithfulness and hope, depends upon God's gift of time and the right attitude toward God's gift and its exercise. A patient person does not rush in before the right time, and does not have a short fuse. In pastoral work *timing* is often more important than a proposed action in itself. Genuine love for the other will wait until the other is ready, especially if love prompts a word of warning or rebuke. The Bible speaks of God and human persons who are "slow to anger" (Prov. 19:11). Love does not blunder in, or blurt out.

The next verb, **show kindness**, clearly matches the modern English equivalent, except that it conveyed more warmth in first-century Greek (Spicq, *Agapē*, vol. 2, p. 151). The Northern English wit Alan Bennet suggests that "He was kind" is so understated as to function well as an epitaph for a compliant husband who never demanded anything of his widow day or night. In Greek the word has none of the faint praise often associated with the word in modern English. In its positive sense, **kindness** is pure and unselfish concern for the well-being of the other.

Love does not burn with envy (v. 4b) admittedly adds **burns** to the Greek, but it serves to indicate the *intensity* of the original Greek *ou zēloi*. It looks back explicitly to the attitude of "jealousy and strife" (3:3) that leads Paul to reject the desire of many in Corinth to be regarded as "spiritual people." The best translation of the next phrase is **does not brag**, which accords with the research and translation suggested by Barrett and by Spicq.

The last term in the verse, **is not inflated with its own importance** (v. 4c), also translates a single verb: "is not inflated" (Collins), "is not puffed up" (AV/KJV), or "is not conceited" (REB, NJB). The important point is that it uses the same metaphor of being **inflated** or *filled with mere air* that Paul uses in 8:1, where *"knowledge" inflates*, but *love builds*. It recalls the self-inflation of the self-important frog in Aesop's *Fables*. "Proud" (NIV) and "arrogant" (NRSV) lose the thread of the metaphor. To be **inflated**, furthermore, is to add attention to the self, to cultivate attention-seeking behavior, and this is precisely what Paul finds so disturbing and so un-Christ-like among the Christians in Corinth. They like to parade their "gifts" and "spirituality."

Verse 5 refers back to the need for respect toward the other that assumes habituated patterns of character in what today we might call "church order." Love **does not behave with ill-mannered impropriety** (v. 5a). However, the application is broader. The occurrence of the adjectival form in 12:23 confirms that good taste, public good manners, and courtesy toward others are at issue. All these things express an attitude of respect for others, and the acceptance of constraints upon self-will and self-advertisement. Genuine love will never elbow its way into conversations or into worship services without observing appropriate courtesies.

Love **is not preoccupied with the interests of the self** (v. 5) identifies the root attitude of heart and mind that prompts this nonintrusive courtesy. The Greek, which AV/KJV renders literally as "seeketh not her own," is more weighty than "is never selfish" (REB), and broader than "does not insist on its own way" (NRSV). "Not self-seeking" (NIV) is nearer, but today's culture might suggest that our equivalent to the Greek should combine *self-interest* and *self-centeredness*. Our translation seeks to convey this double nuance.

Here Nygren's emphasis (noted above) may assist our understanding further. In contrast to characteristic uses of *erōs*, "agapeistic" love never seeks to "possess" the other for its own self-gratification. When a lover (or, in a different idiom, a parent) expresses love in the form of "I *want* you," danger signals begin to emerge suggesting a kind of love that sails too close to the wind of gratifying the "interests" of the self. Genuine love may seek to protect; but genuine love is never manipulative. This addresses many kinds and levels of relationship within marriage and the family; but it also concerns relationships within the church and in other spheres of life. It reflects the love of Christ, who "did not please himself" (Rom. 15:3).

Paul ascribes many of the problems in Corinth to a series of failures to live this out: insisting on one's own way about idol food (10:24, 33); rushing ahead with the Lord's Supper or "hosting" it insensitively (11:21-22); interrupting speakers to intrude sudden revelations, or speaking too long at the expense of listening to others (14:29-33). All these manifestations of preoccupation with self-interest treat "the other person" not as a *person* in their own right *("you")* but as an *object* to serve the self (transposed into an *"it,"* in Martin Buber's idiom). This also signals a major difference between love and lust in the marital, romantic, or sexual sphere.

Love **does not become exasperated into pique** (v. 5b) translates a single Greek verb that draws on the metaphor of *making sharp* or *making acid* to denote the experience of **exasperation** or *irritation*. In the papyri the word often denotes the experience of "being provoked," especially to "irritation." Love, in this sense, Paul declares, "does not overreact." There is much to be said for Barrett's succinct translation, "is not touchy." All the same, this, like most other proposed translations, does not do full justice to the careful use of the passive voice here.

Paul's wording looks back to the positive praise of a love that **waits patiently**. If love lacks *patience* and allows *self-regard* or *self-importance* to creep in, such contaminated love may **become exasperated into pique** or into *bitterness,* in part because self-interest has been affronted and in part because it has overreacted. "Agapeistic" love may degenerate into a self-regarding love that nurses and parades its "hurts." Love then becomes corrupted into a kind of moral blackmail, and becomes manipulative. This seriously threatens the survival and growth of "true" love, for it may generate a cycle of mutual recrimination.

With great pastoral sensitivity and insight Paul anticipates the possibility of such a process. He seeks to nip it in the bud by insisting:

love **does not keep a reckoning up of evil** (v. 5c). Some argue that the Greek word *(logizomai)* means "does not take evil into account," while Spicq follows the traditional "thinks no evil" (AV/KJV). But the verb usually means "to reckon" or **to reckon up**, often in the sense used in accountancy.

REB has "keeps no score of wrongs," but NRSV loses the dynamic thrust with the adjective "resentful." As we have suggested above, deviation and decline occur when love degenerates into mutual recrimination. While the verb probably denotes "adding up" and "counting" supposed wrongs, other translations fill out further nuances of the situation that Paul envisages: the supposed wrongs of the other person or group are counted, noted, brooded upon, and resentfully added into a grand total of supposed "hurt." Each phrase brilliantly unfolds the one that went before in this prophetic meditation.

Love does not take pleasure at wrongdoing (v. 6a) clearly alludes to the wrongdoing of someone else. The competitive temperament, behavior, and situation in Corinth provide circumstances in which someone's failure, mistake, or fall could be a source of secret pleasure to another. Alternatively or additionally, Paul may have in the back of his mind the situation in 5:1-5 where genuine love would never join in the mood of self-congratulation or arrogance concerning tolerance or even warm acceptance of the incestuous man. It would not disregard the effects of self-damage or self-destruction. True love never gloats at someone's failure, nor thrills at the thought of being able to lecture someone on his or her shortcomings. Love never relishes the opportunity to say, "I told you so." A pastor who loves a congregation takes no pleasure in having to say a hard thing. No more is personal satisfaction at criticizing someone's ministry a sign of genuine love for the minister, unless it is done with a heavy and gracious heart.

The last phrase of v. 6 has been largely misunderstood. Many suggest that **truth**, or *the truth* here, denotes gospel truth (Fee, *First Epistle*, p. 639). But this use of the word belongs mainly to the later writings of the New Testament and interrupts the context of thought. However, the use of persuasive rhetoric in Corinth (cf. 2:1-5) suggests an understanding that resonates with postmodern aspects of our culture today. Michel Foucault among others views uses of knowledge and rhetorical "spin" as tools of *power*. From Nietzsche to Foucault and Lyotard interpersonal relations are seen more in terms of rhetoric and power on behalf of the self than in terms of truth. But this emerges also from biblical perceptions of the deceitfulness of the human heart and human fallenness. Hence Paul urges that love seeks not the self-promotion and power interests of spin and rhetorical coloring, but **celebrates** disinterested **truth**.

In accord with this, Spicq rightly understands the compound verb (*chairei*, "rejoices," with the prefix *syn-* or *syg-*) to mean "congratulate . . . felicitate . . . applaud . . . acclaim . . ." in a participatory sense (Spicq, *Agapē*, vol. 2, p. 158). In our view the best translation is **joyfully celebrates truth**, for it discards any hidden interest of its own. This fits well with Nygren's emphasis on love as being disinterested, undistracted by thoughts of personal gain, and creative of value. It needs no subtexts or manipulative devices, for, as the next verse implies, it can face anything.

The grand climax emerges in v. 7: *love **never tires of support, never loses faith, never exhausts hope, never gives up***. The REB, as I observe in my larger commentary, is the only major version to appreciate that English *has to use a double negative* to convey the difference between an exclusive and inclusive use of Paul's term "all things" in the Greek. Paul's "all things" excludes limits, but this does *not* serve to define what love includes. To suggest, for example, that "love believes all things" (AV/KJV) is to transpose the robust **never loses faith** of *agapē* into the credulous blindness of romantic or erotic love, often denoted by *erōs*. Here REB rightly suggests: "there is no limit to its faith," which is accurate, but this also loses the dynamic motion of the Greek verb for "believe," which **never loses faith** attempts to preserve.

The first of these four unlimited qualities of genuine love finds a focus in a word (Greek *stegei*) that may relate to both *a roof as a covering* and *a roof as a protection,* and is also related to *support*. This leads to a difference of emphasis among translators. Paul may be saying that love throws a *protective cover* over everything that another has done that may bring discredit upon them. This is possible. However, NRSV's "bears all things" and NIV's "always protects," are more probable, while NJB hedges its bets by proposing "always ready to make allowances." The problem with these is partly that they leave us with fairly insipid English for a fantastic climax to a robust crescendo of extraordinarily powerful language, climbing to the heights with *"all things . . . all things . . . all things . . ."* or with *"never . . . never . . . never. . . ."*

A further reason lies behind our choice of *love* **never tires of support**. Some interpreters argue that Paul places *himself* in the role of the one who loves (i.e., loves the church in Corinth).* This remains speculative, but if it is correct, the four phrases precisely describe Paul's attitude, which will lead on to 2 Corinthians: *Love* **never tires of support, never loses faith, never exhausts hope, never gives up. Never gives up** points to the third stanza of this chapter in which "love never ends." It is not only Paul's example, however, that inspires these words; the love of Christ **never gives up**: "He loved them to the end" (John 13:1).

36. Suggestions for Possible Reflection on 13:1-7

(1) *On the emptiness of seeking every gift except love (vv. 1-3):* On what do we spend most of our time and energy? What gifts or achievements do we imagine will win us most respect? Will profound wisdom, prophetic insight, or massive self-sacrifice? If the Spirit has not poured God's love into our hearts until it overflows (Rom. 5:5), all these other "achievements" are like covering many sheets of paper with statistics or equations only to end up with zero as the end result. What tempts us to make such illusory and deceptive judgments about the relative value of these different aspects of service? Perhaps respect and care for others ultimately call for more radical transformation of the self than what merely demands time and energy: might this be a key to this overly ready self-deception?

(2) *On avoiding loveless and intrusive "noise" (v. 1):* In acoustics and electronics "noise" carries a technical meaning. It denotes the generating of sound or current that often accompanies a transmitted signal but is not part of it, but rather obscures it and partially drowns it out. This is close to Paul's metaphor of *an acoustic resonator* that amplifies noise but conveys no musical note or signal in its own right. Without love for the other, Christians can unwittingly generate mere "noise." Others may feel that they invade their personal space in obtrusive ways, with no effect except irritation. How can we insure that our presence, words, and deeds are not merely intrusive: like mere "noise" that obscures Christ rather than conveys Christ?

*Technical Note: For example, E. Stuart, "Love Is . . . Paul," *Expository Times* 102 (1991): 264-66. However, Stuart sees this as a manipulative strategy. C. J. Walters rejects this claim (cf. 13:6) but endorses the basic proposal, "'Love Is . . . Paul' — A Response," *Expository Times* 103 (1991-92): 75.

(3) *On pure or mixed motivations that lie behind love and loving action (v. 3):* Whether the manuscript of v. 3 reads *"to glory"* or *"to be burned,"* Paul warns us that people can make extraordinary sacrifices for reasons other than love. Might self-sacrifice spring from dour, half-resentful duty? Might it ever spring from a desperate desire to win respect or recognition, or to make others take us more seriously? When is love *freely given,* and when does love *depend on receiving something* in return? God's love does not depend on whether we are attractive to God: God loves us freely. How can Christians show *that kind* of love that does not love *only the like-minded, congenial, or attractive?* How does all this shed light on the love of Christ?

(4) *On the virtue of waiting patiently (v. 4a):* We spoke of patience as a "temporal virtue" (Doctrine Commission Report, *Being Human,* pp. 121-23). Many examples of great things or events simply cannot be rushed: examples of great music; a growing oak tree; and the maturing of a thinker, scholar, or artist. So why does our "postmodern" era ever demand instantaneousness? Why do we demand instant solutions, instant success, instant cures or answers? Would genuine love for the other seek premature closure of what troubles or challenges the other? How important in pastoral work is judging *the right time* for action (or inaction)? Since God chose to make time, along with space, a dimension of this world, can love fail to respect its timings? Temporal virtue is grounded in God. God will *give* us time for what God wills; if he gives no time, has God willed it?

(5) *On the warmth, generosity, and purity of showing kindness (v. 4a):* We noted that in modern English "kind" often seems bland and insipid. "How kind!" is often a merely conventional reply. Paul deliberately uses a rare verb here to suggest dynamic action, in contrast to the more usual abstract noun "kindness." It occurs only here within the whole New Testament, and otherwise only in Christian writings (Danker, *Greek-English Lexicon,* 3rd edn. p. 1089). But even the noun includes "the quality of being helpful . . . 'readily generous in disposition'" (p. 1090). The quality is ascribed to God (Ps. 30:20; Rom. 2:4; 9:23; 11:22). To "show kindness" (the verb) invites acts of kindness from others (*1 Clement* 13:2; 14:3). How can we more adequately appreciate the warmth, power, and generosity of sheer kindness? How closely does this word bring us to the heart of *love?*

(6) *On the contamination of love by envy, self-importance, and self-interest (vv. 4b, 5):* The context of v. 4b is especially (but not exclusively) the church. If we

genuinely love our fellow Christians, shall we grudge them gifts or ministries that God may choose to give to them? What place has *envy* if we love them? Does not love want the best for the loved one? If God deals with us through sheer gift alone, can we deal with others on a different basis? How important is generosity as an indicator of "pure" love?

(7) *On love under pressure to keep a score of "hurts" (vv. 5b-6):* As J. Moltmann observes, to love is to render oneself vulnerable. Indeed, "a God who cannot suffer cannot love either" (*Trinity and Kingdom*, p. 38). This applies to husbands and wives, parents and children, and lovers. Hence the one who loves is especially open to being wounded through misunderstandings, false assumptions, or disappointments. How do we prevent this from *"becoming exasperated into pique"* (v. 5b)? Where there is *self-regard* and lack of *patience,* this turns readily into "a parade of hurts." This, in turn, provides material for a manipulative blackmail in which the one who is "hurt" seeks redress. Paul perceives that a downward spiral into mutual recrimination can be prevented only if *love does not keep a reckoning up of evil* (v. 5c), or "keeps no score of wrongs" (REB). Love will never seek to identify a grand total of supposed "hurt" or injury. How can we best avoid these pitfalls in the church, in the home, at work, or in society?

(8) *On the nonmanipulative character of love (v. 6):* Love is never glad if another fails. Does love sometimes lose its way, and we are tempted to say, "I told you so," even with relish? How easily might the dynamics of love degenerate into dynamics of manipulative control? Self-deception might pretend that this is for the benefit of the other. But true love persists, and discards false rhetoric in favor of a mutual search for truth, which it then celebrates.

(9) *On the constancy and tirelessness of true love (v. 7):* Love *never tires of support,* . . . *never gives up* (v. 7).

> Love is strong as death. . . .
> Many waters cannot quench love,
> neither can floods drown it.
> If one offered for love
> all the wealth of one's house,
> it would be utterly scorned. (Song of Songs 8:6-7)

Paul's ringing declarations carry no constraints of context, time, or place. God's love for the world and his church *never tires of support . . . never gives up.* Christians are caught up in that love. What encouragement might this suggest for our Christian assurance, trust, and hope? What challenge might it suggest?

2. The Permanence and Solid Futurity of Love (13:8-13)

8 Love never falls apart. Whether there are prophecies, these will be brought to an end; or if it be tongues, these will stop; if it be "knowledge," this will be rendered obsolete. 9 For we know in fragmentary ways, and we prophesy part by part. 10 But when the completed whole comes, what is piece by piece shall be done away. 11 When I was a child, I used to talk like a child, form opinions like a child, count values like a child; when I reached adulthood, I turned my back on the things of childhood. 12 For we are seeing the present only by means of a mirror indirectly; but then it will be face to face. For the present I come to know part by part; but then I shall come to know just as fully as I have been known. 13 So now, there remain faith, hope, love, these three; but the greatest of these is love.

What is true about love at the interpersonal level has even larger implications and applications at the cosmic level, in which it relates to the end time. Describing a state of affairs independent of human perceptions Paul declares, Love **never falls** *down,* **falls** *to the ground,* or **never falls apart** (v. 8a). The NIV (with AV/KJV), "never fails," NRSV, "never ends," and REB, NJB, "never comes to an end," elucidate the metaphor, but since Paul has hitherto used such "physical" metaphors as burning, inflating, sticking a sharp point into someone, and adding up accounts, it would be a pity to part with the metaphor of *falling.* **Falls apart** retains the metaphor and its application.

The three protases of conditional clauses (**whether ... if ... if ...**) underline that the gifts to which **love** stands in contrast as absolute and permanent are relative and temporary: even **if** people have the gift of prophetic speech, this will become obsolete and redundant at the end time; **if** the gift is that of **tongues, these will stop**. The church will no longer need even "**knowledge**," for the Day of the Lord will reveal all, and then this gift **will be rendered obsolete**.

This contrast between the *relativity* of "**knowledge**" and the *absolute* permanence of **love** unfolds further still the contrast of 8:1 between knowledge and love. The contrast looks back to chapters 3 and 8–10, just as the contrast between love and **prophecy** or **tongues** looks forward to chapter 14. The powerful verb translated **brought to an end** and **rendered obsolete** applies respectively to **prophecy** and **knowledge**. (**Stop** is only for stylistic variation.)

The verb is the same as that used in 2:6 (the rulers of this age are "doomed to come to nothing") and 1:28. Will the redeemed in heaven need sermons from **prophets**? Will their resurrection modes of being express praise in **tongues**? No, but **love** will ever remain the interpersonal currency of heaven. It will characterize the relation between God and God's created beings. Other gifts will evaporate as now also redundant, but habituated attitudes and acts of love will survive as part of God's celestial glory. Karl Barth observes that all other gifts are subject to "relativization in the light of [the] . . . future; but their relativization will not overtake love" (*Church Dogmatics* IV/2, sect. 68, p. 837). In my larger commentary I discuss "cessationist" views of tongues, or the view that "tongues" ceased after the close of the biblical canon (*First Epistle*, pp. 1061-64).

The traditional translation of v. 9, "Now we know in part" (AV/KJV, NRSV, NIV) and "partial knowledge" (REB), do not adequately reproduce acquiring knowledge as a *process* suggested by the Greek *(ek merous)*. Paul asserts that in this present life we come to know *bit by bit, piece by piece, part by part*, or in *piecemeal stages*. For stylistic variation we translate **in fragmentary ways** in v. 9a, and as **part by part** in v. 9b: **For we know in fragmentary ways, and we prophesy part by part**.

This has important consequences for theories of knowledge. We cannot reach an integrated wholeness of knowledge on this side of the grave. Because we acquire knowledge "bit by bit," human understanding always retains a provisional dimension. Nevertheless, when knowledge is founded upon revelation, it becomes adequate *in practice* for the *next step on the way*. This is how Luther understood "the clarity of Scripture" in debate with Erasmus: clear enough to take the next step. But Paul rejects the notion current among some in Corinth that "knowledge" can be fully achieved and mastered (3:18; cf. 8:1). Hence he prefers to use, not the noun "knowledge" (*gnōsis*, favored in Corinth), but the verb "to come to know" (*ginōskō*, denoting a *process*).

The completed whole will not **come** (v. 10) until the end time. But then its arrival will be like the sun that eclipses, swamps, or drenches out, the efforts of candles that we needed when it was dark.

Only a fool lights a candle in the full blaze of the sun. In this sense the *"pieces"* of candlelight **shall be done away** (v. 10b). (In philosophical terms Hegel's claim that "only the whole is real," and Pannenberg's discussion of "the whole" and meaning in theology provide a helpful backcloth for understanding this verse, for those of a philosophical cast of mind [Pannenberg, *Basic Questions*, vol. 1, p. 181].) All the same, the **piece-by-piece** knowing of the present may be **done away** in an even stronger sense. Jürgen Moltmann urges that the "new" does not simply "emerge" from the old in a developmental sense: "It makes the old obsolete. It is not simply the old in new form. It is also a new creation" (*The Coming of God,* pp. 27-28).

Many writers seem to miss the point of Paul's analogy: **talk like a child, form opinions like a child, count values like a child** (v. 11). It is unfashionable to follow Augustine's reflections in his *Confessions* that a **child** is not merely immature but also, to a large extent, however "innocent," largely centered on self-concern (with the rest of "fallen" humanity). A child often orders strategies of desire in terms of short-term wishes for the present. **Adulthood** perceives the need to "order" spontaneous, short-term wishes to take account of the impact of one individual's intrusive "fun" on others.

There is keen debate about whether Paul's contrast between **child** and *adult* relates directly to the gift of tongues in chapter 14 and to other gifts of the Spirit in chapters 12 and 14. Understandably many reject the notion that **I turned my back on the things of childhood** (v. 11b) can be understood to mean "**turned my back** on prophecy and tongues." Others insist that this is Paul's meaning, often citing 14:20. But a third view may be more likely. **Forming opinions** or **counting values like a child** applies not to using gifts from the Holy Spirit as such, but *to holding a childishly self-centered view of them.* "Spirituality" in Corinth, the whole epistle suggests, was regarded less as Christ-like holiness involving transformation of life than as receiving toylike gifts that provided status or pleasure in the playroom. *The key point here is that* **love**, *by contrast, decenters the self.* Real **love** sees spiritual gifts as *"for* the church," to build "the other"; not *for* "the self" (14:4).

This verse (v. 11) is a pivotal and climactic one for expounding not how "maturity" affects everything, but how sheer **love** affects everything. After all, this is precisely the thrust of 13:1-3, and the chapter broadly forms a chiasmus in which the third stanza presses home the points made in the first. The second stanza provides an astonishingly powerful explication of the nature, power, and action of love. On this basis the third stanza presses home the point of vv. 1-3 all the more effectively. "Maturity" provides an analogy dependent upon using reflection and greater self-awareness about what springs from self-interest and self-concern or otherwise.

The further analogy of the **mirror** in v. 12 raises one or two difficult questions. Corinth produced and exported some good-quality bronze mirrors, by the standards of the day. Polished bronze could provide a fairly good reflection of the person who looked into the mirror. So how can Paul suggest that such mirrors yield only "a poor reflection" (NIV) or "puzzling reflections" (REB), let alone "seeing through a glass darkly" (AV/KJV)? Convex or concave mirrors might distort an image, but Paul's low assessment of their effectiveness would hardly be seen as tactful in Corinth. The key lies in the contrast with **face to face** (v. 12b). In *relative* terms there is a huge difference between viewing an image **indirectly** and having **face-to-face** eye contact.

Specialist scholars have suggested numerous backgrounds, for example, from Num. 12:8 and Ezek. 43:3, for a Hebrew wordplay on "vision" and "mirror," allusions to "magic" mirrors used by sorcerers, and the role of "image" in Plato's philosophy (discussed in my *First Epistle*, pp. 1067-70). Paul and his audience were not "Platonists," but certain notions found in Plato have a place in later popular thought. One such notion was the inferiority of "image" as an inferior copy of reality; another was Plato's analogy of knowing through "reflections" in a dark cave. But however we understand Paul's use of analogy here, the main thrust is clear. Perfect "knowledge" is not merely by inference or deduction.

In the biblical writings *the shining of God's* **face** provides the supreme model or paradigm of an interpersonal **coming to know just as fully as I have been known** (v. 12c). **Face-to-face** understanding *outshines any other way of seeking to know,* but if the **face** is the **face** of God "shining upon" his people, God's saving, intimate, self-revealed presence becomes *transforming as well as revelatory.* Only here does any opposition or contrast between **knowledge** and **love** vanish away, for here **knowing** is shaped by **being known**, and **love** defines this mutuality.

The line of the hymn that reads "And when I see Thee as Thou art, I'll praise Thee as I ought" expresses the same confidence that the pouring out of God's love in human hearts through the Holy Spirit (Rom. 5:5) will reach perfection at the end time. Here **know** in its verbal form recalls the dimension of intimate personal encounter that we find in Hebrew uses of the word to denote sexual union.

To become *one* with God in **face-to-face** encounter is to receive a drenching in the divine love that nurtures unqualified loving reciprocity. Bornkamm observes, "The cleft between knowing and being known by God is abolished" (Bornkamm, "The More Excellent Way," in *Early Christian Experience*, p. 185). Here also Johannine theology comes close to Paul: "We know that when Christ appears we shall be like him, because we shall see him as he is" (1 John 3:3, REB).

After these rhapsodic heights it is anticlimactic to have to consider two different interpretations of v. 13. But the verse may be read in either of two ways: Do three things *(faith, hope,* and *love)* last forever (with REB and NRSV)? Or does one thing *(love)* last forever (with NIV and NJB)? REB translates: "There are three things that last for ever: faith, hope and love"; and NRSV, Now faith, hope, and love abide." Against this, NJB and NIV understand "abides" or "remains" (Greek *menei*) not in a temporal sense ("lasts") but in a logical sense ("there remains [to be considered]"). NJB translates: "As it is, there remain faith, hope, and love" (NIV is similar).

If the Greek verb has a temporal meaning, it is difficult to reconcile with the implication of vv. 8-12 that *love alone* abides forever. On the other hand, *faith* may perhaps endure in the form of a confident looking to God for everything, while *hope* may await yet more "new things" from the living God. On balance, Paul may well mean: "Taking all into account, we have on the table faith, hope, and love, and the greatest of these is love." Our translation leans toward this, but leaves the door partly open: **So now, there remain faith, hope, love, these three. But the greatest of these is love**.

Since hope vanishes when what we hope for comes firmly into view (Rom. 8:24), and since faith, at least in some of its various meanings, stands in contrast to sight (2 Cor. 5:7), at the very least, even if faith and hope survive forever, these will assume different forms. Barth takes up this point in his ringing declaration about love. Love is "the future eternal light shining in the present. It therefore needs no change of form" (*Church Dogmatics*, IV/2, sect. 68, p. 840). The pastor and theologian may be out of a job at the end time. But the one who learns to love has cultivated habits of mind and attitudes that will never become redundant or obsolete. For love is grounded in the very nature of God.

37. SUGGESTIONS FOR POSSIBLE REFLECTION ON 13:8-13

(1) *On the tenacity of love (v. 8):* In what sense is "love . . . strong as death" (see above, Song of Songs 8:6)? While death has a single fling, and brings a premature end, love "never falls apart" (v. 8) and endures to the ultimate end. Hosea celebrates the tenacity of God's love that grips and holds onto the loved one (11:4 and throughout), even when such love is rejected. Francis Thompson's *Hound of Heaven* portrays the endless pursuit of divine love that never tires and never quits, even incognito. George Mattheson, emerging from a dark period of mental anguish, cries, "O love that wilt not let me go," and relishes its "ocean's depths . . . sunshine's blaze," from which "there blossoms red life that shall endless be." This is covenant love: it will never go back on what love has pledged and promised.

(2) *On the provisional value of prophetic speech, speaking in tongues, and "knowledge" compared with the absolute and ultimate value of love (vv. 8b-10):* There are no "ifs or buts" about showing love. Other gifts depend on the right time and right attitudes to be of any value. Could the timing or application of a "prophecy" be wrong? When could demonstrating "knowledge" merely inflate the person who "knows"? Are we aware of how much hard work is required to build genuine "'knowledge' piece by piece"? But how much more hard work is required by persistent, unselfish habits of love?

(3) *On growing from childhood to maturity (v. 11):* Paul has already alluded to infantile or childish "spirituality" as that which remains self-absorbed (3:1-3). The relative innocence of children brings delight. But how would we characterize Christians of longer years who remain "children" under the illusion that it is attractive to postpone adulthood? In what ways can Christians be "childish" in their faith? Do such qualities as overdependence, instability, short-term goals, and a desire for instantaneous gratification provide further content to this metaphor? On the other hand, need "maturity" bring lack of excitement, apathy, or world-weary, "seen it all" cynicism? How can we retain the zest of youth with the wisdom of age?

(4) *On the beatific vision of loving and being loved in perfect communion (v. 12):* The beatific vision (seeing God face to face) will come at the end time,

when mutual love will need no sacrament or church or Bible, no knowledge by inference, but the vision of God face to face. A lover does not need another to tell them about the loved one when they have met. The nearest experience this side of death is "seeing the glory of the Lord as though reflected in a mirror . . . being transformed into the same image from one degree of glory to another" (2 Cor. 3:18). Only poetry or hymn can hint at the celestial vision: "And when I see Thee as Thou art, I'll praise Thee as I ought."

The Psalms declare that God will "make his face shine upon us" (Ps. 67:1). "God's glory," as Hans Urs von Balthasar explains, is also God's beauty and radiance. Quoting Barth, Balthasar writes that to see God's face is to see him "as the one who arouses *pleasure,* creates desire for himself, and rewards with *delight* . . . the one who as God is both *lovely and loveworthy*" (*The Glory of the Lord,* vol. 1, p. 54). To contemplate God face to face is to see that God "is beautiful, divinely beautiful in His own way . . . as unattainable primal beauty, yet really beautiful" (Barth, *Church Dogmatics* II/1, sect. 31, p. 650).

E. Applying Love to the Gifts of Speech and Speaking in Tongues (14:1-40)

Many commentators seem to write as if chapter 14 introduced a separate topic from chapter 13. But throughout chapter 14 Paul shows how love, in the sense defined in chapter 13, makes a difference for how Christians exercise the gifts of the Spirit, especially the gifts of speech or utterance. Paul affirms the value of speaking in tongues as a vehicle of praise to God (vv. 2, 5), but more strongly asserts the value of prophetic discourse as a way of building up others and implementing a loving concern for the whole church (vv. 1, 4, 5, 19).

This leads to the neglected and sometimes unfashionable truth that "church order" (i.e., acceptance of discipline and restraint in the life of the church), far from suggesting a *lack* of concern for the Spirit's renewal, provides a medium for the expression of love and respect for others inspired by the Spirit. Church order restrains self-centered individualism on the part of some less reticent Christians. Sometimes "structure" can benefit all.

Indeed, this theme of self-discipline for the sake of love has come to the fore already from 8:7-13, chapter 9, parts of chapter 10, and the whole of chapter 11. These principles are now applied to the respective roles of speaking in tongues and prophetic speech, again with further reference to differences between different gifts. The chapter has a single, coherent theme, but (a) 14:1-25 focuses on *intelligibility* as a condition for "building" others, while (b) 14:26-40 focuses on *"controlled"* speech.

1. Only Intelligible Communication Can "Build Up" (14:1-25)

a. Gifts for the Self or Gifts for the Benefit of Others? (14:1-5)

1 Pursue love and then be eager for gifts of the Spirit [for utterance], most particularly that you may prophesy. 2 For the person who speaks in a tongue does not communicate to human beings but speaks to God. For no one understands anything, but he or she utters mysteries in the Spirit. 3 However, when a person prophesies to other people, the speaker thereby builds them up, encourages them, and brings them comfort. 4 For the person who speaks in a tongue "builds up" himself or herself; whereas the one who prophesies builds up the church community. 5 I take pleasure in all of you speaking in tongues, but I would rather that you prophesy. The person who prophesies is of greater importance than the one who speaks in tongues, unless that person articulates the utterance intelligibly for the church community to receive this "building up."

The little conjunction after **Pursue love** can be translated either as "and" or as "but," and in my larger commentary I proposed "but." On further reflection over five more years I conclude that more than a contrast alone is at stake, and follow NRSV's "then," to translate: **Pursue love and then be eager for gifts**. But "strive for" (NRSV) seems inappropriate. Paul affirms an *eagerness* to receive whatever the Spirit may be pleased to give of himself. Since *"love builds"* (8:1), the gift that does the most "for the other" is **prophetic speech**, which itself is characterized as **building up** the Christian community.

Verse 2, **For the person who speaks in a tongue does not communicate to human beings but speaks to God** offers one of the clearest definitions of speaking in tongues in the New Testament, always bearing in mind two provisos: (1) that Paul recognizes various *kinds* of tongues (12:10); and (2) that these are the kind that are at issue in Corinth and probably the Pauline churches. We have suggested that this may take the form of inarticulate praise, or the releasing of divine mysteries in God's presence, akin to the experience of Rom. 8:26. There "groaning" or "sighing" (Greek *stenagmos*) may well denote what springs up from preconscious depths where the Spirit is at work but the conscious mind can scarcely comprehend. Here (14:2) Paul lays emphasis on the point that **no one understands** the sounds that issue forth except God himself.

By contrast, prophetic speech **builds other people up** (v. 3), **encourages them, and brings them comfort**. If the criterion for evaluating gifts, therefore, is **love** for others (v. 1), **prophetic speech** is clearly the more important. Again, we argue above that *prophecy* may include various kinds of God-given, revelatory speech, including applied pastoral preaching. Verses 24-25 suggest that it could also include evangelistic preaching.

"Building up" oneself only is the net effect of speaking in tongues (v. 4). This may be taken at face value, as a simultaneous recognition of its value (Fee, *First Epistle,* p. 657), but also as a condemnation of individualism and self-centeredness. Vielhauer argues at length that "build" here is used ironically to denote a self-indulgent religiosity that brings individual satisfaction but helps no one else (Vielhauer, *Oikodomē,* pp. 86-98; also Garland, *1 Corinthians,* pp. 633-34). **"Building up"** is defined not only in terms of *love* and *prophetic speech,* but also in terms of Paul's self-awareness of the apostolic task. Sandnes develops our understanding of *prophecy* helpfully by relating it to Paul's personal prophetic call to proclaim the death and resurrection of Christ. This is apostolic and prophetic proclamation (Sandnes, *Paul — One of the Prophets?*).

The best way to translate **I take pleasure in all of you speaking in tongues** (v. 5) is widely disputed. REB has "I am happy for you," which fits the context well. NRSV and NIV are more controversial: "I would like every one of you to speak in tongues." The problem arises because the Greek word in question (*thelō*) ranges in meaning from "I want" or "I would like," to "I am willing" or "I am happy for."

Commentators and translators are found at both ends of the spectrum as well as in the middle. For example, (1) NJB, Conzelmann, Bruce, and Héring view it as concessive: Paul "allows" tongues. (2) NIV and Fee view it as a positive wish: Paul "wants" tongues. (3) Some argue that "wish" governs *only the whole sentence,* that is, **I would rather that you prophesy** (Kistemaker, citing Num. 11:29, I wish that all the Lord's people were prophets). (4) In Mark 12:38 the same Greek verb denotes "takes pleasure in" (the scribes take pleasure in walking in long robes). Whatever emphasis we place upon the verb, Paul sums up his chief desire in v. 5b: **I would rather that you prophesy**.

The third part of v. 5 reinforces the point with one proviso. Prophetic speech is a more important medium of utterance than speaking in tongues **unless that person articulates the utterance** [spoken in tongues] **intelligibly**. The text, however, does not make clear or explicit *who* is doing the "articulating" or "interpreting." Most writers see here an allusion to "the interpretation of tongues" as an activity performed by someone other than the tongues speaker. I have argued against this view in several studies, mainly on the basis of 14:13, where there is *no* word for "someone" who interprets in the original Greek (also followed by Garland, *1 Corinthians*, p. 635).

The most natural way of understanding both verses, I argue, is that if the one who speaks in tongues can articulate this profound experience of praise or mystery intelligibly, they would be uttering prophetic speech. However, the notion of a distinct "interpreter" remains entrenched almost as a *cultural* tradition of understanding in many circles today. Whichever view is correct, Paul's central concern is for the *intelligible communication* of gospel truth.

38. Suggestions for Possible Reflection on 14:1-5

(1) *On being eager for God's gifts (v. 1):* While human analogies may be weak and sometimes misleading, can we learn anything from the eagerness of a child for a parental gift as a birthday or Christmas approaches? A child would not offer achievements or qualifications to "earn" the desired gift. But the child might express a present longing for and potential appreciation of a longed-for gift. All the same, a trusting child would not finally question a parental "no" about the gift if the timing and the situation of the child suggest this. How many demands for inappropriate pets have met with "no" from love and wisdom? Do we show genuine eagerness for God's gifts, with measured trust in God's love and wisdom to choose the best for us?

(2) *On the motivation for being eager for the gift of prophetic speech (vv. 1, 3, 4):* Prophetic speech "builds" others (v. 44). Does eagerness for a gift assume a

higher level when this stems largely from a desire to share the gift for the benefit of others? Is this one reason why to desire the gift of prophetic speech seems to rank more highly than a desire to speak in tongues?

(3) *On being careful not to disparage the gift of tongues (vv. 2, 5):* Parts of this chapter appear to "downgrade" tongues only because the comparison is with prophecy or with love. But tongues speaking speaks to *God* (v. 2b), and presumably the welling up of praise to, or longing for, God, gives *God* delight, even if others do not also profit. How can anyone resent the apportioning out (12:4-7) of such a gift, or be envious of it or critical of it? What invites criticism is only its exercise in public worship without its intelligible articulation, or any attitude of self-congratulation or superiority on the part of the tongues speaker. Might God give other ways of liberation, release, and using praise language to those whom he does not choose to give the gift of tongues? Do we eagerly seek these?

(4) *On the goal of "building" others and the wider church (vv. 3-5):* Paul introduced the metaphor of building earlier (3:11-13). If right materials are used on the foundation of Christ, such building lasts forever. Do we perceive building others as shaping the very landscape of eternity? Exercising gifts with love can have an impact on others forever, to become manifest at the Last Day and the life of heaven. In pastoral ministry we call this spiritual *formation.*

b. Four Analogies on the Pointlessness of Making Unintelligible Sounds: Opening the Whole Self (Including the Mind) to God (14:6-19)

6 Well now, dear fellow believers, suppose that when I come to you I come speaking in tongues. What shall I profit you unless I speak to you in terms either of a disclosure or of knowledge, or of prophetic speech or of teaching? 7 Similarly, with reference to an inanimate musical instrument: in the case of either a flute or a lyre, unless these yield distinct differences of pitch, how can what is produced by wind or by string be recognized? 8 Further, if the trumpet produces a sound which is ambiguous as a signal, who will prepare for battle? 9 Even so, if you yourselves do not produce through speaking in a tongue a message which is readily intelligible, how shall what is being said be comprehended? For you are speaking into empty air. 10 It may be that there are varieties of languages within the world, and none fails to use sound. 11 Yet it follows that if I do not know the force of the sound, I shall be an alien to the speaker, and the speaker

will remain an alien in my eyes. 12 You yourselves are in this situation. Since you have a burning concern about the powers of the Spirit, direct this eagerness toward the building up of the church community, to excel in this.

13 Hence the person who prays in a tongue should pray that he or she may put what they have uttered into words. 14 For if I pray in a tongue, my innermost spiritual being prays, but my mind produces no fruit from it. 15 So what follows? I will pray with my deepest spiritual being, but I shall pray with my mind too. I will sing praise with the depths of my being, but I will sing praise with my mind too. 16 Otherwise, if you bless God from the depths of your being only [or *"in the Spirit"*], how can the uninitiated person speak his or her "Amen" to your thanksgiving since he or she does not know what you are saying? 17 For you, on your side, may be giving thanks well enough; but the other, on his or her side, is not being built up. 18 Thank God, I am more gifted in tongues than any of you, 19 but all the same in the assembled congregation I would rather speak five intelligible words to communicate instruction to others than thousands upon thousands in a tongue.

Paul uses vivid, concrete analogies to illustrate a point more often than those who view the epistles as "abstract" readily realize. The first (more negative) half of these dozen or so verses draw on four analogies to bring home the uselessness of unintelligible sounds or speech.

(1) If a preacher were *only* "to speak in tongues," how could the apostolic gospel be heard (v. 6)? In 2:1-5 Paul renounced reliance on professional, high-sounding rhetoric, but equally here he underlines the need for intelligible communicative action. The preacher and audience must share a common language for the gospel to be conveyed, or for Christian **teaching** to have serious effect.

(2) How can an instrument make *music* unless it is capable of producing variations in distinct pitch (v. 7)? This axiom applies to wind instruments (**flute**) and to strings (**lyre**). To **recognize** the melody requires intelligible, patterned distinctions within the productions of sound. Centuries ahead of his time Paul enunciates the axiom associated today with Saussure and Derrida that meaning rests on "difference"; or, in more technical terms, on differences within a sign system that make communication intelligible.

(3) How can military personnel use a trumpet to issue commands unless the trumpeter uses his instrument to produce a recognizable signal (v. 8)? If the notes are confused or blurred, the signal loses its

clarity and becomes ambiguous. With the high stakes of readiness for battle, ambiguity would herald disaster.

(4) How can a foreigner understand or be understood unless those who attempt communication share knowledge of a common language (v. 9)? All languages use **sound**, but sound without sense achieves nothing (vv. 10, 11). To one person the other remains **alien** or barbarian. The language barrier cannot be overcome without thought, reflection, and intelligible speech. **You yourselves are in this situation** (v. 12a).

All this weight of cumulative analogy is to harness **the burning concern about the powers of the Spirit** experienced among Christians in Corinth **toward the building up of the community** rather than the sheer exercise of "gifts" that impress people or bring status or personal satisfaction to the recipient (v. 12b).

This is the governing and determining context for understanding the meaning of v. 13: **The person who prays in a tongue should pray that he or she may put what they have uttered into** [intelligible] **words.** Paul's desire is that the inexpressible delight in God that saturates the preconscious and emotional dimensions of the Christian self may embrace the reflective **mind too** (v. 15). If the speaker-in-tongues who **sings** [or speaks] **praise with the depth of** [his] **being** receives the further gift that **will sing praise with** [his] **mind too** (i.e., by mental reflection and cognitive discernment *make articulate* or *"interpret"* what springs up from **the depths of** [his] **being**), the gift of **tongues** will become transposed through the gift of "articulate utterance" or "interpretation" (12:10) into *prophetic speech*. This articulates what God has revealed, now in an *intelligent form* and in a *shared language*. Then other people can enter into the experience and the praise and add their **"Amen"** to what is said (v. 16).

This understanding of v. 13 provides a *smooth and seamless, coherent, logical flow of argument from 14:1 through to 14:19*. If the "language" remains unshared and private or inarticulate, **you, on your side, may be giving thanks well enough, but the other, on his or her side, is not being built up** (v. 17); or, as REB expresses it, "it is no help to the other person." The NIV, REB, NRSV, and NJB go most of the way toward accepting this understanding of 14:13: "the man who speaks in a tongue should pray that he may interpret what he says" (NIV); or "anyone who speaks in tongues should pray for the ability to interpret" (REB).

It is fundamental to Paul's view of human selfhood that he does *not* set up an opposition or contrast between the **innermost spiritual being** and **the mind**. Both equally are modes of selfhood through which the Holy Spirit is present and active: **I will pray with my deepest spiritual being, but I shall pray with my mind too** (v. 15). Paul encourages careful reflection on the part of Christians, and leads by personal example. We have already alluded to the work of Stanley Stowers, among others, in emphasizing Paul's positive view of "reason" for Christians. On one side Paul perceives that the gospel is "folly" to fallen human reason (1 Cor. 1:18-25); but in openness to Scripture and the Holy Spirit rational reflection is a major instrument or vehicle for good. He does not spare himself the trouble of rigorous rational argument, as Pannenberg reminds us, and he does not resort simply to making declarations under the rubric "Thus says the Lord."

In 14:1-19 the affirmation of rational reflection turns on language, communication, and *intelligibility* as conditions for "building" the church. In 14:20-25 Paul extends this argument by appealing to the role of reflection in promoting *maturity*.

39. SUGGESTIONS FOR POSSIBLE REFLECTION ON 14:6-19

(1) *On the intelligible communication of the Christian faith to others (vv. 6-10):* Paul exclaims, "Woe to me if I do not proclaim the gospel. . . . To the Jews I became as a Jew in order to win Jews. . . . To the weak, I became weak . . . for the sake of the gospel" (9:16, 20, 22-23, NRSV). Do we, like Paul, reflect upon what others are able to "hear"? Are our signs or signals like the voice of a tone-deaf singer, or like the gesticulations of an officer whose directives mean anything or everything? Words, body language, and love all seem to convey a clearer and less ambiguous message than "tongues." How do we seek to communicate the gospel in the clearest and most sensitively appropriate terms?

(2) *On so ordering the church that people are at home (v. 11):* This point is made again more fully in vv. 21-23 (see further under "Suggestions for Possible Reflection" below). Any phenomenon that seems merely bizarre to outsiders, visitors, or other Christians risks making them feel uncomfortable and "not at home." Such patterns of conduct require very special justification. Does any part of our church's ethos, décor, or proceedings, or of our personal conduct, risk *alienating* outsiders or fellow Christians?

(3) On offering the whole self to God, both inmost depths and rational mind (vv. 13-15): John Henry Newman described the eighteenth century as "the age of reason" when love grew cold. Zinzendorf, the Wesleys, and Christian Pietists rightly protested against a religion of reason only, which left the heart untouched and unchanged. But the converse neglects "the whole person" no less. Nietzsche's disparagement of "the bellows of divinity" as merely powering "a heaving heart" has some justification. The use of the mind prevents concern for credibility from becoming sheer credulity. Do I praise and pray "with my deepest spiritual being but . . . with *my mind too*" (v. 15)?

(4) On sharing communal offerings of worship (vv. 16-19): The church in Corinth anticipated to some extent the modern Western vice of undue individualism. God requires and expects the worship of his people *as a people.* Does it matter whether others can say *"Amen"* to praise or prayers that they can fully understand? How might we, or our church, make it harder or easier for everyone to be drawn in as one worshiping people in this way? Might visual texts of common, shared worship facilitate clarity of this kind, or might they inhibit creativity? Do some ways of leading prayer and worship provide a platform for individual performance rather than communal participation? Is there a balance to be sought?

c. Mature Reflection Values the Shared Language of "Home" (14:20-25)

20 My fellow Christians, stop thinking like little children. Be children in matters of wickedness, but begin to think like grown adults. 21 In the Law it is written: "By people of a foreign tongue and by alien lips shall I address this people, and not even then will they hear me, says the Lord." 22 So then, tongues serve not as a sign for believers, but as a sign for judgment for unbelievers; while prophetic speech signals not people who do not believe but those who come to faith. 23 If, therefore, the whole church community comes together and everyone is speaking in tongues, and people who are uninitiated or unbelievers enter, will they not say that you are out of your mind? 24 Suppose, by contrast, that everyone is using prophetic speech, and someone who is an unbeliever or not in the know enters and undergoes conviction and judgment by all that is said. 25 The secret depths of their very being become exposed, and thus they fall to their knees in obeisance and worship God, confessing, "God is indeed really among you."

Paul distinguishes between being *childlike* and *childish*. A childlike character is "innocent" in the sense of being not yet contaminated by **wickedness** (v. 20). But there is nothing attractive about childish ways of *thinking*: **stop thinking like little children . . . but begin to think like grown adults**. (The Greek sets up a contrast between **stop thinking**, the negation of a present imperative, and **begin to think**, the force here of a positive aorist imperative.)

In what sense have Christians in Corinth been in a state of habituated childishness? Where was *mature* reflection absent? Mature, thoughtful Christians, Paul suggests in vv. 21-25, would appreciate that uttering unintelligible sounds, especially if this won approval from those "in the know," tends to make ordinary Christians feel "not at home" in the church. But if Christians belong to the same family (12:12-27), nothing should make them feel that they do not "belong." The "childish," unreflective assumption is that parading the ability to speak in tongues in the public assembly will somehow impress people, whereas mature *reflection* shows that it has the very opposite effect.

Paul cites the scriptural principle exemplified in Isa. 28:11-12 (slightly altered from both Hebrew and LXX versions to emphasize the point) that the experience of being "not at home" was precisely what befell Israel in exile as divine *judgment*. But if Christians stand not under judgment but under grace, those who use tongues in public are thoughtlessly denying the welcome and affirmation due to all Christians who meet together in simple faith, whatever "gifts" they might or might not have. Hence, Paul infers, **tongues serve not as a sign for believers, but as a sign for judgment for unbelievers** (v. 22a). They place the Christian, in effect, in a position more appropriate to unbelievers under judgment, like that of those who do not yet fully belong to the church as *home*.

By contrast, prophetic discourse speaks to them as those who belong: **prophetic speech signals . . . those who come to faith** (v. 22b). Indeed, the greater here includes the less: *anyone* who enters the assembly (**not** those **in the know**) may well draw the conclusion that **if everyone is speaking in tongues, you** [the speakers] **are out of your mind**. What a difference it would make if this were intelligible prophetic discourse! **Suppose, by contrast, that everyone** [who is speaking] **is using prophetic speech. . . . The secret depths of their very being become exposed, and thus they will fall to their knees in obeisance and worship God, confessing, "God is indeed really among you"** (v. 25).

Could any greater contrast be envisaged: *"You are mad,"* or *"God is really here"*? Paul appeals to his Corinthians: "Just *think*."*

40. SUGGESTIONS FOR POSSIBLE REFLECTION ON 14:20-25

(1) *On the peril of trying to impress people, especially if we want them to feel at home:* Can trying to impress people sometimes backfire and have the opposite effect? Sometimes unpretentious "ordinariness" is more effective than anything else. A pastor who invited a non-church couple into his untidy kitchen learned later that they would have run a mile away from his book-lined study. How can we help people to feel more at home with the gospel or the church? Do even Christians feel not at home where we are?

(2) *On signs of the presence of God in our home, community, or church:* Will people say of our church or home, "God is really here" (v. 25)? Recently a group of Christian leaders were discussing what personal "holiness" means. To meet with a *holy* person (in the special sense of this term, it was suggested) somehow leaves the impression that thereby we have also met with God. Dare we hope for this in our case?

(3) *On prophetic speech that reveals the beauty of God:* If prophetic discourse reveals the inner, secret depths of the self, and if this leads to a longing to cast ourselves before God in obeisance (v. 25), does this mean only (or first of all) that prophetic speech exposes sin? Does not prophetic discourse also entail revealing the *beauty* of the Lord God as one who "creates desire for himself and rewards with *delight* . . . the one who as God is both *loving* and *loveworthy*" (Hans Urs von Balthasar, *The Glory of the Lord*, vol. I, p. 54; also citing Karl Barth)?

2. The Value of Controlled Speech (14:26-40)

a. The Ordering of Public Worship (14:26-33a)

26 What follows, then, my dear friends? Suppose that when you assemble together each contributes a hymn, an item of teaching, something disclosed, or

---

*Note on Translation: I have made another very small change from my earlier translation: **those not in the know** better reflects the Greek *idiotēs* than my earlier, accurate but too stilted, *people who are uninitiated*. Similarly, in v. 20 I translated **stop thinking** instead of *do not continue to think* as less clumsy.

speaks in a tongue, or puts the tongues language into words, the point remains: "Let everything serve the building up of the community." 27 If it is in a tongue that someone speaks, let only two or at the most three speak in turn, and let the one who is speaking put it into words. 28 However, if he or she cannot put it into words, let them remain silent in the assembled congregation, and address God privately. 29 In the case of prophets, however, let two or three speak, and let the others sift what is said. 30 If something is disclosed to another person who is sitting down nearby, the first speaker should stop speaking. 31 For you have the power for it to be one by one, every one of you, when you prophesy, in order that all may learn and everyone be encouraged or exhorted. 32 And the spiritual utterances of the prophets are subject to the prophets' control. 33a For God is a God not of disorder but of peace.

Paul explicitly states that what follows is a set of inferences to be drawn from his arguments about intelligible communication and rational reflection in the previous section. **What follows, then** (v. 26a)? or *what does this imply?* What follows is a list of directives for church order.

Some writers perceive "order" as Paul's attempt to repress the liberty of charismatic enthusiasm along the lines of authoritarian "hierarchy" or "paternalism" (Antoinette Wire, *The Corinthian Women Prophets,* 1990). But we have argued that Paul seeks to protect good manners and respect for "the weak" as an outworking of concern for the interests of others, as exemplified in chapter 13. *"Order" is the outworking of love.* It includes restraint and self-discipline, and places individual "autonomy" in question. Paul's belief that "love builds" (8:1, 10) leads to the key point: procedures of public worship fall under the governing axiom **"Let everything serve the building up of the community"** (v. 26b).

It is unfortunate that many commentators interpret the meaning of **each** in v. 26 (Greek *hekastos*) too readily in accordance with their own church traditions. Thus Fee believes that every member of the assembled congregation exercises the gifts or services of v. 26 (Fee, *First Epistle,* p. 684), while Conzelmann, Schrage, and Senft believe that word denotes the person in view at a given time rather than a numerical designation of "every single individual" (Conzelmann, *1 Corinthians,* p. 244; Senft, *Première Epître,* p. 181). The Greek alone cannot determine the matter, but a woodenly literalist understanding of **each** strains the text in this context (Thiselton, *First Epistle,* pp. 1134-35).

Some of the terms used in v. 26 are indeterminate. **Hymn** (Greek *psalmon*) may denote a biblical psalm, a pre-composed hymn, or an innovative utterance sung rather than spoken. Other terms are more akin to their normal modern usage, for example, **teaching. Something disclosed** (Greek *apokalypsis*) may denote a stretch of prophetic speech "given" to a speaker from God, but it may equally include a sermon or even a "given" portion of Scripture as God's revelation. As we have argued, we should be cautious about assuming that **each** in speaking in tongues denotes a different speaker from the one who puts the tongue speaking into words. Hence I have translated v. 27: **If it is in a tongue that someone speaks, let only two or at the most three speak in turn, and let the one who is speaking put it** [their utterance] **into words.**

The NRSV renders v. 28, "But if there is no one to interpret, let them be silent in church and speak to themselves and to God," while NIV similarly has, "If there is no interpreter, the speakers should keep quiet." Since the Greek uses a noun here (NIV, "an interpreter"; Greek *diermēneutēs*), this might seem to favor, after all, the notion of a separate person who interprets, alongside the tongues speaker. But the Greek word occurs only here in the New Testament, and not again until the Byzantine period centuries later (F. W. Danker *Greek-English Lexicon,* 3d edn., p. 244). Some later Western variants (D*, F, G) read *hermēneutēs,* also only here in the New Testament. It would be hazardous to assume that either of these words necessarily denotes one who receives the gift of "interpreting" tongues *spoken by another.* It may simply denote one who has learned by reflection to put his deepest experience into words. In this case, the meaning of v. 28 is: If he or she cannot express this deep experience in words, **let** [that person] **remain silent in the assembled congregation, and address God privately**. This is perhaps the only verse that might just possibly support the more usual view, but it is hazardous to place such weight on a single verse, the meaning of which leaves room for doubt.

Prophets also have the power to control how and what they speak (vv. 29-32). A prophetic discourse is to cease if good cause arises. Similarly, if more than a strictly limited number seek to speak, some may have to wait for another occasion. *Most important of all,* **others** *are to* **sift** *what claims to have been prophetic speech or a "prophecy."* Others must sift whether the discourse or utterance is truly God-given, or whether, perhaps, what began as a God-given utterance degenerated into mere human opinion. This may well be the point of Paul's warning, **the first speaker should stop speaking** (v. 30b), although this may simply reflect the need for courtesy in deferring to another speaker. Paul expects those who claim to utter God-given prophetic discourse also to have *enough critical self-awareness to know when to stop.*

If the practice in Corinth had not been to observe the courtesy of speaking **one by one**, this recalls 13:4-5a: "Love waits patiently . . . is not inflated with its own importance. It does not behave with ill-mannered impropriety." Paul allows no exception to the principle of order: **the spiritual utterances of the prophets are subject to the prophets' control** (v. 32).

If Christians claim that their utterances are "given" or inspired by God, one further test of their genuineness is whether such utterances promote or undermine "order" in the church, for God himself is a God **not of disorder** (Greek *ou . . . estin akatastasias*). This word denotes *disturbance, unruliness* or *opposition to established authority* (F. W. Danker, *Lexicon, BDAG,* 3d edn., p. 35). As Paul will expound in 15:23-28 and 15:38-44, the Creator God is characterized by purposive, ordered activity. Some speak as if the Holy Spirit produced chaos and anarchy, acting in discontinuity rather than continuity with his earlier work. The entire dialectic of unity and diversity from 12:1 to 14:40 exhibits the sovereign purposes of the God of coherence and order, who **builds** the whole, albeit through diversities of gifts and roles.

41. SUGGESTIONS FOR POSSIBLE REFLECTION ON 14:26-33A

(1) *On the constraints of love and the use of rules for the common good (vv. 26-33a):* Respect and courtesy to fellow Christians require that from time to time we readily defer to others. In a group, in the church, in the home, or in any community, "house rules" are needed to insure that necessary constraints operate for the good of the whole. Do we resent rules that have love for others as their aim? Is rule-breaking romantic and courageous, or merely self-centered? However, if rules become obsolete or oppressive, do we share with others a concern to change them to reflect their original purpose? Is there a difference between rules as tools for oppression, and restraints or orderedness grounded in the nature and love of God (v. 33a)?

(2) *On learning to speak in turn (vv. 27-32):* Every chairperson faces the problem of how to give everyone a fair share of speaking, but without inhibiting those whose gifts or wisdom give them something vital to say. Is a speaker always the best judge of how much he or she can contribute? These verses challenge some to speak more readily, but others to more humility and silence.

(3) *On learning to speak more succinctly (vv. 27-32):* How important are the constraints of time? Has everyone time to listen to everything that we want to say? Do we have time to listen to everything that everyone else wants to say? How can a balance be held that insures mutual participation but also the constructive building of the community? In a group we may need the temporal virtue of patience; but a leader or chairperson also needs the virtue of insuring order, and a speaker the virtue of self-control.

(4) *On "ordained" ministry, or leadership, structure, and courtesy (vv. 29-33a):* Every movement that serves a vision needs a structure to support it. Who insures that these third person imperatives *(let him . . .)* have force? Whether the earliest church elected a "chairperson," or whether the apostles appointed or ordained ministers or leaders, structure and order prevent chaos and confusion. Can anarchy or chaos ever be regarded as evidence that the Holy Spirit is at work (v. 33a)? Peace (v. 33a) denotes a harmony derived from mutual courtesy. Do Christians sometimes fail to recognize the distinctively "Christian" basis of courtesy as grounded in the love that accords worth to others?

(5) *On testing prophetic speech (v. 29b):* Paul insists that whether a Christian discourse has come genuinely from God as a prophetic revelation (in part or whole) remains open to *sifting* or testing. Why can we not take a speaker's claim to be inspired by God simply at face value? Can even devout Christians become victims of self-deception and be misled? What criteria of testing should we apply today? What role should we give to the scriptures of the Old and New Testaments? How important is it to ask whether the utterance or sermon coheres with mainline Christian tradition? Does it matter whether it is arguable or "reasonable" in the light of biblical teaching about God, other Christian truth, its context and circumstances? Prayer for the discernment of the Holy Spirit (12:8-11) should always accompany such reflection, meditation, or *sifting*.

b. Further Case Study on Controlled Speech:
Women and Speaking "Out of Order" (14:33b-40)

33b As in all the churches of God's holy people, when congregations meet in public, the women should allow for silence. 34 For there exists no permission for them to speak [*in the way they do*]. Let them keep to their ordered place, as the law indicates. 35 If they want to learn anything, let them interrogate their own husbands at home. For a woman to speak thus in public worship brings disgrace. 36 Or was it from you that the word of God went forth? Or are you the only ones to whom it came?

37 If anyone thinks that he or she is a prophet or "a person of the Spirit," let them recognize that what I write to you is [*a command*] from the Lord. 38 If anyone does not recognize it, he or she is not [*to be*] recognized. 39 So then, my dear friends, continue to be zealously concerned about prophetic speech and do not forbid speaking in tongues. 40 Only, everything should happen fittingly and in an ordered manner.

Paul proceeds to lay down a further rule of church order observed **in all the churches of God's holy people** (v. 33b). The context suggests that "in the churches" (v. 34, NRSV) means **when congregations meet in public**, while "women should be silent" (NRSV; Greek *sigatōsin*) might perhaps invite a broader understanding in keeping with vv. 25-40, with the sense of **the women should allow for silence**. The New English Bible's "should not address the meeting" clearly conflicts with 11:2-16, where "women utter prophetic speech" (v. 5). If, as I have argued, prophetic speech may include pastoral preaching, **silence** in 14:33b-36 can hardly refer to a categorical veto on public preaching or on leading in worship.

Many interpreters have suggested that this supposed contradiction is a genuine contradiction, but that vv. 33b-36 are not from Paul. On this theory they are a non-Pauline piece of material intruded into the text as an interpolation. Fee, Hays, Schrage, and others hold this view on the ground that (1) the verses depart from the main theme of chapters 12-14; (2) they interrupt the argument about prophets; (3) they conflict with 11:5; (4) they appeal to a legal rule; and (5) a few later MSS place the verse after v. 40. One "popular" solution that retains Paul's authorship proposes that 14:33b-36 refers to "chatter," while 11:5 alludes to public speaking. But this cannot be sustained by the Greek.

Patient exegesis suggests a more probable explanation on the assumption that Paul wrote these difficult verses. Since the section here concerns *prophecy*, and the immediate context concerns the *sifting* of prophetic speech, the admonition to curb speech of a certain kind almost certainly refers to contributions from *women who seek to join in the sifting* or *testing of a claim to speak with prophetic authority*. What kind of situation would make such speech "out of order"? This would be exacerbated if the test of daily conduct were cited as undermining such a claim, and if there were any thought of a ganging up of "woman power" to rule a male prophet out of order.

We can only speculate on the nature of the situation, but it is not difficult to imagine scenarios in which the opportunity to take a speaker down a peg might be open to abuse and undermine "order." Ben Witherington similarly imagines the women asking "perhaps inappropriate questions" in the testing of prophecy, "and the worship service was being disrupted" (Witherington, *Conflict and Community*, p. 287). The hypothesis that some women raised questions about prophetic speech *from their own husbands* becomes more plausible in the light of v. 35: **If they want to learn anything** [perhaps expressing doubts about competency and motives], **let them interrogate their own husbands at home** (cf. Thiselton, *First Epistle*, pp. 1146-62).

Paul shows concern not only for respect between husband and wife in public and at home (11:2-16), but also for the effect of ordered or disordered worship upon "outsiders" or unbelievers (14:25). This may corroborate these suggestions. Using public worship as an extension of tensions in the home would have disastrous effects, especially if initiated by the women. Witherington observes, "If women were 'laying down the law' or judging their husbands' prophecy by leading questions . . . worship might become a family feud" (*Women in the Earliest Churches*, p. 102).

The allusion of v. 37, **if anyone thinks that he or she is a prophet or "a person of the Spirit,"** may be to prophets whose claims might be in question. But equally it might well apply to the women who claimed to offer necessary "spiritual" discernment in the criticisms that they made. On the other hand, Paul directs the rebuke of v. 36, **Was it from you that the word of God went forth?** more probably to the leading figures in the church in Corinth who felt themselves free to make up their own "local" rules, whatever the rest of the church "in every place" (1:2) might do.

The force of v. 38a, **If anyone does not recognize it, he or she is not recognized**, performs the speech act of withdrawing recognition of claims. More important still, it reflects the "internal grammar" of 1 Cor. 3:18, "If anyone thinks himself wise, let that person become a fool in order to become wise." This axiom follows 3:17: "If anyone destroys God's temple, that person will God destroy." Each respective action brings a self-defeating axiomatic penalty of self-loss. To step beyond the bounds *is thereby* to show the emptiness or lack of validity of the claim.* This becomes all the clearer when the cross is perceived as both "ground and criterion" of the gospel and the church, especially in 1:18–2:5.

Paul concludes with an encouragement to his **dear friends**, or *brothers and sisters* in Christ, to **continue to be zealously concerned about prophetic speech** (v. 39a). They need not show the same zealous concern about speaking in tongues, although tongues remains an authentic "gift" either for private devotion or to be transposed into public prophecy. They must **not forbid speaking in tongues** (v. 39b). The overriding exhortation about church life, however, is that everything should happen **fittingly** (v. 40, Greek *euschemonōs*, "appropriately"). The word means both *in an orderly, proper sequence* (which would reflect vv. 27-30) and *becomingly, with agreeable, attractive behavior* (which also reflects vv. 20-26). Once again, the term reflects the nature of love in 13:4-7.

The final phrase presses home the point: **fittingly and in an ordered manner** (v. 40b). The Greek phrase *(kata taxin)* reminds readers that this is a quality of God's own nature. We learn in 15:23 that while God brings about resurrection, God enacts this event "each in his own order" *(tō idiō tagmati)*. **Order** and **orderedness** is not confined to the church or even God's creation. It is *the way that God chooses to work because it corresponds with God's nature.*

42. SUGGESTIONS FOR POSSIBLE REFLECTION ON 14:33B-40

(1) *On foregoing possible rights or privileges in the face of sensitive situations (vv. 33b-35, 40):* Paul urges two top priorities: (a) love and respect for the other; and

---

*Technical Note: A. C. Wire claims that Paul makes a cheap rhetorical ploy by claiming "mere thought" for his opponents' claims, and "reality" for his (*Women Prophets*, pp. 14-15 and 149-52). But this misses the subtlety of the "internal grammar" of an inbuilt penalty for a claim that is exposed as simply self-defeating.

(b) all for the sake of the gospel. While he affirms a vocal role for women in public worship (11:2-16), he urges otherwise in circumstances that bring acute sensitivities and threaten these two top priorities. In what ways might these verses constitute a parallel with 8:1-11:1? Does restraint on the part of "the strong" in not eating meat offered to idols parallel the restraint of women not speaking to sift prophecies of men or husbands? What ranking do we accord to respect for others and to furthering the gospel? Are these at all costs?

(2) *On churches or Christian individuals that try to go it alone (vv. 33b, 36, and 38):* The church in Corinth so often wanted to go it alone, in theology and practice. Paul asks: Did a "local" church produce the word of God on its own, or found the gospel (v. 36)? Can a local church invent or reshape the gospel? If it derives biblical and apostolic identity from Christ and from sharing with *all* of God's people, how far can it invent its own rules, even to address a local situation? How far can a church or an individual go it alone before it loses "recognition" as "Christian" (v. 38)?

(3) *On further aspects of testing or sifting prophetic speech (vv. 37-40):* We have already suggested possible reflections on testing prophecy (above, under v. 29b). But these verses may add a further dimension. In addition to such criteria as Scripture, wider church teaching, reflection, and prayer for the wisdom of the Holy Spirit, what part (if any) is played by the "recognition" of a regular, authentic ministry on the part of the speaker? Should manner of life also contribute to these criteria? Can we reach judgements about others or sift what they claim honestly but also with courtesy and respect? Who can make such judgments?

(4) *On doing everything in an ordered manner (v. 40):* If God is a God of *order,* should *"orderedness"* characterize everyday living as God's people? Might some Christians lack a degree of effectiveness because some goals point in different directions, and some of their energies verge on chaos or even self-contradiction?

VIII. The Resurrection of the Dead (15:1-58)

The fifteenth chapter reflects clear and careful logical argument, coherence, and constructive use of resources from the best Roman rheto-

ric of the times. But this does not imply, as some have suggested, that it
stands apart from the rest of the epistle as a separate treatise. It is
worth quoting from Karl Barth. He declares, "The Resurrection of the
Dead is the point from which Paul is speaking and to which he points"
(*The Resurrection of the Dead,* p. 107). "The resurrection . . . forms not
only the close and crown of the whole epistle, but also provides the clue
to its meaning, from which place light is shed on the whole . . . as a
unity" (p. 11).

The resurrection demonstrates more clearly than anything else,
Barth continues, that the "of God" in such passages as "everyone shall
have praise of God" (4:5) is "the secret nerve . . . of the whole epistle"
(p. 18). Resurrection is neither a religious achievement nor an innate
human capacity for postmortal survival, but *a transforming, sovereign gift
of God.* In an earlier chapter Paul questions, "What do you have that you
did not receive?" (4:7). At death, humankind (whether or not Christian
believers) has nothing to offer. Christians simply *receive* a gift of sheer
grace, in accordance with which God as sovereign Creator *raises* them to
life in a *transformed* mode of existence.

To be raised by the power of God in and through Christ is the final outworking of what has hitherto been appropriated by faith,
namely, being placed in a right relation with God. *Justification by grace
and the resurrection of the dead are two sides of the same coin.* Moltmann
shows how the "nothing" *(nihil)* of death matches the "nothing" of the
cross: "The experience of the crucified one as the living Lord . . . annihi-
lates the total *nihil.* . . . It points . . . even beyond Jesus to the coming revelation of God" (*Theology of Hope,* pp. 198 and 201).

The "vacuum" caused both by death and by "the absence of religious ideas" leaves "in all its undisguised harshness" the experience of
"the deadliness of death as compared with the promised life received
from the promise of God" (*Hope,* p. 210). Resurrection is understood
"not as a mere return to life as such but as a conquest of the deadliness
of death — as a conquest of God-forsakenness" (p. 211). This is why (in
Barth's words) "1 Cor. XV could be better described as *the methodology of
the apostle's preaching,* rather than eschatology . . . the nerve of its whole"
(*Resurrection,* his italics, p. 115).

Paul asserts not a humanist belief in postmortal survival by virtue
of the capacities of the human self, but a raising to a transformed
mode of life through the sovereign power of God as a gift. This is why

Luther perceptively observes that to deny the resurrection is to deny "far more . . . in brief, that God is God" (*Luther's Works*, vol. 28, p. 95).

Paul now expounds this key theme in four main acts or logical stages: (a) the reality of the resurrection of Jesus Christ (15:1-11); (b) the unacceptable consequences of denying the resurrection (15:12-34); (c) how the resurrection of the body can be credible or even conceivable (15:35-50); and (d) further inferences for everyday life (15:51-58).

What precisely did some in Corinth doubt or deny? Three (or four) kinds of answers have been given: (1) They denied human existence after death *in any form*. (2) They insisted that "the resurrection" (in some spiritual sense) had *taken place already,* leaving no further event to hope for (cf. 2 Tim. 2:18). (3) They could neither believe in, nor conceive of, the *resurrection of "the body"* (Greek *sōma*). (4) Several writers from Luther onward, including recently Margaret Mitchell, have suggested that different groups in Corinth may have faced all these different problems. This view is probable; Paul addresses different problems within the church. All remain relevant today.

A. The Reality of the Resurrection of Jesus Christ: The Major Premise (15:1-11)

1 Now I want to restore to your full knowledge, dear brothers and sisters, the gospel that I proclaimed to you; the gospel which in turn you received and on which you have taken your stand. 2 Through this gospel you are in process of being saved if you hold fast to the substance of the gospel that I proclaimed to you — unless you believed without coherent consideration. 3 For I handed on to you first and foremost what I, in turn, received, namely:

"Christ died for our sins according to the scriptures;
4 "He was buried;
"He was raised on the third day according to the scriptures;
5 "He appeared to Peter and then to the Twelve."

6 Then he appeared to more than five hundred of our Christian people on a single occasion, most of whom are still alive, although some have died. 7 Then he appeared to James, then to all the apostles. 8 Last of all, he appeared also to me, as if to an aborted foetus. 9 For I am the very least of the apostles; I am not competent to be called an apostle because I persecuted the church of God.

10 But by the grace of God I am what I am, and his grace which he extended to me has not proved fruitless. On the contrary, I labored to an even greater degree than all of them, yet not I, but God's grace working with me. 11 Whether, anyway, it is they or I, it is this that we proclaim and it is this that you came to believe.

Belief in the resurrection of Christ is no mere "Pauline" invention. It is expressed as part of the pre-Pauline bedrock of Christian faith, as a creed or confession of faith, which *both* declares a content of truth (belief *that*) *and* is like nailing one's colors to the mast as a self-involving "Here I stand." The readers **received** (Greek *parelabete*, v. 1) what Paul himself had also first **received** and then **handed on** (Greek *paredōka*, v. 3). These words serve in effect as terms for the reception and transmission of a prior, given tradition that is to be guarded and preserved. It is on this apostolic tradition that believers in Corinth **have taken** [their] **stand**. Creeds perform a double role both as *declarations of a theological content* and as *self-involving personal commitments*, like nailing up one's colors (see Neufeld, *Earliest Christian Confessions*). As an article of faith this very early creed ranks as **first and foremost**: it has first importance.

It is misleading to suggest that only in the later Pastoral Epistles does Paul (or a later writer) show a concern about **holding fast** to gospel truth or Christian doctrine. This is the very ground of their being **in process of being saved** (present tense, as in 1:18). It demands **coherent consideration** (v. 2). The RSV raises needless difficulty by translating "unless you believed in vain." The Greek word *(eikē)* suggests a hasty, ill-thought-out, belief commitment. This well matches Paul's careful explication of the logical entailments of believing or disbelieving in the resurrection in vv. 12-34.

In vv. 3-5 (or in vv. 3-6 or 3-7) Paul quotes the "articles" of this received tradition of gospel truth. The creedal context includes four articles of faith. Each "article" begins with the Greek word *hoti*, which stands partly in lieu of quotation marks.

(1) The first is "**Christ died for our sins according to the scriptures.**" Both this first article (the saving death of Christ) and the third (the resurrection) are "**according to the scriptures.**" This very early confession of Christian and apostolic faith declares that the Scriptures of the Old Testament provide *the frame of reference* or the *interpretive key* for understanding *how* or *in what sense* the events of Christ's death and

resurrection were *saving* events "for us" or **for our sins**. The phrase does not imply that Christ's death and resurrection relate to one specific scriptural reference. The pre-Pauline creed or confession of faith thus reflects the tradition behind Luke 24:27. "Beginning with Moses and all the prophets, he interpreted to them the things about himself in all the scriptures," and 24:44-46, "Everything written about me in the law of Moses, the prophets and the psalms must be fulfilled. . . . It is written that the Messiah is to suffer and to rise from the dead on the third day" (NRSV).

That **Christ died for our sins** in terms of this explanatory framework of understanding (v. 3) belongs to the bedrock of pre-Pauline apostolic doctrine, going back to Jesus himself. In addition to 15:3, parallel pre-Pauline formulas occur in 1 Cor. 11:23-25 (discussed above); Rom. 4:25, "who was handed over to death for our trespasses and was raised for our justification"; and elsewhere. Cullmann and many others rightly identify such passages as pre-Pauline. The use of **sins** (in the plural) is unusual in Paul, and this also points to its earlier pre-Pauline origin. The occurrence of the same phrase in Gal. 1:4 also suggests its very early formulation.

Pannenberg observes, "The traditional formula in Paul (1 Cor. 15:3) . . . undoubtedly means that he [Christ] made expiation for our sins" (*Systematic Theology*, vol. 2, p. 418). The Greek preposition translated as **for** is *hyper*. This usually denotes "benefit on behalf of" someone and sometimes serves as a synonym for *anti*, "in place of." The general sense of the phrase, therefore, is that of putting right the situation caused by human **sins**.

(2) The second component of the early confession of faith is "**He was buried**" (v. 4a). The purpose of this clause is twofold. It demonstrates the *undeniable reality of the death of Jesus;* and it excludes any notion of a "docetic" Christ, namely, one whose flesh and blood were merely "what *appeared* to be the case" but were illusory "clothing" for a being of pure spirit. Such a view rested upon the Greek notion that a flesh-and-blood body would have been an unworthy vehicle for a heavenly Christ figure. But apart from its false assumption about the body, such a view would deny the reality of the suffering and death of Jesus Christ. Hence "**He was buried**" became an important early article of Christian belief.

(3) The third article is "**He was raised on the third day according**

to the scriptures" (v. 4b). It is important to note that the verb **he was raised** (*egēgertai*) is a perfect *passive*. Dahl among others rightly insists that in Paul's theology Christ does not "raise" himself, but is raised by the power of God through the agency of the Holy Spirit (*The Resurrection of the Body*, pp. 96-100). This emphasis is essential if we are fully to appreciate the logical consequence that "If the Spirit of him who raised Jesus from the dead dwells in you, he who raised Christ from the dead will give life to your mortal bodies also through his Spirit that dwells in you" (Rom. 8:11, NRSV). Dahl includes a table of uses of the word "raise" in Paul's epistles that corroborates the point.

Only in John does Jesus speak of his hypothetical power to raise himself, but even in John he does not suggest that this will be the efficient cause of the resurrection event (cf. John 6:39, 40, 54). The transitive sense of *God's* raising Christ occurs in Acts 3:15; 4:10; 5:30; 10:40; 13:30; Rom. 4:21; 8:11; 10:9; 1 Cor. 6:14; 15:15; 2 Cor. 4:14; Gal 1:1; Col. 2:2; 1 Thess. 1:10; and elsewhere. Further, if this were otherwise, our comments above concerning the experience of death as "nothingness," a yielding of the self into the hands of God alone, would not apply to the death of Jesus Christ. But patently this *was* the character of Christ's death. Resurrection springs from God's promise, God's power, God's act of re-creation, and God's grace — and this alone.

The allusion to **the third day** should not be restricted to a single Old Testament passage that includes this exact phrase, such as Hos. 6:2. **According to the scriptures** governs the biblical frame of reference that provides an understanding of *resurrection as such* as God's vindication of his faithful Servant-Son, rather than more narrowly alluding only to **the third day**. The *scriptural pattern* of divine promise, divine faithfulness, and divine vindication of his elect Servant-Son is the focus of emphasis here. Although many explanations have been offered for *the third day*, the most widely accepted view is that the phrase simply records the experiences of the first witnesses who, as a matter of fact, saw the raised Christ or discovered the empty tomb **on the third day** after his crucifixion. Barrett and Hays support this view, along with many others (Barrett, *First Epistle*, p. 340; Hays, *First Corinthians*, p. 256).

One alternative explanation merits serious attention. Weiss and others point out that, according to popular Jewish belief, corruption befalls the body after three days. Hence **the third day** (on this basis) would suggest the genuineness of death, and **according to the scrip-**

tures (if it refers to the third day) might allude to Ps. 16:9-11 (LXX), ". . . not let thy Holy One see corruption." But this second view is less likely than the first.

(4) "**He appeared to Peter and then to the Twelve**" (v. 5). This is the fourth (and last) of the sentences or clauses that are introduced by the Greek word *hoti*, serving as the equivalent of quotation marks. The precise force of **appeared** (Greek *ōphthē*) has been the subject of acute and prolonged controversy in modern theology and in New Testament studies. Traditionally the verb has been understood to denote the *appearing* of the raised Christ to public witnesses. But some have taken it to denote simply a religious or visionary experience.

Marxsen, for example, argues that the phrase has as much to do with the function that the Twelve now have as with "experience" of the raised Christ (*The Resurrection*, p. 84). As part of a creed or confession of faith it expresses the "involvement" of the apostles in the resurrection, or "their present faith," *without determining the truth or falsity of a past event* (pp. 19-20). It remains open ended, Marxsen insists, about Christ's *mode* of appearance. It says more about "finding faith" than offering "factual evidence" (p. 108).

All the same, is Marxsen right? Many scholars take a very different view. Among such writers two stand out: Künneth and Pannenberg. Künneth declares, "[The resurrection] is a primal miracle like the creation of the world"; it exhibits "the qualitative difference" of the appearance of the raised Christ from ecstatic or other "religious" experiences of Christ (*The Theology of the Resurrection*, pp. 75 and 84; cf. pp. 72-91). Pannenberg asserts, "The event took place in this world, namely in the tomb of Jesus in Jerusalem before the visit of the women. . . . [It] implies an historical claim . . ." (*Systematic Theology*, vol. 2, p. 360).

Künneth and Pannenberg rightly insist that the reference to Christ's burial in the previous clause forms part of the context that determines how we should understand "**He appeared**," while the same applies to the specific mention of **Peter and the Twelve** as foundational apostolic witnesses. Both writers hold that the placing together of the articles and their context brings together the "appearances" theme and that of the empty tomb. The former implicitly assumes the latter. Pannenberg observes, "The first Christians could not have successfully preached the resurrection of Jesus if his body had been intact in the tomb" (p. 358). Even if the clause "**He was buried**" tells us "nothing regarding his [Paul's] knowledge of the finding of the empty tomb," nevertheless "for Paul the empty tomb was a self-evident implication of what was said . . ." (p. 359).

The "appearance," Künneth urges, was "neither a phantasy nor a theophany." Christ appears in a "new, living mode of existence" (p. 85). This mode is one of glory, but "corporeality" is built into it. "The account of the empty tomb was definitely included in the apostolic tradition" (pp. 87, 93). (This does not pre-judge what "corporeality" might mean; see under vv. 35-44.)

When we introduced this confession of faith or creed, we noted that these articles function *both* as declarations of a content of belief (belief *that* certain events occurred) *and* as commitments that stake one's own involvement in what is confessed *(belief in)*. Writers who follow Marxsen sometimes denigrate a more "factual" understanding on the grounds that these are expressions of commitment and personal faith. But these are not exclusive alternatives.

Some interpreters argue that the tradition that Paul **received** and **handed on** (v. 3) included v. 6 and perhaps also v. 7. The use of virtual quotation marks (Greek *hoti*), the use of **the Twelve** (which normally does not feature in Paul's writings), and other factors clearly establish vv. 1-5 as "pre-Pauline." It is possible that vv. 6-7 continue the pre-Pauline "received" doctrine, although this is less certain. Christ **appeared to more than five hundred of our Christian people on a single occasion** (v. 6) may no longer be directly verifiable today, but Paul comments (or inserts into the tradition), **most of whom are still alive**, implying that this was still open to verifiability at the time of writing. Pannenberg declares, "Any assertion that an event took place in the past implies an historical claim and exposes itself to testing" (*Systematic Theology*, vol. 2, p. 360). Paul accepts this challenge for this own day. The fact that this multiple testimony occurred **on a single occasion** renders a reference only to personal "vision" surely out of the question, or at least very highly unlikely. E.-B. Allo identifies the occasion with that of Matt. 28:16-20 (*Première Épître*, p. 396; cf. pp. 394-98).

James (v. 7) is not the son of Zebedee, one of the Twelve, but James of Jerusalem, the brother of Jesus (Gal. 1:19). Paul describes him in Gal. 2:9 as both an *apostle* and a *pillar* of the Jerusalem church. Already, therefore, Paul has extended the term *apostle* beyond the Twelve. Künneth rightly emphasizes the effect of the resurrection appearance in restoring and commissioning Peter or **Cephas** (v. 5), who had denied Jesus, and **James**, who had not been among the believers, in the Gospels. The word order for **all the apostles** might better suggest the sense: **to the apostles** as a body — in other words, the emphasis does not lie on **all** in a numerical sense, but on the rounding up of the entire apostolic "college" *except for Paul.*

Paul now adds his personal testimony: **Last of all, he appeared also to me, as if to an aborted foetus** (v. 8). The significance of this emerges in v. 10: **But by the grace of God I am what I am.** As we observed in our introductory paragraphs to this chapter, resurrection is all about God's sovereign power as sheer gift and **grace** that confers life upon the dead and transforms the lifeless. Peter, James, and, above all, Paul needed to be turned around and commissioned by the resurrection appearance of Christ. Hence Paul is only secondarily including himself among the witnesses; an even greater emphasis is placed upon his lack of qualification or merit to be so favored: **I am not competent to be called an apostle because I persecuted the church of God** (v. 9).

The metaphor of **an aborted foetus** (Greek *ektrōma*) suggests (1) the unlikelihood (in human terms) that such a wretched specimen as a **foetus, aborted** before its birth, *could ever live. It also suggests* (2) not only that Paul's birth to the apostolate is a miracle of divine grace but also the *extent* of that grace in bringing to life one who was ugly, misshapen, and ill equipped in the sense that he had **persecuted the church of God.** The language of the NRSV ("as to one untimely born"), REB ("like a sudden, abnormal birth"), and NJB/NIV ("abnormally born") brings out a third aspect: (3) Paul did not, like the other apostles, receive the three-or-so years of apprenticeship training of discipleship from the earthly Jesus.

Aborted foetus, then, emphasizes above all the miracle of undeserved, life-giving, sovereign grace, and this is Paul's main point. Whether or not the term had been hurled at Paul as an insult expressing derision or contempt, *he now uses it as a vehicle through which to glory in God's grace.* Elsewhere in Hellenistic Greek the word may denote a *monster* or *freak;* but more usually it denotes what results from a premature birth or a miscarriage.

Paul **labored to an even greater degree** (v. 10b) to express and to convey his gratitude for such exceptional **grace;** but it was not a fruitless attempt to "pay God back" for it. **Grace** in this way **worked with**

[him]. This reflects closely the maxim of Jesus, "Freely you received, freely give" (Matt. 10:8). But **whether, anyway, it is I or they** (v. 11a), all of the witnesses stand under grace, and all share together in the privilege of the apostolic proclamation that **you came to believe** (v. 11b).

43. SUGGESTIONS FOR POSSIBLE REFLECTION ON 15:1-11

(1) *On assenting to belief carelessly or without careful thought (v. 2):* The Greek word usually translated "in vain" (NRSV, NIV, REB) is better rendered "without careful thought" or "without due consideration" (Danker, *Lexicon*, 3d edn., p. 281, on this verse). Can overly hasty, careless belief be worse than none? Might it seduce us into a false security or illusion that we have appropriated saving truth when in practice it remains doubtful whether we are "in process of being saved" on this basis? Are there resonances here with seed sown in shallow, stony ground in Jesus' parable (Mark 4:5-6, 16-17)? Do we take time and trouble in appropriating Christian truth?

(2) *On the solid foundation of transmitted apostolic truth (vv. 1 and 4-5):* The bedrock of Christian doctrine is the earliest apostolic witness to Jesus Christ and to the saving acts of God in and through Jesus. The foundation is Christ (3:11); Christ's death and resurrection is of "first importance" (15:3); and Christian truth is built on the foundation of the apostles and prophets (Eph. 2:20). The gospel is not a human social construction. Are we sufficiently alert to insure that claims to "Christian" truth today match the doctrine and faith transmitted through the apostles as apostolic doctrine and witness?

(3) *On the saving death and resurrection of Christ as the heart of the gospel (vv. 3-5):* Apostolic witness not only singles out "Christ died for our sins" and "Christ was raised," but in each case adds "according to the scriptures." What counts "first and foremost" (v. 3) is to understand both *these events* and *their meaning* within a scriptural frame of reference. Is it surprising that some find the notion of Christ's death as a sacrifice incredible or bizarre if they have not appropriated the teaching of the Old Testament on sin, sacrifice, and salvation? Does it trouble us that some confuse resurrection and immortality if they have little or no understanding of divine promise, divine vindication, or divine grace as revealed in the Old Testament scriptures? How seriously do we take the axiom that the Old Testament was *the scripture of the earliest church* (cf. Luke 24:27 and 44-46)?

(4) *On holding fast to the gospel in the present process of being saved (v. 2):* As in 1:18, Paul addresses Christians as those "in process of being saved" (present tense). Christians are like those who have been saved from drowning or from shipwreck but who are still traveling in the lifeboat to the harbor and dry land. "To hold fast to the substance of the gospel" (v. 2a) is essential, not optional, for Christians. What God-given resources or supports help us "to hold fast"? Is there any resource that we neglect or forget? Are we actively and deliberately holding fast, or are we, by contrast, passively drifting with the tide?

(5) *On the role of credible witnesses to Christ and to truth (vv. 5-8):* In addition to the more general allusions to witnesses (who include here Peter and the Twelve, v. 5), the four Gospels add more details, for example, the witness of Mary Magdalene and Thomas. The five hundred (v. 6) might, as Allo suggests, be those who witnessed Christ's final Commission, in spite of Matthew's allusion to the clever as the immediate addressees. Lawsuits rely heavily on the testimony of witnesses who were "there" to establish a state of affairs. In this sense the witness of the apostles and of the biblical writings remains primary and unique. But in what sense does Christian witness to the living Christ today still "count"? Are we credible witnesses to Jesus Christ? In what does our witness consist? Is our witness in any sense "apostolic"?

(6) *On the relation between doctrine and experience (vv. 1-5):* In the history of the church, especially in the era from the Reformation to today, some Christians have disparaged doctrine and placed great weight on experience, while others have done the reverse. Would Paul condone elevating either one above the other? Can experience be authentic without apostolic teaching? Or does doctrine profit without the living appropriation that transforms and shapes experience (v. 2a)?

(7) *On worrying whether we have missed the boat (vv. 9-11):* On the face of it, Paul came to faith "too late" to be numbered among the Twelve, whom Jesus had trained as his disciples. But God's sovereign initiative and generous grace placed Paul within the apostolate in almost every sense: "by the grace of God I am what I am" (v. 10). Can we doubt that God has ways to work his will even "against the clock" or "against the calendar"?

(8) *On transforming abuse or past shame into occasions for glorying (v. 8):* We cannot be certain whether Paul coined the term "aborted foetus" to describe

himself, or whether others used it as an abusive insult. The former would not exclude the latter. Paul turns the term of abuse into a ground for *glorying in God's sheer goodness and grace*. Misbegotten he may be, but God chose him, lavished his love upon him, and called him to service. Even the shameful memory of persecuting the church became a foil that shows still more clearly God's generosity and transforming grace. Do we have skeletons in the closet, or public failures, that we can turn to occasions for glorying in God?

B. The Unacceptable Consequences of Denying the Resurrection (15:12-34)

The structure of Paul's argument in this chapter is one of the most striking examples of Paul's use of forms and conventions familiar in Greco-Roman rhetoric. The first section (vv. 1-11) stated a major premise or basic case (Latin *narratio*). Normally this set out common, shared, beliefs or assumptions on which the rest of the argument could be based. This next middle section (vv. 12-34) embodies what rhetoricians called a *refutatio* (the reasons why a denial of the argument leads to unacceptable consequences, vv. 12-19) and a *confirmatio* (a reaffirmation of the logical alternative and its implications, vv. 20-34). Paul begins with the *refutatio*.

1. What Would Follow If the Very Concept of Resurrection Is Denied? (15:12-19)

12 Now if Christ is proclaimed as raised from the dead, how can some of you claim that there is no resurrection of the dead? 13 But if there is no resurrection of the dead, neither can Christ have been raised! 14 Yet if Christ has not been raised, it follows that our proclamation of the gospel is hollow, and empty also is your faith. 15 We too shall be exposed as liars in what we witness about God, because we gave testimony against God that he raised Christ when, if, as they say, it were the case that the dead are not raised, he did not raise him after all. 16 For if the dead are not raised, neither can Christ have been raised. 17 But if Christ has not been raised, your faith is without effect, and you are still in your sins. 18 It also follows, then, that those who were laid to sleep in Christ are lost for good. 19 If in this life we have placed hope in Christ with nothing beyond, we are more to be pitied than all human beings.

We considered in the introduction to this chapter three different problems that troubled some Christians in Corinth. One of these was the very concept of resurrection, which differs from the Greek notion of the immortality of the soul. Paul begins this section *(the refutatio)* by asking how it could make any sense whatever *to deny* that "resurrection" was a viable or credible concept if at the same time their very salvation rested upon the foundational event of the resurrection of Jesus Christ: **Now if Christ is proclaimed as raised from the dead, how can some of you claim that there is no resurrection of the dead?** (v. 12). This question paves the way for the heart of this part of the argument: **But if there is no resurrection of the dead, neither can Christ have been raised!**

From the very start, Paul insists that to deny the *possibility* of resurrection knocks the bottom out of Christian faith. It quite literally destroys by logical exclusion the foundation on which the gospel rests. He elucidates this in vv. 14-15: **if Christ has not been raised, it follows that our proclamation of the gospel is hollow, and empty also is your faith** (v. 14).

In the remainder of this section Paul specifies four sets of unacceptable consequences. However, we must first note the main inference of vv. 12-14: Christ's resurrection is not an isolated event. Neither will the resurrection of Christian believers be an isolated event. The two occurrences are bound together as one, causally, conceptually, and theologically. It makes no sense to conceive of one without the other. For Christians will experience resurrection as an event "together with Christ" (cf. Rom. 6:4). As Thornton vividly expresses it, "When Christ rose, the Church rose from the dead" (*The Common Life in the Body of Christ*, p. 282).

In the proper sense of the term, Christ is the *paradigm case* of resurrection. In other words, what resurrection *is* may be defined with reference to *Christ's* resurrection. The one major difference is that of timing, as Paul makes clear in vv. 20-28. Christ is the "firstfruits" (v. 20), namely, the first sample sheaf of the harvest that is yet to some. Christians *anticipate* this resurrection in the sense of the foretaste of receiving life and transformation through the agency of the Holy Spirit in the present (Rom. 6:4-11), but this is only a hint or "first installment" of the glorious reality of the harvest yet to come in fullness at the end time.

Meanwhile, in vv. 14b-19 Paul sets out four damning consequences that a denial of the resurrection as a concept and reality applicable to Christ and Christians would entail. These are as follows.

(1) **The proclamation of the gospel** [would be] **hollow**, and **your faith** [would be] **empty** (v. 14b). **Hollow** and **empty** translate the same Greek word (*kenos*, "without substance, in vain, empty"). Neither the gospel nor the faith of Christians would retain any substance, authenticity, or effectiveness. They would be a sham and a delusion. Christianity would be no more than a human social construct.

(2) The apostles would be **exposed as liars**. Paul's criterion for preaching, unlike that of the Corinthian sophist rhetoricians, was *truth, not "success."* If the gospel is without foundation, it matters not whether a Christian congregation was founded in Corinth. Paul has no interest in pragmatic "self-adjustment," but in calling for a transformation of thought and life that is based on truth.

(3) A third entailment is that *there is no release from sin:* **you are still in your sins** (v. 17b). Without the resurrection the redemptive, atoning, liberating effect of Christ's death remains ineffective, for his death and resurrection are two sides of the one redemptive event. Redemption *"from"* sin or bondage is not *redemption* without redemption *"to"* the new life.

Christians are *identified with Christ in his death and resurrection. Christ* won for us benefits in his death of which he had no need: forgiveness, justification, reconciliation; these have a *substitutionary, "for us"* aspect. But other aspects are better expressed as *identification: because he lives, we shall live also. The victory* motif, also essential for understanding the meaning of Christ's work, would be hollow without the triumph of resurrection. Paul placed the two aspects together in 1 Cor. 5:7: "Clean out the old leaven, so that you may be a newly begun batch of dough. . . . Christ has been sacrificed, so let us celebrate the Passover festival . . . with the unleavened bread which is purity and truth." Deliverance from the old remains pointless unless it leads to embracing the new.

(4) The fourth consequence would be that *dead believers are lost:* **Those who were laid to sleep in Christ are lost for good** (v. 18). If there is **nothing beyond** the grave (v. 19a), Paul perceives Christians as **more to be pitied than all human beings** (v. 19b). *Pitiable* alludes to the state of Christians if this whole fourfold chain of consequences were to apply to them, especially the climactic **loss** of everything that lies ahead.

Sleep (v. 18) is a word pregnant with the promise of future awakening at the dawn of a new day. Pannenberg comments on this early Christian use of the word: "The familiar experience of being awakened and rising from sleep serves as a parable for the complete unknown destiny expected for the dead" (*Jesus — God and Man*, p. 74). A. G. Hogg gives poetic expression to "the new world" of the inexhaustible possibilities of the future for which Christians are destined, a world that leaves behind the limited and manageable: "it is a kingdom into which none enter but children . . . where the child's little finger becomes stronger than the giant world: a wide kingdom . . . in which the world lies like a foolish, wilful dream in the solid truth of the day" (*Redemption from this World* [Edinburgh: T&T Clark, 1924], pp. 25-26). If there is no resurrection, any notion of a transformed mode of existence after death is reduced to sheer fantasy.

44. Suggestions for Possible Reflection on 15:12-19

(1) *On doubting the very concept (or conceivability) of resurrection (vv. 12-15):* Does the credibility or currency of a concept depend on whether we can imagine it? Can we imagine the square root of minus 1, or a thousand-sided polygon? Resurrection depends not on our ability to imagine it, but on the capacity of the Creator God to design and to activate it. In the end, Paul will argue in this chapter, belief in the resurrection depends upon whether we have "knowledge of God" and God's ways (v. 34). Do we find some things difficult to believe because "our God is too small"?

(2) *On the consequences of confused belief or disbelief (vv. 14-18):* Surveys of religious belief by interviewers yield anomalous results. Some believe in post-mortal existence, but not in God; others believe in "salvation," but not in life after death. Paul places Christian belief in certain levels of logical priority: God is the foundation on the basis of which resurrection becomes credible; the death and resurrection of Christ is the foundation for effective faith, forgiveness of sins, apostolic preaching, future resurrection, and meeting loved ones in the hereafter. Is our own belief system centered on God, or on items or articles of belief? Do we bring the frame of reference to bear on what we can or do believe?

(3) *On "sleep" as bringing an inbuilt promise of waking at dawn (v. 18):* The earliest Christians readily spoke of death as "sleep" (v. 18). For sleep not only

comes to the weary and exhausted as rest but also contains within itself the very promise of *awaking* to a new day. How do we view death? Do we perceive it as an episode *en route* to the dawning of a glorious day when we shall see God face to face (13:13) in glory (15:44)? Christ's death "for us" has absorbed the "sting" of death (15:55).

(4) *On Christians as those by no means to be pitied (v. 19):* If the whole chain of negative consequences dependent upon a denial of the resurrection were to hold sway, Christians are "more to be pitied than all human beings." But this hypothesis is contrary to fact. Do we sometimes act as if we had nothing more in which to glory than unbelievers? Does the glory that lies ahead influence our present attitudes and inspire us to promote the gospel?

2. *A Reaffirmation of the Truth of the Resurrection:* Confirmatio (15:20-28)

20 In reality, however, Christ has been raised from the dead, the firstfruits of the harvest of the dead. 21 For since through a human being death came, so also through a human being comes about the resurrection of the dead. 22 For just as all die in Adam, even so all will be brought to life in Christ. 23 But each in the properly arranged order: Christ the firstfruits; then afterward, at his coming, those who are Christ's. 24 Then is the End, when he hands over the rule to him who is God and Father, when he shall have annihilated every rule and every authority and power. 25 For he must reign until he puts all his enemies under his feet. 26 The last enemy doomed to be brought to nothing is death. For "He has placed all things in subjection under his feet." 27 But when it says "all things are in subjection," it is clear that "all things" excludes the One who has brought all things into submission to him. 28 But when all things have been subjected to him, then will the Son himself also be made subject to the One who placed all things in subjection to him, so that God may be all in all.

In reality, Paul begins by way of *confirmatio*, **Christ has been raised from the dead, the firstfruits of the harvest of the dead.** The **firstfruits** is an agricultural term for the first installment of the harvest that pledges more of the same kind to come. Paul regularly stresses the "sameness," solidarity, or paradigmatic equivalence of the resurrection of Christ and the resurrection of Christians who are "in" Christ, but with the one crucial difference of *timing*. In this sense, Christ is the "firstborn" (Greek *prōtotokon*) among many brothers and sisters (Rom. 8:29; cf. Col. 1:18). Christ's resurrection, therefore, is a *pledge* and *assurance* of the future resurrection of the dead in Christ. The term also denotes a *representative* example of the rest of the crop.

This representative character leads to the thought of vv. 21-22: **Since through a human being death came, so also through a human being comes about the resurrection of the dead.** In v. 21 the Greek uses the word for **human being** *(anthrōpos)*; but v. 22 explicitly names **Adam** and **Christ** as the two respective representative figures of humankind. Fallen humanity is **in Adam**; the new, redeemed humanity is **in Christ**. Paul develops this terminology in 1 Cor. 15:45-48, where Christ is "the last Adam," and will later develop the contrast in still more detail in Rom. 5:12-21.

Three theological themes converge in vv. 21-22. (1) First, the resurrection of Christ is *an event of cosmic significance*, not simply an event in the history and life of Israel and the church. Since resurrection was expected only as an event of the "last days," the resurrection of Christ brings forward the end time to the present as the firstfruits of *the new creation*. In vv. 38-44 Paul will expound resurrection as an act of the sovereign *Creator* God, comparable in formative power and purpose with the act of creation itself, but the active creation of a new, transformed "world." In technical terms it is an "apocalyptic" event. Beker perceives this aspect in 15:20-28 as the very heart of this chapter (*Paul the Apostle*, pp. 168-70).

(2) Second, since the resurrection of Christ is not an isolated event but carries with it the pledge of the future resurrection of believers, the terms **in Adam** and **in Christ** (v. 22) reflect the theological reality of *corporate solidarity*. "Solidarity" was more difficult to explain to a culture of modern Western individualism before the media made sports such an all-pervasive phenomenon in life, and before trade unions took over the term to denote "one for all" and "all for one." If a team member scores a goal, or contrariwise incurs a penalty, the whole team is credited with the gain or made liable for the loss incurred by an individual on the team. In Rom. 5:12-21 Paul explains that we cannot have one (the advantage) without the other (the liability). Yet "the result of one trespass" differs in effect and scope from "the result of one act of righteousness" (5:17) in that *"how much more* did God's grace and the gift that came by the grace of one man, Jesus Christ, overflow to the many" (5:14, NIV).

(3) The third theological theme is *the Lordship of Christ,* or *Christology.* **The resurrection of the dead comes about through a human being.... All will be brought to life in Christ** (vv. 21-22) in a *cosmic* and *corporate* event that rests on "the enthronement of Christ as 'Lord'" (Beker, as cited above; cf. Rom. 1:3-4). Through this cosmic event, Paul goes on to explain, Christ **shall have annihilated every rule and every authority and power. For he must reign until he puts all his enemies under his feet** (vv. 24b and 25).

Christ's reign is decisively established in the resurrection, but inaugurates a process of victory that is not instantaneous. It is vital to understanding the meaning of vv. 20-28 that we give due prominence to the words **each in the properly arranged order** (v. 23). This takes up the theme of chapter 14 on "order" (Greek *tagma,* used of ordered military ranks), in that the resurrection of Christ took place *in advance* as **the firstfruits,** and then **afterward** the resurrection of **those who are Christ's at his coming** (Greek *parousia,* v. 23).

This is one of the three great "last things" (the *parousia,* the **resurrection,** and the *last judgment*) that together signal **the End** (v. 24a). These three "last things" mark the completion of the intermediate era when **Christ must reign** as Vice Regent or Deputy of God prior to the climax **when he hands over the rule to him who is God and Father, when he shall have annihilated every** [competing] **rule and every authority and power** (v. 24).

In vv. 24b-28 Christ as Lord following his resurrection implements his office and work by establishing "the messianic reign" that in turn brings about the consummation of the rule or kingdom of God. The strong, emphatic word **annihilate** (vv. 24 and 26; Greek *katargeō,* "thoroughly to render idle or null") takes up the use of the same word in 1:28 and especially 2:6 (cf. also 6:13; 13:8, 10, 11). It is doubtful whether the Greek behind **to him who is God and Father** should be translated "to God the Father" (with NRSV, REB, NIV, and NJB). The Greek includes the conjunction **and,** probably in the sense of the One who is both **God and Father,** but perhaps in the sense of *his* [Christ's] **God and Father.**

The allusion to **every rule and every authority and power** denotes those forces of structural or corporate evil that threaten to oppose the reign of Christ or to overwhelm God's people. In an apocalyptic context these may include "supernatural" powers, but Paul does not specify their identity any more closely than in terms of their power, which exceeds that of mere human individuals. Often the cumulative effect of evil or the corporate impact of evil generated by "regimes," by anti-Christian cultures, or by global social-economic forces threatens the gospel or the church with powers beyond those of even an influential but wicked individual. (On "the powers," see Wink, *Unmasking the Powers* and *Engaging the Powers*.) Christ will **annihilate** such evil powers. Indeed, in 2:6 they are in process of beginning to crumble. The phrase in v. 25, **puts all his enemies under his feet**, alludes to Ps. 110:1. In vv. 26-27 the thought will move to Ps. 8:6.

Death is the **last enemy doomed to be brought to nothing** (v. 26). The Christian and Hebrew-Jewish attitudes to death are different from that of many Greeks. The Greeks often viewed the release of the soul from the body as a welcome liberation; the physical was left behind as the self became pure spirit. In the Bible, by contrast, death is viewed as a disruption of life that, *apart from resurrection, reduces* the totality of the self as a psychosomatic unity. In this sense it is an *enemy* associated with fallenness, sin, and divine judgment.

Superficial reactions may be to reject such a notion as conflicting with the sheer biological necessity of death in the physical world. However, Paul sees the whole of creation (Greek *hē ktisis*) "waiting with eager longing" to be "set free from its bondage to decay. . . . The whole creation has been groaning in labor pains until now, and not only creation but we ourselves who have the firstfruits of the Spirit groan inwardly while we wait for . . . the redemption of our bodies" (Rom. 8:19-23, NRSV).

Writers who follow Bultmann regard such language as no more than prescientific "myth," but many respected theologians accept its value as "cosmic" spirituality and as "biocentric" rather than merely human-centered. Moltmann writes at length of "the liberation of the earth" and "the preservation of creation" (*God for a Secular Society,* pp. 101-16; *Source of Life,* pp. 118-24; and, in more detail, *God in Creation*).

Paul now cites Ps. 8:6, where the psalmist recalls that the task of humankind (focused in Adam) was to serve as vice regent or deputy ruler of the created order on God's behalf. Yet, as Heb. 2:5-8 explains in a parallel statement, Adam (or humankind) failed in fulfilling this role, and only in Christ do we see "true humanness" as the one who rules and restores creation. Christ thereby serves as the new Adam, or Adam of the last days ("the last Adam," vv. 45-46). Christ bears the true image of God, "humanity" as God willed it to be. As ruler on behalf of God, Christ establishes his authority as Lord over **every authority and power**.

Paul concludes: **But when all things have been subjected to him, then will the Son himself also be made subject to the One who placed all things in subjection to him, so that God may be all in all** (v. 28). This brings to an end the narration of a cosmic eschatology focussed on the reign of **Christ** but culminating in the reign of **God**. In the light of later formulations of a doctrine of the Trinity in which the three persons of the Trinity are coequal in glory, some find themselves troubled by what has been called a "subordinationist" Christology here. But there are two responses.

(1) First, in first-century Hellenistic religions there was often too readily an overly cozy focus on some specific "Lord" *(kyrios)*, which left vague ideas of the supreme, transcendent God as no more than a shadowy figure in the background. **God**, the Creator and Agent of the resurrection of Jesus Christ, is the ultimate *Source* and *Goal* of all. Neil Richardson concludes in a specialist study that 15:24 and 15:28 "are in line with Paul's theology elsewhere" (*Paul's Language about God*, p. 303).

(2) Second, mainline Christian theology has always distinguished between (a) "internal" relations within the Trinity of divine persons and (b) how **God**-as-Trinity acts upon and in the world. To humankind and creation **God** is *God*; believers relate to the Father, the Son, and the Holy Spirit as **God**. Issues about "internal" trinitarian distinctions of role *do not affect the praising doxology of the created order to **God** through **Christin** the power of **the Spirit**.* **God** remains source and goal of **all**; **God** remains **all in all**.

45. Suggestions for Possible Reflection on 15:20-28

(1) *On the Christ-like nature of the new humanity, the church (vv. 20-23):* Language about Christ as the "new" Adam underlines that true "humanness" is found in Christ, in contrast to fallen humanness in Adam. Each "humanity" reflects the character of its representative figure: Adam and Christ. Do we regard "Christ-likeness" as an optional extra for especially holy Christians or as what defines our very *being and identity as Christians?* Everything that Christians are and have is derived from being in Christ. What difference does it make to see things in this way?

(2) *On Christ the Firstfruits (vv. 20 and 23):* Do we see Christ's resurrection as a guarantee of ours? Do we perceive the raised Christ's mode of being as indicating the nature of ours? Christ's raised "body" combined recognizable identity and transformed difference. What does this suggest for the resurrection of Christians? (This also arises more fully in vv. 42-44.)

(3) *On death as the last enemy (v. 26):* Some Christians are perplexed because the effects of Christ's death and resurrection are not implemented all at once. But these saving events set in motion *a process.* Sin and death still bring damage and sorrow; but they are no longer decisive forces. They do not have the last word. Since Christ has removed "the sting" of death (v. 55), death need no longer be fearful, but is a gateway into the immediate presence of God.

(4) *On the Ultimacy of God as Source and Goal (vv. 24-28):* The church worships God as Father, Son, and Holy Spirit, coequal in glory and co-sharing in our creation and salvation. But in their "internal" relations, God has an "ordered" place as the Ultimate Source and Goal of all. God is **all in all**. Do we ever confuse the "penultimates" of faith (Bible, church, sacraments) with the only Ultimate, God himself? Can a Christian be unwittingly seduced into idolatry by according an ultimate place to any person, object, or desire alongside, or in place of, God?

3. Practical Action in Corinth and Also by Paul Presupposes the Truth of the Resurrection (15:29-34)

29 Otherwise what do those people think they are doing who have themselves baptized for the sake of the dead? If the dead are really not raised, what is the point of being baptized for them.

30 Why do we, too, let ourselves be put at risk every hour of the day? 31 From day to day I court fatality — oh yes, by all the pride in you that I hold dear in Christ Jesus our Lord, I so affirm! 32 If it was only within human horizons that I have battled with wild, bestial creatures at Ephesus, what profit could there have been for me? If dead people are not raised,

"Let us eat and drink,
for tomorrow we die."
33 Stop being seduced:
"Belonging to bad 'in-groups' ruins reputable lifestyles."

34 Come to your senses; wake up and sober up! Leave sin alone. Some people, you see, have an utter lack of "knowledge of God." I tell you this to shame you.

Verse 29 is one of the most difficult in this epistle to interpret with certainty. The *general* meaning is clear: "baptism for **the dead**" (whatever this means in detail) would be pointless and senseless if there were no resurrection. But since, evidently, they **have themselves baptized for the sake of the dead**, either some people tacitly assume the truth of the resurrection or else their action is self-contradictory.

More detailed understandings of what this practice involved are legion. Even the translation of the Greek *(hoi baptizomenoi hyper tōn nekrōn)* is disputed: NIV follows AV/KJV with baptism "for the dead"; NRSV, REB, and NJB propose "on behalf of the dead"; my translation follows Findlay, Schnackenburg, and Collins: **for the sake of the dead**. The Greek preposition *hyper* generally has the force of "on behalf of" or "for the benefit of," but its meaning is often broader. (In my larger commentary I listed thirteen interpretations worthy of note, but three or four that most deserve consideration, pp. 1240-49.) Here are the three leading contenders, of which I advocate the third, with the second also possible.

(1) Many interpreters have argued that at face value the phrase seems to refer to a practice of the *vicarious baptism* or *proxy baptism* of those who are now **dead**. Many favored this view in the first half of the twentieth century, but it has since declined. It implies too crude a "cause-effect," sacramental theology on the part of Paul, even if he does not state that he personally supports the practice. Some modify this, suggesting that it applies to those who died seeking "a baptism of desire" that had not been implemented before they died. But as Murphy-O'Connor observes, the whole idea conflicts with "Paul's understanding of the way the sacraments work" (*1 Corinthians,* p. 178).

(2) Possibly the motivations of those who sought baptism were mixed. In part they wanted to be united with their Christian loved ones who had died. Hence they sought baptism **for the sake of the dead** in the sense of their wanting to join them in the future life, which formed part of their motivation for baptism. This view is plausible but speculative.

(3) In my judgment the practice is most likely to reflect the dying

testimony of those who witnessed to Christ with radiant confidence on their deathbeds. These may have been loved ones or simply radiant Christians. Death strips away pretense. If such Christians could face death with joyful anticipation of resurrection with Christ, this may well have led some to full commitment to Christ and to baptism. Paul asks: Do you no longer share their confidence in being raised with Christ? If you doubt the resurrection, why were you baptized?

Common to all explanations remains the foundational axiom that the act of baptism is above all identification with Christ in his death and resurrection (Rom. 6:3-11). *Baptism as such without the dimension of the resurrection would mean nothing.*

In v. 30 Paul turns from the implications drawn from practices among his readers to the resurrection as a foundation for his own (and other apostles') ministry and lifestyle: **Why do we let ourselves be put at risk every hour of the day? From day to day I court fatality** (vv. 30-31a). In 2 Cor. 1:9 Paul speaks of death in a metaphorical sense as "coming to the end of oneself," which leads on to a "resurrection" of the experience of God's power and renewal. In 2 Cor. 4:10 he speaks more theologically of "carrying about the dying of Jesus in my body" in the sense of living out identification with Christ's death and resurrection.

Paul's point here (vv. 30-32) is that if such identification with Christ were to bring only the "death" side, something would have gone badly wrong. He accepts a ministry and lifestyle that brings him regularly to the brink of death in the knowledge that God's resurrection power is also at work, promising in due time the climactic event of resurrection at the last day. In pastoral terms this includes (1) facing death with robust courage; (2) living life in identification with Christ and Christ's work; and (3) accepting vulnerability and fragility in expectation of God's power of resurrection.

The Greek clause (beginning *nē* . . .) expresses an affirmation that would normally take the form of an oath: by Zeus! by Hermes' feet! Paul selects "by — my glorying in you!" My proposed translation, **Yes, by all the pride in you that I hold dear in Christ, . . . I so affirm!** adds **that I hold dear** to the Greek. This is to elucidate his reason for choosing this surprising vehicle for an oath of affirmation. Fee's comment, "He swears by what is dearest to him" (*First Epistle*, p. 770), reflects the convention that in the ancient world people swore "by" what was dearest to them. The added phrase expresses what Paul assumes but might otherwise remain obscure to readers today.

Paul recalls a specific instance of the experience that he describes: **I have battled with wild, bestial creatures at Ephesus** (v. 32). We cannot be certain whether this allusion is literal or metaphorical, but normally as a Roman citizen Paul would not have been forced to fight with wild animals. It clearly denotes an extreme, life-threatening situation, probably precipitated by fanatical obsessive hostility. 2 Cor. 1:9 (cited above) provides a close parallel and may relate to this experience.

Without the truth of the resurrection, Paul affirms, all this would remain empty, fruitless, and pointless. **What profit could there have been for me?** (v. 32) is qualified in three ways. First, he is speaking of the experience as if it were one **within human horizons**. Second, **profit** alludes to what Paul contributes to the work of the gospel, not simply personal "reward," even if it also includes the joy of participation in future resurrection. Above all, third, the gospel itself hinges on the validity of God's promise of vindication and resurrection power.

"**Let us eat and drink, for tomorrow we die**" (v. 32b) comes from either or both of two sources. It probably reflects a loose quotation from Isa. 22:13 (LXX) where the inhabitants of Jerusalem face the Assyrian siege with passive scepticism, "as if there were no tomorrow" (Hays, *First Corinthians,* p. 268). But it may also take up a popular quotation drawn either from Epicurean sceptical philosophy or, possibly, from Stoic-Cynic satire on Epicurean scepticism. Paul uses the quotation to press home the utter futility of a life bounded only by the five senses of the biophysical self with no perception of what lies ahead, beyond the grave. Although this quotation originally came from a comedy by Menander, by Paul's time it had become a popular maxim.

Such a pathetic and sceptical view of human life is the result of error, self-deception, illusion, and seduction: **Stop being seduced** (v. 33a). Such a view is also promoted by Christians in Corinth who go about with the wrong crowd: "**Belonging to bad 'in-groups' ruins reputable lifestyles**" (v. 33b). "**In-groups**" ("gangs" in my larger commentary) may seem an odd word to use here (NRSV, REB, NIV, and NJB all have "bad company"). But the Greek *(homiliai kakai)* conveys the suggestion that *peer pressure* is at the heart of the problem. This peer group or "gang" may be "the wrong sort" or materialists in general.

Paul enjoins the people concerned: **Come to your senses; wake**

**up and sober up! Leave sin alone. Some people, you see, have an ut-
ter lack of "knowledge of God"** (v. 34). NRSV translates the first
clause as "Come to a sober and right mind." But the string of metaphors alludes to waking up from a drunken stupor and sobering up.
They are *to **wake up** to reality* and *to **wake up** to clear thinking* (cf. v. 2b).

Two keys are presented: (1) the need for coherent thinking of the
kind that Paul has demonstrated in 15:1-32; and (2) the need to *come to
know* **God** as the God of creation, grace, power, and promise. The feasi-
bility, possibility, credibility, and conceivability of the resurrection of
the dead all depend upon **God**. Resurrection depends not on human
imagination, not on belief in the capacities of the human self to survive
death, but on the infinite power and infinite resourcefulness of **God**.
Such a **God** will purpose and design an appropriate transformed mode
of existence for the raised community in Christ, has the power to create
anew (if necessary from "nothing"), and will keep faith with his covenant promises in and through Christ. Paul affirms, and will shortly
demonstrate further, that the credibility and conceivability of future
resurrection depends on *what kind of God we believe in or "know."* Do not
those at Corinth claim to have such "knowledge" (1 Cor. 8:1-2, 7)? Yet
their confused belief system shows that they have yet to appropriate
such knowledge of God.

46. SUGGESTIONS FOR POSSIBLE REFLECTION ON 15:29-34

(1) *On the radiant testimony of some Christians in death (v. 29):* I have been privileged to be at the deathbed of Christians who have died in radiant anticipation of "being with the Lord." Such testimony, in the midst of pain, declared utter confidence in the forgiveness of sins, reconciliation with God,
welcome in heaven, and resurrection life. What value do we place on such
testimony when those who know that they are dying have no need of, or
desire for, pretense or deception? Will our dying be marked by such testimony? Shall we have contributed to another's coming to faith?

(2) *On baptism as sharing in Christ's death and resurrection (v. 29):* Is baptism
simply a rite of passage, or in some sense "being clothed with Christ" (Gal.
3:27)? Does our baptism signify for us a genuine ending of life lived for the
self without Christ, and entry into a new world "raised with Christ" (Rom.
6:3-11)? Might saying the Creed be like reaffirming our baptismal vows by

retracing our signature to an agreement "with a dry pen"? Could baptism have any point if there is no resurrection?

(3) *On the testimony of courageous and costly Christian living (vv. 30-32):* Arguably some "religious" people might base their lives on illusion. But could so many different types and temperaments all be self-deceived? Bonhoeffer stresses that self-protective Christian living for "help" and self-affirmation cuts little ice. It could be viewed by others as illusory wish fulfillment. But if faith motivates greater venture and cost to the self, can we regard its beliefs lightly? Who would *choose* to believe what demands everything?

(4) *On the seductive influence of "the wrong crowd" to be "in" with (v. 33).* The people who form our "in" groups or peer group wield enormous power in shaping our worldview, expectations, priorities, and value systems. Belief and conduct are never merely individual affairs. Our choice of friends, of those whom we trust, and, on the other side, whether or not we belong to a church where Christ is Lord, all play their part in shaping our mind-set in more ways than we might realize. What is our situation in such respects?

(5) *On dreaming and drifting unwittingly to disaster (v. 34):* How could the Christians in Corinth have arrived at such confused belief? Paul calls them *to wake up.* Can Christian assurance that "all is well" lull us into a dreamy slumber that drifts to unnoticed disaster? *To wake up and sober up* opens the way for a more serious contemplation of God.

(6) *On "knowing God" as the key to judgments of good sense (v. 34):* To what extent do problems about resurrection depend for an adequate reply on "knowledge of God"? What difference does it make to recall the central doctrine that God is Creator? (Note: the next section has more on this).

C. How Can We Conceive of the Resurrection of the Body? What Kind of "Body" Will God Raise? (15:35-50)

1. Misplaced Scepticism That a Raised "Body" Is Unintelligible and Inconceivable (15:35-44)

35 Nevertheless, someone will voice the objection: How are the dead raised? With what kind of body can they come? 36 You are talking nonsense! What you sow is not brought to life unless it dies. 37 And as to what you sow: it is not the

body which is to come about that you sow but a bare grain, perhaps of wheat, or something else. 38 But God gives to it a "body," just as he purposed, that is, to each of the various kinds of seeds its own perishable body. 39 All flesh is not the same flesh. There is human flesh; a different flesh that pertains to animals, another to birds, and another to fish. 40 There are also super-earthly bodies, and bodies for beings of earth. But what gives to super-earthly bodies their particular splendor is one thing; while that of the bodies of those who live on earth is quite another. 41 The splendor of the sun is one particular thing; the splendor of the moon is another; and the stars have yet another splendor of their own. For one star differs from another star in splendor. 42 Thus it shall be with the resurrection of the dead. What is sown in decay is raised in decay's reversal. 43 It is sown in humiliation; it is raised in splendor. It is sown in weakness; it is raised in power. 44 It is sown an ordinary human body; it is raised a body constituted by the Spirit. If there is a body for the human realm, there is also a body for the realm of the Spirit.

This section resumes a second *refutatio,* which supplements the *refutatio* of vv. 12-19. In the first *refutatio* Paul showed the unacceptable consequences of denying the very notion of resurrection and thereby also denying the resurrection of Christ. Here he exposes claims that the future resurrection of the "body" is unintelligible and unbelievable as indefensible and untenable.

Someone will voice the objection: How are the dead raised? With what kind of body can they come? (v. 35). The sceptic or doubter is thought to offer the difficulty: I can't *conceive* of a future resurrection of the *body;* what kind of event could "resurrection" possibly be? Paul replies on three levels. (1) First, creation or nature itself provides multiple *parables, analogies, or models* of resurrection. Thus what is sown on the earth comes to the end of its own existence *as a seed,* but this *same entity* or *same life* experiences transformation into a new, more glorious mode of existence (vv. 36-37). (2) Second, whether human beings can conceive of resurrection is irrelevant; for it is **God** who will create and will design an appropriate mode of existence or "body" for the transformed state of resurrection (vv. 38-42). (3) Finally, Paul elucidates three sets of contrasts that characterise respectively the preresurrection and postresurrection modes of existence.

It is difficult to find a modern equivalent to the Greek *aphrōn* (v. 36a), traditionally rendered "Fool!" (NRSV). NIV's "How foolish!" and

REB's "What stupid questions!" better convey an equivalent, but the word used is one of address to the questioner. In my larger commentary I proposed, "You nonsense person!" But perhaps **You are talking nonsense!** is less awkward, while still addressing the doubter. The analogy of the seed shows that an entity can come to the *end of its life as such and yet be transformed into something else as the very same entity:* **What you sow is not brought to life unless it dies. And as to what you sow: it is not the body which is to come about that you sow but a bare grain . . .** (v. 37).

Verses 35-44 provide a profound answer to a notoriously persistent question for philosophers and all who wrestle with belief in life after death. Questions about "the soul" fail to address the key problem of whether, if there is life after death, it is "I" who survives or will be raised. Paul tackles the heart of the issue by making two assertions. (1) It is *God alone* who gives the self life in a transformed mode of being after death: **God gives to it a "body," just as he purposed** (v. 38); and (2) it is *the same self,* but *the same self* will assume a *different form,* namely, a glorified mode of existence appropriate to resurrection life.

a. The Analogy of the Seed

This helps us to understand a difficult point. It underlines that (1) the seed comes to the *end* of its own existence *as a seed:* **What you sow is not brought to life unless it dies** (v. 36). (2) The new resurrection "body" is *not the same form* as that which was "sown" (v. 37). (3) God is able to provide *change of form* alongside *continuity of identity:* **What is sown in decay is raised in decay's reversal. It is sown in humiliation; it is raised in splendor** (vv. 42-43).

The Greek word for **its own** body (*idion,* v. 38) underlines the "same" identity, and reflects Gen. 1:11, "seeds according to their kinds." The Greek translated **body** *(sōma)* denotes "whole person." This includes a person's capacity *to be identified, to relate to God,* and *to communicate with others in a "public" environment.* (We discuss this further below, under vv. 42-44.)

Other analogies from everyday life underline the point that *the same self* can pass through *differing forms.* The baby, the infant, the teenager, the middle-aged person, and the fragile, elderly person can be *the same self,* but their *vehicle* of *expression, identity, and communication* may differ radically at the same time. Sometimes a "surprise" feature, often the voice, allows us to recognize an elderly person as the "same" person whom we knew fifty years earlier. An applicant for a job would be foolish to argue that pension rights were of no consequence because they might not even "like" the eighty-year-old who would be drawing the pension fifty years later! *The self is the same self,* even if it has undergone changes of appearance and even changes of character.

All this successfully addresses the issue of "conceivability." But how can this come about? This leads to Paul's second main argument.

b. Everything Depends upon God (15:39)

The whole issue hinges upon God's infinite resourcefulness, demonstrated already in God's resourcefulness as Creator. God has already shown that he created organisms, entities, and modes of being *appropriate for every kind of condition or environment:* **animals** for earth, **fish** for rivers and the sea, **birds** for the sky, planets or flaming gases for space, **stars** of different magnitudes for different places within the galaxy and the universe (vv. 39-41). Using "**flesh**" to denote here *substances-used-in-creation,* Paul declares, **All flesh is not the same flesh** (v. 39a). **Human flesh** differs from that of **animals**; and we can extrapolate through to the **sun, moon,** and **stars,** each of which has a different **splendor,** each a glory of its own: **star differs from star in splendor** (v. 41b). So God will not be caught by some design problem relating to the resurrection.

c. The Preresurrection and Postresurrection Contrasts Explained

Finally, in this marvelous section Paul specifies four key contrasts between the ordinary human body given for this life and the counterpart "body" that shall be in the resurrection of the dead (v. 42a).

(1) **What is sown in decay is raised in decay's reversal** (v. 42b). The NRSV, REB, NIV, and NJB all translate: "perishable . . . imperishable" (cf. KJV/AV "in corruption . . . in incorruption"). This may at first sight appear to do justice to the positive term "imperishable" (Greek *aphtharsia*), which appears simply to negative *phthora,* "perishable." But in this context *phthora* denotes a *process* rather than a *quality.* It denotes *decreasing capacities, increasing weakness,* ready *exhaustion,* and that which finally closes in upon itself as *stagnation.* Anyone who is even beginning to experience symptoms of being well past middle age will know only too well what this contrast of *processes* (not simply states) signifies. Our earthly bodies begin to "die" quite early on in life.

By contrast, *aphtharsia* denotes not simply *negation* of decay, but if decay is a process, the opposite of decay is **reversal of decay**: *increasing* vitality and strength. This is not the negation of *pianissimo* by *double forte;* it is the transformation of *decrescendo* into *crescendo*. It is the recovery of the "youth" of the new resurrection vitality and *life*. For in Hebrew *life* is a *process;* in both Greek and Hebrew *living water* is *running water,* which constantly replaces what flows past or is used with the ever new. (I have discussed the Greek further in my longer commentary, pp. 1271-72.)

(2) **It is sown in humiliation; it is raised in splendor** (v. 43a). The **humiliation** or "dishonor" (NRSV, NIV, AV/KJV) may in part allude to the lowly position of the preresurrection mode of being in contrast to resurrection splendor, but it may equally, indeed more probably, call to mind that in the case of fallen humanity the body has often become a vehicle for unworthy attitudes and actions (cf. v. 50). However, NJB's translation "contemptible" too readily suggests a devaluation of the body. **Splendor** could equally be translated "glory." The Greek *(doxa)* reflects the Hebrew *kabod,* which denotes what makes someone or something *impressive, weighty,* or *majestic,* sometimes with the added nuance of *radiance, light,* or *luminosity.*

This should *not* be taken to mean that the resurrection body will be composed of "light," for these adjectives do not denote composition or material. The resurrection mode of being will be *glorious* and characterized by **splendor** not least because (as v. 44 explains) the Holy Spirit will activate and transform it. It will not be less than *radiant.* We have an inkling of this when the face of a lover or loved one becomes *radiant with joy* in moments of special happiness or tenderness. The last tatters and shreds of sin are no longer present to cloud the sun.

(3) **It is sown in weakness; it is raised in power** (v. 43b). One reason why the old, everyday body is beset with **weakness** is that it is subject to the ravages of time and to the constraints and limitations that mark the whole of creation in space and time. The earthly body is subject to injuries, incapacities, and accidents that may befall it in the *past.* Sometimes this weakness is exacerbated by mistaken or sinful choices made in the past: the abuse of the body through addiction or overindulgence, or the burdens derived from bondage to sin that may produce psychosomatic effects.

By contrast, the **power** of the resurrection mode of existence derives from its *futurity:* what is determinative is not the effects of the causal network of sin, the law, and processes of degeneration and death, but release from the past to appropriate a new future destined by God, which is characterized by transformation "from glory to glory" as believers become fully transformed into the likeness of Christ with "unveiled face," namely, face to face with God (2 Cor. 3:17). There is nothing to weigh down or to exhaust the new "body" of the resurrection, but only **power** *for* the life of the new creation. **Power**, as we have seen above, denotes *effectiveness* to carry out God's will in the strength of God's Spirit.

(4) Hence: **It is sown an ordinary human body; it is raised a body constituted by the Spirit. If there is a body for the human realm, there is also a body for the realm of the Spirit** (v. 44). The NRSV translation, "sown a physical body . . . raised a spiritual body . . . ," is a misleading blunder in a version that is usually reliable and often excellent. The contrast is not between physical and nonphysical. The Greek word *pneumatikos* does *not* mean "composed of nonmaterial spirit." Paul uses the adjective in this epistle to denote that which *reflects or instances the presence, power, and transforming activity of the Holy Spirit.* The raised body is characterized by the uninterrupted, transforming power of the Holy Spirit of God. It stands in contrast with the **ordinary human body** that has been open to the influence of the Holy Spirit, but in partial ways, still marred by human failure, fallibility, and self-interest. The perfect openness to the Holy Spirit characteristic of the resurrection mode of being therefore brings together **decay's reversal, splendor** or "glory," **power**, and a mode of being **constituted by the Spirit** (vv. 42b-44a).

Thus, similarly in v. 44b, such a "body" or mode of being is one designed for the realm or sphere of the presence and resurrection action of the Holy **Spirit**, not merely for the realm of nonmaterial "spirit."

Throughout this section and chapter **body** (Greek *sōma*) includes the physical body when the body in question exists within the universe of space and time as it is now. But Paul has already extended the meaning of **flesh** in v. 39 to include the body substance of fish and birds, and extended the meaning of **body** in v. 40 to include planets and stars. In the resurrection mode of being the **body** will be a transphysical counterpart to what we term "body" on earth, namely, a means of personal expression, identity, appreciation, communication, and interaction with God, with others, and with the environment of the resurrection world.

While Paul speaks of the resurrection body of Jesus Christ as the **firstfruits** or anticipatory model of the resurrection of the dead, it should not be forgotten that in the Gospels Jesus appeared to his disciples *within the conditions of the space-time universe.* These passages do not therefore indicate the full character of the resurrection mode of being within a set of conditions outside the present world order. The resurrection **body** is capable of assuming various forms in accordance with its immediate environment; in this respect it is *more* than "physical," but not less.

47. SUGGESTIONS FOR POSSIBLE REFLECTION ON 15:35-44

(1) *On learning to listen with patience and understanding (vv. 35-39):* Ultimately the problem raised by the doubter (v. 35) does not make sense (v. 36). But Paul *listens* to the problem, and addresses it with a series of analogies, pictures, parallels, and a shift in theological perspective that unblocks a barrier and allows everything to fall into place. Do we really *listen* to what troubles others, whether or not their problems make sense? Do we seek to help them with simplicity, clarity, imagination, and theological insight? How can we improve in this?

(2) *On the raised "body" as characterized by contrast, continuity, and change (vv. 36-38 and 42-44):* How seriously (or joyfully) do we appropriate God's firm promise of decay's reversal and of a crescendo of life, power, and glory in the future resurrection? Can we rest confidently on God's promise of a mode of being in which we and our loved ones are still *we* but also radically changed? Do analogies from life help to explain how God can allow us to be recognized and identified yet also to share God's beauty in glory?

(3) *On the ultimate basis on which such a promise can be fulfilled (vv. 38-41):* Does such a destiny seem too good to be true? God's work as Creator already demonstrates his resourcefulness as Designer, Creator, and Artist to build a universe wondrous and yet multiform beyond human imagining. Is not this sufficient guarantee that God has resources of wisdom and power to raise us "different but the same," differing "as one star differs from another in splendor"?

2. The New Order of Being Derives Its Character from Christ as the "Last" Adam (15:45-50)

45 In this sense it is written, "The first human being," Adam, "became a living human person." The last Adam became a life-giving Spirit. 46 However, it is not the One who is of the Spirit that came first, but the one who was purely human, and after that the One of the Spirit. 47 The first man is "from earth's soil, made from dust"; the second man is from heaven. 48 The one from dust is the model for people of dust; the One from heaven models those who pertain to heaven. 49 Even as we have worn the image of him who was formed from earth's dust, so we shall wear the image of the heavenly one. 50 This I affirm, my dear friends: flesh and blood cannot inherit the kingdom of God; neither can decay come into possession of that which is free from decay.

Paul and first-century Judaism thought in less individualistic terms than does the modern Western world. The natural order of creation, as it stands at present, fulfills the divine decree of Gen. 2:7: **"The first human being," Adam, "became a living human person"** (v. 45a). Paul inserts the words **first** and **Adam** into the Genesis quotation to clarify the contrast that he is about to make: **the last Adam became a life-giving Spirit** (v. 45b). The Hebrew of Gen. 2:7 uses *chayyah* for **living** (LXX Greek *zōsan*), and *nephesh* for **human person** (often translated *soul*, but broader than *soul* in meaning; Greek *psychē*). These terms provide an emphatic contrast between the old order (derived from our representative human parents) and Christ as **the life-giving Spirit**, who stands as the **last** Adam, or the **Adam** of the "last days." Christ is Head and representative of the *new* humanity and *new order of being.*

The following verses (vv. 46-48) probably address a Hellenistic-Jewish theology of the day such as we find in Paul's near-contemporary Philo. Philo draws on the philosophical tradition of Plato to suggest that God first created an Ideal, "heavenly" Adam, and then instantiated this ideal nonmaterial model in the earthly Adam as a physical or material copy of the Idea (or of the Ideal, disembodied Form). Paul distances himself from such a notion: **the first man** was **"from earth's soil, made from dust"** (v. 47a, quoting Gen. 2:7). The **second man**, Christ, is **from heaven** (v. 47b).

The old order of humankind is mortal: "From dust humankind came; to dust it returns" (Gen. 3:19). The new order of redeemed humanity derives its character and its futurity from Christ as the Adam of the "last days" and from the Holy Spirit of life. The Greek uses pronouns denoting "of such a quality" to convey the point that the old humanity is characterized by old-Adam qualities; the new humanity is characterized by new-Adam qualities. Thus: **the One from heaven models those who pertain to heaven** (v. 48b).

If these verses seem a little obscure, this is mainly because they address a mistaken speculation of the time about Adam. But v. 49 makes everything clear: **Even as we have worn the image of him who was formed from earth's dust, so we shall wear the image of the heavenly one.** This serves in part as a commentary on 15:22: "For just as all die in Adam, even so all will be brought to life in Christ." But it goes further. Christ as the new Adam is not only the *source* of life for those "in Christ" but also the one who shapes and determines the *quality and character* of that life. Hence the resurrection life will be holy and Christ-like, as might be expected from those whose mode of being is utterly open to the Holy Spirit. Christians will **wear** Christ's **image** like a badge of identity or a coat of arms.

This characterizes the life of **heaven** (v. 49b). Paul gives this term a double meaning. The life of **heaven** is holy, Christ-like, and loving (13:13), but **heaven** also denotes the realm from which Christ appears at the Parousia or the Last Day. He is **the last Adam** (or the "last day" Adam), who will appear publicly at the End.

Verses 45-49 make it clear that v. 50 is *not* discussing the need for a nonmaterial form. Paul does *not* mean that **flesh and blood cannot inherit the kingdom of God** *because of its fragility or physicality;* he means that God requires *holiness in place of sin.* God requires *transformation of the self through resurrection and the Holy Spirit.* Only the holy and pure in heart can see God face to face and be granted the beatific vision. The second part of the verse makes the complementary point that God's gift of resurrection brings liberation from weakness and decay.

48. SUGGESTIONS FOR POSSIBLE REFLECTION ON 15:45-50

(1) *On the image of God, restored in Christ as the Last Adam (vv. 45-49):* God created humankind in his image (Gen. 1:26-27), but Adam-shaped humanity marred this image through fallenness. God prohibits images of wood or

stone (Exod. 20:4) not only because God is greater than these, but also because humanity itself has the task of being an image or mirror of God. "Objects" cannot substitute for this. If Christians will "wear" a restored image of God, do we yet to any extent "image" God to the world? Do we see God also mirrored in other Christian people?

(2) *On being "purely human" (v. 46):* Paul rejects philosophical theories of his day about a nonmaterial Adam. The biblical writings celebrate flesh-and-blood, embodied humanness. While we seek to live as the "new," Christ-shaped humanity, do we still celebrate "being human" as God's chosen created order for us with all its earthly frailty, constraints, and given time and place? Jesus shared such constraints as our "new" Adam.

(3) *On the transformation of "flesh and blood" to enter the kingdom (v. 50):* Nothing could show more clearly the differences between general ideas and Christian ideas of death and resurrection than how we understand "flesh and blood." Is the main issue for us a need for transformation from the physical to the nonphysical? Or is our greater concern our need for holiness to meet God face to face? If the resurrection mode of being is characterized by the action of the Holy Spirit, can we doubt that the Spirit will both clothe us in the righteousness of Christ and transform us into whatever is required to meet God face to face?

D. The Vision of Future Glory and Its Practical Consequences (15:51-58)

51 Look! I am telling you a mystery. Not all of us humans will fall asleep in death, but all of us will undergo transformation: in an instant, in the blinking of an eye, at the sound of the last trumpet. 52 For the trumpet will give its signal, and the dead will be raised without degenerating decay, and we shall be transfigured into another form. 53 For this body which is subject to decay must become clothed in that which cannot wear out, and this mortal body shall put on what is incapable of dying. 54 When this body subject to decay comes to put on that which will not decay, and when this mortal body comes to put on what cannot die, then shall come into force the declaration of scripture: "Death has been swallowed up in victory. 55 Death — where is your victory? Death — where is your sting?" 56 Now the sting of death is sin, and the power of sin comes from the law. 57 But thanks be to God, who gives us the victory through our Lord Jesus Christ. 58 Therefore, my very dear fellow Christians, stand firm, immovable,

287

abounding more and more without measure in the work of the Lord always, knowing that your labor is not fruitless in the work of the Lord.

In 2:7 we translated the Greek for "mystery" (NRSV, REB, NIV) as "too profound for merely human discovery." This is the meaning of the word in v. 51. Paul's disclosure goes beyond human discovery and derives from revelation. The heart of this revelation is that **all of us will undergo transformation: in an instant, in the blinking of an eye, at the sound of the last trumpet** (v. 51). Transformation at the last day is not a long process of change; it takes place *in a flash*. The Greek word denotes what is the smallest conceivable moment of time (*atomon*, "indivisible"). The metaphor of the **last trumpet** underlines the instantaneous character of the event: a *sudden signal* announces a new situation; for example, it awakens a sleeping army in an instant. The army leaps to its feet in readiness for immediate action.

The phrase **not all of us humans will fall asleep in death** (v. 51a) says nothing about how soon the final coming of Christ will take place, unless we interpret **us** with wooden literalism to mean the first readers rather than *people* or *Christians*. Paul is simply saying that there will be a "last generation" for whom the great last events will intervene before they are to die. The main point here is that **all of us**, whether we have died before the Parousia or are the "last generation," will experience the very same **transformation**. The second part of v. 52 amplifies what the great **transformation** of v. 51 will entail: **The dead will be raised without degenerating decay, and we shall be transfigured into another form.** Verse 53 expounds the resultant condition further: in place of **decay** we shall receive a mode of being **which cannot wear out** and **is incapable of dying**. We have discussed these terms above, especially in our comments on vv. 41-44.

The net result finds expression in vv. 54-57: "**Death has been swallowed up in victory. Death — where is you victory? Death — where is your sting?**" (v. 55). Paul draws on Isa. 25:8, probably in conjunction with Hos. 13:14. (The relation to the Hebrew and LXX is complex, but it need not detain us; see Thiselton, *First Epistle*, pp. 1298-1300.) The **victory** or *triumph* relates directly to the finished work of Christ. Through his atoning work Christ has removed death's **sting**. The word denotes the bite of a venomous animal or the sting of a scorpion's tail. Death has poison fangs if we encounter it in the context of **sin** and **the**

law (v. 56). But because Christ has dealt with **sin** and **the law**, it now faces Christians as a *stingless death:* as a cup of poison from which an antidote has neutralized and removed the poison. For Christ himself has absorbed in his own person the sting and the poison of death.

Cullmann provides a vivid comment on this. In Gethsemane Jesus approached death as a terror and a horror with trembling and distress, for death separates us from God (*Immortality of the Soul or Resurrection of the Dead?* p. 24). By contrast Socrates faced death with equanimity as a release from "the prison" of the body. He does not fear death (p. 20). Was Christ less courageous? Jesus faced death as *God-forsakenness,* as a sacrament of God's wrath upon sin, absorbing the sting of death "for us." Thereby Christians may face death not, like Socrates, under the *illusion* that death has not to be feared, but under the *truth* that for those who "follow after Jesus" death has *lost its horror.* Death has been transformed into a gateway to the nearer presence of God, for "with Christ" believers face resurrection and victory over death's sting. "**Death has been swallowed up in victory.**"

The comments on **sin** and **the law** in v. 56 have been described as an epigram or summary of all that Paul says on these matters in Romans 4-7 and Galatians 3. The interrelation between sin, law, and death makes death a terror. **The law** provides a cause-effect framework that makes the consequences of human **sin** irreversible. But through Christ's death and resurrection the Christian passes out of the realm where **the law** holds sway and **sin** remains a determinative **power** (v. 56) into the realm of resurrection newness where **victory** over these powers prevails **through our Lord Jesus Christ** (v. 57). Paul can exclaim only, **Thanks be to God, who gives us the victory** (v. 57). The **victory** is *given* by grace.

Paul concludes with practical inferences that look back in positive terms to his reflections on Christian labor and struggle in vv. 30-32: **Therefore . . . stand firm . . . abounding more and more without measure in the work of the Lord always, knowing that your labor is not fruitless in the work of the Lord** (v. 58). **Standing** looks back to 15:1, where they "took their stand on" the gospel, but also were in danger of believing "without coherent consideration" (v. 2). Paul has unfolded a coherent account of the resurrection of Christ and of the future resurrection of the dead. This gives every ground for Christians **to abound more and more . . . in the work of the Lord**, knowing that their present and no less their future owe everything to God's grace that also **abounds more and more** (cf. Luke 6:38: no grudging measure on either side).

49. SUGGESTIONS FOR POSSIBLE REFLECTION ON 15:51-58

(1) *On instantaneous transformation as the beginning of a new world (vv. 51-52):* Whether we die before the Parousia of Christ or are still alive when this End event occurs, the same experience of instantaneous transformation will be granted to all Christian people. Do we see death simply as an ending, or as more like a starting pistol that signals an "off" to the new, transformed, ongoing resurrection mode of being? Does the transfiguration of Jesus on the mountaintop provide any analogy with what transformation might imply?

(2) *On the ending of degeneration and the reversal of decay (vv. 53-54):* The Second Law of Thermodynamics (on the irreversible flow of heat), and the related principle of entropy underline the "running down" of our universe (matching the Big Bang theory in astrophysics), although some scholars apply this only to a present stage of our universe (the Oscillating Universe model). (Might the latter have something to do with cosmic bondage and deliverance in theology, or is this fanciful? Cf. Rom. 8:19-23a.) To return to solid ground, can we allow ourselves to be excited at the prospect of a reversal of direction and dynamic in the postresurrection "world"? It will move from strength to strength (without entropy) in a crescendo of glory. It will hardly be even static, for the *living* God is always "on the move."

(3) *On death without a sting (vv. 55-57):* Through his saving work Jesus "absorbed" the poisonous sting of sin and annihilated its cause-effect entanglement with law and penalty. In what spirit should Christians now face death? With what confident hope should we approach death? Has a former terror become *victory*?

(4) *On the prospect of resurrection as a multiple motivation for action (v. 58):* How many motivations for service lie hidden or stated in v. 58? Is gratitude one? "Freely you have received, freely give." If everything comes from God's overflowing grace, can we measure service to Christ grudgingly? What difference does it make that Christian "building" (3:12-15) has lasting effects? How does the prospect of the beatific vision shape our service and inspire us to offer all and to venture all? No work "for the Lord" is "fruitless."

IX. The Collection, Travel Plans, and Greetings (16:1-24)

A. *The Collection as an Act of Solidarity, Care, and Mutuality among God's People (16:1-4)*

1 Now concerning the collection for God's people, as I directed the churches of Galatia, even so you should do likewise. 2 Every Sunday each of you should put aside at home an accumulation of savings in accordance with how you may fare, so that collections are not left to whatever moment I may come. 3 But whenever I arrive, I will send by means of letters of authorization whatever delegates you approve as tried and true to carry your gift to Jerusalem. 4 If it seems right for me to go as well, they can accompany me.

The issues about "the collection" constitute more than an appendix or afterthought to the rest of the epistle. An exposition of the resurrection of "the *body*" leads on to a matter of responsibility or *action* in the public world of relations between Christians. In particular the collection represents a practical expression of *respect for "the other,"* for *mutuality,* and for *solidarity,* which Paul has been promoting throughout the epistle, and especially from 7:1 through to 14:40.

Two theological principles govern the importance of the collection. First, as Paul explains in more detail in 2 Corinthians 8–9, it reflects "the economy of abundance" that embodies obedience to Christ as Lord, who, "though he was rich, yet for your sakes he became poor" (2 Cor. 8:9; see Ford, "The Economy of God," pp. 171-85). Second, in accordance with Gal. 2:10, the collection of funds by Gentile churches for the Jewish Christians in Jerusalem serves as an important *pledge of solidarity and mutuality between Gentile and Jewish Christians.* This offers a parallel today with obligations on the part of better-off churches, parishes, and dioceses to give substance to their co-sharing and common identity with poorer churches, not least by sharing financial resources with those fellow believers who stand in greater need.

It is entirely likely (as Weiss suggests) that the effect of "selling their possessions" to have "all things in common" in the earliest days of the Jerusalem church (Acts 4:32-37) resulted in the collapse of various business enterprises that might otherwise have provided better long-term income for the Jerusalem church. Whatever the cause (and there were other external causes also), the gift of financial assistance to the

Christians in Jerusalem had a double significance: in part, as support for those in need or poverty; in part, as an act of solidarity with those Christians who came from Jewish roots.

Paul uses an unusual word for **the collection** (v. 1). It alludes here to a particular **collection** for a specific purpose in contrast to the regular giving of the Christian community. **The churches of Galatia**, whom Paul **directed**, similarly (v. 1) included Antioch of Pisidia, Iconium, Lystra, and Derbe, namely, the churches founded on Paul's first missionary journey (Acts 13-14). The theological basis emerges in Gal. 2:10. Each of the major epistles of Paul has something about giving, financial support, and **the collection**: Rom. 15:25-28; 1 Cor. 16:1-4; 2 Corinthians 8–9; Gal. 2:10.

A weekly **putting aside** of appropriate **savings** is to take place **at home** on **every Sunday** (v. 2). This is one of the earliest allusions to **Sunday** (strictly, *every first day of the week*). A very similar term denotes the day of the appearance of the raised Jesus Christ to Mary Magdalene and the other women (Mark 16:2; cf. Luke 24:1). **Sunday** thus looks back to the "day of resurrection" and forward to the *Day of the Lord*, which relates closely to "the Lord's Day" in Rev. 1:10. We do not know for certain how early in the life of the church Christians began to meet for worship on a Sunday rather than on the *Sabbath*. R. T. Beckwith and Wilfred Stott argue that this occurred during the apostolic age, but others are less convinced. Probably it was a gradual process that *began* in the age of the apostles (details in Thiselton, *First Epistle*, pp. 1321-23).

Paul's qualifying phrase **in accordance with how you may fare** adds flexibility to the direction in the case of individuals for whom financial setbacks may have occurred. But he reminds the Corinthians in 2 Cor. 9:6, "Whoever sows sparingly will also reap sparingly." He is firm about the discipline of a weekly review, however, lest there should be any last-minute scraping around for what they can give at the last moment. *Planned, disciplined, regular giving* remains the basic principle.

In v. 3 Paul shows his pastoral wisdom, sensitivity, and awareness of the need for demonstrable, "public" accountability. He invites the church to **approve delegates** whom they trust as **tried and true** to ensure the safe passage of the church's accumulated gift, and Paul will countersign due **letters of authorization**. Everything will be above board, or, in the technical administrative terminology of the twenty-first century, will be "transparent" as well as "rigorous." (Strictly the Greek word behind **tried and true** means only "approved": but *dokimos* in this epistle has carried greater weight, which our translation expresses. Cf. 3:13; 11:19, 29.) NJB, NIV, and REB translate "letter of introduction," and NRSV simply "letters," but the thought behind the word or phrase remains the same: the concern for accountability and transparency. Even apostles have to consider the "best practice" in administration. Paul leaves open whether **it seems right for me to go as well** (v. 4), since he does not wish to preempt the decision of where his greatest priorities lie in advance of what circumstances may arise.

50. Suggestions for Possible Reflection on 16:1-4

(1) *On transparent discipleship in the public world (vv. 1-2):* Christian discipleship is no more "inner" or "private" than the resurrection of the body. As one writer expresses this, one indication of whether discipleship is genuine is what Christians do with their pockets and pocketbooks. Do we see our giving of time, talents, and money as a public expression of our response to God's grace? Does this reflect Christian authenticity?

(2) *On contributing financial support to those who are needy in mutuality and solidarity (vv. 1-2):* Support for the church in Jerusalem was more than a gift to the poor. Paul saw it as a solemn pledge bound up with the legitimacy of bringing the gospel to the Gentiles. Such gifts pledged solidarity from Gentile Christians to Jerusalem Christians, and recognized the heritage received from the Jews. Is our giving to Christian work in part an act of identifying with where the recipients stand?

(3) *On giving out of abundance or in relation to "how we have fared" (v. 2):* Giving is a response to "grace abounding" from God. But it also springs from an awareness of the need to address inequalities. If "how you fare" leaves us in difficulties, we are not expected to give what we do not have. But how rigorously do we measure our resources against those in real need? Do these verses suggest that wealthy churches should support poorer ones? Where should this principle begin, and where (if at all) should it end?

(4) *On giving as a planned and regular activity (vv. 1-2):* As well as hinting at an authorized observance of "Sunday" (perhaps no longer Sabbath), Paul advocates "putting aside" gifts on this day of resurrection. How can we re-

spond at the last minute if we have already used up our budget? How can giving best be planned?

(5) *On accountability and transparency in management or leadership (v. 4):* Paul is at pains to insure not only that everything financial is above board, but also that it is *seen* to be so. How scrupulous are those of us in leadership or management to exercise transparency and to show accountability for our actions?

B. Strategic Plans for Travel: Paul, Timothy, and Apollos (16:5-12)

5 I shall come to you when I have passed through Macedonia, for I plan to go through Macedonia. 6 It may be that I shall stay with you for a time, or even spend the winter with you, so that you can send me wherever I go next with practical support. 7 For it is not my wish to see you just in passing, for I hope to spend some time with you, if the Lord permits. 8 But I shall remain at Ephesus until Pentecost. 9 For a great and effective door stands open to me, and many opponents stand against me. 10 Whenever Timothy comes, take care that he is free from fear when he is with you. For he continues the Lord's work, just as I do. 11 Let no one belittle him as a nobody. Help him on his way with practical support and in peace, for his return to me. For I am waiting for him, with the brothers and sisters. 12 Now concerning our brother Apollos: I besought him earnestly to travel with the others to be with you, but he was fully determined not to go yet. He will go as soon as the time is right.

These verses reveal Paul as an apostle who "has the care of all the churches" (2 Cor. 11:28) who are "Pauline" communities. In his responsibilities he stands in part parallel with senior bishops, superintendents, or pastors today who have *episkopē* over a number of local church-communities. Here he shares his strategies, plans, and hopes for revisiting and reviewing churches to whom he has already brought the gospel, with the possibility of extending further outreach. Paul combines the work of apostle, pastor, theologian, and evangelist or missionary. Corinth remains the most strategic cosmopolitan center of Greece, spanning north and south and east and west. Ephesus represents his strategic center for Asia Minor. Philippi and Thessalonica are key centers for Macedonia. Rome and further west find a place in his thoughts of outreach.

Yet, contrary to some popular assumptions, Paul never sees himself as a freelance, lone evangelist. He is "sent out" not only by God but also by supporting churches, and not alone but collaboratively with such co-workers as Timothy, Luke, Silas, or Apollos. In Pauline scholarship and in modern ecclesiology there is an increasing emphasis upon "co-workers" in Paul's epistles, as a pattern of corporate and collaborative ministry.

Currently Paul is ministering in his Asian "base center" in Ephesus. Dangers and threats to the church in Philippi (Phil. 3:2–4:1) suggest that he should visit Macedonia before returning to Corinth. However, if news from Corinth implies an even greater threat there, he may change this provisional plan. One compromise is to send Timothy to explore further how serious the respective problems may be (1 Cor. 4:17-18; cf. vv. 14-21). This receives elucidation in 16:10-11. Paul also hoped that Apollos would revisit Corinth (16:12), but either because of their attempts to misuse Apollos as a party figure against Paul or because of other priorities, Apollos judges it the wrong time for him to go (v. 12). The basic strategy has been planned; the specific tactics and sequence of operations remain necessarily fluid and flexible until circumstances become clarified or changed.

The pastoral visit to **Macedonia** (primarily Philippi and probably Thessalonica) may be a shorter one than the ultimate destination of Corinth since Paul plans to **stay with you for a time, or even spend the winter with you** (v. 6). Paul's visit to Corinth prior to writing 1 Corinthians lasted for some eighteen months, and the two visits together would amount to up to two years. His pastoral and missionary work in and from Ephesus was longer still. This dispels any notion that Paul merely "jetted" from one place to another preaching the gospel, with little concern for pastoral follow-up.

Part of the effect of this will be for Corinth to have a part in **sending** [Paul] **wherever** he **goes next**, and to do so **with practical support** (v. 6). Part is no less because genuine pastoral support cannot be given and received **just in passing** (v. 7). Such is Paul's concern that he repeats the same thought twice (vv. 6 and 7: Greek *katamenē . . . chronon tina epimeinai . . .*). The **practical support** to which Paul alludes denotes *help on the journey,* and often denotes such provisions as food and names of contacts for hospitality and accommodation. But there may well be an added nuance derived from **sending** that includes spiritual responsibility in "standing behind" Paul and praying for him.

Everything depends ultimately upon **if the Lord permits** (v. 7b). With this proviso Paul plans to **remain at Ephesus until Pentecost** (v. 8). For the situation in Ephesus is one of high stakes. On one side a **great and effective door stands open** for Paul and the gospel; on the other side **many opponents stand against** Paul and the gospel (v. 9). Overseas missionaries often borrow Paul's metaphor of an **open door** of opportunity (cf. 2 Corinthians 12 and Col. 4:3), but in the everyday parlance of business or office administration we more often speak of a *window* of opportunity, to the same effect. At the same time opportunities are balanced against threats: **opponents** set up opposition to the gospel. For the present, on both counts Paul is needed in Ephesus, but this does not mean that he has ceased to give *Corinth* and **Macedonia** a place in his plans at a later date. All this points to planned, reflective, proactive strategy, not to reactive, instantaneous attention only to the problem of the present moment.

The penultimate subsection of these verses expresses Paul's concern for **Timothy**, who is to serve as Paul's agent or deputy in a more immediate visit to Corinth. The readers in Corinth are to **take care that he is free from fear when he is with you** (v. 10). Given the arrogance and disparagement of leaders other than those selectively chosen in Corinth, not surprisingly Paul declares, **Let no one belittle him as a nobody** (v. 11). Timothy may be acting as Paul's deputy, but **he continues the Lord's work, just as I do** (v. 10b). The two thoughts look back to Paul's earlier language about regarding a person as a "nobody" (1 Cor. 1:28) and about sharing different functions within the same ministry (3:6-9).

Again, the church in Corinth is to **help** [Timothy] **on his way with practical support** (v. 11b), just as they are to do this for Paul (v. 6b). Paul also expresses his *need* for Timothy's assistance: **For I am waiting for him** (v. 11b). His collaboration with co-workers is not a matter of lip service to "collaborative ministry" as an antiauthoritarian or anti-monarchic gesture, but a real sharing of the burden for the benefit of all.

The final verse of this section concerns **Apollos** (v. 12), and is very revealing about both Paul and **Apollos**. Paul **besought him earnestly to travel with the others to be with you**. He fears nothing from

Apollos's personal presence in Corinth. He trusts **Apollos** utterly not to succumb to Corinthian flattery, but to defend his openness in the same work with Paul. On **Apollos's** side, far from any eagerness to enjoy the adulation of a so-called pro-Apollos group, his mood is more likely to have been sorrow, if not exasperation. How could they pit him against his beloved co-worker Paul when their vision was one in the Lord's work? **Apollos** looks to greater priorities, and will return to Corinth only when other obligations permit this. But he does care: **He will go as soon as the time is right** (v. 12b).

51. SUGGESTIONS FOR POSSIBLE REFLECTION ON 16:5-8

(1) *On sharing and communicating hopes and plans (vv. 5-12):* Paul recognizes that wishes and intentions do not always work out as one hopes, even for an apostle. God does not always protect Christians against "random" events in travel or circumstances. Hence as a wise pastor Paul shares his hopes, allowing for possible changes, to avoid subsequent misunderstandings or accusations or changing his mind. Is it always wise to keep too much to ourselves?

(2) *On planting the gospel in strategic centers (vv. 5-9):* Geographical factors affect churches greatly. Although many are cautious about the notion of Paul's choosing strategic centers, the great centers of Corinth, Ephesus, Thessalonica, and Philippi were clearly of strategic importance for spreading the gospel. How much care should clergy and churches invest in proactive strategic planning? Would such planning "quench" the Holy Spirit, or reflect the Spirit's promptings? Do we spend too much time only reacting to what others have planned?

(3) *On collaborative leadership and partnership (vv. 7-12):* Paul is not an independent, "freelance" evangelist. He was commissioned by the apostles, and worked in close collaboration with Barnabas, Silas, Apollos, Timothy, and others. He revisits churches to provide sustained pastoral support (eighteen months in Corinth with subsequent visits; probably longer in Ephesus). Is there a danger that some like to "be in control" and devalue collaborative ministry?

(4) *On the need for courage where a door of opportunity stands open (v. 9):* Paul does not shirk facing "opponents" if an "effective door" of opportunity

opens. Could we show such courage in parallel situations? Or would we trust God to stand by us?

(5) *On respect for younger leaders and ministers (vv. 10-11):* If Paul found problems in Corinth with his greater weight and experience, how would Timothy fare as his deputy? Paul's plea for respect matches his concerns in chapters 8-10 and 11-14. Do we show respect equally to all?

(6) *On sensitivity and trust (v. 12):* Paul trusts Apollos fully enough to ask him to visit the very church where his "admirers" caused trouble. Apollos responds to such trust with sensitivity. He does not want to risk compounding the problem. Do these examples suggest anything for our situations?

C. Final Parting, Comments, Injunctions, and Greetings (16:13-24)

13 Keep alert; stand firm in the faith; show mature courage; increase your strength. 14 Let everything you do be done in love. 15 I have another request to ask you, dear Christian brothers and sisters. You know that the Stephanas household was the first of more converts to come in Achaia, and that they assigned themselves to the service of God's people. 16 You yourselves should please be subject to such people as these and to everyone who shares in hard toil in our common work. 17 I am delighted that Stephanas and Fortunatus and Achaicus have arrived because they have made up for my missing you here. 18 They have raised my spirits, just as they do yours. You should show due recognition, then, to people of such a kind. 19 The churches of Asia send greetings to you. Aquila and Prisca send warm greetings to you in the Lord, together with the church that meets in their house. 20 Greetings from all your fellow Christians! Greet one another with a holy kiss. 21 The greeting in my — Paul's — hand. 22 If anyone does not love the Lord, let that person be anathema. "Our Lord, come!" 23 The grace of the Lord Jesus be with you. 24 My love be with you all in Christ Jesus.

In outline Paul broadly follows a conventional form for closure in Greek and Roman letter writing, just as he observed conventional forms of address and opening in 1:1-4. As in the opening he fills the conventional form with distinctively Christian content, in this epistle above all others stressing the importance of **love** no fewer than three times (vv. 14, 22, 24). The use of **anathema** is also unusual (only in 16:22 and Gal. 1:8-9).

As in all judicious rhetoric, the conclusion (or rhetorical *peroratio*) picks up aspects of the key theme (or rhetorical *propositio*) of the epistle, which, we must remind ourselves, would have been read aloud to a listening congregation or audience rather than be read by individual readers in seclusion.

Let everything you do be done in love (v. 14) complements the need for action and courage but also supplements and fills out the injunction not to relapse into childishness. For, as we saw, putting away what is "childish" (13:11) entails discarding short-term wishes, wants, and interests for the sake of the longer-term good of all. A **mature** adult sees the larger picture and respects its demands.

The next cluster of injunctions develops the theme of *respect for others* with specific reference to "senior" Christians of longer standing in the church, of whom **the Stephanas household** represents a major example (vv. 15-16). The Greek for "ask" or "request" *(parakalō)* here probably has the force of **please** in modern English (v. 16). As 1:16 also implies, the **Stephanas household** were perhaps the earliest people from **Achaia** to become Christians in Corinth. They constituted a welcome *firstfruits* (Greek *aparchē*) or *vanguard* in the sense of their being **the first of more converts to come**. As among the earliest generation of church members, they had a long and faithful record in **the service of God's people** and as those who **shared in hard toil in our common work** (v. 16b). It is churlish not to give special respect to those who welcomed newer Christians into the church and offered support and nurture while they found their feet as newly baptized Christians and church members. It is all too easy to overlook the loyal service and leadership of "older" members.

Paul expresses his personal delight for the Christian support, friendship, and solidarity enjoyed with the arrival of **Stephanas, Fortunatus, and Achaicus** in Ephesus. Their **arrival** brought genuine refreshment of heart: **They have raised my spirits, just as they do yours** (v. 18). NIV's "they have supplied what was lacking from you" (v. 18b) may mislead us about Paul's meaning. Paul means that **they made up for my missing you here** in the sense that, as Robertson and Plummer express it, they were "a little bit of Corinth" come to Paul, which flooded him with memories and a sense that his troublesome but beloved people of Corinth were **here** in the person of these three.

It is difficult for modern Westerners with instant electronic communications, including instant e-mails and mobile phones, to imagine the heartache of waiting for news from those traveling by land or sea, amid the difficulties of checking the truth of unconfirmed rumors and garbled reports, even with occasional letters carried also over land and sea. Now Paul could catch up with all the news from trusted fellow Christians who knew the church in Corinth inside out. This prompts him again to remind the church how lucky they are to have three people of such a kind among them, and to urge a second time that they **show them due recognition** and *respect* (v. 18b).

All the same, Paul never restricts his attention and concern only to a single local church. Paul is never obsessed with "my" patch alone. Clearly he has talked of Corinth to the Christians in Ephesus, and *vice versa*. Now he tells Corinth that **The churches of Asia send greetings to you** (v. 19). **Asia** denotes the Roman province surrounding Ephesus as its capital.

Not surprisingly those Christians who had been with Paul in Corinth and are still at his side in Ephesus receive special mention. Of course, Aquila and **Prisca** (or *Priscilla*) want to **send warm greetings to you** [Corinth] **in the Lord** (v. 19). Paul mentions "Prisca and Aquila" as his "co-workers" in Rom. 16:3, and they may well have become Christians in Rome prior to moving to Corinth where they met Paul. When Paul traveled from Corinth to Ephesus, once again this husband-wife team were ahead of him in Ephesus (cf. Acts 18:26-28). With Paul, they look back with warm affection to their sharing with fellow believers in Corinth the victories and struggles of Christian life in a pagan, pluralist city, and of witnessing and worshiping together in that challenging context. I have translated the Greek behind "many greetings" (REB) as an intensifier of quality, not quantity, to denote **warm greetings** (with NIV and NRSV, "greet you warmly"; but *not* NJB's more formal and remote "best wishes": they *must* have meant more than that!).

The church that meets in their house (v. 19b) can mean only the gathering of Christians who met as a church in the house owned by **Aquila** and **Prisca**. Priscilla was highly educated (she instructed Apollos in the Scriptures), Aquila and Priscilla were clearly businesspeople in an area that dealt with leather goods, tents, sails, and related goods, and they moved from Rome to Corinth, Corinth to Ephesus, and probably back to Rome, owning their premises and perhaps expanding their business as they moved on.

Travel was only for the wealthy or for productive businesspeople. By around A.D. 53 it is entirely probable that they could own a house large enough to accommodate a worshiping community of up to fifty or sixty Christians if both the *atrium* and *triclinium* were used, and people stood in the *atrium*. Paul owed them a special debt of gratitude. In Rom. 16:4 we are told that they "risked their necks" for Paul, perhaps in this period in Ephesus. F. F. Bruce dryly remarks that the articulate Priscilla would hardly have been likely to do so for an *alleged* unlovable misogynist!

Others may well have asked Paul to send greetings to Christians of whom they may have heard, or to the "friend of a friend" in Corinth. As a wise pastor, Paul includes **greetings from all your fellow Christians!** which leaves no one out through memory lapse or lack of space in the letter. The **kiss** was a sign of both respect and honor. It is possible but less certain that it conveys personal affection. The parting **kiss** of the Ephesian elders (Acts 20:37) is a sign of their respect and gratitude to Paul. Research on the significance of the formal **kiss** in the Greco-Roman world shows that it might be used to signify a variety of acts and attitudes. Hence Paul couples with it the adjective **holy** to denote a kind of greeting appropriate to an expression of solidarity, mutuality, and respect among the people of God. Negatively it excludes its use for erotic expression or overfamiliarity; positively it includes reciprocal respect and (where needed) reconciliation. As time passes, it becomes *the kiss of peace* in public liturgy.

The greeting in my — Paul's — hand (v. 21) follows Barrett's excellent translation of the Greek. Paul has dictated the letter up to this verse, in keeping with the common custom for letter writers who have written more than very briefly. Tertius, for example, penned Romans, (Rom. 16:23), and Sosthenes presumably 1 Cor. 1:1–16:20. Paul on several occasions chooses to add his personal signature and a few lines in his own, different, larger handwriting (see Gal. 6:11; cf. also Col. 4:18, Philemon 19, and 2 Thess. 3:17).

Some scholars insist that "**Our Lord, come**" in conjunction with **If anyone does not love the Lord, let that person be anathema** (v. 22) decisively implies a context of reading this epistle aloud in the Eucharist or Lord's Supper (Lietzmann and Bornkamm). But others convincingly reject this theory, notably C. F. D. Moule and, most recently, Anders Eriksson. (I consider their arguments in *First Epistle*, pp. 1348-52.)

Moule argues with care that "**Our Lord, come!**" is not an invocation at the Eucharist but an eschatological prayer for the Lord's coming at the Parousia. Eriksson shows conclusively that vv. 13-24 gather up key themes from the whole epistle. In v. 13 **keep alert** introduces the tone picked up in "**Our Lord, come!**": both allude to Christ's final coming. **Stand firm** relates to *building* on solid foundations and to maintaining apostolic *tradition*. Finally, **anathema** and **loving the Lord** sum up covenant curse and covenant blessing, which take up the major theme of the covenant implicit in many chapters but explicit in 10:1-22 and 11:23-32. **Love** here includes covenant loyalty.

When the love command is placed in a covenant setting, Eriksson concludes, Paul re-preaches the proclamation of the cross (1:18-25) as that which brings destruction or *a curse* to those who declare it folly, but salvation to those who appropriate its effect as *believers*, as Paul states in 1:18. In rhetorical *and* epistolary terms, Eriksson adds, the ending combines recapitulation of the heart of the epistle with a final emotional appeal. It is as if Paul concludes: "Come on, then, are you 'in' or 'out' when confronted by the proclamation of the cross?"*

Yet the final word of all takes up the other core theme of the epistle, namely, **grace**. "What do you have that you did not receive?" (4:7); "By the **grace** of God I am what I am" (15:10); "Grace and peace to you from God . . ." (1:3); **The grace of the Lord Jesus be with you** (v. 23). In this epistle, as in Romans but arguably even more so, **grace** remains the central theme from first to last. This undeserved gift of sheer generosity flows through Paul and other agents of the gospel so that their hearts, in turn, overflow with this abundance. Thus Paul adds from the heart: **My love be with you all in Christ Jesus** (v. 24). He attaches no strings and no reserve.

52. Suggestions for Possible Reflection on 16:13-24

(1) *On the further use of convention, but with a Christian content (vv. 14-21):* As we observed on 1:1-3 and 4-9, Paul uses conventional letter forms of the day in his opening, and here he does so again in his ending. He is not counter-

---

*Anders Eriksson, "Maranatha in the Letter's Peroratio," in Eriksson, *Tradition as Rhetorical Proof: Paul's Argumentation in 1 Corinthians* (Stockholm: Almqvist & Wiksell, 1998), pp. 279-98.

cultural provided that a cultural convention does not run counter to the gospel. But he enhances accepted forms with deeply Christian content. As Christians do we still respect the normal courtesies of society, but always with an eye to the gospel?

(2) *On special respect for long-standing Christians (vv. 15-18):* In most churches there are "those who have borne the burden and heat of the day," like the Stephanas household. Do such Christians receive proper respect (v. 18), especially from younger leaders? The church "belongs" to *God* (1:1-2), but do recent arrivals (or sometimes older members) think of it as "theirs"? Christian service is a *common work* (v. 16) in which *all* share with *mutual* respect.

(3) *On gratitude for those who raise our spirits by their witness and faith (vv. 17-18):* Stephanas was probably Paul's first convert from Achaia (1:16; 16:15). No doubt Paul shared with him (and with Fortunatus and Achaicus) varied memories of eighteen months in Corinth. They had not only given devoted Christian service (v. 15), but also presumably came with buoyant, glad, and thankful hearts that lifted Paul's spirits (v. 18a). Are we sufficiently thankful for buoyant, faithful people who lift our spirits? Do we try to lift the spirits of others likewise?

(4) *On Paul's parting words "grace" and "love" (vv. 23-24):* This epistle is no less about God's undeserved, overflowing grace than is Romans. The role that this epistle accords to love also goes deep, and it dominates chapters 8 to 14, especially in the climactic chapter 13. Such love is not a matter of mere feeling, but issues creatively in respect, courtesy, sensitivity, and a practical desire for the welfare of the other. What are our final impressions of the heart of this epistle? Can we identify its most transforming effects for Christian thought and life today?

A Bibliography of Works Cited

A. General Works and Studies Cited

Aageson, J. W. *Written Also for Our Sake.* Louisville: Westminster/John Knox, 1993.

Balthasar, Hans Urs von. *The Glory of the Lord,* vol. 1. Edinburgh: T&T Clark, 1982.

Balz, Horst, and Gerhard Schneider. *Exegetical Dictionary of the New Testament,* 3 vols. Eng. tr. Grand Rapids: Eerdmans, 1993.

Barrett, C. K. *The Signs of an Apostle.* London: Epworth, 1970.

Barth, Karl. *The Resurrection of the Dead.* Eng. tr. London: Hodder, 1933.

———. *Church Dogmatics,* II/1. Edinburgh: T&T Clark, 1957.

———. *Church Dogmatics,* IV/2. Edinburgh: T&T Clark, 1958.

Barthes, Roland. *Elements of Semiology.* London: Cape, 1967.

———. *Mythologies.* London: Cape, 1972

Beker, J. Christiaan. *Paul the Apostle.* Philadelphia: Fortress, 1980.

Blomberg, Craig L. *1 Corinthians.* Grand Rapids: Zondervan, 1994.

Bockmuehl, M. *Revelation and Mystery in Ancient Judaism and Pauline Christianity.* Tübingen: Mohr, 1990.

Bonhoeffer, Dietrich. *Meditating on the Word.* Cambridge, Mass.: Cowley, 1986.

Bornkamm, G. "Lord's Supper and Church in Paul." Pp. 123-60 in *Early Christian Experience.* London: SCM, 1969.

———. "The More Excellent Way (1 Cor. 13)." Pp. 180-93 in *Early Christian Experience.* Eng. tr. London: SCM, 1969.

Brown, Alexandra R. *The Cross in Human Transformation.* Minneapolis: Fortress, 1995.

Bruce, F. F. *Paul: Apostle of the Free Spirit.* Exeter: Paternoster, 1977.

Bullimore, M. A. *St. Paul's Rhetorical Style: An Examination of 1 Cor 2:1-5.* San Francisco: International Scholars, 1995.

Bultmann, Rudolf. *Theology of the New Testament,* vol. 1. English tr. London: SCM, 1952.

Caird, George B. *The Language and Imagery of the Bible.* London: Duckworth, 1980.

Carson, Don. "Pauline Inconsistency: Reflections in 1 Cor. 9:19-23 and Gal. 2:11-14." *Churchman* 100 (1986): 6-45.

Castelli, Elizabeth. *Imitating Paul: A Discourse of Power.* Louisville: Westminster/John Knox, 1991.

Clarke, Andrew D. *Secular and Christian Leadership in Corinth.* Leiden: Brill, 1993.

Collins, G. D. "That We Might Not Crave Evil. . . ." *Journal for the Study of the New Testament* 55 (1994): 55-75.

Collins, John N. *Diakonia: Re-Interpreting the Ancient Sources.* New York and Oxford: Oxford University Press, 1990.

Crafton, J. A. *The Agency of the Apostle.* Sheffield: Sheffield Academic Press, 1991.

Crocker, Cornelia Cyss. *Reading 1 Corinthians in the Twenty-First Century.* London and New York: T&T Clark International/Continuum, 2004.

Cullmann, Oscar. *Immortality of the Soul or Resurrection of the Dead?* Eng. tr. London: Epworth, 1958.

Dahl, M. E., *The Resurrection of the Body.* London: SCM, 1962.

Danker, Frederick W. (ed.). *A Greek-English Lexicon of the New Testament and Other Early Christian Literature,* 3d edn. [BDAG]. Chicago: University of Chicago Press, 2000.

Dautzenberg, G. *Urchristliche Prophetie.* Stuttgart: Kolhammer, 1975.

Deissmann, Adolf. *Light from the Ancient East.* Eng. tr. London: Hodder & Stoughton, 1927.

Deming, William. *Paul on Marriage and Celibacy: The Hellenistic Background of 1 Cor. 7.* Cambridge: Cambridge University Press, 1995.

Dungan, D. L. *The Sayings of Jesus to the Churches of Paul.* Oxford: Blackwell, 1971.

Dunn, James D. G. *Baptism in the Holy Spirit.* London: SCM 1970.

————. *Jesus and the Spirit.* London: SCM, 1975.

————. *The Theology of the Apostle Paul.* Grand Rapids: Eerdmans and Edinburgh: T&T Clark, 1998.

Eckstein, Hans-Joachim. *Der Begriff Syneidēsis bei Paulus.* Tübingen: Mohr, 1983.

Elliott, Neil. *Liberating Paul.* Maryknoll, N.Y.: Orbis, 1994.

Ellis, E. E. "'Spiritual' Gifts in the Pauline Community." Pp. 25-44 in Ellis, *Prophecy and Hermeneutic in Early Christianity.* Grand Rapids: Eerdmans, 1978.

Engels, Donald. *Roman Corinth.* Chicago: University of Chicago Press, 1990.

Eriksson, Anders. *Traditions as Rhetorical Proof: Pauline Argumentation in 1 Corinthians.* Stockholm: Almqvist & Wiksell, 1998.

Fish, Stanley. "Rhetoric." Pp. 471-502 in *Doing What Comes Naturally.* Oxford: Clarendon, 1989.

Ford, David F. "The Economy of God." In F. Young and D. F. Ford, *Meaning and Truth in 2 Corinthians*. London: SPCK, 1987.

Fuchs, E. *Christus und der Geist bei Paulus*. Leipzig: Hinrichs, 1932.

Gardner, Paul D. *The Gifts of God and the Authentication of a Christian: An Exegetical Study of 1 Cor. 8:1–11:1*. Lanham, Md.: University Press of America, 1994.

Gee, Donald. *Spiritual Gifts in the Work of the Ministry Today*. Springfield, Mo.: Gospel, 1963.

Gill, D. W. "The Meat Market at Corinth [1 Cor. 10:25]." *Tyndale Bulletin* 43 (1992): 389-93.

Gillespie, Thomas W. *The First Theologians: A Study in Early Christian Prophecy*. Grand Rapids: Eerdmans, 1994.

Glad, C. E. *Paul and Philodemus: Adaptability in Epicurean and Early Christian Psychology*. Leiden: Brill, 1995.

Grenz, Stanley. *The Social God and the Relational Self*. Louisville & London: Westminster/John Knox, 2001.

Gundry-Volf, Judith. "Gender and Creation in 1 Cor. 11:2-16." Pp. 151-77 in J. Adna and others (eds.). *Evangelium, Schriftauslegung, Kirche: Festschrift für Peter Stuhlmacher*. Göttingen: Vandenhoeck & Ruprecht, 1997.

Hall, David R. *The Unity of the Corinthian Correspondence*. London and New York: T&T Clark International/Continuum, 2003.

Hainz, J. *Koinonia*. Regensburg: Pustet, 1982.

Hanson, Anthony T. *Studies in Paul's Technique and Theology*. London: SPCK, 1974.

Harris, W. V. "'Sounding Brass' and Hellenistic Technology." *Biblical Archaeologist Reader* 8 (1982): 38-41.

Harrisville, R. A. *The Concept of Newness in the New Testament*. Minneapolis: Augsburg, 1960.

Hengel, Martin. *The Cross of the Son of God*. Eng. tr. London: SCM, 1986.

Hill, David. *New Testament Prophecy*. London: Marshall, 1979.

Holland, Tom. *Contours of Pauline Theology*. Fearn: Mentor/Christian Focus, 2004.

Hooker, Morna D. "Beyond the Things Which Are Written." *New Testament Studies* 10 (1963-64): 127-32.

———. "Authority on Her Head: An Examination of 1 Cor. 11:10." *New Testament Studies* 10 (1964): 410-16; also reprinted in Hooker, *From Adam to Christ: Essays on Paul*. Cambridge: Cambridge University Press, 1990, pp. 113-20.

Horsley, R. A. "Consciousness and Freedom among the Corinthians: 1 Cor. 8–10." *Catholic Biblical Quarterly* 40 (1978): 574-89.

Hurd, John C., Jr. *The Origin of 1 Corinthians*. London: SPCK, 1965.

Judge, E. A. *The Social Patterns of the Christian Groups in the First Century.* London: Tyndale, 1960.

Jüngel, E. *God as the Mystery of the World.* Eng. tr. Edinburgh: T&T Clark, 1983.

Käsemann, Ernst. "Sentences of Holy Law in the New Testament." Pp. 66-81 in *New Testament Questions of Today.* Eng. tr. London: SCM, 1969.

Klein, W. W. "Noisy Gong or Acoustic Vase? A Note on 1 Cor. 13:1." *New Testament Studies* 32 (1986): 286-89.

Künneth, Walter. *The Theology of the Resurrection.* Eng. tr. London: SCM, 1965.

Lanci, J. R. *A New Temple for Corinth.* New York & Bern: Lang, 1997.

Lietzmann, H. *An die Korinther 1/2.* Tübingen: Mohr, 1949.

Litfin, D. *St Paul's Theology of Proclamation.* Cambridge: Cambridge University Press, 1994.

Loader, William. *The Septuagint, Sexuality, and the New Testament: Case Studies on the Impact of the LXX on Philo and the New Testament.* Grand Rapids: Eerdmans, 2004.

Luther, Martin. *Heidelberg Disputation,* in *Early Theological Works.* Library of Christian Classics, vol. 16. London: SCM, 1962.

McCant, Jerry W. "Paul's Parodic Apologia." Pp. 175-92 in James D. Hester and J. David Hester (eds.), *Rhetorics and Hermeneutics.* New York & Edinburgh: T&T Clark/Continuum, 2004.

Macchia, F. D. "Tongues and Prophecy: A Pentecostal Perspective." *Concilium* 3 (1996): 63-69.

———. "Groans Too Deep for Words." *Asian Journal of Pentecostal Studies* 1 (1998): 149-73.

Malina, Bruce. *The New Testament World: Insights from Cultural Anthropology.* Louisville: Westminster/John Knox, 2d edn. 1993.

Martin, Dale. *The Corinthian Body.* New Haven, Conn.: Yale University Press, 1995.

Marxsen, Willi. *The Resurrection of Jesus of Nazareth.* London: SCM, 1970.

Mitchell, Margaret M. *Paul and the Rhetoric of Reconciliation.* Louisville: Westminster/John Knox, 1992.

Moltmann, Jürgen. *Theology of Hope.* Eng. tr. London: SCM, 1967.

———. *The Crucified God.* Eng. tr. London: SCM, 1974.

———. *The Trinity and the Kingdom of God.* Eng. tr. London: SCM, 1981.

———. *God in Creation.* Eng. tr. London: SCM, 1985.

———. *The Spirit of Life: A Universal Affirmation.* Eng. tr. London: SCM, 1992.

———. *The Coming of God.* Eng. tr. London: SCM, 1996.

———. *The Source of Life.* Eng. tr. London: SCM, 1997.

———. *God for a Secular Society.* Eng. tr. London: SCM, 1999.

Moores, John D. *Wrestling with Rationality in Paul.* Cambridge: Cambridge University Press, 1995

Moule, C. F. D. "The Judgment Theme in the Sacraments." Pp. 464-81 in W. D.

Davies and D. Daube (eds.). *Background to the New Testament and of Eschatology*. Cambridge: Cambridge University Press, 1956.

Müller, U. B. *Prophetie und Predigt im Neuen Testament*. Gütersloh: Mohn, 1975.

Murphy-O'Connor, Jerome. "Corinthian Slogans in 1 Cor. 6:12-20." *Catholic Biblical Quarterly* 40 (1978): 391-96.

―――. *St. Paul's Corinth: Texts and Archaeology*. Wilmington: Glazier, 1983.

―――. *Paul: A Critical Life*. Oxford: Oxford University Press, 1997.

Neufeld, Vernon H. *Earliest Christian Confessions*. Leiden: Brill, 1963.

Nietzsche, F. *The Complete Works*. 18 vols. Eng. tr. London: Allen & Unwin, 1909-13. *The Antichrist. Aphorism* 43.

Nock, A. D. *St. Paul*. New York: Harper, 1938.

Nygren, Anders. *Agapē and Eros*. Eng. tr. London: SPCK, 1957.

Økland, Jorunn. *Women in Their Place: Paul and the Corinthian Discourse of Gender and Sanctuary Space*. London and New York: T&T Clark International/ Continuum, 2004.

Panikulam, G. *Koinonia in the New Testament*. Rome: Pontifical Biblical Institute Press, 1979.

Pannenberg, Wolfhart. *Jesus — God and Man*. Eng. tr. London: SCM, 1968.

―――. *Basic Questions in Theology*, vol. 1. Eng. tr. London: SCM, 1970.

―――. *Systematic Theology*, vol. 2. Edinburgh: T&T Clark and Grand Rapids: Eerdmans, 1994.

Pierce, C. A. *Conscience in the New Testament*. London: SCM, 1955.

Pogoloff, Stephen M. *Logos and Sophia: The Rhetorical Situation of 1 Corinthians*. Atlanta: Scholars, 1992.

Ramsey, Ian. *Religious Language*. London: SCM, 1957.

Richardson, Neil. *Paul's Language about God*. Sheffield: Sheffield Academic Press, 1994.

Ricoeur, Paul. *The Symbolism of Evil*. Boston: Beacon Press, 1967.

―――. *Interpretation Theory*. Fort Worth: Texas Christian University Press, 1975.

Robinson, J. A. T. *The Body*. London: SCM, 1957.

Rorty, Richard. *Truth and Progress: Philosophical Papers*, vol. 3. Cambridge: Cambridge University Press, 1998.

Rosner, Brian. *Paul, Scripture and Ethics: A Study of 1 Cor. 5–7*. Leiden: Brill, 1994.

Rousselle, Aline. "Body Politics in Ancient Rome." Pp. 296-337 in G. Duby and M. Perrot (eds.). *A History of Women in the West*, vol. 1. Cambridge, Mass.: Harvard University Press, 1992.

Routledge, Robin. "Passover and Last Supper." *Tyndale Bulletin* 53 (2002): 203-21.

Sandnes, K. O. *Paul — One of the Prophets?* Tübingen: Mohr, 1991.

Shanor, J. "Paul as Master Builder." *New Testament Studies* 34 (1988): 461-71.

Spicq, C. *Agapē in the New Testament*, 3 vols. Eng. tr. London: Herder, 1963.

Stanley, C. D. *Paul and the Language of Scripture*. Cambridge: Cambridge University Press, 1992.

Stendahl, K. "Glossolalia — The New Testament Evidence." In Stendahl, *Paul among Jews and Gentiles*. London: SCM, 1977.

Stowers, Stanley. "Paul on the Use and Abuse of Reason." Pp. 253-86 in D. L. Balch, E. Ferguson, and W. A. Meeks (eds.). *Greeks, Romans, and Christians: Essays in Honour of Abraham J. Malherbe*. Minneapolis: Augsburg, 1990.

Theissen, Gerd. *The Social Setting of Pauline Christianity*. Eng. tr. Philadelphia: Fortress, 1982.

———. *Psychological Aspects of Pauline Theology*. Eng. tr. Edinburgh: T&T Clark, 1987.

Thiselton, Anthony C. "The 'Interpretation' of Tongues?" *Journal of Theological Studies* 30 (1979): 15-36.

———. *Interpreting God and the Postmodern Self*. Grand Rapids: Eerdmans and Edinburgh: T&T Clark, 1995.

———. "Part VI: Philosophy, Language, Theology, and Postmodernity." Pp. 523-682 in *Thiselton on Hermeneutics: The Collected Works and New Essays of Anthony Thiselton*. London: Ashgate and Grand Rapids: Eerdmans, 2006.

Thornton, Lionel S. *The Common Life in the Body of Christ*. London: Dacre, 3d edn. 1950.

Vielhauer, P. *Oikodomē: Das Bild vom Bau*. Karlsruhe: Harrassowitz, 1940.

Watson, D. F. "1 Cor. 10:23–11:1 in the Light of Graeco-Roman Rhetoric: The Role of Rhetorical Questions." *Journal of Biblical Literature* 108 (1989): 1-18.

Welborn, L. L. *Politics and Rhetoric in the Corinthian Epistles*. Macon, Ga.: Mercer University Press, 1997.

———. *Paul the Fool of Christ: A Study of 1 Corinthians 1–4 in the Comic-Philosophic Tradition*. London and New York: T&T Clark International/Continuum, 2005.

Willis, W. L. *Idol-Meat in Corinth*. Chico, Calif.: Scholars, 1985.

Wimbush, V. *Paul, the Worldly Ascetic: Response to the World and Self-Understanding according to 1 Corinthians 7*. Macon, Ga: Mercer University Press, 1987.

Wink, Walter. *Unmasking the Powers: The Invisible Forces That Determine Human Existence*. Philadelphia: Fortress, 1986.

———. *Engaging the Powers*. Minneapolis: Fortress, 1992.

Winter, Bruce. "The Lord's Supper at Corinth." *Reformed Theological Review* 37 (1978): 73-82.

———. "Secular and Christian Responses to Corinthian Famine." *Tyndale Bulletin* 40 (1989): 86-106

———. *Philo and Paul among the Sophists*. Cambridge: Cambridge University Press, 1997.

———. "Religious Curses and Christian Vindictiveness, 1 Cor. 12–14." Pp. 164-83 in *After Paul Left Corinth*. Grand Rapids: Eerdmans, 2001.

Wire, Antoinette C. *The Corinthian Women Prophets*. Minneapolis: Fortress, 1990.

Wischmeyer, O. *Der höchste Weg: Das 13 Kapitel des 1 Kor.* Gütersloh: Mohn, 1981.

Wiseman, J. "Corinth and Rome I." *Aufstieg und Niedergang der römischischen Welt* 2:7:1 (1979): 438-548.

Witherington, Ben. *Women in the Earliest Churches*. Cambridge: Cambridge University Press, 1988.

―――. *Conflict and Community in Corinth*. Grand Rapids: Eerdmans, 1995.

Wright, N. T. *The Resurrection of the Son of God*. London: SPCK, 2003.

Zodhiates, S. *1 Cor. 12*. 2 vols. Chattanooga, Tenn.: AMG Publishers, 1983.

B. Commentaries Cited in the Text

Allo, E.-B. *Première Épître aux Corinthiens*. Paris: Gabalda, 2d edn. 1956.

Ambrose, *Commentarius in epistolam Beati Pauli ad Corinthios primam*. Vol. 17 in J. P. Migne (ed.). *Patrologia Latina*. Paris: Petit-Montrouge, 1857-86.

Barrett, C. K. *A Commentary on the First Epistle to the Corinthians*. London: Black, 2d edn. 1971.

Bengel, J. A. *Gnomon Novi Testamenti*. Stuttgart: Steinkopf and London: Dulau (from 3d edn. 1773), 1886.

Bruce, F. F. *1 and 2 Corinthians*. London: Oliphants, 1971.

Calvin, John. *The First Epistle of Paul to the Corinthians*. Eng. tr. Edinburgh: Oliver & Boyd and St. Andrews, 1960.

Chrysostom, John. *Homilies on 1 and 2 Corinthians*. Edinburgh: T&T Clark and Grand Rapids: Eerdmans, rpt. 1989.

Collins, R. F. *First Corinthians*. Collegeville, Minn.: Glazier, 1999.

Conzelmann, Hans. *1 Corinthians*. Philadelphia: Fortress, 1975.

Craig, C. T. "The First Epistle to the Corinthians." Pp. 3-262 in *The Interpreter's Bible*, vol. 10. New York and Nashville: Abingdon, 1953.

Deluz, Gaston. *Companion to 1 Corinthians*. Eng. tr. London: Darton, Longman & Todd, 1963.

Edwards, T. C. *A Commentary on the First Epistle to the Corinthians*. London: Hodder, 2d edn. 1885.

Fee, Gordon D. *The First Epistle to the Corinthians*. Grand Rapids: Eerdmans, 1987.

Garland, David E. *1 Corinthians*. Grand Rapids: Baker Academic, 2003.

Hays, Richard B. *First Corinthians*. Louisville: John Knox, 1997.

Heinrici, C. F. G. *Das erste Sendschreiben des Apostel Paulus an die Korinther*. Berlin: Hertz, 1880.

Héring, Jean. *First Epistle of St Paul to the Corinthians*. Eng. tr. London: Epworth, 1962.

Horsley, R. A. *1 Corinthians*. Nashville: Abingdon, 1998.

Johnson, Alan F. *1 Corinthians*. Downers Grove, Ill.: InterVarsity Press, 2004

Kistemaker, Simon J. *1 Corinthians*. Grand Rapids: Baker Book House, 1993.

Lightfoot, J. B. *Notes on the Epistles of St. Paul.* London: Macmillan, 1895.

Luther, Martin. *Works: Vol. 28, Commentary on 1 Corinthians 7 and 15.* St Louis: Concordia, 1973.

Merklein, H. *Der erste Brief and die Korinther Kapitel 1–4.* Gütersloh: Gütersloher and Mohr: Echter, 1992-2005.

Moffatt, James. *The First Epistle of Paul to the Corinthians.* London: Hodder, 1938.

Murphy-O'Connor, Jerome. *1 Corinthians.* Wilmington, Del.: Glazier, 1979 and Oxford: Oxford University Press, 1997.

Robertson, A. T., and A. Plummer. *A Critical and Exegetical Commentary on the First Epistle of St Paul to the Corinthians.* Edinburgh: T&T Clark, 2d edn. 1914.

Senft, C. *La Première Epître de Saint Paul aux Corinthiens.* Commentaire du Nouveau Testament. Geneva: Labor et Fides, 2d rev. ed. 1990 (1979).

Schrage, Wolfgang. *Der erste Brief an die Korinther,* 4 vols. Zürich: Benziger and Neukirchen-Vluyn: Neukirchener, 1991-2001.

Thiselton, Anthony C. *The First Epistle to the Corinthians: A Commentary on the Greek Text.* Grand Rapids: Eerdmans and Carlisle: Paternoster, 2000.

Weiss, Johannes. *Der erste Korintherbrief.* Göttingen: Vandenhoeck & Ruprecht, 1910, rpt. 1977.

Index of Names

Index of Subjects

Index of Biblical References

Note: Passages from 1 Corinthians that occur sequentially in the text are not listed below.

323